D1570101

No Precedent, No Plan

No Precedent, No Plan

Inside Russia's 1998 Default

Martin Gilman

The MIT Press
Cambridge, Massachusetts
London, England

For information about special quantity discounts, please email <special_sales@ mitpress.mit.edu>.

This book was set in Sabon by Toppan Best-set Premedia Limited. Printed and bound in the United States of America.

Library of Congress Cataloging-in-Publication Data

Gilman, Martin G.
No precedent, no plan : inside Russia's 1998 default / Martin Gilman.
   p.   cm.
Includes bibliographical references and index.
ISBN 978-0-262-01465-6 (hardcover : alk. paper)
1. Russia (Federation)—Economic conditions—1991– 2. Financial crises—Russia (Federation)—21st century. I. Title.
HC340.12.G54   2010
330.947'0861—dc22

                                                        2010008279

10   9   8   7   6   5   4   3   2   1

To the memory of my parents, Rosalind and Seymour, who encouraged me to live my dreams, and to Tanya, who has made those dreams come true.

Contents

Foreword

Michel Camdessus[1]

Chou En-lai once said that two hundred years later, it was a little bit premature to try to write the true story of the French Revolution. He was possibly right. Martin Gilman, in offering *No Precedent, No Plan* to the public, is nevertheless demonstrating that when you have been both a key actor and an acute observer of unfolding events, if you go through all the existing records and patiently confront the testimonies of the other eyewitnesses, you can achieve the performance Chou En-lai would have dreamed about. And the story is worth telling.

Modern history is replete with unanticipated events in one country or region that presented challenges to the collective will, talents, and resources of the world community. The sudden dissolution of the Soviet Union on Christmas 1991 and the collapse of its economy starting in the late Gorbachev period shook the global order that had existed since the end of the Second World War.

How the new Russia, emerging from the foremost social experiment of the twentieth century, would cope with its vastly different circumstances was a key challenge not only for the Russian people and their immediate neighbors but also for everyone else. Not the least was the fact that the country controlled thousands of nuclear missiles. No one could be sure that the chain of command would work or that the country would not splinter, or worse.

The imagination can only begin to apprehend the enormous task that such a challenge posed for the other major powers and international institutions in trying to find an effective and positive response. There was no precedent, no plan, no easy solutions, but there was plenty of controversy—not surprising in view of the enormous stakes at risk.

President Boris Yeltsin and world leaders turned to the International Monetary Fund (IMF) for a coordinated response. At the time the IMF was not the only possibility, and indeed other parallel paths were pursued.

In retrospect, I wish that the World Bank had been able to play a more effective role at an earlier stage. In a sense, the IMF became the main focus of external efforts to assist Russia in its transformation more or less by default.

Gilman's book is as close as you can come to actually being there at the time and participating in the events leading up to the August 1998 default by Russia on its domestic sovereign ruble securities as well as the aftermath.

The publication of this book is long overdue. It has been "in the making" for an extended period and thus permanently enriched. Its publication now is all the more timely because the author's vast experience with Russian economic issues enabled him to explore the legacy of that earlier crisis in the more recent period, when another economic collapse, also precipitated by external factors, weighed on Russia. His analysis of the lessons learned from 1998 and how they have been applied in the context of the more recent global crisis is insightful. With the dramatic impact of the first major crisis of the "global village" in the twenty-first century, the resilience of the Russian authorities has been tested along with other countries. This allows us a perspective with which to assess how Russia is coping with the new challenges both in relation to the previous crisis and compared with other countries.

Twelve years ago, Russia experienced a financial meltdown that brought the economy to the edge of the precipice. The prospects were dim, and the political fallout seemed ominous for the future of Russia and the world. The resurrection of Russia's economy from a bankrupt pariah to an integral part of the world system has been perhaps the most extraordinary recovery story in global finance of the past decade.

A critical issue is whether the recent financial crisis has been a replay of the meltdown of August 1998. After all, plummeting oil prices and financial contagion were also at play some twelve years ago. Financial assets have plummeted in value, and the ruble exchange rate came under pressure. In that regard, it seems that the Russians, or at least those veterans of 1998 who still dominate economic policy, clearly internalized the lessons from their earlier crisis.

Russia's fiscal policy—its Achilles' heel in the 1990s—has been prudent, with a consistent focus on the nonoil deficit. At the same time Russia has become a tax haven with its low, flat income tax. Even in the face of some apparent initial skepticism by the IMF and other outsiders, it created an oil stabilization fund in 2004 that cushioned the economy from the brunt of the global crisis and helped to prevent Dutch disease.

Russia has also displayed pragmatism in adjusting the exchange rate at the outset of the crisis, unlike in 1997 when it was considered too sensitive to touch. Lastly, there has been political stability, and ministers have now been in office long enough to learn their jobs and accept the responsibility for the outcomes of their actions.

This book is unique not only in its narrative on Russia and the role of the IMF. It also provides a tangible sense of how the IMF works in practice. I hope that what is appreciated is the extent to which the IMF is a pragmatic institution, attempting to find effective solutions to multilateral and national challenges. This may seem at odds with the outside view of the fund as a monolithic structure following a doctrinaire model applied in all cases. Nothing could be further from the truth.

In fact, while the Russian story really was sui generis, the IMF constantly strives to work with the authorities in any country to figure out what will work best, at the lowest economic and human cost, on a case-by-case basis. Since the recent global crisis has engulfed a number of countries, putting them in a severe financial bind, the IMF—like a fire department that seemed redundant because of a lack of fires—is once again playing a critical role.

No Precedent, No Plan is unique for several reasons. Obviously, it records a crucial turning point in history. More important, it explains how the fund works in practice even when confronted with what turned out to be one of the greatest challenges it ever faced. And finally, speaking as the man in charge of the fund during this key decade, this book offers a convincing and exciting demonstration of something that I have been adamantly convinced of: the admirable capacity of Russia to find in its history, its culture, and the virtues and talents of its people, the resources needed to overcome the most difficult challenges. To have worked with Russia, doing the essential job of the IMF—"to give confidence to its members"—even under the most adverse circumstances, remains one of the most rewarding experiences of my career as an international civil servant.

Preface

The basic premise of my book is that the Russian government default on its domestic financial obligations in August 1998 and the subsequent economic collapse were not inevitable, and but for a series of missteps recent history might have been very different. Once it happened, however, its sovereign debt crisis had a cathartic effect that has endured, helping the country to adjust to the recent global financial meltdown and influencing the country that Russia has now become. The narrative recounts a unique historical experience in Russia, its causes and consequences, and the people and policies behind these events as witnessed by an insider, albeit from the International Monetary Fund (IMF). The book describes how a promising beginning, following Boris Yeltsin's reelection as president in mid-1996, was increasingly compromised by domestic political intrigues against a background of a sharp deterioration in external economic conditions. After discussing the ordeal of the August 1998 crisis itself, it goes on to recount how an even greater catastrophe was averted and eventually how Russia emerged from its tutelage under the IMF. Finally, it traces the legacy of that crisis on subsequent Russian economic policy and argues that Russia, as a result, was better prepared to withstand the impact of the recent global great recession.

One could ask why write another book about Russia, much less about an economic crisis that took place more than twelve years ago? After all is said and done, that crisis—whatever its immediate costs in human and financial terms—seemed to leave little trace over a decade later. Yet the sudden drop in international oil prices in late 2008 and the abrupt reversal of capital flows during the recent global recession revived with a vengeance the memories of this seemingly now somewhat forgotten event. The crash of August 1998 needs to be appreciated if one is interested in understanding contemporary Russia, how it coped with the recent global crisis, and where it is headed. Furthermore, an understanding of the 1998 default is key to appreciating the antipathy that most Russians still harbor to the 1990s, and the solace they have found since Vladimir Putin and subsequently Dmitry Medvedev came to power.

It should also not be forgotten that Russia is the largest country in the world in terms of land area and the seventh largest in population. In 2009 it was considered to be the eighth-largest economy in the world at the current exchange rates—and climbing in the rankings. But with Russia now thoroughly integrated into the global economy, it is no longer insulated from financial turbulences that seize up the world.

The narrative related here should bring an unusual perspective to those already familiar with the events of over twelve years ago. Moreover, the lessons drawn from this case study could be important even for those presumably conversant with this saga of modern economic crises. Those lessons are particularly relevant in the context of the recent global financial crisis even for countries well beyond Russia. In fact, for those countries that have turned to the IMF for financial support, the insights from the Russian experience may be especially useful.

In preparing the book, it was obvious that there were many important, although largely technical, issues that would have to be left to one side. Among these were how the Russian crisis of 1998 related to the preceding Asian crisis and the subsequent one in Brazil, and more generally how the Russian crisis relates to the vast economic crisis literature. It would have been interesting to relate the story told here to the research on the IMF's role, the issues of international crisis contagion, the "oil" curse, exchange rate policy analysis in emerging market economies, capital market development theory, and multicountry comparisons, especially in the Commonwealth of Independent States (CIS) and East European regions. Had I done so, the risk was that the story itself would have been diluted. Hopefully many research projects will spawn from the present work. Since the list of characters seems to rival a Tolstoy novel, I have attached an appendix about the principal Russian participants and their activities around the time of the 1998 default as well as a list of abbreviations and a selected data set for those so inclined.

This seems to be the first book of its kind. I am not aware of any senior IMF staff members who are writing chronicles of key events in which they participated professionally, even from the relative security of retirement. This would appear to be a curiosity since especially in this modern era of greater openness concerning government policy, you would think that other senior IMF people would have riveting stories to tell of other countries in the past.[1] Understandably, I am not suggesting that active IMF staff members should write their personal views about the member countries to which they are currently assigned. I will not belabor the point: both the IMF's external relations policy and a strong collegiate identity within the institution are indeed interesting issues for future research.[2]

To my surprise, none of the key Russian or foreign participants in the 1998 crisis had any plans to set pen to paper, so it seemed that it was left up to me to tell the story before it fades into the oblivion of eternity. My book will likely be the definitive history of those events, immodest as that may sound. Writing this book has been more than just an opportunity to try to set the historical record straight, or an attempt to justify earlier actions or even to collect my thoughts. In truth, I am now at an age where I am conscious of the legacy that we leave to our children—the kind of world that we will bequeath to them in the not-too-distant future.

In this regard it is important to avoid a newly entrenched conventional wisdom about Russia in the United States and Europe, which could in turn lead to major misinterpretations by policymakers and investors alike in the period ahead. If we do not correctly understand what happened—including the mistakes that were made—we may have trouble avoiding future pitfalls. And given Russia's still-lethal military prowess, its geologic and geographic centrality, not to mention its historical role as a pivotal state, we cannot ignore what may happen in the years ahead. Especially in light of the tensions and indeed misunderstandings that have emerged between Russia and the West over a range of issues in recent years, this plea for objectivity rather than stereotypes is no banality.

This chronicle is a result of my ongoing Russian experience. It is not a systematic study of all sides of the issues facing Russia and the IMF during the period under review.[3] In 1993, I was appointed a senior member of the IMF's Russia team, shuttling back and forth between Washington, DC, and Moscow, increasingly on a monthly basis. In November 1996, I moved to Moscow to become the IMF's senior representative, and lived there until my return to Washington in July 2002. The idea of a book of this kind started to take shape during a sabbatical from the IMF at the State University–Higher School of Economics toward the end of that sojourn in Moscow. Subsequently, after retiring from the IMF, I returned to live in Moscow in July 2005 as a professor at the Higher School of Economics.

For over thirty years I worked on the economic problems of many countries from an international viewpoint, first with the Organization for Economic Cooperation and Development in Paris, and then with the IMF, mostly in its central policy department, but also participating in negotiating missions to seventeen other countries in Eastern Europe, Asia, Africa, and the Middle East. By virtue of my position, I was thrust into the center of decision making on most major economic questions facing the Russian authorities for almost eight years. Unlike writers who have to use secondary sources, I used my own notes and recollections of meetings, discussions, and incidents over that period. I also had access to internal IMF documents, communications with the Russian authorities, the officials rescheduling Russia's debt through the Paris Club, and background notes prepared by the IMF for the Group of Seven (G-7)—although I am constrained from quoting internal IMF sources in this book.

I also had the full cooperation of the key former senior IMF officials at the time, most notably Michel Camdessus, the IMF's managing director until early 2000, Stanley Fischer, his deputy, who left in late 2001, and John Odling-Smee, the director of the European II Department until October 2003. It should be noted that this is the first time that Camdessus has gone on public record with many of the views expressed in this book. I was also able to verify my own recollections through conversations with many senior Russian officials who I know well, and some of whom have subsequently become good friends. Finally, and perhaps most important, my marriage to Tatiana Malkina, one of Russia's most prominent political columnists at the time and a senior member of the Kremlin press corps until our move to Washington in 2002, has provided me not only with easy and privileged access to the highest levels of power but also a special insight into the way that Russians really see their world.

More significant than the narration, much of which is already known, is the interpretation of these events, which at times will appear at odds with the received wisdom. Indeed, even now, more than twelve years since the crisis and its aftermath, external perceptions in some cases still seem to get stuck with erroneous notions of what happened. In the process, reputations have been lost, lives ruined, and dangerous stereotypes established of Russia as a land misruled by the mafia, oligarchs, and security cronies.[4] The reality is more complex, and perhaps more troubling.

This analytic narrative presents my understanding of what happened. It was neither authorized nor even seen by anyone at the IMF or within the Russian government. Since I am no longer working for the IMF, I am not subject to the rules that could inhibit staff members from publishing such a work. An earlier and different manuscript was, in effect, censored by the IMF. Clearly, some IMF staff members were concerned that the publication of such a book might reveal too much about how the IMF works in practice. They were able to contrive to have the Russian authorities request that the book not be published at that time. With a totally new management in place in spring 2003, that book was put aside. At the time Camdessus wrote that such an action was unfortunate since unlike a good bottle of French wine, this work should not be left too long in the cellar.

That in itself was a curiosity that reflects poorly on the institution as overly defensive and hypocritical in view of its own consistent call for openness and transparency on the part of its membership. IMF policies are criticized where warranted. But in the last analysis I believe that I am saved from the charge of undue bias by virtue of my argument that in any case, little credit for Russia's relative economic failure and success in recent years goes to the IMF. As we will see, the lion's share of the credit (and blame) should go to the Russians themselves.

Acknowledgments

This is a book about the economic policies pursued by Russia in the latter part of the 1990s and early in the 2000s as well as the people making the decisions. I am indebted to many of these people, who devoted their time during the book's long gestation to discuss their reflections on the events covered. Such a list includes, among others, Sergei Aleksashenko, Anders Aslund, Andrei Bugrov, Oleg Buklemishev, Michel Camdessus, Jerry Evensky, Stanley Fischer, Allan Hirst, Evgeny Gavrilenkov, Yusuke Horiguchi, Mikhail Kasyanov, Yaroslav Kouzminov, Lawrence Malkin, Aleksei Mozhin, Elvira Nabiullina, John Odling-Smee, Alexander Potemkin, Anton Stroutchenevski, Daniel Treisman, Mikhail Tsypkin, Oleg Viugin, Alexander Voloshin, and Evgeny Yasin. Thanks also to Samuel Charap, who convinced me to revisit the earlier manuscript that had been censored by the IMF; to my editor at MIT Press, Jane Macdonald, who patiently worked with me to render the manuscript more reader-friendly; and to my assistant Elena Lavrenuk, for her help with the text. The book would have never materialized without the comprehensive and astute contributions of Andrei Denisov and Dmitry Volkov.

I am also indebted to those Russian authors—cited in the chapters to follow—who have written important articles and books covering some of the events described in this book. I hope to supplement their work from a different angle on some of the same questions. There are also a number of well-informed and no doubt much-better-written books by foreign journalists who lived in Moscow, but who were not direct participants and so relied on the use of secondhand sources. Then there were those works written from farther away, mostly by academics or other Russia experts. Many of these books provide excellent background material and analysis for Western readers. Most important, unlike all of the other books by foreigners, as mentioned earlier, this one is written by a direct participant in the events described. That said, I would like to note in particular a useful and argumentative book published late in 2007 by Anders Aslund, *Russia's Capitalist Revolution: Why Market Reform Succeeded and Democracy Failed*, which covers much of the background and saves me from unnecessary repetition.

No Precedent, No Plan

Introduction

As a country, the Russian Federation is not even a generation old. At the outset, coinciding roughly with the beginning of 1992, it inherited an unusually large amount of historical baggage—such as the Russian Orthodox religion, Russia's separation from Europe during the Mongolian period, the rule of the czars, and the pervasive experiment with Soviet Communism. The Russia that emerged from the latter experience was in a shambles, but, more important, it was dangerous. The West had little choice but to get involved. It used the IMF as its primary vehicle.

The 1998 financial crisis represents a critical juncture in Russia's emergence from its historical straitjacket, and how it has handled that legacy says much about its future. Overall I contend that Russia has learned important lessons, and has opted to join the global economy and political system as a partner. There are those who do not seem to share that view, however, instead interpreting the past decade or so since the 1998 crisis as a temporary aberration fueled by high energy prices perhaps in conjunction with some unusually good luck. I hope to show that most critics have a tendency either to oversimplify a complex reality or more often prematurely jump to conclusions that they are then reluctant to reconsider when more complete information becomes available.[1]

This book follows roughly a chronology of events, and also includes my commentary and analysis. I hope that the structure of the book will convey a sense of the way in which some generally smart but inexperienced people who happened to be in a position to make decisions, based on their perceived interests along with the motives and expectations of others, and all operating with only partial information, tried to do their best—in most cases. Sometimes their decisions worked, and sometimes they didn't. There was nothing inevitable about the outcome; historical determinism according to some misguided Hegelian approach did not play a role. And while national character may mold or influence events, this book is really a story about how individuals, improvising as they went along, forged the beginnings of a new national experience.

Russia is a country that provokes extreme views, and the mood swings seem to intensify with the distance from Moscow. Indeed, in summer 1997, when even modest individual investors in the U.S. Midwest were, on the advice of their stockbrokers, buying up high-yield ruble-denominated regional commercial notes (veksels), investors inside Russia were skeptical, putting their money into dollar assets abroad. After the August 1998 default, when some foreigners decided that Russian assets were as dangerous as nuclear waste, Russian investors remained more sanguine, including some investment banks in Moscow. Moreover, much of what has been published, especially in the West, has contributed to a clichéd image of a Russia run by self-serving oligarchs, the mafia, and former security agents.

This image in part lingers because of the legacy of some purported financial scandals that emerged in the wake of the 1998 financial collapse, indirectly playing a role in the waning of the IMF's involvement. The two biggest ones were largely bogus: the US$4.8 billion IMF tranche released in July 1998 was not stolen, nor was there evidence that the Bank of New York laundered billions of dollars from the Russian mafia (although there were some minor transgressions). Yet the media bear much of the responsibility for this enduring legacy. Front-page stories, headline television news, and congressional investigations launched on the basis of the allegations are all that the public remembers. How would it know that stories were retracted, and charges settled or cases closed, if this information was buried in the inside pages of just a few major newspapers?

The book is directed at a public skeptical not only about Russia but also about the IMF. While acknowledging mistakes, it will challenge those critics such as Nobel laureate Joseph Stiglitz who allege that the IMF made major mistakes in Russia that could have been readily avoided. At the same time it will demonstrate that Russia was trying to cope with seemingly insurmountable problems simultaneously, and in that context, as messy as it was, acquitted itself better than could have been expected. This is a very different Russia than portrayed by Edward Lucas in his 2008 book about a new cold war.[2]

Interestingly, when I began writing this book, I—and it seems most others, including in the IMF itself—thought that bailouts for countries in sovereign debt crises were a thing of the past. So I expected that the story related here of the intimate workings between the IMF and Russia would be a case study of mainly historical interest. The swift spread of the global mass deleveraging of debt since the bankruptcy of Lehman Brothers in mid-September 2008 forced a whole new set of countries to beseech an ill-prepared IMF for financial assistance and urgent advice. And here lay perhaps some of the book's greatest insights. For how the IMF operated in Russia, although a special case in many ways, reveals many aspects of the practical issues in making the hard political economy choices recently faced by countries as diverse as Belarus, Hungary, Latvia, Pakistan, Serbia, and Ukraine, and to a lesser extent Colombia, Mexico, and Poland, which are using a newly created IMF credit line. In fact, the overhang of sovereign debt issued in domestic currencies when revenues are collapsing, as witnessed even within the European Union in 2010, starting with Greece, has been a stark reminder of Russia's predicament in 1998. Again the IMF has had a central role to play.

The Daunting Task of Reforming Russia: What If?

To understand that the August 1998 default was avoidable and yet nevertheless why it occurred, we need to go back to its origins. For the story of the default cannot be understood without appreciating the starting conditions of post-Soviet Russia, at least in brief, and tracing some of the main elements that formed the background of Russia's traumatic development as a modern country.[3]

This is in large part a story of Russia's reintegration into the globalized, Western-dominated economy after an absence of over seventy years. In 1991, hardly any Russian alive was an adult at the time that the country last enjoyed full participation in the outside world. Of course, the Soviet Union itself as well as its extensive system of satellite and comrade countries after World War II—the second world—was an international network of trade, but based entirely on the notion of state-to-state relations. This highly regulated approach also applied to economic relations beyond the Soviet bloc.

Seen from the perspective of 2010, it is hard to appreciate the extent to which the Soviet Union, and especially its Russian territory, was decoupled from the events of the Western-dominated global economy. When the Western world was enduring the Great Depression, there was little impact on Russia. With the construction of its postwar empire, alliances, and state-trading system based on the transferable ruble accounting scheme and state planning, Russia was largely impervious to developments in the Western market economies—even if Soviet oil sales and hard currency borrowing had become increasingly important for the financing of the Soviet economy in its final years. An alternative economic reality—only occasionally punctuated by black markets and other economic "crimes"—took hold over the long reign of the Soviet experiment.

In a sense, Russia's membership in the IMF, beginning formally in June 1992, traces the path of this reintegration, with the relationship reaching its apogee by the time of the August 1998 crisis.

I could start almost anywhere with the story of Russia in the past eighteen years or so. For instance, what if the Russian army had not remained loyal to Yeltsin in the context of his dissolution of the Supreme Soviet in September 1993? Imagine the kind of state that Russia might have become under the control of those nostalgic to reinstate the Soviet Union and punish the West for its role in supporting both Mikhail Gorbachev and then Yeltsin. Or what if Yeltsin, under the influence of his confidants, Oleg Soskovets and Alexander Korzhakov, had decided to cancel the presidential elections of 1996 and suspend the constitution of 1993? What kind of country would Russia be now? Perhaps General Alexander Lebed, the tough and independent-minded paratrooper who challenged Yeltsin in the first round of that election and received 15 percent of the vote, would have successfully rallied opposition to impeach a sick and unpopular Yeltsin. Maybe Russia would be now ruled by a junta à la Augusto Pinochet.

Fortunately, history did not turn out like that. And in a country emerging out of modern history's most thorough, persistent, and perverse social experiment involving the lives (and deaths) of tens of millions of people over seventy years, and armed with a nuclear force of almost six thousand active warheads (at that time), many on hair trigger launch alert, the fact that we are still here and I can write this book is a testament to our luck. For it was luck. There was nothing inevitable about the relatively happy ending, thus far, resulting from that turbulent period.

The Starting Conditions Were Unfavorable

There may be no single, simple explanation for why the transformation of the Russian economy seemingly took so long, and was so apparently fitful and unpredictable. Why did we in the West expect that the "recoupling" after the collapse of the Soviet Union would be swift? Many contended that either the transformation of Russia should have followed the pattern seen earlier in Eastern Europe, as I also originally thought, or at the other extreme, that the country would be locked forever in a hopeless pattern dictated by the heavy weight of culture and history.[4] No doubt at least part of the explanation stems from the unrealistic expectations of so many observers at the outset—and hence the ferocity of the debate on the sequencing of the reforms, with the assumption being that if the reforms could be implemented in a certain order, then Russia could quickly join the ranks of forerunners like Poland, Hungary, and the former Czechoslovakia.

The heated debate about the reforms effectively revolved around the question of the appropriate sequencing of economic and social policies in order to move from a state-controlled economy to one where the private sector dominates. This involved a highly complex set of issues about freeing prices in the face of a shortage of goods, privatizing enterprises belonging to the state, introducing market-determined interest and exchange rates, substituting a social safety net as enterprises withdrew services, making real estate tradable, and so on. All of these steps presumably should have been done in the context of new laws and institutions with a whole new set of leaders, as witnessed in all of Central Europe after 1989.

To my mind, if there is one single factor that could be identified, at least in retrospect, that explains the difficulties that Russia almost uniquely faced and why those initial expectations proved to be so unrealistic, it would be the effective collapse of the state. Indeed, the disappointing "potential" of the 1990s in Russia points to this key insight from those fateful years. It is contended here that this potential was limited, or much more circumscribed than was initially imagined. The fitful nature of post-Soviet Russian economic policy was a consequence of the sudden, and potentially dangerous, vacuum of power and loss of decision-making capacity that resulted from the collapse of the Soviet Union and the disintegration of the centralized authority of the Communist Party of the Soviet Union (CPSU).

Post-Soviet Russia cannot be really be understood, in my view, without acknowledging the key role played by the collapse and temporary ban of the CPSU. In the West, most observers were seemingly oblivious to such causality. It was just too hard to believe that the strong, centralized control that had literally defined Soviet power simply vanished. An inability to even see this fact led Western leaders, the IMF, and the media to mislead themselves as to what could be done. The Russians did a poor job in trying to convey this new reality, to the extent that they themselves really understood it. The events of the 1990s graphically revealed the incongruence of seemingly normal political structures—at least as viewed from the outside—with an almost total absence of real authority to make and implement decisions, as seen, for instance, in the inability to implement needed economic reforms.

The events of the entire transition period result from the historical fact, as Michael McFaul (now with the National Security Council) put it in his introduction to the English edition of the late, former Russian acting prime minister Yegor Gaidar's book, that the Russia that emerged from the breakup of the Soviet Union at the end of December 1991 "was not a sovereign state, as it had no sovereign borders, no sovereign currency, no sovereign army, and weak, ill-defined government institutions."[5] I concur with McFaul that modern Russia inherited a unique set of starting conditions. In many ways, it would have almost been better had the country started with a completely new political class and institutions. Instead President Yeltsin and Gaidar, as his first prime minister, had to address all the problems of the collapse of empire and the economy with the practices, institutions, officials, and most of the laws of the Soviet system still in place. These included a state-controlled and planned system for all economic transactions in principle, almost no legal markets at the beginning but a pervasive, criminalized black market, a huge military-industrial complex, massive corruption, a legal vacuum, and more. Perhaps most critical, because by choice the revolutionary events that caused the old regime to implode did not involve the violent liquidation of its leaders, Yeltsin and the new reformers had to contend with the old guard and its many sympathizers at every step on the need and pace of reforms in the economy and political system. And unlike in other parts of the Soviet empire, there was no preexisting consensus on the need for democratic and market transformation. On the contrary, the Russian political class and society were divided and polarized.

In that same book, Gaidar added that "in my view, what we witnessed then was a revolution—one comparable, in terms of its influence on the historical process, to the French revolution, the 1917 Russian revolution, and the Chinese revolution of 1949. The country saw its economic and political foundations collapse, its socioeconomic structure and its ruling ideology radically change."

The Second Russian Revolution Was Traumatic

The insightful extension of the theory of revolution published by Vladimir Mau and Irina Starodubrovskaya is a tour de force in explaining the economic basis for revolution and the specific nature of Russia's relatively bloodless second revolution of the twentieth century.[6] The difficulties and inconsistency of the Russian reforms under Yeltsin are usually described as a result of the mistakes made by the new government. Rather, I agree with Mau and Starodubrovskaya's thesis that these problems should be considered as a natural consequence of a "weak state." In a revolution, the weakness of state power is inevitable—resulting from social fragmentation, the transformation of property rights, and changes in the interests of various social groups. They maintain convincingly that most of the transitional problems in Russia were unavoidable.

In his analysis of Russia, Anders Aslund writes that "in a revolution, the old institutions cease to function. For a short time, this hiatus offers political leaders much greater opportunities than in ordinary times. The drawback is that the tools of government are rudimentary."[7]

Arguably, had more Western observers understood the truly revolutionary nature of Communism's collapse and its aftermath, the crisis-ridden and occasionally violent nature of Russian politics in the post-Soviet era would have come as far less of a shock. We in the West made the mistake of thinking that Russian "reform" could unfold through ordinary, not extraordinary, means since we didn't appreciate the revolutionary character of the upheaval. It is as if we suffered from collective myopia in believing that a few years would suffice to start turning things around.

In fact, the dominant viewpoint during the 1990s among Russia experts, especially in the West, was that Russia was, or should have been, in the midst of a "transition to democracy and market society," with the metaphor of transition implying both a preordained outcome and a relatively smooth path between the Soviet past and a liberal market future. After all, this is a path that was being trodden in a number of other countries in Central and Eastern Europe. This is a critical point, as much of the nostalgia expressed by Western observers about former Russian president Putin and his supposed reversal of democracy seemed to stem from, at best, a romanticized view of what actually was the situation on the ground in the 1990s combined with inertial thinking from the simpler context of the cold war.

Some foreign experts on Russia such as McFaul propose an alternative view.[8] McFaul repeatedly stresses the revolutionary nature of Russia's post-Communist transformation. Likewise, for instance, in a monograph Thomas Graham (then at the American Enterprise Institute, but now at Kissinger Associates) analyzed the sources of Russia's decline during the Soviet era, and the dangerous fragmentation and erosion of state power in the 1990s. Russia's descent to the brink of disintegration was, he notes, "a story of political shortsightedness, unprincipled political struggle, ill health, greed, and bad fortune." The Soviet collapse abruptly ended the cold war, but also resulted in a decade of chaos and impoverishment for the Russian people.[9]

Other Views Have Dominated the Debate

I have nothing against noneconomists analyzing major economic and political upheavals. It is perfectly normal, and presumably they are good at their professions. Nevertheless, when even the best of them turn their attention to complex economic issues, the results can often be disappointingly superficial, and occasionally insulting to one's intelligence if you happen to be an economist.[10] A typical example of a well-meaning but myopic interpretation of events in Russia as a democratic and prosperous transition usurped by Yeltsin and his entourage with the connivance of the United States is Stephen Cohen's observation that the new government rejected alternative policies that could have been at least as effective with far less suffering.[11] Cohen, like other writers with more of a political perspective, sees obvious alternatives that in his view should have existed and could have been exercised, but attributes either personal ambition or the greed of Yeltsin and his entourage to the fact that they were not even attempted. He never seems to consider the possibility that most other alternatives were either nonexistent or totally utopian (such as entirely new institutional structures springing miraculously from a spontaneous democratic movement or a "Marshall Plan" for Russia).

Some, like Lilian Shevtsova, made the facile lament that Yeltsin's "worst mistake, both for Russia and for himself, has been his failure to establish strong political institutions and stable rules of the game."[12] Others, like Peter Reddaway and Dmitri Glinski, interpret developments perhaps in a more patronizing tone, noting that "the Yeltsin regime's persistent attempts to strengthen its grip without addressing the legitimacy problem produced a vicious circle of escalating autocratic centralization of executive powers within a government whose administrative capacity was progressively declining."[13] All of these observers of course have a point, but they seem to dismiss or minimize the inherited weakness and dispersion of state authority as well as the virtual absence of mechanisms for effective decision making.

The depiction of modern Russia as a morality play has continued, as seen in Lucas's 2008 polemic, *The New Cold War: Putin's Russia and the Threat to the West*, in which he recognizes the enormous economic progress achieved, but warns repeatedly and unconvincingly that Russia is provoking a new cold war.[14] Russia, he argues, is aggressively waging a global war for influence with its vast natural resources and massive financial reserves, and only the United States and Britain are trying to resist the overt pressure exerted by Russia's aggressive posture. His assertions appear seductive to those blinkered by the past, but are detached from reality.

In contrast to the implausible and jingoistic politicized views of Lucas, Stephen Kotkin contends that "Russia was not a liberal democracy under Yeltsin, and neither has it reverted to totalitarianism under Putin."[15]

Perhaps a key factor distinguishing Russia's post-Communist revolution from all previous great revolutions, while simultaneously obscuring its revolutionary nature, was that it was the first one in history consciously directed against an officially "revolutionary" regime. The Soviet Union at all times paid homage to its revolutionary objectives—however hollow those claims appeared to most Soviet citizens in the regime's latter years. Even Soviet president Gorbachev firmly insisted that his plan for perestroika (restructuring) constituted a continuation of the romantic revolutionary traditions of Vladimir Ilyich Lenin and was directly linked to reestablishing the ideals of the original Bolshevik revolution of 1917. So as the truly revolutionary currents under Gorbachev began to undermine the coherence of the Soviet regime itself, ironically they could not explicitly be called revolutionary without alienating most of the population. The dilemmas of the "antirevolutionary revolution" have bedeviled post-Soviet Russia ever since.

Surviving Economic Collapse

If Yeltsin, without fully realizing it, was indeed riding the crest of a revolution, he understood enough that institutionalizing a genuinely democratic and capitalist system in Russia would necessarily have required revolutionary upheaval in practically every sphere of social life. Yet under the circumstances this was not even vaguely realistic—and had it been, the risks would have been enormous. Throughout the country, former Communist apparatchiks remained in control of the most important state bureaucracies and regional governments, and the nearly bankrupt economy was almost entirely dominated by inefficient military industries and collective farms. It seems that the military, already demoralized and stretched by the totally unprepared and unfinanced repatriation from the former German Democratic Republic (GDR) and other Warsaw Pact countries, could not be fully trusted. Moreover, in the Gorbachev period after 1985, various partial attempts at ad hoc reforms in combination with the growing power vacuum created opportunities for asset grabs, asset stripping, pyramid schemes, and shuttle trade—all a telling symptom of power slipping away from the state and creating centripetal forces that Yeltsin somehow admirably managed to contain.

On a political level, the idealized creation of a genuinely democratic regime would have required a new constitution, new governmental institutions, new presidential and parliamentary elections, and a thorough reform of the laws governing relations between Moscow and Russia's regions and ethnic republics. I might add somewhat facetiously that it probably would have necessitated a different country with a different history, or at least a different generation and better starting conditions.

The creation of a market economy presented itself as the most promising—and maybe only—course available given the bankrupted state apparatus that the Russian Federation inherited and the lack of conceivable financing. In fact, in view of the dire financial situation, where no feasible financing scenario was realistically available, a coordinated economic shock therapy would have been appropriate: calling for the almost simultaneous immediate freeing of prices, the transformation of the ruble from an artificial, state-issued coupon into a reliable market-determined currency, the end of explicit and implicit state subsidies, and the wholesale breakup and privatization of state-owned enterprises. But such a shock therapy did not even have a chance.

At every turn, Yeltsin had to try to accommodate powerful factions and interests—some motivated by a sense of greed, others by fear, and still others by self-preservation. Operating in a power vacuum with few levers to pull, he sometimes groped in anger or despair to effect change.[16] Shock therapy as a policy package was never even attempted. Only the relatively easier to implement macroeconomic elements were applied, thereby creating ever-new distortions in the process. Earlier, for instance, the 1988 law on cooperatives allowed private companies and unregulated banks to be formed while price controls remained in place, leading to sudden wealth for those state enterprise managers with access to price-controlled goods.

In view of the dominant political pressures, the formulation, much less the pursuit, of economic reforms was marginalized. In order to understand how the collapse of the state exacerbated the critical fiscal problem faced by Russia, it is important to appreciate the extent to which the tough starting conditions resulted from accumulated financial problems during the late Communist period, and not from the stabilization policy per se (meaning a coordinated set of monetary and fiscal policies aimed to reduce inflation and other financial imbalances). In other words, if there was a shock therapy aspect of the stabilization program, it was for the most part administered inadvertently through the policies of the last Communist government. Certainly the oil price collapse in the 1980s deprived the Soviet Union of vital foreign exchange and budget revenue, just as demands were increasing from both the military and the civilian population. With his back against the wall, Gorbachev decided to deplete the foreign exchange and gold reserves, and borrow massively from Western governments and banks. History is littered with cases where new leaders inherit a catastrophic situation after defeat in war—think of postwar Germany or Japan—but not usually after a near-bloodless revolution.

As Gaidar pointed out, in post-Communist countries there was a clear connection between the duration of a period of high inflation and the extent of a budget crisis. The longer there is high inflation, the stronger is the addiction of the government and the economy to an inflation tax (which while hidden, effectively confiscates the resources of holders of monetary instruments); the greater the inflation tax, the further the tax system degenerates. Incomplete macroeconomic stabilization then caused the erosion of fiscal resources available to the budget, the crisis in the budget sphere, and hence the need for domestic borrowing in the form of treasury bonds. This, in turn, set in motion a deep crisis within the developing institutional structure and within the government itself.[17]

In her perceptive book *The Meltdown of the Russian State*, my former IMF colleague Piroskha Nagy focused on the economic causes and consequences of Russia's enfeebled beginnings as an independent state.[18] While she ascribes no doubt more significance to choices made by Yeltsin during the early reform period than authors such as Gaidar or Mau, Nagy arrives at similar conclusions that arbitrary and unpredictable policies are a sign of a weak government that also cannot establish institutions, especially those necessary for the protection of property rights and the enforcement of legal contracts, essential for the functioning of markets. In trying to work around these chaotic formal sets of legal requirements in the context of dysfunctional institutions under the control of low-paid government bureaucrats, corruption flourished.

Again, one of the most cogent and comprehensive analyses of the role of economics in the second Russian revolution is contained in the book by Mau and Starodubrovskaya. Placing the budgetary crisis of 1998 in a longer perspective, they note that "although its roots are to be found in the second half of the 1980s, it became particularly acute in the mid-1990s."[19] They go on to describe this as a typical crisis of the end of a revolution. The state had recovered just enough strength in a few areas, notably monetary control by the Central Bank of Russia (CBR), to bring inflation down and stabilize the ruble. This actually exacerbated the budgetary problem, however, since inflation could no longer be relied on to increase revenues while reducing the real value of nominal spending fixed in the budget.

Nobel laureate Joseph Stiglitz, who interpreted the Russian experience as a lost opportunity to apply the lessons of Chinese reforms and make structural/institutional reform the central focus, has been a vociferous critic of the IMF's role in Russia.[20] He was particularly outspoken in his criticism of the "Washington consensus" with its erroneous fascination with macroeconomic stabilization at the expense of all the really necessary microeconomic reforms. Stiglitz maintained that the IMF and others ignored the lessons of Russian history and culture, imposing an inappropriate shock therapy on the country. The problem with his analysis, as brilliantly analyzed by Mau, is that he seems to forget that the reformers and those supporting them, such as the IMF, were not conducting a social experiment where they could set the starting conditions and constraints.[21] Instead, they had to start where they were—a point that left them few options.

An appreciation of the kinds of societal choices that Russians were confronting really does hinge on an appropriate perspective on the historical context. As former President Putin alluded in his 2005 annual address to the Federal Assembly, "The collapse of the Soviet Union was a major geopolitical disaster of the century. As for the Russian nation, it became a genuine drama." While shocking for Western commentators when taken out of context, most Russians understood the sense that the collapse of empire—especially in the absence of war and military defeat—creates dislocation, confusion, and insecurity.

Gaidar warned that imperial collapse can be disorienting and dispiriting to the empire's subjects, even if the empire brutally repressed them. Using historical analogies, he remarked that demagogues and revanchists can exploit this disorientation and depression to achieve power. Those suffering from postempire depression are susceptible to demagogic myths that imperial glory was destroyed by "stabs in the back" from enemies foreign and domestic, and that a restoration of this glory requires the people to unite behind an authoritarian leader who will ruthlessly pursue traitors at home and take revenge on foreign foes.[22] Such was the fate, for instance, of Weimar Germany under the Nazis. Gaidar believed that such a myth is dangerous for Russia and the world.

And What Came Next?

As Gaidar noted, the fall of an empire seems anything but common sense to those who lived through it. During his two presidential terms from 2000 to 2008, Putin (and his colleagues) played on such sentiments at times, perpetrating the myth that the collapse of the Soviet Union, and the economic and social chaos that followed, was not due to the inherent defects of the Soviet economic system but instead resulted from malign external forces.

Using the revolution approach to understand the Soviet Union's collapse and the rise of post-Soviet Russia, in retrospect the Putin period can be understood as a classic Thermidor—that period during the French Revolution when the Reign of Terror gave way to a desire for stability. Although I have no real claim as a political scientist, it does seem to me plausible that all people, not just Russians, within the context of the modern nation-state, trade some freedom for some economic stability and security. The Patriot Act in the United States comes to mind as a consequence of the 9/11 terrorist attacks. Things were so bad in Russia and so absolutely difficult to endure that some discipline and a more controlled process of development had to be instituted. It was just indescribably hard for people to survive, and endure the mental anguish and physical hardship of the 1990s, during the collapse of the Soviet Union and its aftermath. In hindsight, it may be considered fortunate for the world that it was Putin who led the country back to some form of self-confidence and global identity. It could have been a lot worse.

Another highly regarded British journalist, Anatole Kaletsky—who unlike Lucas, does not strive to interpret twenty-first-century prospects through the prism of twentieth-century thinking but instead actually tries to understand the dynamics in light of what history teaches us—has an equally provocative though much more relevant interpretation of current Russian thinking. According to Kaletsky, "America and Europe, regardless of their warm words about Russia, are treating it objectively as an enemy, taking every opportunity to cut it down to size. After 15 years of this experience, is it really surprising if the Russians, emboldened by their newfound oil wealth, now respond in kind? In other words, it is not Russia but America and Europe that have restarted the Cold War."[23]

Historians will have to decide whether the mistakes of Russia's transition in the 1990s could have been avoided. The mistakes themselves were obvious in retrospect. These were the mistakes of omission—lost opportunities or rather nonexistent possibilities in many cases—hence, perhaps not so much mistakes as a muddle, and a dangerous one at that. In what follows, it is assumed that the reader is at least sufficiently open-minded to consider that powerful social forces had been released in a vacuum, resulting in discordance at the supposed center and in the dispersion of power. These conditions were hardly propitious to the kind of drastic institution building, law making, and implementation of tough economic policies necessitated by the circumstances, especially while trying to protect the population from unnecessary pain. This is not presented as an alibi but rather as the unfortunate yardstick that should be used in assessing blame or praise relative to other hypothetical alternatives.

1
Russia and the IMF

Looking back on the Russian financial crisis that culminated in the sovereign default on domestic debt obligations on August 17, 1998, it would be convenient—although wrong—to categorize the crisis as just one in a series, sandwiched between the Asian crisis of late 1997 and the Brazilian one of early 1999. It was not just that Russia's default was the first major one of its kind since the 1930s, as no foreign debt was involved. Rather, Russia was just too dangerous to fail. The West, having won the cold war, could not risk placing the so-called peace dividend, much less world peace itself, in jeopardy. The IMF, along with the World Bank, had been assigned the role of the West's bulwark against such a fate. It almost failed, but the West got quite a bargain in the end.

An Independent Russia Emerges from the Detritus of the USSR

Too many people, who perhaps should have known better, expected the independent Russia emerging from the debris of the Soviet Union to become a normal country rapidly. To their credit, this was a pattern that had already been observed in the other transition economies in the 1980s. These unrealistic expectations, fed by Russian and Western political leaders, set goals and even standards of behavior that could only lead to disappointment and frustration on both sides. For example, Lucas, the Moscow correspondent for the *Economist* from 1997 to 2002, was a persistent critic of Russian domestic and external policy during his stay (and subsequently), arguing that Russia—unlike China—should be judged by Western standards of behavior since the Russian political class invited such comparisons. The G-7 leaders from the major advanced economies wanted quick results, and while using the IMF as a politically convenient tool to support parts of their own agenda, were sometimes frustrated with the IMF as much as with the Russians. This was further complicated by the fact that the G-7 as a political grouping representing the interests of the major creditors in the latter part of the twentieth century was not monolithic and had divergent views, especially beyond the realm of economics.

Symptomatic of this misplaced emphasis on the short run was the key role that the IMF was called on to play in this drama. Its managing director (since 1987), Camdessus, wanted to demonstrate that the IMF could rise to such a historical challenge. Many of the IMF's twenty-four executive directors, in theory acting as individuals but in practice representing their governments, had always expressed concern that Russia was receiving favorable treatment relative to other countries that were members of the fund. Their positions, moreover, often reflected their own country's historical stance concerning Russia and were further complicated by inclusion or exclusion from the G-7 deliberations.

As originally conceived by its founders at Bretton Woods in New Hampshire in 1944, the IMF was created as a fund of pooled resources to help member countries adjust to macroeconomic imbalances. In conjunction with its financial support, the IMF helps these countries in devising economic adjustment programs to correct the imbalance. Relatively short-term financing is provided at market-related interest rates in order to cushion the impact of these adjustment policies.[1] In its history, the IMF has played a significant role in helping countries to restore their balance of payments, and guide appropriate fiscal and monetary policies. It was understandable that the West would turn to the IMF for a resolution to the complex set of issues raised by the collapse of the Soviet Empire.

As Camdessus explained to me, "In retrospect, with its short-term focus and lack of expertise in microeconomic issues, it was clear that the IMF was not the appropriate organization to come to Russia's aid in the 1990s, or at least not to take the 'lead' role." But the World Bank did not take up the gauntlet, nor did others. The IMF rose to the challenge, faute de mieux. This book contends that you get what you pay for; the end result was not bad, considering the possible alternatives, and the basis at least was laid for future generations to develop Russia as a modern, even democratic country.

So during the 1990s the IMF was intensely involved with the Russian authorities—meaning effectively the government and the central bank. Indeed, the intimacy between the IMF at senior levels and these Russian officials was close, albeit contentious. IMF staff members and management were consulted on most aspects of fiscal and monetary policies, although the IMF also sometimes complained that the belated nature of the consultation, such as when the exchange rate corridor policy was prematurely announced for three more years in November 1997, was tantamount to a fait accompli.

On their side, senior Russian officials were sometimes running professional and even personal risks in circumventing the country's Soviet-era secrecy acts and laws—for instance, in discussing budget parameters for the next fiscal exercise (budget year) with IMF staff members when even the minister, much less the government or the State Duma (parliament), had not seen them. Despite this close involvement between the IMF and Russian officials, one of the great ironies of the relationship was that in the end, the IMF played only a marginal part in influencing Russia's transition from a Soviet command economy to a market economy increasingly integrated with the rest of the world. Suffice it to say that the policies recommended by the IMF can only be as effective as the government that is implementing them.

An Unlikely Partnership Starts to Take Shape

Thinking back to the kind of world that existed at the time of the Soviet Union, even under President Gorbachev, it is hard to imagine a more unlikely partnership than that between Russia and the IMF. Such a possibility seemed inconceivable almost until the time it actually happened. Although the Soviet Union, as one of the victorious allied countries emerging from the Great Patriotic War (as the Russians call it), had participated in the establishment of the IMF, it declined to become a member. It later forced Czechoslovakia to withdraw from the fund after the Communist takeover, and demonstrated consistently its hostility to the philosophy and policies of the IMF throughout its history.[2] In essence, the Soviet leadership saw the IMF as a tool of Western capitalism and especially U.S. foreign policy. It seems to be one of the ironies of contemporary history that this view, earlier confined to the leadership of the Soviet Union and its like-minded satellites, now appears to have become virtually an article of faith in the antiglobalization camp.

This book has no pretense to present a comprehensive history of Russia's relationship with the IMF. A number of others have already covered this ground in whole or in part.[3] As background to the extraordinary events in Russia leading up to the 1998 crisis, however, it is important to mention some of the relevant issues that emerged beforehand.

The IMF was clearly abhorrent to the Soviet Union. After the collapse of oil prices starting in the mid-1980s and the growing importance of borrowing abroad to sustain domestic consumption, though, some Soviet strategists, especially in the then–Ministry of Foreign Economic Relations, were starting to have second thoughts about the arm's-length relations with the IMF and World Bank. Having seen the financial support provided to Council for Mutual Economic Assistance (COMECON) members such as Hungary, it dawned on some Soviet observers that under certain conditions, some relationship with the IMF might be in the country's interest. It can be recalled that the COMECON was established as an extension of Soviet planning for the allocation and exchange of trade, investments, and finance between the Soviet Union and its satellite countries.

In 1988 already, it seems that some technical suggestions had been put forward on an informal basis to the CPSU's Central Committee (the real decision-making body in the Soviet Union, under the guidance of the party's politburo) to have the issue of economic cooperation tabled at the G-7 Summit in 1989. Discreet contacts were apparently made through a Soviet embassy in Europe, and a long-serving executive director in the IMF from Belgium, Jacques de Groote, was consulted about various aspects of a possible relationship. The issue was tabled too late for the mid-July G-7 Summit in Paris; French president François Mitterrand only referred to a Soviet request to look into the matter further. With the surge of East Germans a few weeks later across the recently opened border between Hungary and Austria, and the fall of the Berlin wall in November, the immediate concern of the West turned to the remnants of the Soviet Empire in Central Europe.

The economic situation of the Soviet Union itself became ever-more desperate, especially given the disruption of trade and finance with its former satellites and the disintegration of the COMECON. At the G-7 Summit in Houston in July 1990, Gorbachev was invited as a guest and presented his request for unprecedented Western assistance. As a result, a crash study of the situation and prospects was prepared jointly by the IMF, the World Bank, the Organization for Economic Cooperation and Development (OECD), and the new European Bank for Reconstruction and Development (EBRD), in association with the European Union (EU).

The G-7 political solution to have all of these international institutions—each with its own established rules, traditions, and hierarchies—cooperate effectively under demanding time constraints and in the public limelight was a recipe for producing a bureaucratic soup. In the end, in order to avoid delay, it was agreed that the IMF would be named the "convener" of the study by the G-7. No doubt because of its phenomenal ability to quickly redeploy its human resources and centralized management structure, at least relative to the other institutions, the IMF took the lead in this process. Camdessus' decisiveness in sensing the historical significance of the endeavor was also no doubt an ingredient. Yet the contributions of the other institutions on microeconomic and structural policies were significant, especially over a longer time frame.

Even though countries such as China, Vietnam, and Poland were already IMF members, the problems in trying to forge a normal relationship with the Soviet Union were considered formidable. These were primarily of a political and ideological nature, evoked by the Soviet leadership but a real concern for Western leaders as well. At that time, there was no question of an application for membership from the Soviet Union; rather, the idea was to create a structure for cooperation with the IMF from scratch. The Soviet Union thus was approved for a "special association" with the IMF in October 1991, which would have allowed the IMF to begin normal monitoring of the Soviet economy. The IMF established, at first informally, a Moscow office in early November 1991, initially located in a couple of rooms on the second floor of the Metropol Hotel. Jean Foglizzo, an acquaintance of Camdessus from Paris who had never worked in the IMF, set up the office.

It was somewhat ironic that this innovative procedure for trying to cope with an extraordinary institutional challenge to the IMF, and more important, how to start to integrate the Soviet Union into the international system of trade, payments, and investment, fell apart two months later when the Soviet Union was dissolved on Christmas (in the West) 1991. Amid the ensuing chaos, in both the West and the East, all those involved, as it were, had to start again almost afresh. The IMF had by that time at least fielded missions to visit each of the USSR republics before the day of the dissolution, and so had a base on which to build future relations with each of the new countries.

The Russian Federation, which emerged as a sovereign entity at the beginning of 1992, with Yeltsin as president and Gaidar as the acting prime minister, was in terrible shape. First, Russia had a unique historical inheritance; transforming a huge economy in a huge territory without suitable institutions or central control proved to be an almost-insuperable task. With the collapse of the CPSU command structure, there was a total power vacuum at all levels. Second, the economy inherited from the Soviet Union was in a state of advanced decay. Third, the simultaneous loss of economic and trading relationships, alliances, and integration with other members of the union made it necessary to find urgent stopgap solutions across-the-board in order to avoid starvation that winter.

Already in fall 1991, the shelves of shops were hopelessly bare, far worse than the normal postwar Soviet experience of shortages. The specter of chaos was near. This wasn't just a shortage of, say, butter with some bread still to be bought after standing in a line for an hour. This was a total absence of goods. This was also a clear and final result of the Soviet legacy of cumulative system failure that could no longer be mended. It could not be blamed merely on Gorbachev's inability to deal with the economy.

The policy response of the Gorbachev government under Soviet prime minister Nikolai Ryzhkov was a wave of product rationing, which had become ubiquitous throughout the Russian territory of the Soviet Union by 1991. Then Valentin Pavlov served from January 1991 until the time of the aborted putsch against Gorbachev in August 1991. An important element in Pavlov's economic policy was to increase the general price level to regulate money and commodity supply. This reform took place on April 2, 1991, and temporarily helped to fill Soviet stores with essential commodities, at least in some regions. Yet this price increase (for the first time since 1961), which happened nine months before Gaidar's price liberalization, was highly unpopular and probably undermined any residual authority that Gorbachev may have had as a political leader.

A vociferous but seemingly fruitless debate about the direction and pace of reforms was conducted on the Russian side during early winter 1992. Most of the members of a special commission in the Russian Supreme Soviet (parliament) were quite skeptical of the advice of the so-called Harvard boys, who favored immediate price liberalization. The Harvard boys, fielded by Harvard's Institute of Development Economics, were among the earliest foreign advisers to the Gaidar government, and notably included Jeffrey Sachs, David Lipton, Jonathan Hay, and Andrei Shleifer. An additional problem was that the commission's time and effort were dedicated to organizing food convoys to Moscow and other places where hunger loomed menacingly close.

Obviously, Soviet academicians had some proposals—but somebody had to choose one of them. Most of the alternatives discussed in public debate and among the Russian population concerned a basic reliance on a gradualistic approach, which should be financed by the West for the most part. But the feeling of many in Moscow and elsewhere was that there was no time for gradualism. And this feeling seemed to be shared by many people outside the political or academic establishment.

In this regard, it really is important to try to appreciate the initial conditions in post-Soviet Russia and just how much the economic misery was a legacy of the Soviet period. The threat of starvation—a prospect not encountered in Moscow and other major cities since the time of the Nazi invasion in 1941—was real. The population was getting desperate. Debates about the appropriate pace of reforms, the ideal sequencing of policies, and the degree of gradualism seemed implausibly academic.

To make matters even worse for the frantic policymakers in the new Russian Federation, the possibility of borrowing from markets abroad to finance emergency food imports was virtually nil. Earlier, in an effort to avert catastrophe (but that merely delayed needed policies), Gorbachev's government—after having already immobilized the savings of much of the population through so-called monetary reform and the mandatory issue of commodity bonds—spent the bulk of the Soviet Union's reputed gold and foreign exchange reserves on trying to finance imported consumer goods.[4] Not only that, but in the late 1980s, it also borrowed massive amounts from a grateful German government—in exchange for facilitating reunification—and also from banks and other creditors.

Until that time, the Soviet Union enjoyed an impeccable payments record and high international credit ratings. Then in November 1991, Vneshekonombank (VEB), the foreign trade bank of the Soviet Union, could no longer service the country's foreign debt and defaulted on its debt payments since the foreign exchange savings of the population and enterprises (about US$11 billion) had effectively been squandered by a despairing Soviet regime. Only foreign governments, motivated by political considerations, were in a position to assist the new Russian authorities during winter 1992, but the largest G-7 members were insisting that the outstanding debt issues—in the wake of the VEB default—be resolved first and then an agreement reached with the IMF.

This was the situation that the incoming Russian government inherited. The debate about whether it could have done things differently or not has been a particularly virulent one. In all of the criticisms of the policies actually implemented at the time, it is not clear what specific proposals would have been better in view of the actual, as opposed to hypothetical, circumstances.

Given the extreme views of the critics of the policies pursued under the Gaidar and then Chernomyrdin governments in Russia, and only conjecture as to what alternative outcomes might have occurred under the prevailing constraints, it is unlikely that this historical debate can ever be satisfactorily resolved.[5] A stoic approach to the issue seems to be warranted, giving the benefit of the doubt to those actually trying to implement policies in totally uncharted circumstances and without the advantage of hindsight.

Of course, it would have been better to have ensured a transition into the post-Soviet era with less social and economic disruption, without calling into question the efforts of millions of people whose education and training had prepared them to live in a different world, and without destroying the limited savings that could have provided a cushion and been so valuable in laying the basis for an emerging middle class during those difficult years. The problem is that all of these unfortunate developments were already evident before the rise of Yeltsin and the policies of his Russian governments.[6]

Of seeming greater interest is the counterfactual in the other direction. I think that the Russian authorities had real choices, and the rest of the world was fortunate in that some of the more likely roads were indeed not taken. In the context of Russia's second revolution of the twentieth century, the choices made were not self-evident. Russia could have been a Yugoslavia, and a Russian "Slobodan Milošević" could have emerged, but it didn't happen. At the very least, it could have been expected that Yeltsin—like his erstwhile Soviet colleagues in Turkmenistan and Uzbekistan—would have turned increasingly autocratic after an initial flirtation with democratic ideas. Or like the president of Belarus, Alexander Lukashenko, President Yeltsin could have aspired to an entirely different approach by trying to maintain state control over most economic activity; or like former president Leonid Kuchma of Ukraine, he could have tolerated a degree of cronyism, undermining the economy's performance.

The IMF Tries to Adapt to the Challenge

Partly in view of the high political drama of the time, partly because of the chronic financing situation, and partly no doubt owing to the recognition of the need for urgent technical advice, the IMF—along with other Western donors and institutions—became quickly involved in the post-Soviet Russian project. Already in spring 1992, at the same time that Russia was preparing to become a member of the IMF, an economic policy program was being devised by the Gaidar government with IMF input. On June 1, 1992, the Russian Federation became the 162nd member of the IMF with a shareholding (called a "quota") equivalent to a little less than 3 percent of the IMF's capital. A country's quota in the IMF is important not only for voting but especially for establishing the maximum amount of money that the member can borrow. Determining Russia's quota, along with other former Soviet countries, was particularly fraught with difficulties because of the lack of data and the artificial exchange rates prevalent in Soviet times.

I think it is fair to characterize the IMF as a conservative institution that evolves slowly, since the executive directors as country representatives need to reach a consensus (formal voting is rare) on policies. For the most part, it is prepared to innovate when the IMF managing director proposes new policy initiatives, which is usually after much behind-the-scenes discussions involving some of the largest, current key members. The fact is that major organizational changes in recent decades have been rare. The collapse and dismemberment of the Soviet Union was one of those occasions where a major and immediate institutional response was required. A new department, European II, was created in January 1992 to take primary responsibility within the IMF for the fifteen new resulting countries, including Russia. The new department sought to address many of the unresolved regional issues—from ruble monetary reform, intraregional trade, and financing and debt issues, to ownership and investment flows, although these synergies declined over time as the individual states, most notably the Baltic ones, forged new external economic and political relations. A former high-level British Treasury mandarin, John Odling-Smee, who had worked in the IMF previously, became the director of the new department. In 2003, European II was disbanded and the IMF reverted to the earlier five area department model with Russia under the European Department.

The new Chernomyrdin government finalized an economic stabilization program for 1992 with the liberalization and unification of the foreign exchange market for the ruble on July 1 as a key condition for a one-year IMF credit, which was approved in June.

In the strict sense, the IMF does not loan money. It is not a bank. As a revolving fund, it provides foreign exchange resources on a temporary basis against an equivalent amount of domestic currency, which must be repurchased within a predetermined time frame. Once approved, the money is available automatically on a standby basis so long as the member remains eligible under the conditions of the arrangement.[7]

The Russian government drew down the full amount of one billion U.S. dollars in December 1992.

The program started to deviate substantially from its objectives shortly after it was approved, however. That experience with failed program performance quickly made the IMF realize that its standard policies developed to assist members with temporary payment difficulties were not up to the task of confronting the seemingly intractable problems of a country like Russia. Russia was almost in category of its own. There was a realization that the process would take longer, and would require a much greater emphasis on technical assistance and institution building than would normally be the case. In tandem with fragile institutions, poorly trained officials, a lack of market signals, and little political will, it was also understood that IMF financial support would have to be considerably greater than could be provided under normal procedures, and yet the accompanying policy conditionality, at best, could not be too demanding. It took some time—and the early experience with Russia—to develop a consensus among IMF members that a new approach was warranted.

Thus, a special new lending facility was created by the IMF on a temporary basis to be used to facilitate the transition for Russia and similar countries. It was called, appropriately, the systemic transformation facility (STF). An economic program covering 1993 for Russia was negotiated in late spring with a crucial condition being the liberalization of the interest rate structure. It was approved by the IMF on July 6, 1993, and the first tranche of US$1.5 billion was disbursed.

The second STF tranche of an equal amount was disbursed in April 1994. The program performance was poor, even relative to the low conditionality requirements. No attempt to analyze these programs was made here.[8] Interestingly, the IMF and the Russian authorities kept looking for ways to ensure better program performance. Or perhaps it would be more accurate to say that the IMF kept looking.

One of the insights into IMF collaboration with the Russian officials was just how one-sided it seemed to be in those early days. And this experience was quite unusual in IMF practice. In most countries, even small ones, senior officials are often well trained in economics (frequently as well as their IMF counterparts), and have thoroughly debated internally their various priorities and options, even in crisis situations. There is usually a fairly clear policy line handed down by the country's leadership. Thus the discussions with the IMF are substantive, with disagreements prevailing at the outset, and each side learning from the other until

an agreed economic program is produced. At the very least, IMF officials—with a good understanding of economics and what has worked in
similar circumstances elsewhere, but less well-informed about the details
of local conditions—confront country officials, who while possibly
unaware of comparative economic dynamics, can impart clear views
about economic and legal constraints, institutional mechanisms, and
political and social realities.

In Russia, oddly enough, these elements were missing. In retrospect,
it is remarkable how few disagreements there were over issues of program
design—that is, what was needed to address a specific problem or achieve
an objective. Perhaps experienced IMF staff members should have been
more skeptical about the surprising lack of disagreement with their proposals. In Russia, maybe even more than in other countries since it had
been isolated for so long, we (as I had joined the IMF Russia team
already in June 1993) had a difficult task in understanding the local
conditions, history, institutions, laws, and so forth. No doubt like many
outsiders, we succumbed to an obvious stereotype about the Soviet
Union, which was its reputedly highly centralized control. Had we understood better the legacy of the disintegration of that central authority, we
might have been able to better appreciate the daunting tasks ahead.
Hence, both the IMF and its G-7 shareholders continued to blame a lack
of political will for poor program implementation rather than any inherent managerial and administrative inabilities.

In fact, it was all the more necessary in Russia that the local officials
should play a dynamic role in defending their country's interests against
the foreigners from Washington who were obviously less familiar with
local conditions. This startling lack of codetermination seemed to
stem from the dramatic collapse of centralized decision making in early
post-Soviet Russian governments, a lack of familiarity with the issues
and negotiating process when there is not a "zero-sum" outcome, and a
total lack of tradition for officials to take any initiative without top-
level sanction. In Soviet times, there was the often-used expression that
"initiative is punished."

It seems that a key to understanding the dynamics of the Russia-IMF
relationship, especially in those early years, was the apparent innocence
or insouciance of the IMF's Russian counterparts, who did not realize
how much had to be done (or if they did, they failed to say so) to trans-
late programs on paper into action on the ground.

Not in all cases, however. I recall a heated discussion in late 1993
with Ministry of Finance (MinFin) first deputy minister Andrei Vavilov

in which the IMF team was pleading with him to include explicit policies and budgetary support for an extensive social safety net to cushion the harsh impact that economic dislocation was causing for much of the population. Vavilov was disdainful of our arguments, replying forcefully that "we had over seventy years of failed social experimentation. It's enough!"

It did not help that the fractious nature of government authority was not conducive to the formulation of forward-thinking policy, much less agreement on negotiating instructions for the Russian side. Finally, the constant change of finance ministers was also a problem as the new incumbent never felt responsible for what had been agreed to by his predecessor. Between 1993 and 2000, there were a total of nine ministers of finance, which was hardly a recipe for either consistent policy formulation or implementation. Individual ambitions also muddled the focus. For instance, it was well-known that Gazprom, the natural gas monopoly, was sacrosanct—under the personal protection of the prime minister. It was long considered obvious in the final years of the Chernomyrdin government that the main reason that deputy economy minister, Sergey Vasiliev, did not become minister, despite his qualifications, was his all-too-attentive focus on Gazprom as essential to resolving Russia's fiscal and structural problems.

In such circumstances, it was hardly surprising that Russia's economic programs of the early 1990s had an unreal quality to them, and were both hard to implement and hard to monitor objectively. Even when the IMF tried to stretch its existing policies to accommodate Russia's needs or create new, almost tailor-made policies like the STF, the programs were of dubious success. Indeed, Camdessus explained to me that "more than any other member country, the attempt to find solutions for Russia's problems created constant tensions with other members in an effort to fit Russia into the framework of established IMF policies."

IMF executive directors and their country authorities expressed continuing concerns with what they viewed as the exceptional treatment of Russia—in terms of staff resources, management and board time, technical assistance, the amount of financial support, and especially on the application of the IMF's policy of conditionality. In essence, countries using IMF money should achieve predefined targets to show that their economic program was on track. This policy of conditionality is central to IMF operations to ensure timely repayment so that the revolving nature of the fund resources is preserved.

It was long contended that the usual standards of conditionality were relaxed in the case of Russia, where there appeared to be a tendency to sign documents, take the money, and limit policy measures to the "prior actions" negotiated in the agreement. In fact, with little confidence that policies would be sustained, the focus of negotiations shifted to the prior actions as the only measures that could be relied on. Yet even here, the Russian authorities seemed to have perfected a "salami" approach in reaching agreements, where they would agree with the policy principle, but then whittle down the scope of its practical application with legislative, administrative, or procedural qualifications. It meant that in the end, you only get a thin slice of what you thought had been agreed to, but accept this outcome as better than nothing. The salami approach was applied on many occasions whether calculating tax yields, agreeing on targets for foreign exchange reserves, identifying tax delinquents, removing tax exemptions, or setting financial conditions for pre-winter deliveries to the Northern Territories.

By 1995, though, Russia was perhaps getting past the worst part of the transition process. Russia seemed ready to embark on an economic program supported by the normal financial facilities of the IMF. The Russian government and central bank approved an ambitious disinflationary program for 1995 that was financed in part by a one-year standby credit approved by the IMF in April. An innovation introduced for the first time in an IMF arrangement was the use of monthly tranching of the money based on monthly performance requirements as well as quarterly reviews of the program. Performance criteria acted as automatic off-on triggers with respect to a country's continuing right to draw on IMF financial resources. If the prespecified quantitative targets were met, the member could draw more from the fund; if not, there were a series of steps to be taken to check whether the deviation was small, temporary, and reversible, in which case the IMF could grant a waiver so that the resources could be drawn, or additional measures would be required to bring the program back to its projected trajectory, sometimes in combination with a modification of the trajectory itself as updated information became available. This was a recognition that uncertainty about the economic environment (because of inadequate data) and a poor track record of program implementation required flexibility in order to make quick corrections to the program before it could veer definitively off track.

Despite the earlier poor program performance and weak leadership, the Russian authorities were able to meet their targets month after month during 1995. Overall, the performance under the standby was exemplary—even by IMF standards. Most remarkable, inflation decelerated from an annual average of 214 percent in 1994 to 132 percent in 1995, and 22 percent by 1996. Russia's foreign exchange reserves (including gold) rose from US$6.5 billion at the end of 1994 to US$17.2 billion by the end of 1995. And the federal budget deficit was narrowed from 9.8 percent of the gross domestic product (GDP) in 1994 to 5.9 percent of the GDP in 1995. There seemed to be light at the end of the tunnel.

During the early days of IMF involvement in Russia (and later as well), the G-7 was trying to orchestrate events for its own political purposes. I thought at the time that the Italians and the British were motivated primarily by a desire to establish business relations, the Germans to recover their large loans to the former Soviet Union, the French to play a major regional role as a conduit for Russian integration with the West (and perhaps to eventually reestablish their historic alliance with Russia, no longer as a counterweight to Germany—as was the case a hundred years ago, but rather to the United States), and the Japanese to finally reach an agreement on a peace treaty to formally end World War II. Most of all, the United States was keen to promote the normalization and transformation of Russia. Both presidents George Bush senior and then Bill Clinton promoted the rapid assimilation of Russia with U.S. interests in the world.

In its early guises, the G-7 played a major role. The problem was the need for consensus on what needed to be done, and in 1991–1993, the Germans drove the agenda through their lowest common denominator insistence on the regularization of the debt situation as a precondition for any further assistance. The IMF was then drawn into a supporting role because of the G-7's insistence, and Paris Club rules, concerning the need for an IMF program before considering a restructuring of the maturities of debt obligations falling due.

The slow pace of progress was frustrating for those G-7 members who pushed for a larger role for the fund, not least as a conduit for large-scale financing (since funding from the IMF was beyond the immediate scrutiny of parliaments), and to move beyond the G-7 consensus rules. Tensions also quickly emerged between the IMF and the G-7 as the United States in particular grew impatient with the perceived slowness in engaging and financing Russian reforms.

This frustration reached a peak when the United States, acting through the G-7, decided to take matters into its own hands and circumvent the IMF by establishing its own office in Moscow to coordinate G-7 efforts.

Called the G-7 Support Implementation Group, it was created at the Tokyo Summit in July 1993. It was supposed to facilitate the effective implementation of G7 assistance to the Russian Federation—first, through promoting information sharing and coordination among the G7 countries; and second, through communication and consultation with Russian authorities. With the other G-7 wary of this U.S.-inspired operation, it was quickly assimilated into the U.S. embassy operations, and most of its resources were directed at trying to justify its continuing existence through the creation of a time-consuming database on bilateral assistance and lobbying the Russian government concerning the "taxation of assistance" issue. The G-7 Support Implementation Group essentially became a lobby to have the G7 and other donors exempted from Russian taxes and customs duties. Its operation was curtailed starting in 1997.

How Much Did the West Have to Pay to Support Russia's Transition?

For those who followed the policy discussions in the West after the fall of the Berlin wall in late 1989, and especially after the dissolution of the Soviet Union on December 25, 1991, one of the prevalent themes was the use of the peace dividend. For instance, in 1992, former U.S. president Richard Nixon alleged that the Yeltsin government was in mortal danger from an unholy alliance of ex-Communists and ultranationalists that would be a prescription for the beginning of a new cold war. Asserting that "the Yeltsin Government will not survive unless it receives a major new economic assistance package," he warned that the peace dividend, which the Clinton administration was counting on to help finance its new domestic policies, would then "be down the tube," as it would be necessary to increase defense spending by billions of dollars.[9]

One thing is clear: the peace dividend—such as it was—was not spent helping Russia or the other states emerging from the Soviet Union. Aslund observes that the United States was able to halve its defense spending as a percent of its GDP from the 6 percent level prevailing in the 1980s by the time of the 9/11 terrorist attacks.[10] Given the minimal level of actual Western financial support and in view of the risks incurred by such a minimalist approach, the results of a less than ideal but peaceful and prosperous Russia should be considered the bargain of the century.

Clearly there was little new financing for Russia from Western governments on a bilateral basis, and multilateral finance from the Bretton

Woods institutions was only a part of the story. Russia's reintegration into the global economy became increasingly important in the 1990s as witnessed by the 1998 crisis itself. Without a developed banking sector or attractive financial instruments, and with endemic mistrust of their own government, most Russian nouveaux riches understandably diversified their assets abroad. At the same time, Western investors, ever in search of higher returns, relentlessly poured funds into short-term Russian treasury bonds and the stock market even before they were legally permitted to do so. This form of carry trade was characteristic of normal investor behavior during the period that economists call the "Great Moderation," from about 1985 to 2005, when inflation, interest rates, and risk premia were unusually low, and so investors were anxious to find novel ways to increase yields on assets. The result was a pendulum swing in Western perceptions of Russia, set against the abiding stoicism of the Russians themselves.

First, let's look at Russian investors. With a tiny equity market, few fixed-interest securities available (except for the treasury bond market between 1995 and 1998), a risky commercial paper market, and negative real interest rates on bank deposits, it was—for the most part—hardly surprising that the majority of Russian citizens and companies generally minimized their ruble holdings to what were needed for transaction purposes. Moreover, tax legislation was confusing and subject to interpretation, with statutory rates, if fully paid, that could be considered confiscatory in some cases. Any surplus funds were invested in mainly U.S. dollar assets, depending on the amount and sophistication of the saver. For households, cash dollars were held at home (that is, as mattress money). A household survey conducted by the U.S. Treasury in anticipation of the introduction of the new U.S. hundred dollar banknote showed that in February 1996, the average Russian family held four hundred dollars in banknotes, or over twenty billion U.S. dollars. For wealthier individuals, dollars might be held in a Russian bank dollar account, but when they had much larger sums, they held them in banks abroad and invested them in short-term instruments. For businesses, much the same pattern was repeated.

Until 2002, when the requirement for CBR authorization to hold a bank account abroad was lifted, most of these offshore operations were not legal under Russian law. Although too often confused with money laundering, they reflected perfectly rational behavior and, apparently in almost all cases, were legal in the host countries. In fact, a number of foreign banks, notably the Bank of New York (BONY) and UBS, developed solid reputations in Russia, Eastern Europe, and elsewhere as credible, efficient, and reliable alternatives in the absence of a functioning domestic payments system. As a result, most interenterprise payments and settlements were effected through such an offshore payments system. Tax evasion was also rampant, and I suppose that some crime-sourced money must have been laundered in the process.

These operations made sense for several reasons: after decades in which Russians could not hold assets abroad, there was a natural desire to diversify; given the paucity of savings instruments in Russia and their poor returns, investing abroad was seen as more profitable; Russian government financial policy, not to mention in Soviet times, was seen as erratic and possibly confiscatory; financial institutions in Russia were seen as weak, untrustworthy, and expensive; and given the poor level of banking services, enterprises found payments and settlements could be effected more efficiently offshore, even among Russian companies. As if higher profit and much lower risks were not good enough reasons to transfer savings offshore, it was likely that tax evasion was an additional motivation for holding assets abroad. One misunderstanding that has arisen in discussions about capital flows from Russia concerns the timing of the liberalization of capital account operations. Russia introduced convertibility only on current account operations on June 1, 1996 (when it accepted the obligations of IMF Article VIII), but introduced full ruble convertibility, including capital account operations, only a full decade later on July 1, 2006.

For foreign investors, Russia up until 1998 figured increasingly prominently in emerging market financial portfolios. Ironically, in early 1998, the relative weight of Russia was raised in the MSCI, a leading index for investment in emerging market economies. The equity market had always been a source of interest to foreign investors, even though periodic scandals surrounding governance issues meant that such investments were probably seen as speculative ones. For fixed-interest securities, the high yields and stable ruble encouraged a massive inflow of funds starting in 1995, at first through "gray" schemes and increasingly through CBR-authorized transactions. By summer 1997, nonresident investors appeared ready to buy just about any asset with Russia stamped on it.

But foreign investors have proved fickle, subject to wide mood swings. Interestingly, political attitudes in the West also followed the instincts of their countries' business communities. Thus, after an initial phase of euphoria in 1993 when Russia seemed destined to imitate the United States, there was a period of abject gloom by late 1994 after disappointing economic results, combined with the outbreak of the first Chechen war and a reaction against reforms, dashed the earlier elation. Then, following Yeltsin's election and especially into 1997, the mood swung wildly back to euphoria, only to come crashing down with the ruble after the August 1998 crisis. The mood hit rock bottom by the end of 1999. But starting in 2002, cautious investors once again shifted gears, ready to reconsider Russia in their portfolios. Capital inflows escalated by 2007 and early 2008, only to reverse abruptly in August 2008. In contrast, Russian investors rarely budged from their long-term skepticism, and therefore mostly stuck to the offshore investment strategy.

Thus far, the reference is really to portfolio investors who limited their exposure to the purchase of paper assets. There has also been a significant community of mostly European companies with direct investments in Russia, buying and/or building companies, and investing in tangible assets like equipment and inventories. But the tangle of outdated laws, regulations, and (until recently) the tax burden with its seemingly arbitrary and even discriminatory treatment have, along with the above mood swings, tended to minimize the enthusiasm of even those companies that recognize the significant potential of the Russian market. Many foreign investors at the time cited the customs procedures as particularly burdensome, time-consuming, and corrupt. In fact, pervasive corruption and arbitrary administrative procedures continue to deter foreign investors.

Finally, in view of what was at stake, it is almost unconscionable how little the rest of the world was ready to provide in support of the country's heavy post-Soviet transition. Each major G-7 country had a good excuse, but as a consequence, no peace dividend was spent on grants to help the Russian people. There has been considerable controversy over how Russian reforms were financed. Early on, some advocated a kind of Marshall Plan for Russia, while at another extreme, others considered that any money supplied by Western taxpayers would be inevitably wasted. During late Soviet times, an estimated forty billion U.S. dollars was borrowed from Western governments, banks, and other creditors. After the breakup of the Soviet Union and until the responsibility for these debts was acknowledged, Western official creditors insisted that there could be no progress in restructuring these liabilities and making them manageable. Moreover, most creditor rules made it impossible to disburse new credits until the old ones were regularized. As Richard Layard pointedly notes, the West sent in its "debt collectors." Creditor insistence that the debt continue to be serviced in full until a rescheduling could be agreed on was partly responsible for VEB's default in November 1991.[11]

The Russian government, after some attempts to work out a sharing formula with the other constituent parts of the former Soviet Union, agreed to be fully responsible for the debts in September 1992—and agreed on "zero-option" deals with the other states emerging out of the Soviet Union that it alone would assume all union liabilities as well as any assets. While it turns out that those liabilities were large, in excess of US$120 billion, the inherited assets turned out to be little more than a few embassy properties abroad—maybe about US$4 billion in gold, including nonbullion gold, and claims on debtors of significant paper value (perhaps about US$10 billion valued using the 1997 "Memorandum of Understanding" with the Paris Club), but of dubious value in terms of collectability. Such was the degree of mistrust that several of the states hesitated in signing a zero-option agreement with Russia, convinced that there were huge assets hidden away.

It is important for my story about the 1998 default to underscore that the Russians, from the outset, made a clear distinction between what they considered Soviet-era debt assumed by the Russian Federation under the zero-option agreements and the external sovereign debt of Russia. The latter liabilities, with respect to foreign currency loans and credits contracted as well as disbursed after January 1, 1992, have been considered sacrosanct. No Russian politician of stature has ever suggested, even during the 1998 crisis, that these latter amounts might even be restructured, much less forgiven.

In contrast, Soviet debts were considered fair game for restructuring, since they were inherited from a juridically different political entity, which included the debts of former Soviet states other than Russia, and were mostly contracted in the final years of the Soviet era in a desperate attempt to forestall an economic collapse. The Western creditors were therefore seen as at least complicit in these debts, which were also essentially considered compensation money from Germany to facilitate the withdrawal of Soviet troops from the former GDR.

This distinction between the two sorts of external debt was not always obvious to many observers. For instance, around the time of the 1998 crisis, there was intense speculation within the London-based investment banking community that Russia might default on its Eurobonds, when such a proposal was never even considered by the Russian side. As in any relatively free society, of course, there was occasional conjecture by individuals that even Russian external debt might have to be restructured or canceled, but this was never considered seriously at an official level. Russians' attachment to the maintenance of an impeccable payment record on Russian external debt was a source of national pride as well as pragmatism. There was no abiding tradition in Soviet Russia to uphold the value of ruble-denominated debt. In Soviet times and sometimes even now, the U.S. dollar (and other currencies) was considered "real" money with purchasing power over goods. Witness the Beriozhka shops that enjoyed such popularity among the *nomenclatura* in Soviet times. Hence, the default and eventual restructuring of the stock of the government's treasury bonds in 1998. Such was the legacy of the Soviet idea of financial obligations. While associated with then–deputy finance minister Mikhail Kasyanov, who kept this key objective in sight even in the dark days of 1998–1999, the commitment to honor the repayment of external debt was in truth a deeply felt value among Russia's political class.

Thus, Soviet-era debt was considered second-class. Some suggested that since the union debt was assumed under duress to some extent in 1992, and in any case was a political gesture, it should be forgiven. Alexander Shokhin, then a deputy prime minister responsible for economic issues, was the foremost proponent of this approach, already proposing in 1994 that Soviet debt should not just be rescheduled but instead forgiven. He cited the treatment by the Allies of Weimar debt (including mostly the accumulated debts with respect to reparation payments ensuing from the Treaty of Versailles) after the Second World War, in which most of the liabilities were canceled, as a historical precedent. The forgiveness of much of Germany's prewar debt was formalized in the Treaty of London in 1953.

Creditors themselves seemed to accept this distinction, since the cutoff date for the Paris Club effectively coincides with the demise of the Soviet Union and the establishment of a sovereign Russia. Official creditors rescheduled Russia's Soviet-era obligations on an annual basis—in parallel with IMF arrangements—from 1992 to 1999. Russia also reached agreement with its commercial bank creditors under the auspices of the London Club in 1997, and later reached agreements with unsecured suppliers and non–Paris Club official creditors with respect to Soviet debts.

The idea of a political settlement of Soviet debt, however, never vanished. The G-7 heads of state recognized the principle of a definitive settlement of these debts in their communiqué at the Cologne Summit in 1999. The communiqué stated: "In order to support Russia's efforts towards macroeconomic stability and sustainable growth, we encourage the Paris Club to continue to deal with the problem of the Russian debt arising from Soviet era obligations, aiming at comprehensive solutions at a later stage once Russia has established conditions that enable it to implement a more ambitious economic reform program."

In dealing with the issue of financing post-Soviet Russia, the discussion would not be complete without addressing how much money was actually provided. Again, views seem to be exaggerated, especially in the West, with claims that huge sums were supplied, which were then wasted or stolen.[12] On the first point, about the amount, Western politicians themselves were mainly to blame for this misconception. It was Bush senior and German chancellor Helmut Kohl who announced a twenty-four billion U.S. dollar "aid" package in 1992, and again Clinton and the G-7 that announced a further package of forty-three billion dollars in 1993. With Yeltsin under a seemingly serious threat from the domestic opposition, the first announcement was made on the day before the Congress of People's Deputies, which promised to offer a showdown over political and economic reforms. The G7 made the twenty-four billion dollar package, including six billion dollars to stabilize the ruble, linked to efforts to fix the exchange rate. The second announcement was made shortly before the crucial referendum on how the country should be governed that was held in April 1993. On April 3, presidents Clinton and Yeltsin met in Vancouver, and ten days later, in Tokyo, where the G7 promised to put up a total of twenty-eight billion dollars (plus fifteen billion dollars in debt deferral).

These numbers are readily dissected.[13] The bulk of the money consisted of debt payments falling due, which could not be paid at that time anyway and so were rescheduled at market interest rates (in other words, no new inflows were involved); another large chunk consisted of wildly optimistic projected disbursements by the IMF and World Bank if programs could be agreed on and fully implemented; and the final portion was the possible use of lines of credit to buy expensive, specific types of imports from creditor countries (and that in reality, should have been considered export promotion). There was almost no grant component— in the normal use of the word aid—nor were there any freely usable funds. Even nontrade bilateral loans, and a few grants, were targeted specifically at the storage and removal of nuclear weapons, scientific research programs, and military resettlement—all areas where the Western countries had a keen self-interest. The U.S. Nunn-Lugar grants for the dismantling, storage, and security of nuclear material from weapons are a case in point.

It is well beyond the scope of this book to analyze how these funds were used. In addition to program (that is, budget support) and project loans, there were numerous technical assistance programs financed by a plethora of international, regional, and bilateral agencies as well as a significant number of government-guaranteed export credits provided by the Paris Club and other governments. But it should be clear by now that the scope for abuse was limited. Perhaps the exception that proves the rule was some early agricultural loans—so-called commodity loans stemming from the Houston Summit in 1991—used to finance imports, which may have disappeared. We do not know for sure what happened to these agricultural loans, but due to widespread convictions that something was amiss in this case, all foreign lending became suspect. Similar suspicions were expressed about the accounting for funds provided by Germany for the housing of officers repatriated from the GDR, which continued after the dissolution of the USSR.

Otherwise, there was little untargeted financing. The bulk, in the form of debt relief, was not even "new" money. IMF and World Bank money either went toward the budget, into reserves, or in the latter case, into specific projects. These disbursements were tightly controlled, and the funds could not, in principle, be misused with respect to their intended purpose. Still, the budget itself or a project might have involved waste or mismanagement, in which case money, being fungible, could have been misallocated. But presumably such spending would have taken place irrespective of the source of financing, so foreign funds could not have been wasted in the narrow sense. That said, clearly there were many projects and expenditures that should have never been authorized.

Interestingly, the one area where there certainly was scope for real abuse was the very one where bilateral creditors were most implicated: in the disbursement of tied trade credits where a Russian enterprise would import goods from a designated list of eligible goods from a particular country. The exporting firm was happy to ship against a full guarantee of its own government's export credit insurance agency. If the importer did not pay, the exporter could collect the insurance readily from the export credit agency. But it was also a free ride—indeed a virtual, nonbudgeted subsidy—for the importer as well. Since the credit was backed by a sovereign guarantee of the Russian government, the importer simply didn't pay, although it received the imported goods.

Until Aleksei Kudrin joined the ministry, MinFin had little means to ensure reimbursement by those importers. Kasyanov had tried since 1995 to end the practice of granting sovereign guarantees, but the pressure from importers, and especially from major exporter governments, was enormous. It took him until he became prime minister, with Kudrin as finance minister, to dispense with this pernicious habit. Obviously the scope for corruption and waste was large as long as this scheme existed. As an example, considerable controversy still surrounds the provision of food aid in the early 1990s by the United States. MinFin contended that the loans were not approved by the government and that the Ministry of Agriculture acted on its own. Critically, it seems that in addition to spurring corruption and stifling the development of a private farm sector, the U.S. food supplies were often simply wasted.

In fact, the main point about the foreign financing to post-Soviet Russia was how small the amount really was. The total amount of loans and grants disbursed to Russia as a sovereign borrower (other than short-tem trade credits) from 1992 to the end of 2002 only amounted to US$20 billion, or about US$2 billion a year on average. In order to avoid double counting, debt reschedulings (which were only a postponement of repayment) are excluded from this figure, as they were all subsequently repaid, as well as loans disbursed but repaid during the period (with interest). The amount is less than 0.5 percent of Russian GDP over that period, and so a fraction of the amount provided to Europe (in terms of GDP) under the Marshall Plan between 1949 and 1954. It represents less than 1 percent on average of the U.S. defense budget alone during those years. Yet the so-called peace dividend to Western nations stemming from the end of the cold war was a significant multiple of this amount. Aslund calculates that the accumulated peace dividend for the United States alone in the 1990s amounted to US$1.4 trillion.[14]

The conclusion has to be that the West got a bargain in Russia but was also lucky. If one considers that all of the external loans and bonds contracted by the Russian Federation have been, and continue to be, repaid in full without disruption even in 1998, and that Soviet-era debts assumed in full by Russia (for seemingly little in the form of compensation in inherited assets of any significant market value) have also been repaid in full after having the time frame for repayment pushed back through restructuring with additional interest to be paid on the rescheduled amounts, the net contribution to Russia from official sources in the 1990s would come to less than US$10 billion, or less than federal grants in the United States to compensate states for armed force base closures over the same period.

Not only was there no Marshall Plan for Russia, it received only limited amounts of grants, especially when considering that much of the aid was not disinterested, and a proportion provided in the form of technical assistance was not always considered high value-added by the Russians. For the West, in retrospect, such a stance vis-à-vis a massively nuclear-armed country with a disintegrating political and social structure looks reckless. The dependence on IMF programs and financing as the major element of a strategy to assist Russia in its post-Soviet transformation was a poor insurance policy against potential calamity.

What did the West and the world get in return? After a fitful start, and most of a decade groping for a clear sense of direction and enormous but immeasurable human costs, a Russia emerged that was no longer a plausible threat and was now a member of the G-20; it was also, at least formally, associated with the EU and the North Atlantic Treaty Organization (NATO), although often at loggerheads. Furthermore, it was a successful emerging market economy—and continues to be, despite the latest global crisis—and displayed problematic but recognizable steps toward some form of democratic system with an embryonic civil society. By any measure, this is a good deal—whatever the ideal that might be desired.

2

Growing IMF Involvement

As the IMF sought to normalize its involvement in Russia, it had to confront the realities of a largely dysfunctional state in which internal rivalries, divergent institutional interests, and bureaucratic infighting made a consensus on policies such as tax collection hard to achieve and sustain, especially in the atmosphere of complacency following Yeltsin's reelection in mid-1996.

Planning for Success

In light of the success in achieving progress toward macroeconomic stabilization under their 1995 economic program, the Russian officials starting working on a much more ambitious successor program that would further stabilization combined with a major emphasis on structural reforms such as privatization, tax reform, social policies, land reform, antimonopoly policies, and so on. For the first time, the World Bank staff members who had the expertise in these areas of structural policies were called in explicitly to help the Russian officials and the IMF team in assisting in the preparation of the Russian economic program that was approved by the IMF in March 1996 under a three-year extended fund facility—the most ambitious of the IMF's lending operations—totaling US$10.1 billion. The World Bank endorsed the identical program with its first structural adjustment loan for Russia at the same time.

One of the popular myths in circulation about the early history of Russia-IMF relations is the notion that the West was blatantly trying to use the IMF to help secure the June 1996 presidential election for Yeltsin. It would seem that some observers looked at the timing of the three-year IMF credit approved in March and concluded that it was too much of a coincidence, especially in light of the large bilateral loans from the

Germans in particular but also from the French around the same time that were no doubt good examples of politically inspired credits.

The timing was in fact largely coincidental even if interpreted by critics as opportunistic on the part of the G-7. Skeptical observers ignored a couple key points, aside from the obvious one that the IMF is not in the business of trying to influence election results for its members. A more subtle point is true: the IMF is an intergovernmental organization, and most of those governments face periodic elections. It is understandable that many of these governments pursue policies that would be considered helpful to future election prospects. Because the IMF is sometimes viewed as an objective outsider, governments may seek an endorsement of their policies by the fund. And given the range of acceptable policies consistent with the objectives of sustainable growth, it should not be surprising that the IMF does often support those policies. First, it is normal IMF policy, provided that there is a financing need, to give a member country the "benefit of the doubt" if it requests that a new program follow on the heels of a successful one-year program, which in Russia's case, was laying the basis for a more ambitious three-year extended fund facility (EFF) program. Second, it is normal fund policy not to require a pause for monitoring performance when a one-year program is seen as being almost impeccably implemented.

It would have been a discrete political act on the part of the IMF to have denied or delayed a new program for Russia in early 1996, just because of the timing of the presidential elections mandated by the country's constitution. Indeed, whether Yeltsin had won or lost, it would still have been incumbent on the new government formed after the elections to endorse and then implement the agreed-on program if disbursements were to continue. The monthly tranching, with all but the first two tranches to be disbursed only after the elections, ensured that risks would be minimized should a president be elected who did not totally endorse the economic program supported by the IMF. For instance, in Bulgaria in 1997 and Korea in 1998, where a change of government seemed likely, the various candidates expressed their intentions to abide by the programs, thus facilitating IMF board approval in advance of the elections. Imagine a counterfactual alternative if the 1995 program had been a failure; the approval of an ambitious follow-up program would have been inconceivable irrespective of political pressure.

In terms of design, Russia's EFF program was overly ambitious in scope. It was conceived to consolidate macroeconomic stabilization with low inflation and a stable exchange rate, while laying the basis for economic growth and completing the transition to a market economy. It contained twelve chapters devoted to structural reforms. The experience of Central and Eastern Europe, and other formerly controlled economies, was incorporated. Expertise was drawn from the World Bank and other institutions. Seminars were organized by the Russian government to consult with experts in each area. If anything, the program concept suffered from overload—what some of us in the IMF staff called a "Christmas tree" approach, with too many baubles and streamers detracting from the main focus. The Russians understood quickly that with so many program measures, they could pick and choose, making it hard to conclude that the program was not working when, say, more than half of the policies were satisfactory, although perhaps not the most crucial ones.

Monthly tranching was to continue for an initial period to take into account the uncertainty surrounding the period of the presidential election ending at the beginning of July, before Russia would "graduate" to a more normal, quarterly monitoring regime in 1997. A particular innovation introduced for the first time in an IMF program was conditionality on revenue (meaning that a monthly minimum target was agreed on for revenue collection that had to be met before Russia could qualify for money). This was done in recognition of the continuing weakness in revenue collection and the difficulties in controlling spending. Until at least 1999 when a nascent treasury system began to function, the Russian government did not know how much it was spending on what budget items, leading to the result, under tight resource constraints, that commitments were unpaid, arrears accumulated, and money was misspent.

It should not be forgotten that for the IMF, Russia was by far its single largest country operation at the time, involving more staff members assigned to it than any other member. Whereas a typical IMF country team might consist of two person-years, and an important country operation might require four to five person-years, the IMF Russia team is estimated to have involved about fifteen person-years at its peak, excluding senior staff members and management time. Likewise, the amount of IMF resources disbursed was considerable. Russia was the largest single exposure of the IMF from 1997 to 2000, and at one time had a gross borrowing of nineteen billion U.S. dollars, or 360 percent of its quota in the IMF. To put this in perspective, it could be noted that a single quarterly tranche for Russia under the EFF was the equivalent of the total amount disbursed to the forty-three countries of Africa in an entire year, on average, from 1996 to 1998.

Politics and People as the Drivers

The interference of domestic politics in the Russian reform process may seem to be too obvious an explanation for what followed, although too frequently overlooked by observers searching for some deus ex machina like collapsing oil prices to explain the unfortunate outcomes of the Russian economy during the 1990s. Much has already been written on the subject, and this book makes no pretense at a political analysis. It is worthwhile to recall again the difficult starting conditions stemming from the collapse of the state.

Suffice it to say that the domestic politics of post-Soviet Russia were messy and byzantine, with competing factions and centers of power. Enormous wealth was being concentrated by a few individuals taking advantage—sometimes legally, but often not—of the distorted relative price structure and monumental bureaucratic inefficiencies in Russia. With a porous legal structure largely inherited from Soviet times, a fiercely partisan and frequently unprofessional media, and extensive corruption at all levels, and without a civil society, it was remarkable that the economy did as well as it did.

Aside from diffuse federal power and unclear ministerial responsibilities, the persons selected to lead Russia in its transformation left much to be desired. Both managerial qualities and public spirit seemed to be in short supply, and these individuals were more beholden to their narrow sectoral interests than to the country as a whole.

Even aside from the so-called oligarchs and red directors (that is, the powerful managers of large productive facilities left over from Soviet times, often in collusion with the regional authorities in which their operations were located), Viktor Chernomyrdin, prime minister from December 1992 to March 1998, was a quintessential apparatchik.[1] The same was true of other high-level officials like Security Council chair Oleg Lobov, and first deputy prime ministers Oleg Soskovets and Vladimir Kadannikov. The inclusion of people in government such as Vladimir Potanin, as the first deputy prime minister responsible for the economy, in his grasping days as an oligarch, was shocking in retrospect. Of course, Potanin was not alone among senior officials in terms of the conflict between business interests and governmental responsibilities. But such appointments were merely the tip of the iceberg. Rare was the appointment of well-intended and competent individuals, albeit with complex motivations, like Gaidar and Anatoly Chubais.

In his position since late 1992, Chernomyrdin was a symbol of stability, seen by many Russians as reassuring after the partially implemented "radical" reforms under his predecessor, Gaidar. Perhaps the best that could be said of his government was that the main players were viewed as men (there were no women) with at least some managerial experience, having been in Soviet or post-Soviet business operations. While such a limited background might sound off-putting for senior government service in much of the world, in Russia, in some quarters, it was at least reassuring that these men might know what they were doing. Such was the legacy of the disintegration of the state.

Ironically, although not intentionally, many of these men were responsible for the collapse of the Soviet system. Chernomyrdin himself epitomized this phenomenon since he used the limited decentralization begun by Gorbachev to spin off most parts of his then-Soviet ministry into the gas monopoly, Gazprom. The initially modest enterprise and fiscal reforms of the late 1980s provided greater autonomy to high officials and local bureaucrats alike, who found themselves able to opportunistically pursue self-interested agendas. Institutional resources were openly employed to generate private gains or defy threats of sanctions. The pillars of the Soviet system crumbled as doubts about the control of resources undermined the authority of organizational structures.

As Steven Solnick, a political scientist who used to represent the Ford Foundation in Moscow, aptly describes in his book, Soviet institutions were victimized by the organizational equivalent of a colossal "bank run," in which local officials rushed to claim their assets before the bureaucratic doors shut for good. As in a bank run, the loss of confidence in the institution makes its demise a self-fulfilling prophecy. Unlike a bank run, the defecting officials were not depositors claiming their rightful assets but rather employees of the state appropriating state assets. Thus, Soviet institutions did not simply atrophy or dissolve but were instead actively pulled apart by officials at all levels seeking to extract assets that were in many ways fungible. The catalysts of state collapse were the agents of the state itself. Once the bank run was on, these officials were not merely stealing resources from the state; they were stealing the state itself.[2]

These men also had to live with the consequences of the "revolution" that they had unintentionally started. They were in positions of leadership in a government where central authority had disintegrated. In late 1998, after the August crisis, there was an ironic incident with Yuri Maslyukov, who had become the first deputy prime minister in charge of the economy in the Primakov government. While a longtime Communist deputy in the State Duma, Maslyukov's previous position in government (except for a brief stint in Sergei Kiriyenko's cabinet) had been as the last Soviet minister of the Gosplan, the state planning agency that organized and managed economic activity throughout the whole country. In a meeting with the IMF, Maslyukov vented his sense of frustration as to how the world had changed. He lamented that when he was in charge of Gosplan, he would push a button or make a call, and things would immediately happen. Afterward, he said forlornly, he gave orders, even pleaded, and no one listened. Some observers of the Russian drama, such as Camdessus, understood the seemingly overwhelming difficulty in dealing with a "failed" state, but there appeared to be no other way ahead, even in the midst of a power vacuum.

The rebuilding of state functions and institutions had to proceed in tandem with the ensuing chaos of economic collapse, disintegration of empire, loss of trading relationships, and disappearance of the very political and economic system itself. As the then–key deputy finance minister, Oleg Viugin, explained to me, "The IMF played a critical role in convincing the widely dispersed holders of bits of power in the emerging post-Soviet Russia that a central authority was necessary if Russia was to develop the functions of a modern state."

In fact, one of the main problems in trying to move beyond the initial stabilization phase of economic policy to tackle the broader agenda of necessary structural reforms, in order to ensure that market capitalism could function efficiently and fairly, was the Russian reality of this power vacuum. It was maybe not so much a vacuum as a disparate group of competing factions for power, where these factions would function in an opaque manner to pursue their various objectives, too often in a narrow self-serving sense.

There was also a fusion of a new layer of emerging entrepreneurs with the institutions of the state, as the weak state sought the support of the new, economically strong and influential class of national entrepreneurs, who came to be called oligarchs. Thus a comfortable environment was created for big business (no matter whether private or quasi-state), where the struggle for survival was superseded by potential support from institutions of the state.

At least it has to be said of Chernomyrdin that he was willing to learn. The only problem is that his learning curve, going from senior apparatchik to self-serving industrialist to a committed reformer, took a long time. But it did seem that by the time he was dismissed in March 1998, he had become a devout monetarist, determined to pursue the virtues of macroeconomic stabilization. Camdessus felt that investing in their personal relationship would yield tangible benefits: if the prime minister trusted him, then he might accept the IMF's well-meaning advice more readily. Although no great fan of the Russian *banya* (sauna) or the hunt, he went along with Chernomyrdin's enthusiasm in the hope of promoting better mutual understanding.

This weak and divided state function also helps to explain a seeming contradiction about the relationship between Russia and the IMF in the 1990s. It should be obvious to the reader by now that the IMF had a somewhat special role as economic adviser and financier in Russia during much of the 1990s. The World Bank staff members and those of other international agencies, some Western think tank and academic advisers such as Aslund, Layard, and Sachs, and the G-7 financial attachés based in Moscow also had privileged access, but none were able to have such a comprehensive overview of the macroeconomic situation on a continuing basis as the IMF.

Perhaps this was because, ultimately, the IMF was the only one with significant financial resources to back up its policy recommendations. Indeed, it was one of the most often repeated inside jokes of IMF staff members involved in the Russia program in the 1990s, especially when explaining the seemingly haphazard commitment of the authorities to policy implementation, that "they were only doing it for the money." Avoiding the limelight, the IMF staff team was an almost constant presence in Moscow, and had access to confidential data, worked on drafts of policy proposals, and advised on alternative strategies based on instructions from IMF management and informed by its experience working in other countries on related issues. Given the intensity and insider nature of the relationship, how is it possible to contend—as Camdessus does, and as reflected in this book—that in the end, the IMF had only a marginal influence on the outcome?

The simple explanation, of course, derives from what has already been said about the weakness of state authority in post-Soviet Russia. As Viugin notes astutely, "How could the IMF be any more effective than the decision-making and implementation capacity of the government whose policies it was supporting?" This is indeed the crux of understanding both the complicity of the two sides collaborating on Russia's economic program and yet the poor track record of the programs themselves. Hence the conclusion that the effectiveness of the IMF in Russia was marginal.

What was also interesting to an outside observer of Russia in the 1990s was the political seasonality. An example here illustrates this observation. When the IMF team was working on balance of payments projections in early 1998 and trying to decide whether a targeted buildup of foreign reserves was feasible, government officials disagreed vigorously. They suggested that reserves always plummet in September and again in January. There was strong seasonality, in their view, which was supported by econometric analysis. It was difficult to pretend that a pattern had been established already for the post-Soviet Russian balance of payments, especially since even-rudimentary balance of payments estimates only existed starting in 1995. But it was the causation that was interesting because it was evident that what they were observing was coincidental political seasonality. Being political, it did not have to repeat itself.

What was really happening was the outcome of poor policy implementation, which usually became apparent by September, leading eventually to a sell-off in the ruble; likewise, a rush of politically motivated budgetary spending and the settlement of outstanding payment arrears at the year-end resulted in a surge in liquidity in January with a consequent downward pressure on the ruble. Thus, the politically driven economic cycle observed in Russia consistently between 1992 and 1998 could be described as: a second quarter of serious implementation of policies under a new program (IMF approval was normally during that period) with initially encouraging results; a third quarter of complacency and complications leading to the program going off track; a fourth quarter where resignation reigns and efforts are seriously relaxed with increasingly worrisome results; and a first quarter in which the political establishment becomes alarmed and starts to grit its teeth, attempting to formulate a new program to tackle the problems. Then the cycle would repeat itself. The governments of Evgeny Primakov, Sergey Stepashin, and Putin—all in 1999—had the daunting task to call a halt to this cycle.

Once the presidential election of 1996 was out of the way, the IMF and its Russian negotiating counterparts recognized reluctantly that valuable time had been lost to domestic politics—although that had been considered almost inevitable. Now, swift progress could finally be made. Had it not been for Yeltsin's chronic health problems at the time, perhaps this would have been the case. That said, Russia still had to live with the legacy of the December 1995 Duma elections in which the Communists and their allies dominated, Chubais's rush to push "loans for shares," and the controversial presidential election itself. In fact, at the time the principal justification for the loans for shares scheme was directly related to the prospect of a Communist victory in the Duma elections and the likelihood that the twelve targeted companies would remain in the state sector permanently.

In hindsight, the scheme was reprehensible since it systematically favored groups with ties to government interests in the transfer of control of the companies. Its implementation cast a long shadow on the reputation of the government and its relations with business, even though Daniel Treisman's analysis demonstrated that the amounts involved relative to the size of the economy were not so large and the underpayment for the assets acquired was not in most cases so outrageous considering the actual market conditions as well as political prospects at the time. Subsequent privatizations have generally been seen as conducted at fair market values.[3]

The IMF was taken by surprise at the time by the manner in which the scheme was implemented. Nevertheless, it is reprehensible to attribute subsequent remarks by the most junior of the IMF's Moscow office expatriate staff members at that time as an admission of the IMF's guilt in this regard, as Stefan Hedlund does, since this was clearly not the IMF's view in that period or since.[4]

There was also the legacy of dealing with men like bankers Mikhail Khodorkovsky (at that time with Bank Menatep), Alexander Smolensky, and Potanin, self-styled power broker Boris Berezovsky, and banking and media magnate Vladimir Gusinsky, who became wealthy seemingly overnight in the early years of the 1990s. By the middle of the decade, they owned or controlled much of the media, and seemed to have been rewarded with influence supposedly based on privileged access to the Kremlin. Yeltsin sometimes at least gave the appearance of being an indecisive or even reclusive leader who had grown dependent on their wealth and power to fend off his political enemies, and especially to get reelected in 1996.[5]

International Politics Were Involved, Too

The relationship between Russia and the West was inherently political, and neither side could escape the legacy of decades of belligerence and mistrust. Despite their misgivings, Western policymakers were determined to be involved in Russian affairs, but at a minimum cost. For the United States, this no doubt reflected the wait-and-see approach that was propounded by Brent Scowcroft, the National Security adviser to

President Bush senior, in 1989–1992 and has shaped a large part of Western policy toward Russia ever since. It has become a cliché for many observers, both inside and outside Russia, that the foreign policy interests of the major shareholders of the IMF dictate the institution's agenda.[6] No country is perceived to pursue its self-serving policies through the IMF more blatantly than the United States.

It may be the case that the United States, in particular, sought a key role for itself in bilateral relations with Russia and through the IMF—so much so that the IMF was seen by some as an agent of the U.S. Treasury. To what extent was this true? In conversations while preparing this book, Camdessus vigorously denied ever succumbing to political pressure with regard to IMF policy on Russia. A few poignant examples are provided in successive chapters. At this point, it is useful to shed some light on the more general issue of an apparent contradiction about political influence on the IMF.

Camdessus explained this point quite well:

[The IMF] management is in an almost constant dialogue with members of the Executive Board and representatives of the major shareholders. And, of course, one listens to what they have to say. It is often the case that on important issues there is a common approach and even emphasis, and sometimes they even have new ideas or thoughts to share, which management can take into consideration. In fact, disagreements are rare as to the preferred course of action, and often even to the timing.

In such circumstances, senior officials in some member countries were tempted to take credit for having influenced the IMF to adopt a particular approach. In some cases, in order to look good to political superiors or legislatures, especially ambitious officials even splashed their so-called exploits in the media. The fact is that "getting" the IMF to do what it was going to do anyway was no tall achievement. The tactic worked, and Camdessus and Stanley Fischer both tolerated it as an inevitable result of dealing with the big egos of some officials.

I would concur with Camdessus as far as *direct* political pressure was involved. As a senior member of the IMF's negotiating team from 1993 to 2001, I perceived no obvious political interference. In view of my position, it would have been virtually impossible for such political actions to have taken place without my being aware of it. That said, given that the IMF is an international institution that reflects the policy priorities of its membership, weighted by the size of their quotas in the fund, it would be naive to contend that political considerations had no role in at least an indirect way through lobbying and research as well as discussions of priorities. In light of the constant dialogue within the IMF at all levels, however, it is virtually impossible to distinguish indirect political influence from other forms of interaction.

Indeed, with all due respect to what Camdessus said about direct political interference, it can be surmised that this indirect or more subtle form of political suasion was operative. It could not have been otherwise. One could well imagine that the IMF would become either marginalized or immobilized if its management was not sensitive to the views of its major shareholders. Camdessus and Fischer thus were fully aware that the United States and its G-7 partners wanted the IMF to keep Russia engaged in a program mode, and as a consequence, they possibly settled for less, earlier (rather than holding out longer, for more) and more often than they would have done if the major shareholders had been disinterested. In such cases, no overt pressure was necessary. This might explain (in the context of the Russian political cycle) why Camdessus would arrive in Moscow in a late winter flourish almost every year to announce to the world that a new agreement was at hand.

Yet even if it can be legitimately contended that the IMF was not politically motivated in its work on Russia, this was clearly not the perception of the Russians. The predominant Russian view in the 1990s was inherited directly from the Soviet Union: all negotiations were a zero-sum game. If the IMF did well in getting its way, this inevitably must have been a loss for Russia. Most of the time, and no more so than in the Primakov era, Russians could not really believe that the IMF's only motive was to try to help Russia establish a viable, growing economy for its people and assume its rightful place in the international community. Many Russians could only imagine that the IMF was a surrogate for the major Western powers, which had their own secret agenda to keep Russia weak and dependent. From their perspective, all the main steps taken by the IMF were politically orchestrated in line with the political objectives of the major shareholders.

The most ironic aspect of the role of the IMF is just how limited a part it played in Russia's transition from the Soviet mode. Indeed, even Camdessus exaggerated only a little when he explained that "the outcome of what has happened in Russia depended 99 percent on Russia and only 1 percent on the IMF." In view of the modest marginal effect, it is ironic that governments and international organizations fought for prominence, including the IMF's sister organization, the World Bank.

Among the infighting, Camdessus ensured that the IMF predominated. This was relatively easy given that the IMF controls large amounts of quick-disbursing resources and can redeploy its staff in a flexible manner. As Camdessus said, it also reflected the philosophy of the IMF staff that it rises to and even welcomes new challenges. This was—in a historical sense—ironic. Here was the IMF, mandated to deal with helping countries correct financial imbalances in the short term, struggling to understand and advise a country in critical need of a vast societal restructuring, involving virtually all institutions and economic sectors. As Harvard economics professor Andrei Shleifer and his UCLA colleague Treisman noted in a slightly different context, we were "without a compass."[7]

When I asked Camdessus how this happened, he answered with a rhetorical question: "Who else?"

The World Bank Plays a Supporting Role

The obvious answer to my question, as Camdessus eagerly agreed, was the World Bank. No other institution could have such a global reach, deep pocket, and long-term perspective, or such extensive in-house experience with institution building, administrative reform, and microeconomic restructuring. Other multilateral agencies, notably the EBRD and the International Finance Corporation (a subsidiary of the World Bank Group), played a useful but more limited role, especially in the critical area of private sector development, including the promotion of small and midsize enterprises—the latter being a perennial weakness in Russia's economic infrastructure. In retrospect, Russia should have been the historic challenge for the World Bank—the greatest opportunity to apply its wisdom and experience in shepherding a stricken country like Russia through an unprecedented and treacherous transition.

But it didn't turn out that way. Instead, if anything, the World Bank played a role of junior partner to the IMF, at least until 1996. Up to that time, the World Bank had only been involved in more narrowly targeted projects and sectoral issues backed by its loans. As Andrei Bugrov, the perceptive and skilled ex-diplomat who was Russia's executive director on the bank's board from 1993 to 2002, explained to me, it was ironic that by the time the World Bank had geared itself up to play a major role at the advent of the Putin era, Russian priorities had changed, with a lower priority assigned to foreign-financed programs and advice.

There are several ways of trying to understand the bank's role as junior partner in Russia in the 1990s. First, it needs to be recognized that the bank, in many ways, had a much tougher job in Russia than the IMF. Macroeconomic stabilization is easier to assess than the difficult job of correcting fundamental microeconomic misallocations and distortions, and devising the right policies in a coherent manner. The IMF also had natural counterparts in the MinFin and CBR, whereas the holdovers from the Gosplan were hardly ideal counterparts for the World Bank, and it took time to change. The bank's limited initial involvement in Russia is also reflected in the numbers. Whereas by the end of 1998 the IMF had disbursed a total of eighteen billion U.S. dollars, the bank had only disbursed three billion dollars, and much of it was parallel financing with the IMF-supported program. Finally, it certainly could not have helped that Lewis Preston was the bank's president from September 1991 to March 1995, since he was in poor and deteriorating health. He died in May 1995.

An analysis of this issue would probably require a book unto itself, and the nuances would undoubtedly escape even the most knowledgeable outsiders. Suffice it to say that Camdessus described the bank's relatively limited early role in terms of what he saw as two fundamental aspects of its operations. One aspect was a preoccupation with the AAA credit rating that the bank enjoyed on the world's capital markets, at least until James Wolfensohn assumed the World Bank presidency in 1996. Ernest Stern, at the time the bank's executive vice president, effectively running the institution, was determined to do whatever was necessary, including keeping Russia at bay, to avoid jeopardizing that rating. Stern understood that Russia would have to be a huge operation to have any chance of success, necessarily disrupting the rest of the bank, for a highly uncertain outcome at best. The bank's prized AAA credit rating could have been adversely affected.

Second, and more important in Camdessus' view for explaining the bank's early reticence to get heavily involved in Russia, was the culture of the bank itself. Most of the World Bank staff members were geared to traditional development issues: Africa, South Asia, and Latin America were their natural constituencies. In the absence of visionary leadership at the top, bank staff members were less than eager to plunge into the quagmire of Russian issues. Bugrov, in a recent discussion, broadly concurred. He observes that the bank, by the end of the 1980s, had moved beyond what he saw as a broad mandate supporting Western interests in the cold war with the Soviet Union. The senior management of the bank, in his view, entered the 1990s with a bold emphasis on the eradication of poverty. The focus was on the provision of the basic necessities—food, water, basic health care, and education—especially for children in mainly the dirt-poor rural areas of the third world. Russia, and the other states emerging out of the disintegration of the Soviet Union, just did not fit into this conceptual framework. It took several years to broaden the focus in practice.

In fact, as Wolfensohn found, given the highly decentralized nature of the bank, even a strong push from the top didn't always go far. Viugin suggests that the virtual absence of the bank from a major role in Russia in the initial years of reform and a larger, yet still modest role later can be explained by the fact that the World Bank essentially operates as a bank, not as an effective intergovernmental institution focused on the top policy concerns of the membership. Thus, the bank is cautious and risk averse, worries about the creditworthiness of its assets, judges career success on the basis of new loans rather than program monitoring, and finds its development mandate quite sufficient.

Moreover, Bugrov underscores a parallel problem associated with the bank's decentralized lending operations whether for programs (budget support—but tied to ministry or sector-specific implementation conditions) or projects: a form of "clientitis." He contends that the bank's programs in Russia did not always reflect the structural policy priorities of the federal authorities so much as the professional interests of the bank staff and the lobbying efforts of various line ministries, or some combination of the two. A major blunder, in his opinion, was also caused by the bank's reluctance to support programs for small and midsize enterprises as a poverty-prevention measure and stimuli for the emergence of a middle class.

In late 1997, Elvira Nabiullina, the then–deputy economy minister responsible for liaison with the World Bank, and Evgeny Yasin, the then–minister of the economy and the intellectual mentor of the Russian reformers, complained to Bugrov. Their ploy was to try to get around the bank's country team by inviting other senior bank staff members who were outside the bureaucratic hierarchy dealing with Russia to visit Moscow and then appeal to them to listen to local concerns. Stiglitz, the bank's controversial chief economist at the time, did indeed travel to Moscow with two high-level bank colleagues. Their trip turned out to be poorly timed, however; the brunt of the financial crisis hit during their visit in May 1998. Although the Russians had been hoping to get the bank to change its work priorities and methods, the message was lost in the ensuing crisis.

An example might help to underscore the problem. In December 1999, the bank and fund jointly proposed to then–prime minister Putin a seminar organized by then-professor Yasin to assist the new government in the formulation of its economic strategy. The date was set for early April 2000, but then the bank staff members started to find excuses to postpone the seminar. Again it was Nabiullina who complained that the bank staff members just were not prepared and so were making up excuses. The bottom line was that despite repeated attempts, including the Stiglitz visit, to try to make the bank more responsive to the Russians' own priorities and program that work—like the budget—on a calendar-year basis, the bank always insisted on starting discussions on structural programs in the late spring/early summer. The result was an inevitable conflict, since the authorities would have almost always been obliged to set their structural policies (including privatization priorities) by the time the bank staff members were ready. So not only was potentially helpful bank expert advice not available but much time and effort also would be lost when the bank would act offended that the Russian authorities had already proceeded on their own. In this case, the date was not post-poned, largely because Russian government officials insisted that they were under direct instructions to hold the seminar at the originally agreed-on time.

To be fair, World Bank staff members saw the situation differently. One senior bank staff member complained to me that the IMF was arrogant, and considered the bank as just another financing source or perhaps a consultant on some specific questions. He rightly remarked that the fund staff members did not fully trust the bank, and did not respect the internal constraints and procedures of the bank in formulating programs with the Russian authorities. He noted that there was resentment at the power and privileged access of the IMF staff members, who were suspected of purposely relegating the World Bank to a supporting role in the eyes of the Russians. Although sympathetic to his arguments, I observed that the size and decentralized nature of the bank did make quality control and confidentiality a problem, even if many individuals were highly qualified.

No One Could Solve Russia's Tax Problem

Following the final round of the presidential election in early July 1996, the widespread expectation, abstracting from Yeltsin's obvious health problems, was that the danger of a policy reversal having been definitively averted, now progress could finally be made in the transformation of the economy as well as the encouragement of new investment and growth. The Russian elite went off to their dachas to savor the prospects to come. The oligarchs decided to cash in on their efforts to promote Yeltsin's reelection, by either withholding tax payments in view of other services that they considered rendered and/or cutting back on areas previously used as vehicles to promote their political causes. For instance, Gusinsky, the owner of the then-top-quality daily newspaper *Segodnya* through his Media-Most holding, told his staff that he was tired of losing money and no longer needed the influence that owning a quality newspaper brought with it, and urged them to refocus on the "man on the metro." The editorial board and most of the staff resigned, eventually establishing a new independent liberal newspaper called *Vremya Novostei*.

On August 23, 1996, Chernomyrdin was asked to form a new government. It looked much like the previous one, despite a few new faces. Alexander Livshits, until then the president's economic adviser, succeeded Vladimir Panskov at MinFin, and Potanin succeeded Kadannikov as first deputy prime minister in charge of the economy. Former finance minister Sergei Dubinin and former deputy finance minister Sergey Alexashenko—who both joined the CBR in early 1995—continued as chair and first deputy chair, transforming it into a modern, professional central bank, and increasingly taking charge of macroeconomic policy, using monetary policy to offset fiscal laxity.

MinFin, still largely run by Vavilov as first deputy minister, remained a weak institution. Not only was Vavilov a powerful first deputy minister, no doubt in part owing to his reputed close relationship to Chernomyrdin, but also he served as minister after the 20 percent drop in the ruble on "Black Tuesday," October 19, 1994, and until the appointment of Panskov as minister on November 4, 1994. In fact, Vavilov remained the power center of MinFin, closely controlling all of its foreign operations during the ministries of Panskov and later of Livshits. It was only with the arrival of Chubais and Kudrin in March 1997 that Vavilov was removed from MinFin. MinFin's operations, especially its foreign ones, were opaque, and the budget under another first deputy minister, Vladimir Petrov, was equally nontransparent. Livshits, to his regret, was unable to get rid of either person. The CBR became the most professional official institution in Russia. Indeed, as Camdessus later told me, he took some pride in this, along with getting the CBR accepted into the exclusive

Basel "club" of central banks. The CBR chair was invited to attend the monthly meeting of the world's lending central banks, held at the Bank for International Settlements headquarters in Basel starting in June 1997. Of course, the high real interest costs involved in such a policy mix, tight money and loose fiscal policies, were initially viewed as a tolerable price to be paid, while the fiscal situation was to be brought gradually under control. As will be seen below, partly for reasons beyond Russia's control, time ran out.

Returning from their holidays, the Russian authorities were shocked at the disastrous cash tax collection of September 1996. Even government wages could not be paid in full, and Yeltsin was reported to be furious. Combined with the rapid disinflation, exposing the weakness of many enterprises in a fractious and largely unregulated market environment, the bitter vicious cycle of nonpayments exploded. After all, a government that cannot even honor its own obligations sends a negative signal to other economic agents.

As a result, or more perhaps in a panic to satisfy the Kremlin and presumably to impress the IMF, Chernomyrdin announced in October 1996 the creation of the Temporary Emergency Tax Commission (VChK) to exert maximum high-level and public pressure on major tax delinquents. The experiment was a monumental failure (although its use still featured in economic programs through 1998). Kudrin, who had been in charge of the Kremlin's financial control department at the time, later lamented that it would have been better to never have raised the ante in such a public manner. No large taxpayers ever received more than a public tongue-lashing from the VChK.

So although the Russian authorities had demonstrated the previous year that they could pursue better macroeconomic policy, by 1996, in retrospect it seems that the easy part was done. Relative to the real—but poorly understood—nature of the daunting problems facing post-Soviet Russia, the difficulties of bringing inflation under control were relatively simple—largely a question of assertive monetary management based on an exchange rate anchor. Besides, the IMF was well equipped, technically and institutionally, to assist the Russian authorities in this limited endeavor. But disinflation had exposed the failure to address the revenue, spending, and financing aspects of budgetary policy.

The key task facing policymakers in 1996 was to build on the success of the 1995 program. It appeared to me and my colleagues as a logical progression. But the institutional, administrative, managerial, and political problems inherited from the collapse of the state thwarted implementation at every step. Thus, success in accomplishing this task was mixed at best. The continuation of a firm policy of monetary restraint by the CBR led to a further decline in inflation. Also, the exchange rate was maintained within its corridor in spite of considerable pressures associated with the presidential elections, but the real rate of the ruble was appreciating rapidly.

Economic activity did not pick up as projected, however, partly owing to the impact on investor confidence of uncertainties about the outcome of the elections and the president's health, but also because of poor policy performance, including the failure to accelerate structural reforms. The weak fiscal performance not only contributed to high interest rates but also to growing general uncertainty about policy sustainability. By the end of the year, it was clear that much work remained to be done to secure a lasting stabilization, and a recovery of living standards in Russia was still nowhere in sight.

The fiscal situation in Russia by the end of 1996 was disturbing. In the 1996 program, the federal government deficit was not to exceed 4.2 percent of GDP. This deficit was projected to decline by about a percentage point per year during the three-year program period. Revenues in 1996 were projected at 11.3 percent of GDP (up from 10.3 percent of GDP in 1995). It was many months into 1997 before the seriousness of the problem became apparent, with the deficit reaching 7.8 percent of GDP and cash revenues only 9.1 percent of GDP.

The problems in Russia were not unique, and in fact were found in other transition economies, as Gaidar noted in the introduction. A substantial revenue shortfall, a distorted structure of expenditures with payment arrears, and significant weaknesses in the institutional arrangements that underpin revenue and expenditure management together made fiscal issues the main economic policy challenge in Russia in the late 1990s. Tax reforms lagged, on both the policy and administrative sides, resulting in a downward trend in revenue.

Of the many problems confronting the Russian authorities on the threshold of 1997, clearly the inability to collect sufficient revenue to finance the state and correspondingly reduce the state's spending commitments was the Achilles' heel of economic policy. What was Russia's tax problem? In a real sense, the Russian tax system needed to be reconstructed, not reformed. Tax concepts, accounting rules, and procedures for taxation did not keep pace with the rapid transition to the market economy. The tax system was thus an unhealthy mix of modern market taxation principles combined with outdated procedures that were designed to control physical production, rather than monitor and enhance tax compliance.

One example of this problem was the interrelationship between modern enterprise tax concepts and the Soviet accounting system. Taxpayers were required to maintain standardized accounts, regardless of whether or not the accounts accurately reflected their economic activity, and in particular services. Emphasis was also based on cost computations because cost formed the basis for the markup pricing system under the old regime. Such an emphasis created adverse tax rules where businesses that sold below cost (however measured) were taxed on the negative difference; that is, the rules under the prior regime assumed that it was impossible for producers to sell at less than cost, regardless of changes in demand or cost structures. These rules, combined with few deductions such as advertising and interest expense, resulted in a tax base that did not reflect the value of the activity and generally in a overstatement of enterprise profits relative to modern accounting systems.

Also, in tax administration, as in most areas involving the use of statistics, there was an almost automatic Soviet tendency to count totals rather than focusing on the main parameters. Hence, the tax authorities wasted their efforts in a hopeless attempt to control all taxpayers rather than to monitor, say, the largest 5 percent, which accounted for the bulk of tax revenues. The same was true for customs, exchange control, or banking supervision. This factor, combined with others, created a tax system that could not be effectively administered. In fact, many of these procedures were not necessary in a market economy where the stress is placed on value, not volume, and administration is designed to monitor, not control.

A mentality resulted where it was assumed that taxpayers were cheats and stole from the state. In part, this became a self-fulfilling prophecy, because taxpayers could not comply with all the tax rules, did not understand the basic procedures, and were penalized severely for computational mistakes. It became cheaper not to comply at all by entering the informal sector, reducing investment, or attempting to influence the process by bribery. Revenues fell, and the system became increasingly corrupt.

The revenue collection problem was compounded by two factors, which themselves stemmed from low revenues, thereby inducing a vicious cycle. One was what could be called the "Krisha" factor, or in other words, a protection racket, which became especially pervasive at the local level. The simple fact was that taxpayers, in the process of honoring their legally mandated tax commitments, expected the state to provide protection and public services in exchange. With a resource-starved, inefficient, and relatively powerless state, but a reasonably well-organized criminal power, taxpayers preferred to pay "taxes" in exchange for the real services supplied by criminal gangs. Needless to say, taxpayers did not tolerate well the notion of double taxation, so that the more paid to the Krisha rackets, the less received by the state, and hence even fewer services that could be financed by the state, even assuming that it was sufficiently organized.

The pervasive and perverse effects of corruption and economic inefficiency also manifested themselves in a second self-defeating factor in terms of revenue collection: the problem of nonmonetary forms of settlement. The disinflation process in the mid-1990s exposed some inherent weaknesses in the post-Soviet Russian economy: inefficient enterprises producing too little value-added (or even negative value-added) output in a market economy. With insufficient demand and inadequate cash flow to meet expenditure commitments, these enterprises engaged in various forms of barter. Wage arrears and other types of spending arrears were just one particularly blatant aspect of this phenomenon.

The Russian state itself, even at the federal level, set the worst possible example by compensating for inadequate cash revenue by paying for goods and services with tax offsets in various forms. Tax offsets, in their simplest form, allowed the state to settle its spending commitment by considering the amount payable (often inflated for the purpose) as the equivalent of tax receipts. Trading in tax offsets not only became a major business activity in itself but taxpayers also had an incentive to use offsets (at a discount) to pay tax obligations rather than cash, thereby further exacerbating the revenue problem.

As a result of the poor cash tax collection, Russian finance ministers, starting with the late Boris Fedorov in 1993, were forced to resort to the practice of sequestration, whereby MinFin would simply not provide the financing to carry out budgetary expenditure. In part this could be done in the early 1990s because there was genuine confusion between what was budgeted, what was authorized but not budgeted (especially by the so-called power ministries), and the spending promises (frequently made by political figures on the stump, including Yeltsin). Later, sequestration provisions were explicitly incorporated into the budget (until 2001), recognizing that spending should not exceed actual financing.

The problem was that in the absence of a treasury system (which was only extended to the power ministries in 2002), budgetary control over expenditure commitments was lacking. Budget arrears were eliminated at the federal level in 2000, but still persisted in some regions into 2002. Hence, even with the sequestration of cash financing, budget arrears could still proliferate, further promoting the disincentives for tax compliance, including the recourse to nonmonetary means of settlement.

In fact, even more than the revenue problem, the lack of effective budgetary expenditure control was the fundamental shortcoming of the Russian fiscal system. Without a treasury system to authorize and monitor both budgetary expenditure commitments and payments, the federal government simply did not know what it—and the other levels of government—was committed to spend nor what it was actually paying for. This meant that government spending was a veritable black box. Since spending was opaque, those who manipulate the black box for their own purposes also had a keen interest in its perpetuation. Thus, even though a basic functional treasury system is an essential feature of government operations throughout the world, and despite the large amounts of bilateral and multilateral technical assistance provided even early in Russia's economic transition, progress in even starting seriously the implementation of the federal treasury was slow until late 1997. Some degree of control was asserted on a progressive basis: for instance, in 1994, a decree was issued requiring the explicit authorization of the minister of finance for any external loan contract or guarantee; in 1995, surveys were developed to monitor federal spending arrears ex post facto of the nonpower ministries. This survey system was improved further, and by mid-1997 it was possible to monitor all government spending arrears other than those of power ministries, where more aggregated data were provided to MinFin.

One of the obvious and major problems confronting the IMF and the Russian authorities, while trying to tackle these issues over the medium term (since there were no quick fixes), was what to do in the meantime. This was a particular problem for the IMF. Its experience elsewhere had been to insist on concrete measures whose effects were quantifiable and verifiable. As Viugin explained, the IMF kept insisting on new revenue measures, including higher tax rates, even when it was clear that the medium-term fiscal reforms had to move in the opposite direction. The IMF, in his view, was caught in the trap of having to focus on revenue (known) versus expenditure (unknown), and on the federal level rather than the general government. But Viugin acknowledged that there was probably no other way to approach the problems at that time.

Banking Is Also a Problem

On the eve of 1997, there were at least two other areas of official policy under the CBR's control. One was Russia's poor excuse for a banking system. Much has been written about the nature of the pre-1998 banking system, with over two thousand banks, most tiny or so-called pocket banks, essentially the treasury department of an enterprise. Many of these banks easily obtained a license, including a general foreign exchange license in the lax environment of the early 1990s, and conducted unlimited opaque operations for their owners. Under Dubinin and Alexashenko, the CBR set up a special unit, the operations department (OPERU II), to monitor the conditions of the largest fifty banks. The process of improving reporting was gradual, and when it counted, it was clear that even the CBR management did not have a complete up-to-date picture of short-term exposure, especially off–balance sheet liabilities denominated in foreign exchange.

Against considerable opposition, beginning in 1996 the CBR management imposed minimum capital requirements on existing banks. Yet the CBR law gave commercial banks three years to comply before the provisions would be binding, and the requirement was duly withdrawn by the new CBR board under Viktor Gerashchenko in 1999, just before it was to take effect. Only since mid-2002, under the management of Sergei Ignatiev, has a minimum capital requirement for banks operating in Russia been introduced by the CBR, subject to the three-year application delay.

Lastly, there was the issue of exchange control and the liberalization of capital operations. There has been an undue amount of controversy around this issue—with accusations that a premature opening of Russian financial markets precipitated the August 1998 crisis. The thrust of the criticism was that a premature opening of the Russian capital market, especially the ability of risk-sensitive emerging market traders to invest (and divest) in government treasury bonds, was doomed to collapse in the absence of a strong banking system and prudent fiscal policy. Too much of this controversy seems to ignore both the facts and the likely counterfactual outcomes with highly constrained domestic and external financing. Russia introduced current account convertibility in June 1996. This meant that it freely allowed documented current operations such as trade, tourism, and payments for services, including interest payments.

The IMF did not advocate, nor did the Russian authorities implement, a liberalization of capital account controls—although clearly some rationalization was called for to address persistent complaints about corruption and arbitrary administrative interference by the various government agencies involved (and that were competing for economic rents) in the application of exchange controls. In fact, it would have been inconsistent to argue for the removal of capital controls—even if they were seen to be largely ineffective—since external creditors, who were providing Russia with exceptional balance of payments support in the form of loans to the budget and debt rescheduling, expected the authorities to take steps to keep the financing provided in the country, including through the recourse to capital controls.

The first point to stress, although it is widely ignored, is that Russian exchange controls—despite (or because of) the several institutions devoted to trying to control capital flight—were broadly ineffective. During the 1990s, Russian capital freely flowed abroad. Only small, unsophisticated operators, or the many economic agents trying to conduct their international transactions according to the confusing legal and administrative procedures (including most nonresident investors), ever seemed to get caught or even deal with the exchange-control authorities. Moreover, large-scale transfer pricing using an offshore marketing office was perfectly legal and widely abused. The notion of relying on capital controls to stem capital flight was therefore all form and virtually no substance. While in terms of numbers of operations foiled or controlled, the controllers could point to their increasing good work, relative to the size of the flows, their actions were nevertheless insignificant. In fact, I had long maintained that a relaxation of controls might actually help to stem net capital outflow by engendering greater confidence and removing one of the risks in holding funds onshore.

Second, as a practical matter, in the case of the opening of the government domestic treasury bills and bonds (GKO/OFZ) market to nonresident investment in the latter half of 1996, there was nothing new. Most of the large nonresident investors who wanted to be in the market could already do so through gray schemes. Indeed, the proliferation of these unregulated gray schemes was a major incentive for the CBR liberalization action.

Lastly, there was also a strategic consideration. To bring inflation down and ensure continued macroeconomic stabilization, it was important to finance the Russian budget as in other countries through nonmonetary means. There was thus a two-pronged approach. One was to bring the deficits down so that less and less financing would be required. Under the EFF, the federal deficit target for 1998, for example, was no more than 2 percent of the GDP, and the other prong of the strategy was to broaden and deepen the domestic financial market through integration with international capital markets. This would also have the double advantage of lowering the relative cost of borrowing. Unfortunately, only the latter prong was put into practice.

That said, it has to be noted that there were risks. The international capital market, as Fischer explained to me, had assumed rapidly the key financing role in Russia, including as a disciplining factor. And the market was much tougher—and less forgiving—than the IMF. Hence, the opening of the domestic market, which was already a fact in practice, was purposeful, even if the conditions for making it work did not materialize. In the story that follows, the inherent weakness of Russia's budget along with the political moves that kept interfering with possible timely responses, combined with a deteriorating global environment, became Russia's undoing in the financial crisis that did not have to happen.

3

Russia Seems to Be Turning a Corner

Despite the heavy legacy, at the IMF we were hopeful that 1997 would be more promising for resolving Russia's economic problems. The elections were out of the way, a three-year economic program supported by the IMF and World Bank was in place, and the global financial environment was benign. It seemed to us that if the Russian political class could harness and sustain sufficient political will to implement the policies in its program, then a corner really could be turned. Of course, life is often a question of whether opportunities are seized or missed. The same is true for countries.

An Inauspicious Beginning

As Russians started to sober up from their extended new year holiday period, the mood was appropriately somber. On the economic front, they had little to show—at the beginning of 1997—for years of sacrifice, despite the many promises and high expectations, except perhaps a more stable currency and lower inflation. This was small comfort when the road to prosperity seemed increasingly forlorn. Output had continued to decline in 1996, for the seventh year in a row—or no doubt even longer, since the growth statistics of the late Soviet era were inaccurate and misleading, as cogently argued by Aslund.[1] In fact, contrary to the expectation that Russia's economic program, supported by the IMF, would produce—finally—a modest growth of 2.4 percent in 1996, it actually fell by 3.6 percent. The postelection rebound didn't happen, and confidence was so low that the bulk of large private and business transactions still took place in dollars. Russia was falling further and further behind the "output collapse followed by strong recovery" model of other transition economies, even in some parts of the former Soviet Union such as the Baltic states.

On the political side, the lineup at the higher levels of government provided little comfort that dynamic and innovative new policies, appropriate to the challenges, were under preparation. Indeed, the fractious team under Prime Minister Chernomyrdin seemed uninspired and rudderless, more intent on the continuing pursuit of its own narrow interests. If anything, the government appeared to have drifted toward a complacent form of crony capitalism based on the discretionary allocation of various favors and concessions by the federal and local authorities, in exchange for backing by powerful groups and factions.

A Sick President Adds to the Gloom

Adding to the somber mood was a report circulating that Yeltsin had caught a cold and canceled appearances. Then it was acknowledged, after wild rumors started to circulate, that he had been hospitalized on the evening of January 8, 1997, with pneumonia. Yeltsin wasn't released from the Central Clinical Hospital until Monday evening, January 20, and then went to his suburban Moscow dacha to continue recovery from what turned out to have been double pneumonia. After Yeltsin's long convalescence from his heart attack the previous June and quintuple heart bypass surgery the previous November 5, people in Moscow seemed to be on a deathwatch. After all, Yeltsin had only returned to work in his office at the Kremlin on December 23, saying, "I feel good." In the State Duma, there were repeated calls for Yeltsin to step down, or at least make his health records public. Both the Communist leader Gennady Zyuganov and General Alexander Lebed, the popular military leader turned politician who challenged Yeltsin in the 1996 election, said that Yeltsin was too ill to rule, and repeatedly demanded that he resign.

Furthermore, all during the year and beyond, the Yeltsin health issue never went away, and was destined to continue as a source of uncertainty. Russia still had a vast nuclear arsenal, which Yeltsin controlled, and foreign investors still considered him the guardian of economic reforms. At every turn, speculation over the president's health weighed on the economy, and especially on the formulation and implementation of policy.

In most cases, they were false alarms. Yet there were real grounds for concern in view of the quintuple heart bypass operation and the double pneumonia episode, not to mention that Yeltsin, at 66 years old, was already beyond the average longevity of his cohorts born in 1931. The speculation and concerns continued throughout the year. For instance, after a period of intense market speculation against the ruble late in 1997, the Kremlin (that is, then–presidential spokesman Sergei Yastrzhembsky) tried to delicately explain to the public that Yeltsin had developed an acute respiratory infection and was hospitalized on December 10. It was alleged that Yeltsin caught a cold the previous week while visiting Sweden and that his doctors, fearing it could turn into something more serious, advised the president to rest.

Despite official reassurances that Yeltsin was not seriously ill, reaction to the news served as a reminder of how much almost everything in Russian politics ultimately depended on him. An important roundtable meeting scheduled for the next day between ministers and parliamentarians—intended to seek resolution of a logjam over whether to allow private sales of land—was canceled. And just when Yeltsin told the country on December 18, 1997, that he was going back to work, his doctors advised him to remain in a sanatorium for another week. Having previously reported Yeltsin's heart attacks as simple colds, the Kremlin had a credibility problem when it came to the president's health. News of the extended hospitalization and a worse-than-expected currency forecast from Standard and Poor's sent the Russian Trading System (RTS) share index falling by 7.6 percent on December 19, 1997.

A mood of uncertainty hung over the country. It seemed to me that most people by that time were thoroughly frustrated with Yeltsin. You couldn't see much compassion in the streets for his condition. This was worsened by official attempts to hide his health problems from the public eye. But the public remained passive—and no real alternative was visible. The lack of reaction was even surprising; every day in the then-opposition-dominated Duma, somebody was warning that the president was ill and that the country was being run by his administration, yet the nation seemed resigned and submissive with respect to who would be the next leader. Immediately following the 1996 election, nobody believed the incumbent Kremlin regime would allow a change in power. This was different from a later feeling of agitation and uncertainty in 1999—perhaps because the mass media was more or less unified in support of Yeltsin during the earlier period, whereas it was split between rival parties when then–Prime Minister Primakov and Moscow mayor Yuri Luzhkov were both trying to get ahold of power.

Promising Potential versus Political Reality

Despite this somber atmosphere as the year began, 1997—the first following the presidential election under the new 1993 constitution—represented the first year of the poststabilization development of the economy. The principal conditions for a transition from delayed stabilization to sustained economic growth had been created. Inflation was brought down to a level consistent with the beginning of investment in the real sector, GKO yields came down and a positive dynamic for a range of social indicators was in evidence—all of which bore witness to the arrival of a new stage. In October 1996, Russia received credit ratings from both Moody's and Standard and Poor's (the former being Ba2, and the latter BB-, which was better than Brazil and Argentina, but below Poland and Hungary), implying that the doors were now open for the Russian government to venture into the Eurobond market. The first, highly successful, one billion U.S. dollar issue was made in November 1996 (for five years at 9.25 percent). In March 1997, there was an equally successful two billion deutsche mark Eurobond (for seven years at 9 percent), and in June there was a further two billion U.S. dollar issue (for ten years at 10 percent). At the same time, however, it showed that the main factors holding back the start of economic growth began to shift into the institutional sphere: budgetary problems and problems associated with stimulating economic growth came to the fore.

In retrospect, it seems that as a result of apparent political infighting, the authorities unconsciously opted for the wrong policy mix: instead of adjusting the macroeconomic policy to rely less on a tight monetary policy combined with a tighter fiscal adjustment, the government further softened its budgetary position, thus giving rise to a severe fiscal crisis. The crisis was aggravated by the fact that because of its successful anti-inflation measures, the government deprived itself of the inflation tax characteristic of all postsocialist countries that had gone through prolonged periods of high inflation. The existing tax system had degenerated further. In addition, delays in implementing structural reforms of the budget itself caused a crisis of government expenditure. Cuts in government spending had, in turn, an extremely negative effect on the social safety net, nonmanufacturing branches of the economy, and the army. In hindsight, the IMF staff members were too inclined to respect the preferences of the authorities and failed to warn sufficiently on the inherent costs of the strategy's adoption.

The unfolding of the budgetary crisis in 1997 was the direct consequence of adopting an absolutely unrealistic and unimplementable budget for that year. This is unusual for a postelection period characterized elsewhere in the world by a display of a reasonable measure of toughness on the part of governments. The government formed in August 1996, and the financial block in particular showed an unprecedented docility when faced with demands by various lobbies. This was not surprising in view of the myriad favors owed to those interests in exchange for their role in supporting those in power, and especially in bankrolling and organizing Yeltsin's reelection. At the same time, the tax system was being undermined by mutual offset operations, which provoked the accumulation of arrears and the reduction of "live money" as a share of budgetary revenue. The offset operations varied over time, but allowed taxpayers to dispense their outstanding tax liabilities, including tax arrears, by using their outstanding claims on government. The latter were usually budgetary arrears, which could be acquired at a significant discount in practice and were traded actively.

My impression was that the parliamentary majority in the State Duma saw a continuation of the sluggish economy as a means to pressure and shift blame to the government, on the one hand, while the coalition nature of the government that had arisen by dint of a compromise between the state and business, on the other, caused a policy deadlock, with conflicting private interests impeding the conduct of a coherent economic policy. The Communist Party, in particular, as the largest faction had little incentive to cooperate with the government. Short of provoking a new parliamentary election where it would likely lose seats, the party systematically blocked government policies—although its deputies demonstrated pragmatism in collaborating with other factions and the Duma leadership when it was a question of preserving their own privileges.

At the beginning of 1997, two scenarios for the future seemed to be possible. The first consisted in breaking the deadlock and intensifying the reform process, by taking steps toward overcoming the budgetary crisis, restructuring natural monopolies, resolving the nonpayments issue, improving the social sphere, and so forth. The second scenario involved moving toward an oligarchic system (that is, a form of crony capitalism where a few key business figures can influence government policy in pursuit of their own interests), with the risk that a state of permanent crisis might in the end lead to a victory for the opposition or to undemocratic developments. It was unclear in which direction the ground would shift. The government tried ostensibly to move in the first direction, and ended up going in the second.

An early sign of a possible change of direction came when Anatoly Kulikov, the wily and ambitious interior minister, was named the deputy prime minister responsible for the State Customs Committee (SCC) and the Tax Police on February 4, in addition to his existing responsibilities. It seemed that the Kremlin's answer was going to be a desperate attempt to use strong-arm tactics to collect more revenue. If so, as sympathetic observers despaired, the hope of moving toward an open market economy under the transparent rule of law appeared to be fading fast.

A few days later, in the absence of IMF managing director Camdessus, Fischer, the IMF's number two, met with Chernomyrdin when he visited Washington, DC, in the context of the eighth meeting of the so-called Gore-Chernomyrdin Commission. In principle, the U.S. vice president and Russian prime minister met every six months (altering between Washington and Moscow) under the Clinton administration to oversee a jointly agreed-on policy agenda between the two countries. Fischer bluntly told the prime minister that the fund could do little if Russia was not prepared to help itself. Chernomyrdin, in turn, complained to the U.S. authorities about how little the IMF understood the realities of life. The United States said that it would do what it could to help, but that the Russian authorities needed to work in a cooperative spirit with the IMF. Chernomyrdin left Washington feeling misunderstood and even angry.

Finally, a Return of the Reformers to Government

Then, confounding the moribund conventional wisdom, a vigorous and confident-sounding Yeltsin presented his annual state of the nation address to the Federal Assembly of both houses of parliament on March 6, 1997. In his focused thirty-minute speech, the president observed that Russia entered 1997 with a heavy burden of problems and the economic situation in the country was critical. The decline in production had continued, and investment had not recovered. People were suffering from delays in payments of wages, pensions, and benefits, and it was time to put things in order. Yeltsin bluntly criticized the parliamentarians for using their positions to "fatten" themselves, and promised that a change of course for Russia was imminent.

Tellingly, he deplored the fact that "the state interferes in the economy where it shouldn't, while where it should, it does nothing." He went on to stress that he would personally take control over the preparation of the 1998 budget (as the 1997 budget was unrealistic and difficult to execute), tax reform would be the top priority for economic policy, and increasing attention would be focused on the operations of the natural monopolies, pension system reform, and reform of the utilities. Shortly thereafter, he declared that the structure and personnel of the government would be changed—new, energetic, and competent people would join the government within days.

The next day, on March 23, 1997, Yeltsin proceeded to all but sack the dithering government of Chernomyrdin, the prime minister since December 1992, appointing a team of ambitious reformers, with his chief of staff Chubais not only holding the finance ministry portfolio but also initially the sole first deputy prime minister seat. (Keeping Chernomyrdin as the emasculated figurehead was seen as an astute move to forestall a time-consuming fight with the State Duma, whose approval is only required when the head of government is changed.) Chubais used this unique opportunity of full presidential support to appoint several liberal allies to key ministries. Lawrence Summers, then the deputy secretary of the U.S. Treasury and the economic ideas' man of the Clinton administration, referred to them as the "dream team." Was this virtual change of government a sign of astuteness or desperation? Maybe it contained elements of both.

Boris Nemtsov, then thirty-seven, the erstwhile progressive governor of the Nizhny Novgorod region to the east of Moscow and a recent protégé of the president, was first designated a deputy prime minister, but then, at Nemtsov's insistence, was also appointed as a "first" deputy prime minister on March 27. Nemtsov was placed in charge of social welfare, housing reform, and reorganizing government monopolies—a tough assignment that Nemtsov himself called a "kamikaze mission."

Nemtsov, in a populist mode, launched high-visibility campaigns that made him a quick enemy of parliament and even backfired with much of the population, who greeted his seemingly naive efforts with humor and even cynicism. He tried to force state officials to declare their incomes and said they should give up expensive foreign cars for official use. Both efforts were quickly abandoned. Nemtsov also placed a close associate in charge of reforming RAO UES, the electricity monopoly, tried to rein in the fuel and energy sector, and even flew to Tokyo to demystify the new Russia with wary Japanese investors.

Although social actions in post-Soviet Russia had a feeble track record with virtually no political influence, the threat of strikes was nevertheless a cause for concern in government circles. Thus, as some groups of key workers across the country prepared to strike on March 27, 1997, over unpaid back wages, and pensioners in many regions were complaining more vocally about their increasing sense of desperation and hunger, Nemtsov and the government's new economic team had to implement a program of reforms that although urgently needed, would bring few immediate benefits and might even temporarily worsen the situation. Nemtsov's attempt to ride the populist horse to change opinion and influence policy was to prove increasingly short-lived as the year progressed.

The reorganization of the government was extensive. The new team was determined to learn finally from earlier mistakes and move quickly with a bold reform agenda. To accomplish these tasks, the reformers needed direct control over the main agencies. Chubais had proposed Kudrin as the minister of finance and took the position himself when he failed to have his candidate for the post accepted. He was convinced that this critical ministry must be brought under his direct control, and envisaged that Kudrin as the new first deputy minister would not only run it but eventually take over as well once the political situation calmed down and he proved himself in the job. In appointing Kudrin as his deputy, Chubais achieved a coup in dislodging his predecessor, Vavilov. Earlier in 1996, Livshits, who had insisted on firing Vavilov as a condition for his appointment the previous August, gave up and accepted the position of minister with Vavilov still in place—a decision that he was to regret. Alfred Kokh, another Chubais loyalist from Saint Petersburg, was appointed deputy prime minister responsible for privatization, and the liberal Yakov Urinson replaced Yasin at the Ministry of Economy, while Yasin became a minister without portfolio. Vasiliev became the first deputy head of the government administration, so taking control of the critical flow of official acts, and Nabiullina became deputy economy minister responsible for the coordination of the government's structural program. A little-known regional banker, the young Kiriyenko, was brought in from Nizhny Novgorod to become Nemstov's first deputy at the Ministry for Fuel and Energy (MFE) on April 24 (Nemstov, like Chubais, held a double portfolio with a major line ministry in addition to his first deputy prime minister position).

Surprisingly Tough Negotiations with the IMF Ensue

Once Chubais had taken over the responsibilities for financial policies, his expectation that the IMF would provide its financial support, because of his well-won reputation as a reformer and his intended policy actions, was quickly disappointed. For instance, when the IMF mission, headed by the diminutive and unusually outspoken Japanese, Yusuke Horiguchi, came to Moscow on March 26, 1997, the new Russian authorities were anxious to move rapidly in concluding an agreement with the fund on a program for 1997. Chubais and his team hoped that Horiguchi's mission could reach broad agreement on that program before the arrival of Camdessus on April 1. They expected no less.

In keeping with the usual practice of IMF staff members, not just in Russia, there was a virtual frenzy within the mission to try to get all the loose ends tied up before the boss arrived. The living dread of any IMF negotiator is to have the managing director arrive in the midst of a complex and sensitive negotiation, and seemingly hijack the discussion.

An illustrative example was when, in March 1994, while negotiating the second tranche of the STF, Camdessus arrived in Moscow and virtually stole the discussions from the IMF negotiator of the day, Ernesto Hernandez-Cata. In one instance, when the mission was back at the Metropol Hotel and totally unaware that the managing director had returned from the prime minister's hunting dacha ahead of schedule, Camdessus was in acting finance minister Dubinin's office negotiating basic aspects of the 1994 budget. The mission only learned about this when Camdessus called about an outstanding technical point.

Since Camdessus was seen as being focused on a few salient issues, the mission feared that anything he might negotiate would not necessarily cohere at a more technical level. And of course, the incentive for the Russian authorities was in some ways just the opposite: to string things out until the IMF management arrived and concluded a deal without many bells and whistles.

On this occasion, though, Horiguchi was in no rush to tie things up. The disappointments in recent months and the deflated expectations following the 1996 presidential elections were cause for some serious reflection of what went wrong as well as what needed to be done. There was sympathy that perhaps the main obstacle had already been removed with the dramatic changes in personnel, and there was a real desire to try to work quickly with the first group of liberals to clearly hold the reins of power in post-Soviet Russia since the early Gaidar government of January–April 1992. From April 1992 until the end of that year, the Gaidar team had been increasingly constrained. This is not to deny that individual reformers were not in key positions to affect policy, such as Fedorov as finance minister in 1993, Dubinin as acting finance minister in 1994, or when Chubais was deputy prime minister in 1995.

In his initial meeting with Chubais on March 28, 2007, Horiguchi stressed the need to reassess the revenue situation, and the sustainability and realism of Russia's fiscal policy in general. It is worth noting the thrust of his remarks. The Russian side sat back, not believing what they were hearing.

Horiguchi told Chubais that Camdessus was deeply worried about Russia's revenue performance during the previous nine to twelve months, and he was not confident about any of the projections for 1997 that were made in the last three months. At first the projection was 360 trillion old rubles, then 320 trillion old rubles, and then 305 trillion. Where was the bottom? Horiguchi was uncomfortable with any revenue target, and suggested that the new government take stock of the situation and deepen its understanding of why the revenue had been so weak. As a result of this process the Russian authorities should devise their own action plan, which was expected to include Duma approval of certain key tax measures (such as part of the tax code and an increase in the oil excise tax), thereby increasing confidence in the prospects for the implementation of the plan.

As Horiguchi spoke, Chubais started to glare. He was annoyed that Horiguchi was not ready to deal and asked how long all of this would take. Chubais became exasperated when Horiguchi mentioned the possibility of a board meeting only by late May, if all went well. Then, discussing Camdessus' forthcoming visit, Chubais was visibly agitated, and retorted that if the managing director wanted the Duma to increase oil excises, he should never go near the Duma.

In fact, in a meeting with me on March 24, 1997, Gaidar, who was working hard behind the scenes to push the new tax reforms through the Duma, also cautioned in a much more moderate tone that "the less the IMF is seen publicly as pressuring Russia on tax reforms, the better the chances of Duma approval in a timely manner." In that same meeting, while generally supportive of IMF efforts, he regretted the premature demise of the oil export tax since it was one of the few sure and transparent sources of federal revenue. In his view, the IMF forced the elimination of this tax in the name of a theoretical first-best principle and a misunderstanding of how things really work in Russia. And as so often, especially on tax issues, Gaidar was right that we had assumed too much in the vacuum.

I recall that at this point, Chubais exclaimed that since the last mission left,

We have spent a lot of time and energy expediting the process of implementing the prior actions agreed, including revenue collection measures and tax reform plans; and working toward the new—more realistic—budget. Despite the fact that not all senior officials in the government have been appointed and that even the distribution of power is still under discussion, we have worked strenuously on all the actions that we agreed should be done. I am at a loss to understand the IMF's position in this context. True, we have a problem with fiscal revenues. But let's be clear: this is a greater problem for Russia than for the IMF and that was precisely the reason for the recent change in government. We have to act immediately and we are ready. It is ironic that after these changes, and having reached a certain consensus with major political groups, including the coal miners, we lose the support of the IMF. Sure, we could wait several months as you suggest. But the signal this would send would be extremely negative. Not everybody in Russia supports what we are doing, and we will soon hear from those who do not agree with us: "Not even the IMF—your friend— supports you." The same negative reaction may result from financial markets, complicating—among other things—our planned placement of Eurobonds.

Chubais continued, saying frankly, "This could undermine relations between Russia and the IMF for years. You know that under adverse circumstances in 1995 we were able to deliver excellent results under an IMF program—and everybody agrees on that. Now it is quite ironic that you say you do not believe that the new government wants to solve the current problems."

They were all clearly worried by the prospect of Camdessus arriving empty-handed, and the negative signal it would send if he came to simply confirm that it was necessary to wait. And as in many countries where the IMF finds itself in tense negotiations in which various domestic political factions have strong vested interests, Chubais and others were not beneath attempts to use hyperbole and even threats to achieve what they saw as their objectives. In point of fact, they were generally world-class in this distinction.

Camdessus Visits Moscow

A visit by IMF management usually helps to focus the host government on what needs to be done to get a publicly announced clean bill of health. Camdessus' visit to Moscow was no exception. On the eve of the managing director's arrival, the mission's assessment was that the authorities' federal revenue target of 9 percent of GDP in 1997 (already drastically reduced from a target of 10.5 percent of GDP just three months earlier) could be missed by up to 1.5 percent of GDP in the absence of additional policy actions in the coming months that would demonstrate a firm commitment to strengthening taxpayer compliance. While there were, in principle, additional tax policy measures that could have been adopted, some of which would have had an effect on revenues in 1997, these were doubtful in light of the likely difficulties in securing Duma approval. On expenditures, while the mission supported the tough target sought by the authorities, it also insisted that it was important for the authorities to be seen as pushing for this target in the context of a revised budget and obtain the Duma's political support.

Camdessus arrived in Moscow on April 1, accompanied by Odling-Smee, who was nominally the boss of the IMF's chief negotiators on Russia, such as Horiguchi. Odling-Smee, having served as the department director since it was formed in 1992, had the longest continuing institutional memory in the fund on Russia at the time.

Camdessus was greeted on his arrival at Sheremetyevo Airport, outside Moscow, by a high-level Russian delegation consisting of Chubais, Dubinin, and Aleksei Mozhin, Russia's still-long-serving representative to the IMF. As one of twenty-four executive directors in the fund, Mozhin can vote the country's almost 3 percent of the equity in decisions taken by the IMF, including disbursements to Russia itself. Like the IMF's representative in Russia, part of whose function is to ensure effective communication, Russia's executive director, who resides in Washington, DC, also facilitates understanding—a double-edged sword if ever there was one since the presentation of each side's views at a senior level may not always be appreciated.[2]

Camdessus and Odling-Smee did not dawdle at the airport. After some pleasantries with the Russian delegation about the hard work to be accomplished in such a short time, they were whisked away in a Zil limousine and then by helicopter for a private rendezvous with Chernomyrdin at one of his favorite hunting retreats outside Moscow. There, in an informal atmosphere of hunt and vodka, they relaxed, and continued building a relationship of trust that would come in handy in the treacherous period ahead. Chernomyrdin, in particular, was of that old Soviet school that sincerely believed that forging a close relationship among powerful individuals was the way to get things done. It is a school of thought that remained potent. Camdessus knew that backslapping and camaraderie could help to facilitate trust, but could not in any way serve as a substitute for good policy.

Camdessus went along with Chernomyrdin's enthusiasm for the hunt in the hope that the latter would come to better understand that there were no miracle palliatives for Russia's myriad problems, and that financing from the IMF and others was only a cushion to dampen the inevitable pain in the policies that would have to be taken if the country were to regain its lost glory.

Camdessus was not a hunter and did not relish these jaunts. That said, he was a reasonable marksman and acquired somewhat of a reputation in senior Russian security circles, where news of his prowess spread.

They returned to Moscow the next afternoon, and Camdessus launched into a whirlwind of meetings, first with Nemtsov and Kokh, and then with Chubais, accompanied by Vasiliev and Viugin. He later met with Dubinin and Alexashenko at the CBR. Camdessus pressed all the officials on the critical issue of fiscal policy and how they envisaged handling it. At a dinner hosted by Chubais, Nemtsov, Kulikov, Kokh, and Dubinin in a palatial government dacha on a hill overlooking Moscow, they tried to grapple with the problems from many angles. Kulikov, in a private meeting with the managing director after dinner, suggested that he had his own plan for ensuring tax collection that he would propose in the near future. Whatever it was, we never heard any more of it.

In addition to meetings with Patriarch Alexei II (Camdessus, as a devout Catholic, had a habit of calling on religious leaders in the countries he visited—a practice that in this case was viewed by many in the Russian media with puzzlement as it just did not fit their preconceived image of the "soulless" head of the IMF), the media, and G-7 ambassadors at the Spaso House (the impressive, domed mansion that serves as the residence of the U.S. ambassador), Camdessus also gave a major speech at the Moscow State Institute for International Relations.

In all of his discussions (and his speech), after noting the significant progress made in grappling with Russia's economic problems, Camdessus called attention to the state of crisis that continued to prevail, notably concerning growth, the nonpayment of taxes, and corruption. His recipe was to accelerate institutional reforms of the state, and he suggested specific solutions in line with the extensive IMF experience of what had worked elsewhere: tax administration reforms on the revenue side, and the treasury control system on the spending side. He understood too well that the future of Russia was in the hands of its people and leaders, and was particularly concerned, with prescience as it transpired, that the State Duma would not cooperate. Camdessus' views helped to both position the IMF in its further discussions with the authorities and set the tone for the IMF's relations with Russia as seen in the rest of the world.

Before leaving Moscow, Camdessus met with President Yeltsin at the Kremlin. Yeltsin warmly greeted the managing director, saying, as I recall, that "you, personally, and the experts who visit Russia on your instructions have saved us from making many mistakes in carrying out our reforms." They discussed the problems at hand, and a well-briefed Yeltsin vowed to do what was necessary to pursue stabilization and structural reform. Camdessus said that the IMF would work with Russia, and provide continuing support to a well-devised and implemented program. Obviously pleasing the president, Camdessus noted that a reformist Russia could become an "economic superpower," although he cautioned that the Duma had a major role to play to ensure that the conditions were right.

Camdessus had pointedly raised these concerns about the Duma's support following meetings with various Duma leaders, ignoring Chubais's advice to stay away. He was especially worried after meeting with the leftist faction leaders who controlled the majority of votes in the lower house at that time. Although his meeting with Communist party head Zyuganov, Ryzhkov from the Narodovlastie Party, and Nikolai Kharitonov from the Agrarian Party was portrayed in the press as a somewhat successful charm offensive, Camdessus came away thinking that their seeming basic lack of understanding of the causes of Russia's problems and possible remedies could be a constant source of difficulties for the government's program, where so much depended, at least in the first instance, in transforming the formal and legal infrastructure. An example is an article in *Segodnya* on April 4, 1997, by Alexander Bekker, in which the journalist comments that "it is unlikely that Mr. Camdessus convinced the orthodox communists, but from an ideological standpoint, he gave a fine performance."

Camdessus' concerns were later underscored when he received a letter a few days later from Ryzhkov, who had been prime minister of the USSR under Gorbachev from 1985 to 1990, that portrayed either a profoundly flawed analysis of the situation or abject hypocrisy. Namely, the letter did not recognize that the dire starting conditions in which Russia had to extricate itself were, in fact, Ryzhkov's direct legacy. That said, Ryzhkov's letter reflected a popular view, broadly represented in the Duma. He wrote that the Soviet Union was not a member of the IMF. However, the situation of the USSR's economy was assessed as fairly stable. After the Russian authorities approved the strategic course of market reforms in 1991 and started implementing a package of measures in that sense, at the recommendation and with the support from the IMF, my country's economic situation has been incessantly deteriorating. Not only I myself, but many people in my country have serious questions related to the IMF's responsibility for the outcome of following its recommendations.

Another revealing incident from his encounters with the Duma took place during an earlier meeting with members of the Budget Committee's leadership on April 3. One of the deputy chairs of the committee, Communist Yuri Voronin, attacked Camdessus in relation to the declining output in the country, boasting that he had made a bet of a bottle of cognac with Fischer that growth would continue to be negative in 1997. The bet had been made in a discussion in Vienna the previous August, with Fischer arguing that growth would be positive in 1997 if the economic program were followed. Fischer later won the bet, on a GDP growth of 1.4 percent. Camdessus stated that not only would Fischer win but also that he himself would bet his best French cognac that Russia would experience at least a 5 percent growth in 2000 if the authorities had sufficient political will to complete what they had begun. When challenged by Deputy Oksana Dmitrieva that he was being too optimistic, Camdessus responded, "Madam, I am not used to losing bets."

Camdessus left that evening having obtained a promise by the government to take additional measures to meet its federal government revenue target of 304 trillion old rubles for 1997 and submit the tax code provisions for immediate passage in the Duma.[3]

Russia's 1997 Economic Program Belatedly Agreed On

Clearly the new government team wanted to show rapid progress in dealing with the financial situation and, maybe even more, demonstrate that it enjoyed the confidence of the international community, to which an IMF agreement was key. Russian officials assured the staff team that the most recent revenue target for 1997 could be readily achieved, although there might be some uncertainty depending on how rapidly the IMF insisted on the elimination of nonmonetary forms of tax settlement. Even though acknowledging that nonmonetary schemes simply foster the growth of tax arrears and a culture of nonpayment, the officials expressed concern that the GKO market could not handle the large amounts of new borrowing that might be needed to clear the budgetary arrears without driving up yields.

Horiguchi and his team returned to Moscow in late April to wrap up the discussions on the program. The government's financial position was already under pressure, and rumors circulated that MinFin was seeking bridge financing from its colead managers, SBC Warburg and J.P. Morgan, with respect to a large Eurobond placement that they were preparing for June. The Eurobond was finally issued in June in the amount of US$250 million, and the bridge was repaid. When I observed to Kasyanov, the then-responsible deputy finance minister, that the secret bridge from Deutschebank to the deutsche mark Eurobond may have adversely affected the terms of that issue and could lead to a toughening of terms for the U.S. dollar placement, he said that without the April tranche from the IMF, his authorities had to weigh the consequences of what I was suggesting with the likely costs of excessive reliance on GKO financing.

The 1997 program was belatedly but quickly finalized with Chubais. It foresaw a real GDP growth of 3.0 percent and the annual inflation rate declining to no more than 14 percent. Chubais argued for a steeply sloped revenue projection for the year, using the logic that the second-quarter revenue performance was already history in the sense of it being too late to take any measures that could seriously affect the outcome, but tangible results would start in the third quarter. Following a similar reasoning, he also projected a steep upward slope for structural reform. A list of prior actions to be implemented and verified before the IMF board could meet to consider Russia's request was also agreed on. The board was supposed to meet on May 16.

In retrospect, it may seem naive to have accepted the steep-slope argument for policy implementation and performance. Since the prevailing view in the IMF at the time was that the poor track record thus far under the EFF was related primarily to a lack of political will, however, it was logical to accept that a sea change in political will, as represented by the arrival of the dream team, would be sufficient to not only break the prevailing political seasonality but to provide a meaningful basis for improved policy performance as well.

I think that the IMF board went along with the staff members' view that the new dream team could belatedly address program shortcomings with determination, and so while expressing its doubts and concerns, reluctantly approved the tranche of US$640 million, which was disbursed to Russia on May 21, 1997, with all the proceeds being credited to the Russian Treasury's account at the CBR.

Intriguingly, around the same time, the new IMF mission chief for Russia, Jorge Marquez-Ruarte, held a meeting with some leading Russian nongovernment economists to gain a better sense of perspective. These economists told him that while nonresident investors appeared to be optimistic, little seemed to have changed with regard to residents. There was only limited confidence in the stability of the ruble and the banking system. This was reflected in residents requiring wage payments in cash dollars, keeping savings outside the banking system, and using the U.S. dollar as the store of value. In the meantime, Horiguchi left to become the head of the IMF's Asia Department a few months later.

Marquez-Ruarte, a citizen of Argentina and with a PhD from the University of Chicago, quickly grasped the problem. From then on, he kept watching to see if Russian residents would change their perceptions, even at the margin. He quickly became a skeptic about the scope and especially the time frame for a real transformation of the Russian economy. As the new chief negotiator for the IMF and successor of the by now almost legendary Horiguchi, however, he was ready to work against his instincts in trying to assist the Russian authorities in their Herculean tasks.

As of June 1, 1997, the economic situation was improving with inflation coming down, some positive signs of growth, fiscal performance on track, and reserves rising rapidly. Reserves rose to US$18.2 billion by June 1, up from US$15.3 billion at the beginning of the year.

The only dark cloud on the horizon at that point was, as Camdessus had worried, the Duma's rejection of the government's proposals on a revised 1997 budget. Duma members wanted to see revenue estimates raised to maintain spending. Chubais and other senior officials told the IMF staff that spending would be maintained in line with the proposed sequestration budget regardless of Duma opposition, and Viugin confirmed that this spending level would be respected in continuing negotiations with the Duma.

With money flowing in, market interest rates continued to decline, with interbank rates in mid-June averaging 10 to 15 percent and taxable GKO yields at around 20 percent. On June 16, the CBR cut its refinance rate from 36 to 24 percent. The nominal depreciation within the corridor had slowed markedly since the spring, and forward market rates implied that the reduction in the rate of depreciation was expected to continue, suggesting that the band regime was fully credible.

In fact, the sharp falls in interest rates and the rapid growth of base money raised concerns as to possible overheating. Although the fund staff team had some qualms about this large amount of liquidity, it did not argue with success. And although reserve performance was well above program levels (and thus the concern with the rapid expansion of base money), it should be noted that even at twenty billion U.S. dollars by July 1, gross reserves were relatively low by international standards, not even covering three months worth of imports at that time. Mexico had an import coverage of about seven months a few months before the 1994 crisis began; Argentina had close to twelve months when the Mexican crisis erupted, and was under severe market pressure but managed to maintain its currency board at that time. The low import coverage would make the balance of payments vulnerable to a crisis, especially as exchange controls—ineffective though they might have been—were relaxed.

The clock was already ticking. Chubais had promised to solve the most acute problems of unpaid pensions and salaries by June 30. It was the conventional wisdom then that the "new" government had to jump-start reforms before the end of 1997 to produce a healthy, growing economy by the time parliamentary and presidential elections were due in late 1999 and mid-2000, respectively. Chubais, ever one to appreciate the critical importance of timing, acknowledged the need for speed before the many enemies of reform could regain their balance. As he portrayed the situation, the new team understood that macroeconomic stabilization in Russia had come at a great cost to the population, partly because the government let social spending plummet in real terms as well as tolerated a sharp rise in wage arrears at the federal and especially local levels in an effort to meet tight budget deficits targets, and partly because reforms were never completed.

The "structural" reforms advocated by the IMF and World Bank, and broadly endorsed by the Russian liberal reformers, were urgently needed to generate revenues, cut waste, remove distortions and disincentives, and set the stage for growth. Among the most vital areas for reform, and the ones that had been prioritized by the government, were taxation, natural monopolies (such as electricity), and housing. Beyond that, an array of areas required attention: the army, the judiciary, the pension system, the treasury, budget procedures, land privatization, the labor market, and business deregulation. Chubais and Nemstov knew that their window of opportunity would close fast as the vested interests and Yeltsin's system of political counterweights would try to dilute any real attempt at reform.

The dash for market reform needed to be bold and quick, before the opposing factions in and around the government could coalesce. In perhaps simplistic terms, the emerging business elite themselves were divided between those early movers who wanted to consolidate their already-accumulated assets under a regime increasingly represented by the rule of law and market forces, as opposed to opaque administrative actions. Others, however, felt strongly that the initial allocation of assets was either unfair or incomplete, and so were not yet prepared for a government committed to the economics of reform. These powerful forces started to bring their conflict into the open over the course of summer 1997.

Especially at the time when these events took place, I had only a limited understanding of these forces that were competing for power and resources. Like many, but not all, outsiders, I tended to emphasize institutions and underestimate the role of individuals, particularly those motivated by greed, revenge, or fear. No doubt, this is an area where journalists have a clear advantage over economists and other analysts. Their contributions of books and articles have helped to shed light, even if speculative in some cases, on the machinations behind the scenes.

In retrospect, it is stunning just how naive most outside observers really were. No doubt this was partly due to the outward appearance of a normally functioning government. More generally, I suspect that most outsiders tended to project their own, perhaps more civilized experiences on Russian reality in order to make some sense of what was happening. Historically this is not unusual, and many international misunderstandings have been founded on the misuse of such projections.

How could we miss even obvious signals? For instance, before Berezovsky (who then controlled the car dealer LogoVAZ, the oil company Sibneft, the national television station ORT, and the international airline Aeroflot) teamed up with Gusinsky (head of the Most Group, including a major bank and media) in 1997 to try to gain control over the privatization of Svyazinvest, the two had been bitter enemies. It had reached such a point earlier that Berezovsky was publicly accusing Gusinsky of attempting to have him killed. Such feuding was only the tip of the iceberg. The fight over the spoils and assets left in limbo from Soviet days led to conflicts that we simply did not imagine could so directly impact public policy. In fairness, when we would ask, our government counterparts would categorically deny any impact from such conflicts. Not being an investigative agency and taking IMF member governments at their word, we had little choice but to accept their relatively rosy interpretation of events, unless it was directly contradicted by the facts.

The problem was that such facts did not readily appear in the data at an aggregated level, and even if the data were accurate, we would not have known what to look for.

These conflicts involved oligarchs, red directors of state companies, government officials, businesspeople, and even reformers. There were factions without well-designated representatives such as the power ministries, whose influence waned after the end of the first Chechen war in 1996. General Lebed took it on himself to negotiate an end to the war after Yeltsin appointed him as secretary of the Kremlin Security Council following Lebed's endorsement of Yeltsin after the first round of the presidential election in June 1996. The military and security forces still maintained considerable input behind the scenes in the policy debate, mostly as a brake. But their ability to interfere, like that of the Communists and nationalists, could usually be bought—for a price. This group, or groups, became known as the "siloviki" and was considered the major force behind Kremlin policies during Putin's second term—namely, the policy of state capitalism and so-called sovereign democracy.

The key point to stress as these various factions competed for power in the post-Soviet vacuum was the way in which they viewed Chubais. In the West, Chubais was seen as one of the only really effective reformers; in much of Russia, he was considered an ogre, as a scapegoat for the reforms that were attributed to him and his team. Yet the other factions and especially the oligarchs considered him just another competing head of a rival faction, and not "the road to the future." Despite the bitter feuds behind the scenes, there really was the appearance of progress and some hopeful signs of normality with the approach of summer 1997. These "green shoots" proved to be short-lived.

A Summer Full of False Hopes

By late spring, the economy was starting to revive and foreign capital began to flow in. This was facilitated by a CBR announcement of measures to liberalize nonresident access to the GKO/OFZ market in a series of phased steps starting on May 1, 1997, and leading to full liberalization from January 1, 1998. This meant that the obligation of nonresidents to hold forward contracts when investing in GKO was phased out, and the CBR even offered its own contracts in a voluntary scheme, the logic of the latter being that a forward market might not develop without CBR participation.

The IMF staff tried to discourage the CBR from becoming directly involved in the provision of forward contract guarantees, not only alluding to the risks, but also the fact that a fairly active market already existed and it would be difficult for the CBR to get the pricing right. It turned out that the CBR contracts did appear generous relative to, say, dollar-denominated Eurobonds, but the CBR went ahead with its scheme anyway. It was expected at that time that the continued net inflows into the GKO market would depress yields further, cutting into the profitability of the domestic banking system, but making the debt dynamics of the budget more sustainable.

Aside from the struggle among oligarchs, the domestic political situation seemed to be calming down as well. On May 12, 1997, a Chechen delegation led by President Aslan Maskhadov met Yeltsin in the Kremlin to sign a peace agreement proclaiming an end to centuries of hostilities between the two sides. Yeltsin even called the region Ichkeria—the name that independence-minded Chechens used for the republic. Maskhadov's right to govern Chechnya was thus legitimized by Russia, although the republic's future status was not discussed. Yeltsin seemed to close the chapter on what he once called his greatest political mistake: the twenty-one-month war in Chechnya. Admittedly, he made this statement in a highly charged atmosphere between the two rounds of the presidential election in 1996.

On May 22, 1997, Yeltsin fired Defense Minister Igor Rodionov after accusing him of failing to implement urgent army reforms. Insisting on a leaner army, he eventually put Chubais in charge of military financing and appointed a loyal ally, Igor Sergeyev, until then head of the rocket forces, as the new defense minister. Then finally, on May 30, Yeltsin made his first official visit to Kiev to sign a much-delayed friendship treaty with Ukraine. Coming on the heels of the Chechen peace deal and a successful summit with Chinese president Jiang Zemin, the accord presumably demonstrated Russia's desire to make peace with all its neighbors.

The story of summer 1997 on the economic front was about the increasing euphoria as money flowed into Russia and fawning Western investment bankers fell over themselves trying to invest in Russian assets. Already the CBR had made net purchases of foreign exchange in the amount of US$1.5 billion in March, US$1.6 billion in April, and US$1.7 billion in May. Capital was starting to flow in, in part for reasons little related to Russia, but rather reflecting an influx of funds into emerging markets more generally as global investors searched for higher yields than then available in the more mature markets of most OECD countries.

And capital was flowing into Russia in particular because the perceived country risk was declining. The feeling at that time was that unless the authorities were to do something really outrageous, the change in perception was permanent and would continue to improve in the foreseeable future. Thus, the idea gained ground that Russia might be experiencing a virtuous circle for a while. In fact, given the stability of the exchange rate, the unlikely change in policy, and the limited scope for exchange rate volatility, the expectation was that foreign investors would bring money to bid down GKO yields until it conformed to their revised risk perceptions. All the flights to Moscow from Western Europe were full of pin-striped bankers trying to find investment opportunities.

In this regard, the story about the agricultural promissory notes serves as a cautionary tale. One of the actions taken by Kudrin in terms of confronting the opaqueness of budget expenditure control and the confusion about spending commitments was to force regional governments to issue securities to collateralize their debt to the federal government for commodity credits issued in 1996. This was an extrabudgetary operation, whereby the federal government allowed oil companies to "pay" their taxes in the form of fuel oil shipped to agricultural enterprises, and whereby those enterprises received the goods as a "commodity credit" from the federal government that the regional government had to guarantee. Under the threat of not receiving budgeted federal transfers, the regional governments securitized this debt—220 billion old rubles was placed in a couple of auctions in late June 1997, and more was subsequently added, up to about 9 trillion old rubles altogether. The proceeds to the treasury were placed into a revolving budget fund for concessional finance to agriculture.

Most intriguing, in light of the euphoria displayed by Western investors to acquire Russian assets that summer, was how investment banks, with little effort, were placing these issues of agricultural *veksels* (promissory notes) with, among others, completely innocent midwestern U.S. investors because of their high yields. Those investors did not understand that the yields represented a high probability of default, though, since the reason that Kudrin forced the regions to securitize the debt was because it was not being paid by the agricultural enterprises that were the recipients of the loans in the first place.

Russia Joins the Paris Club

While the new government was trying to take control of policy, fend off its enemies, and push reforms through before it was too late, Yeltsin made his first trip to Europe since the mid-1996 election. Presidents Clinton and Yeltsin held a bilateral summit in Helsinki on March 21, 1997. Ironically, although the summit was moved from the United States, ostensibly to make the voyage easier on Yeltsin, he was the one who looked healthy and sharp, as he upstaged Clinton, who was confined to a wheelchair because of a knee injury.[4] Clinton won Yeltsin's grudging acquiescence to NATO's eastern expansion plans, setting the stage for the Russian president to visit Paris in May and sign an accord supposedly giving Moscow a voice in future NATO deliberations. In exchange, Yeltsin won Clinton's backing for Russian membership in key world economic clubs, like the OECD, the Paris Club, and the World Trade Organization (WTO). Now, more than thirteen years later, it is noteworthy that only one of the three has been realized, and Russia's alleged NATO role was emasculated. The atmospherics were good, and the decisive recent changes in his government allowed Yeltsin to hold his head high.

Yeltsin clearly relished his more central role in what was renamed the "Summit of the Eight," which was held in Denver and hosted by his friend Clinton on June 20–22, 1997. The leaders' final communiqué underscored this by noting that "the Denver Summit of the Eight marks a new and deeper participation by Russia in our efforts. Russia has taken bold measures to complete an historic transformation into a democratic state with a market economy." It went on to emphasize that "cooperation to integrate Russia's economy into the global economic system represents one of our most important priorities. We welcome the understanding reached between Russia and the Chairman of the Paris Club on the basis for Russia's participation and look forward to the Paris Club and Russia finalizing an agreement in the near future."

As had been foreseen at Yeltsin's bilateral meeting with Clinton in Helsinki and the G-8 summit in Denver in June, progress was being made in Russia's request to participate in the Paris Club as a creditor. The logic was that having reached a definitive restructuring of all the Soviet-era debt in 1996 with both the London and Paris clubs, there were no further issues between the Paris Club and Russia as a debtor. Yet Russia was also a major creditor country, with respect to both Soviet-era credits and loans provided by Russia itself as a sovereign creditor, mostly to countries that were part of the former Soviet Union. In regard to both groups of debtors, Russia was having difficulty getting repaid. The problem was compounded by the fact that many of the debtor countries were undertaking economic adjustment programs supported by the IMF and discussing their debt repayment problems with the Paris Club creditors only. In some cases, debts owed to Russia constituted the bulk of payments due (or overdue), yet Russia itself was not included in the discussions.

An understanding was reached between participants in the Paris Club and Russia on September 16, 1997, on Russia's future participation (since the Paris Club, despite its name, is not an organization but merely a framework for groups of creditors to address common issues, there was no formal agreement but rather a memorandum of understanding that would be respected by all parties concerning Russia's participation). One of the major issues had been how to value the Soviet-era claims, which were primarily denominated in Soviet rubles or transferable rubles as well as the nature of the underlying transactions, including military debt. Russia agreed to value its claims at what was considered a more realistic level (in view of market valuations where they existed, and the nature and exchange rates used in the original deals). The official exchange rate of the Soviet ruble, which was not a convertible currency, was long considered by many as seriously overvalued, as the author discovered for himself when he first visited Moscow in January 1981. In return, as a Paris Club participant, Russia would no longer be the subject of exclusion or less favorable treatment than any other Paris Club member, and the IMF itself, in keeping with its policy, would not lend to any country with outstanding arrears to Russia.

Kasyanov, as the responsible deputy minister, in particular had worked hard to make this happen, in the face of political maneuverings on all sides since the time of the solemn declaration at the G-7 Summit in in Lyon in June 1996 to explore Russia's participation. The opposition at home was formidable, and many interests pushed for a further delay in Russia joining the Paris Club. A number of senior officials and bankers used the delays while also playing on nationalistic feelings in the Duma for separate deals with debtors, which could be highly profitable in personal terms. In fact, one of the original reasons that the IMF lent its support to Russia's efforts to join was to help promote reform in debt management and policy, and in the process, make all of these operations more transparent. Chubais showed up in Paris on September 16 to sign the agreement with Christian Noyer, the then president of the Paris Club, and announced that Russia had become a full-fledged member. Chubais was clearly addressing himself to a Russian audience by pointing out that "Russia would triple annual collections from debtor countries from $100–150 million to some $500 million." This was mostly bravado. In reality the amounts were never more than some tens of millions of dollars, even after Russia became a Paris Club member. It is ironic that in the early 1990s, the delay in finalizing a so-called zero-option agreement with Ukraine (where Russia assumed all the debt obligations of the Soviet Union as well as the claims) was that the Ukrainians seemed convinced that Soviet claims (and gold) were worth tens of billions of dollars.

A Race against Time to Get the Reform Agenda in Place

With the aim of balancing the budget, the government directed its efforts toward several key objectives. Since difficulties in tax collection became the main factor driving the considerable growth of the budget deficit and the increasing dependence of the government on borrowing on the domestic market, the government's top priority was to improve tax collection in practice and then lower the cost of budget financing, while making efforts to restructure enterprise debts to the budget. Similarly, the tax code submitted to the Duma was meant to increase the level of fairness and neutrality of the tax system by reducing tax preferences and fighting tax evasion.

At the same time, a package dealing with social reform, including the reform of housing and the army, was oriented toward increasing the efficiency of budgetary expenditure. Another prong included measures to overcome the nonpayment crisis by reforming the system of prices and tariffs. By summer 1997, it appeared that Russia was caught in a vicious and deepening cycle of barter and nonpayment. It was estimated by the IMF at the time that 40 percent of transactions were conducted using nonmonetary means and that wage arrears in the nongovernment sector were growing. In their analysis, Cliff Gaddy and Barry Ickles conclude that Russia was in large part a virtual economy with large unrehabilitated industries producing negative value-added goods.[5]

The World Bank and the IMF focused on the nonpayment problem as a crucial structural problem. In hindsight, we did not fully appreciate the extent to which the phenomenon stemmed from inadequate budget controls and a lack of hard budget constraints, starting with the federal budget, so that earlier programs instead focused on the emergence of interenterprise arrears.

The first half of 1997 marked a new stage in the fight against corruption. The essential novelty of this approach was that it included an acknowledgment that corruption should no longer be tolerated as business as usual, and a promise to introduce government measures to identify and punish corrupt officials as well as eliminate opportunities for abuse of office by trying to establish clear rules of the game. It also shows just how pervasive and entrenched the problem of corruption was, given the attention paid to it thirteen years later by President Dmitry Medvedev.

In this regard, a curious episode—because it became public knowledge —arose in July 1997 when CBR chair Dubinin accused former first deputy finance minister Vavilov of massive fraud, charging that Vavilov purposely misused MinFin appropriations to assist a financially troubled bank, Unikombank. It seems that the Kremlin finally asked the CBR chair to be quiet, Vavilov went abroad, and the event was forgotten.

The policy to achieve the program's structural objectives was two pronged. First, the government was supposed to pay particular attention to tax collection, notwithstanding the fact that the largest debtors were enterprises in one way or another associated with the leading financial-industrial groups. Second, the government was supposed to strengthen the fiscal dimension of privatization; that is, it proposed to abandon the by-then-established principle in its relations with the leading groups: "property in exchange for political support."

It became subsequently clear that the other factions led by the so-called oligarchs did not appreciate this change in the rules of the game. Potanin may to some extent have realized this, since he was apparently prepared to pay a market price at the next big privatization auction. But it is not apparent why he allegedly might have arranged for one of his companies to provide a book advance later in 1997 for Chubais and his team.

Attempts to implement these policies on a practical level engendered stiff opposition from all the interested parties. The concomitant increase in political pressure on the executive branch caused an effective halt to the work of the government, then reeling under the weight of mounting conflicts within the cabinet and its administration. This situation was becoming all-the-more dangerous since it coincided by the late summer with the beginning of the Asian financial crisis, which required clear, timely, and effective responses from the government.

In fact, that the government's program was in tatters was already apparent in mid-1997, when the Duma rejected a package of draft social laws. The government had by then shown itself to be indecisive in pursuing a consistent reform-oriented policy, which was evident in lower tax revenues, its reluctance to take tough measures against debtors unwilling to restructure their debts to the government, an absence of efforts to restructure government spending, and so on. In line with the typical seasonality of Russia's political cycle, the failure of the government's economic program in a broad sense did not become evident until autumn. Until then, the early signs of failure were masked by a continuing optimism about the new economic team and buoyant financial markets.

With their own channels of influence, their own people in key positions, and direct access to almost all figures who were really decision makers in Russia, two opposing camps seemed to form: one headed by Potanin, president of then Uneximbank, and the other by Berezovsky. Potanin took the initiative by going on an aggressive buying spree in July by paying US$1.875 billion for 25 percent of the telecommunications holding company Svyazinvest and publicly announcing that he had every intention of buying more. The financier, George Soros, in partnership with Potanin for the deal, bought a block of shares, which he later declared to be "the worst investment of his career."[6]

The Svyazinvest deal marked the first time that a major Russian bank had paid the government what was perceived by outsiders to be a fair market value for its property. The loans-for-shares privatizations in 1995, designed by Potanin and adopted by Chubais, had gone to insiders at below-market prices, although as estimated by Treisman, the issue may warrant a more nuanced reaction than is usually associated with it.[7]

In brief, Chubais, at the time the deputy prime minister, supported the scheme as suggested by Potanin as a clever piece of financial engineering that could provide the government with some temporary but urgent financing until after the scheduled Duma elections in December 1995, by which time the government could reacquire the shares, as the new economic program would result in higher tax revenue or transfer ownership in line with the loans should the Communists win those elections. Thus, Chubais justified the deals as the only way under the legislative restrictions placed by the State Duma on the sale of designated "strategic enterprises" to prevent the Communists from getting their hands on the companies in the likelihood that they won the Duma elections (seen as an almost certainty at the time). Like many policies in Russia in the

1990s, the scheme was well intended, but its execution was fraught with egregious irregularities. It also had the unfortunate consequence of setting the moral tone for the future and institutionalizing the gaming of the system to control state assets. Not only is the legitimacy of privatized assets, such as Domodedovo International Airport which was only recently settled, open to question but the moral example of state seizure endures as well.

The deal polarized the Russian financial elite, putting Potanin nominally on the side of Chubais and Nemtsov, who had been trying to squeeze more money out of state assets and encourage more open competition, and Berezovsky on the side of other bankers and officials such as Chernomyrdin, who had vested interests in the status quo. Berezovsky, who was reported to have been part of a consortium that lost the auction, accused Chubais of cutting an insider deal with the winners. The "young reformers" countered that Svyazinvest went to the highest bidder at a fair auction and that Berezovsky's complaints were just sour grapes.

The hostility grew as Berezovsky used his control of ORT television and a chain of newspapers to attack the reformers. Berezovsky was reportedly angling for a piece of a number of major oil company privatizations, including Rosneft, planned in the following year. The balance of the country's financial elite stood between these two extremes: Mikhail Fridman of the Alfa Group, Khodorkovsky of Menatep/Yukos, Smolensky of SBS-Agro, and Gusinsky. Gusinsky, who was on the losing side of the Svyazinvest auction, and also controlled influential print and television media, allied himself with Berezovsky, and Smolensky had long been Berezovsky's business partner. The others appeared to stay on the sidelines.

On August 19, 1997, Nemtsov launched a public attack, which appeared to be a response to strong criticism in the Russian media of the results of that Svyazinvest auction, on Berezovsky, who was also the deputy secretary of the State Security Council in the Kremlin. In an interview published in the Moscow daily *Moskovsky Komsomolets*, Nemtsov said that Berezovsky had orchestrated the media attack on the Svyazinvest sale using his official Kremlin position and his alleged control of ORT television. He also claimed that Berezovsky was part of the consortium that lost in the sale. "While formally he is not engaged in business activities, that is all he does," said Nemtsov. "It is bad when a person involved in business has privileges purely because he has direct access to the state's leadership." Asked if Berezovsky was the right person for the Security Council job, Nemtsov replied, "In my opinion, no. You cannot combine business activity with government."

Then, on September 5, Yeltsin fired Berezovsky from his official post, ending a bitter public feud over economic policy between the businessmen and the young reformers in the government. Berezovsky made it clear he would not go quietly, launching a personal attack on Chubais, whom he blamed for his dismissal, and pledging to fight for his business interests. Yeltsin signed the decree dismissing Berezovsky from his post as deputy secretary of the Security Council after meeting with Chubais and Nemtsov.

A Kremlin spokesperson said that Yeltsin had signed the decree at the urging of both first deputy prime ministers who pledged to improve the state's finances and end sweetheart deals with big business. "The president took such a decision in accordance with his convictions," *Itar-Tass* quoted Nemtsov as saying. "He has regularly warned all officials they could not mix their duties." "I think this is an important step away from oligarchical capitalism in Russia," Nemtsov explained. As deputy secretary of the Security Council since October 1996, Berezovsky said that he had concentrated his efforts on talks with the breakaway republic of Chechnya. Berezovsky claimed that he had transferred to an arm's-length trust the management of his businesses.

After his dismissal, Berezovsky unleashed a fierce tirade against Chubais. "By his mentality, his way of working, Anatoly Borisovich Chubais is a bolshevik because he believes that any means are justified by the ends," Berezovsky remarked on an Ekho Moskvy radio show. Berezovsky accused Chubais of hypocrisy over his promise that privatization auctions would no longer be tainted by sweetheart deals and he alleged that Chubais was already rigging the sell-off of oil company Rosneft in favor of Uneximbank. Berezovsky's Sibneft was reported to have participated in the sale. "Chubais' words are at odds with his actions," Berezovsky said. In the end, he used a book royalties' scandal to unseat Chubais. In so doing, he unwittingly paved the way for the policy paralysis that ensued, just as Russia's external environment started to deteriorate. He also discredited the idea of oligarchy as a viable political model in Russia.

The IMF Is Not Monolithic

A fund mission visited Moscow in late July 1997, headed by Marquez-Ruarte. Its intention was to focus the discussions more on monetary issues in view of the large capital inflows. But with both the sovereign Eurobond issue and the disbursement of a World Bank loan in June, coming on top of the accelerating inflows from nonresident purchases of Russian assets, notably GKO, the CBR purchased almost two billion U.S. dollars in June, a part of which was sterilized through open market operations. Nevertheless, base money was expanding much more rapidly than foreseen under the program, and there was concern surrounding the uncertainty of inflation prospects. While difficult to gauge, the downward trend in the inflation rate appeared to have come to a halt. Before the mission left Washington, DC, there was active debate within the IMF about the appropriate policies to recommend under such circumstances. Views about Russia and its program were far from monolithic within the IMF.

Michael Mussa, the gregarious, blunt-speaking director who headed the IMF's research department, worried a lot about Russia. I recall that at the time, he noted that one of the most regrettable implications, in his view, of the past year's decline in fiscal revenues was the increasingly skewed policy mix: the deficit was large compared to program projections and the monetary policy remained tight, contributing to high real interest rates. Mussa felt that the current environment of good news on structural reforms, external confidence, and declining interest rates offered a unique opportunity to correct the policy mix with minimal risks to stabilization.

While the monetary program did not entail formal targets on base money, in the event that large capital inflows continued to exceed the program assumption, the IMF management instructed the mission to negotiate with the CBR to reduce credit expansion below the pace envisaged under the program so as to contain money growth. The extent of such offsetting action would depend on inflation developments, but a priori, full sterilization would not be advocated in order to keep monetary growth exactly in line with program projections. Fischer added that the mission needed to work with the authorities to figure out how much of the capital inflow equated to an increase in money demand.

At that point in time, the IMF staff saw no basis for assuming any reversal of the net capital inflows (that is, a change in the stock). In view of a disappointing performance in the first half, though, the mission did revise its projection for real growth downward to 1.5 percent under the program in 1997, still assuming a sharp projected acceleration of growth in this second half—that is, the same assumption that was being applied to the growth of revenues. In fact, the GDP grew at 1.4 percent.

Meanwhile, the view from the markets was almost ecstatic about Russia. As a *Business Week* feature of September 15, 1997, noted, "Bond bulls maintain that, at current prices, investors are more than compensated for the risks they're taking. They seem especially confident about Russia, which is swiftly becoming such an enticing draw that Merrill Lynch & Co. estimates it has accounted for 7% of total emerging market debt issued this year alone." The feature went on to stress that with "spreads between the yield on Russian debt and those of Western government issues . . . narrowing as the country's economic and political situation stabilizes and Moscow establishes a debt repayment track record, . . . investors are gaining 'confidence in buying new issues out of the region,'" quoting the London-based head of capital markets for Credit Suisse First Boston (CSFB). It also highlighted that "another frontier for yield-hunting investors is debt issued in local currencies. In Russia, for example, ruble yields on short-term government bonds reach 20% to 30%, while riskier corporate paper can yield as much as 100%."

And It Seemed Too Good to Last

Due to the healthy capital inflows, the mission spent most of its time preoccupied with worrying evidence of continuing weakness in the budgetary situation. Marquez-Ruarte, in his concluding meeting with Chubais on July 31, underscored concerns with the weak revenue situation, evidenced by the fact that even the conservative target for federal government cash revenue in the first six months of 1997 had been missed. The mission said that it would nevertheless recommend to the IMF management that the review be completed, because the target had only been missed by a small margin, the revenue in the second quarter had been close to target (the breach was due to a downward revision of the first-quarter revenue), the deficit target itself had been observed, there were strong efforts to improve revenue collection, and all other targets for end-June under the program had been observed.

Chubais responded that he was not happy with the revenue collections in the early part of 1997 but was confident that the changes in management at the State Tax Service (STS) and SCC were starting to yield better results already in the second quarter. Moreover, the new team at the STS, with the full support of the government, would be able to reach the ambitious targets for the year as a whole, especially as the new STS team had resolved how to treat tax arrears. In a major institutional shake-up, the old management of the STS was dismissed, and Alexander Pochinok was appointed to reform and reorient tax administration and collection.

Marquez-Ruarte and Chubais also discussed the improvements in expenditure control initiated under Chubais and Kudrin, including the attempt to conduct a systematic inventory of budgetary arrears in order to clear or securitize them. Ironically, this first attempt by Chubais and Kudrin to take stock of the government's spending arrears—trying to distinguish between the federal governments' unfulfilled budgetary obligations, the legitimate spending arrears of local governments, unbudgeted but legal commitments, and political promises—actually created the impression that the arrears' situation was worsening, when in actuality it was the first step toward bringing some order and control to what had been a chaotic and almost-unrecorded morass of spending commitments dating back to late Soviet times, when the previous control system had broken down.

Chubais assured the mission that the unfortunate practice of the use of nonmonetary forms of tax settlement would be terminated, finally, by the end of the year once a few remaining in the pipeline had been cleared. Indeed, he noted that the root cause of the need for these tax offsets was weak expenditure control and that the government was finalizing preparations to make the treasury system operational by January 1, 1998.

They finally agreed to keep the preparation of the draft 1998 budget under close review. Chubais expressed his confidence that the government would now go ahead with bold reforms without being compromised by political interference. Confident that the reform process was now seen as "irreversible," most Russian officials went off to their dachas and holidays abroad to enjoy a well-deserved rest.

Meanwhile, Marquez-Ruarte reported about developments in Moscow to IMF headquarters. In addition to the revenue situation, where Chubais had promised to spare no effort, Marquez-Ruarte reported that the problem of budgetary arrears had become increasingly apparent and would require attention. The CBR, at the same time, was pursuing a tight credit policy to limit the potential price effects of large capital inflows. Overall, it seemed that the new economic team appointed in the spring had clearly taken ownership of and been able to reinvigorate the structural reform process, with progress achieved in all major areas, which was broadly consistent with the program.

The IMF board approved a disbursement of US$640 million under the 1997 program on September 3. The board was increasingly worried. Reflecting its view, Camdessus sent a letter to Chernomyrdin on September 11, 1997, in which he mentioned that the directors were concerned about the persistent fragility of the budgetary situation. Following a small shortfall in relation to the January–June EFF program target for federal government cash revenue, cash revenue performed poorly in July and August. Although acknowledging the government's intensified efforts, more was needed, especially since program targets for the remainder of 1997 foresaw a major improvement in cash revenue collections. At the same time, given the revenue weakness, strict expenditure control was essential if budgetary arrears were to be eliminated; the key was to move forward decisively to fully adopt the treasury system.

Complacency Reigns in Hong Kong

The setting for the 1997 IMF annual meeting was Hong Kong, in late September 1997. Unlike Prague three years later, with its throngs of antiglobalization protesters, Hong Kong, having just recently reverted to China, was the ideal venue for the IMF meeting. The IMF usually holds its annual meeting in Washington, DC, but once every three years it is (expensively) held abroad. Hong Kong's recent reversion to China made it an obvious candidate, like Madrid in 1994 following Spain's democratic revival and Prague in 2000. With no protesters to distract attention, the mood was largely self-congratulatory. Despite some seemingly local problems in Thailand and the neighboring region, the fallout from the Mexican financial crisis in 1995 had been successfully weathered and the global economy was poised to continue an already-long period of sustained growth.[8] The prospects for emerging markets were seen as positive, and even the outlook for the poorer developing countries was encouraging.

Chubais, who by the time of the Hong Kong IMF meeting was the finance minister, led a large delegation. The delegation was feted by bankers, businesspeople, international bureaucrats, and the press as the success story of the decade, if not the century.

Chubais's normally placid expression was transformed into an almost-permanent grin as he received compliments. Of all people, he knew the human and political costs of what had been achieved. But at last he could reassure himself that his daring had been worth it. Russia was finally breaking free of its lugubrious past under the chains of the Bolsheviks. The "evil empire" had been destroyed, or more accurately had self-destructed, but every day was still a challenge to combat its corrupt and negative legacy. Nevertheless, economic reforms, so clumsily put in place as the Soviet state crumbled, were irreversible. Russia was finally on its way to becoming a normal country.

Seventy percent of Russia's workers were in the private sector. The ruble was stable, and the foreign exchange reserves were rising. Inflation was heading toward single digits, the economy was growing, and the stock and bond markets were booming. Yeltsin, elected to a second term as president and recovered from his illness, including the double pneumonia of January of that year, was fully in charge and now a member of that most exclusive of clubs—the G-7 industrial powers now expanded to eight to include Yeltsin at the head table to discuss political issues.

Indeed, at the time of the IMF annual meeting, Chubais was honored as the finance minister of the year by the prestigious financial magazine *Euromoney*. Chubais accepted the award at a reception in his honor in Hong Kong on September 22, 1997. He told the gathering of bankers and financiers from around the world that he was proud that Russia's reforms were being given international recognition. Chubais reminded the group that reforming Russia would not be an easy thing, "because it is so hard on the people." But he also said that it would be worse if no reforms were undertaken. He lauded the "brilliant" team of economists who would lead the country to a better life, and affirmed that they had the full support of President Yeltsin, and that the economists in turn support Yeltsin as president.

The new government had the momentum and political will to reform the Russian economy. At a meeting with Camdessus in a spacious, minimalist room at the Hong Kong Convention Center earlier that afternoon, Chubais had predicted what he called Russia's "friendly divorce" from the fund when the financial arrangements between the two were due to expire in about eighteen months.

Chubais was literally banking on his prospective reforms to privatize the old Soviet structure and liberalize the economy—tax reform and control of budget expenditure through the Finance Ministry, banking supervision, and breaking up the monopolies in natural gas, electricity, and the railroads. Society itself, he reckoned, would follow; commercial life would be more open and transparent, crime would become a marginal rather than a central problem, courts would function independently as they do in other countries, and Russia would at last become a nation of laws in which individuals were paramount and not the state. Little did he—or others—suspect then that he would barely have time in office to plant the seeds of those reforms, much less reap the results.

Chubais's mention of a divorce was merely an offhand remark, but Camdessus was not pleased with such bravado. Others in the room noticed it too. It was not that Camdessus wanted to keep Russia as an indebted client, although serving as the lifeline to the previously enfeebled Russian economy certainly did nothing to diminish the prestige of the IMF or its managing director—at least at that time.

What bothered Camdessus was something else. His extensive experience managing the IMF for a decade, and the French central bank and treasury before that, had endowed him with almost a sixth sense for when a country might be tempting fate—and he may have felt that the pendulum of market perceptions in Russia was swinging too far, too fast, to the optimistic side to be credible. He had seen, and indeed had been perceived by many observers to have been implicated in, what happened after unforeseen crises laid low economies that had appeared invulnerable; the Mexican crisis of early 1995 was still fresh in his mind.

The IMF meeting in 1997 was being held in Hong Kong, the very center of the east and southeast Asia region that seemed to have perfected the formula for a country to get rich. Even at that late September financial jamboree, complacency and even smugness was still pervasive. Yet the edifice of capitalist enrichment was about to crumble under the feet of the financial elite. Thailand had been forced to devalue its currency only two months before. Korea was in trouble. While these still seemed like local difficulties, Camdessus' instincts warned him against complacency even as, right in front of him, the normally cautious Chubais succumbed to euphoria and even repeated his remarks in public.

In less than a year, contagion from Asia and the collapse of energy prices—in conjunction with continuing political interference that prevented sensible policies from being enacted to confront the change in fortunes—would dash Chubais's hopes, discredit the reform process in Russia for years to come, and sully the prestige of the IMF itself. Fischer conceded that the failure of Russia's economic program was nothing less than spectacular. These unanticipated external shocks exposed the fundamental vulnerability of a country with a weak political structure in the presence of lax fiscal policy and significant amounts of debt held by nonresidents—a ready reminder of Greece's predicament some thirteen years later.

The crisis in Russia was not inevitable and probably could have been avoided, as mentioned earlier. Yet at every opportunity, when Russia could have stepped back from the brink and made better choices, domestic politics seemed to get in the way.

When the Russian delegation met with Camdessus in Hong Kong on September 23, 1997, it seemed oblivious to the undercurrents back at home. In that meeting, Chubais noted that the revenue situation remained difficult, but that energetic steps were under way. The Russian government was not waiting for the new tax code or even the 1998 budget to take effect. It was moving to declare a big company bankrupt, thereby sending the strongest possible signal of a sea change in attitudes (it was rumored at the time that the target was Nizhnevartovsk NefteGaz). Chubais stressed that the pressure from Yeltsin and Chernomyrdin was great, and it was clear that there was support for more fundamental changes. Yeltsin added his own voice to Chubais's reference of a friendly divorce from the fund. On a visit to Oryol, outside his suburban Moscow sanatorium, on September 18, 1997, the president also said that Russia would stop borrowing from the IMF once its current loan expired in 1999.

On the monetary side, after the inflows of the first half of 1997, Dubinin was sanguine about the second half, noting that in addition to seasonal outflows, there would be some precautionary shift of money holdings into foreign currency prior to the monetary conversion scheduled for January 1, 1998. As a sign of confidence with the definitive taming of inflation, the CBR had announced on August 4 that the ruble would be redenominated from January 1, 1998, by dropping the last three digits, so that one thousand old rubles would become one new ruble. Dubinin stressed the need for continuing exchange rate stability, while contending that some flexibility was also needed.

Even more, the Russian delegation in Hong Kong appeared to ignore what was happening right in front of its eyes in Asia. For the delegation and indeed most observers perched in Hong Kong, what had happened in Thailand seemed like a local difficulty with few broader implications. Chubais even had the temerity to wonder at the time whether emerging market investors, disenchanted with Asian markets, might not consider Russia as a "safe haven" for their investments—so that Russia might actually be a beneficiary of the problems in Asia. The time bomb in Korea exploded only a couple weeks later.[9]

In fact, such was the strength of the myth about the Asian miracle that no one was anticipating what was about to happen next. The tsunami that resulted from the looming Asian crisis, which in turn triggered a collapse in oil and other commodity prices as imports into the leading Asian markets were slashed, was blamed directly by Yasin for the crisis that then seemed to move next to Russia.

None other than Fischer made a presentation at a seminar in Hong Kong on September 19, in which he strongly endorsed the need to amend the fund's articles of agreement to enable the IMF to play its full part in promoting the orderly liberalization of international capital markets. In that presentation, Fischer highlighted the recent turbulence in the region—the attacks on the Thai baht and its devaluation, the subsequent devaluations of other currencies in the region, and the contagion effects that seemed present in east Asia, just as they had been in Latin America in 1995, and perhaps in Europe in 1993. Contrary to the view of those who would contend that the capital account was more often the source of economic difficulties and risk rather than benefit, Fischer tried to persuade those skeptics that managing a liberalized system was in the best interests of the membership.

4

Hope Disappointed

In retrospect, 1997 was a key period, in which a combination of bad luck in the external economic environment combined with intensified political infighting within the Russian governing class conspired to miss the opportunity for an early escape from penury. And practically no one foresaw where this lethal mix would lead.

The View from the IMF

The difficult prospects for 1997 should not have come as such a surprise to the IMF. From the outset, there were indications that the combination of continuing economic dislocation, an ineffectual government operating in a power vacuum, and a newly reelected but virtually invisible president would not augur well for the period ahead. Yet we were not deterred. Relatively speaking, the economic situation had stabilized. Presumably the worst was over. What was needed now was a strong boost to structural reform, including critical aspects of fiscal reform and tax administration. If this next step seemed obvious, it was not clear how to get there.

On January 9, 1997, Fischer had set out his assessment of prospects in a seminar at Harvard University. Fischer said that "five years following the onset of the transition process in Russia, it might be safe to say that the fight to stabilize has been won."

Fischer noted that this success was due in large part to a sharp slowdown in central bank credit, facilitated by a new central bank law that strengthened the bank's independence, and discontinued the practice of direct credit to the budget and enterprises. He also referred to a marked tightening of fiscal policy. Based on a preliminary assessment, it was thought at that point that the 1996 deficit was about 6 percent of GDP, which occurred in an environment of sharply higher interest rates owing in particular to political uncertainties prior to the presidential elections. It later turned out that the actual deficit was the equivalent of 8.5 percent of GDP. Finally, while signaling the favorable prospects for further disinflation and some modest growth for the first time since the transition began, Fischer underscored that the main challenge for 1997 in the macroeconomic area remained the need for fiscal consolidation by improving revenue performance and addressing the imbalances in the pension system.

A few days after that Harvard seminar, arriving just before the last monthly mission in January 1997, Fischer visited Moscow. On his arrival, I joined Fischer for a private dinner with Chubais, still head of the Presidential Administration, and Maxim Boycko, his deputy. We dined at a corner table in the Lobster Grill, then located next to the Teatro restaurant in the basement of the Metropol Hotel. There, Fischer's message was blunt: following the impressive performance month after month in the context of the 1995 program, Russia's mixed performance in policy implementation in 1996 had become a source of significant disappointment to the IMF.

Fischer went on to observe that the discussions of Russia's program at the IMF's board in recent months had been characterized by increasing and serious concern. The directors viewed the recent trend in policy implementation as one of drift, lack of leadership, and a waning commitment to the agreed-on economic program. Without a substantial improvement in performance in 1997, continued support from the IMF could not be assured.

Chubais gravely underscored the message and the warning. He said that he would discuss it with his boss—that is, the president—once Yeltsin's health would allow. While acknowledging that the conduct of economic policy could not afford to remain adrift, Chubais, despite his lofty position as Kremlin chief of staff, could not promise more.

Chubais was all too aware of the snake pit of Russian politics, with his many enemies waiting to pounce on any false move, especially one that might be construed as emanating from foreign sources. Indeed, having been accused of acting as a regent for the ailing Yeltsin in recent months, Chubais was determined to keep a low profile as the best way—for the moment—to ensure that the so-called red directors did not seize all the levers of power. Later it turned out that Chubais had succeeded in getting the message across.

As it was, other than parts of the Kremlin under Chubais's direct sway (such as the financial control office under Kudrin, whom he had brought in from Saint Petersburg), Boycko's Privatization Center, Dmitry Vasiliev at the Federal Commission for the Securities Market, and a few allies in Yasin's Ministry of Economy, notably the dynamic and liberal deputy minister Vasiliev and his then-deputy Nabiullina), the only professionally run official institution in the economic area was the CBR. Even there, however, a fundamental problem emerged in that in the absence of a strong Finance Ministry, Dubinin and Aleksashenko (the chair and first deputy chair, respectively) were shouldering the entire burden of macro-economic stabilization. Unlike many central bankers, they still assessed the situation from their broader focus based on their earlier collaboration at the Ministry of Finance.

At this initial dinner, and in almost all of his subsequent meetings, Fischer stressed that while private markets had responded positively to the major strides made by Russia over the previous two years taken as a whole, this market response was unlikely to be a lasting vote of confidence in the authorities' policy performance. In his view, it reflected rather the benefit of the doubt accorded by the market to the authorities for the progress made thus far. If this assessment was right, it was probable that the market would turn even more positive if the authorities made further progress, while the response would be a marked turn in the negative direction if only sluggish progress were to be made in policy implementation.

Even before the dream team arrived, considerable efforts were made to find workable solutions to this challenge. The IMF team lead by Horiguchi, and the Russian officials—from Potanin, as deputy prime minister, and Livshits, as finance minister, on down—continued program negotiations during late winter 1997, and the IMF Moscow office, now under my direction (I moved to Moscow in November 1996), ensured a constant policy dialogue and prepared the technical work to facilitate the negotiations on a 1997 economic program. Horiguchi, no doubt because of his formidable combination of astute analysis, inventiveness, daring, stubbornness, and human insight, became somewhat of a legend in Russian financial circles, within the IMF, and later in international finance more broadly.

But as the final numbers for end-1996 performance started to appear and, more worryingly, the concerns with weak revenue performance in early 1997 started to mount, the IMF management grew increasingly skeptical of real progress and, as a precaution, suggested for the first time the idea of introducing monthly revenue floors as program conditionality.

As 1997 unfolded, we were operating with the sense that the previous year's performance was extremely disappointing. To be sure, impressive success was achieved in the fight against inflation and the maintenance of exchange rate stability in the face of the pressure associated with the presidential elections. At the same time, fiscal goals for the year were missed, exchange rate stability was maintained at the expense of a significant loss of reserves, and a large debt was accumulated (including with the IMF, German loans, Eurobond issues, and large GKO issues). Furthermore, structural reforms were not pursued with the vigor that was expected, much less required. We needed to do better.

Of course we understood that the disappointing fiscal performance could be blamed, to some extent, on the impact of uncertainties related to the election outcome, which pushed up interest costs to the budget. More fundamentally, however, fiscal slippages were attributable to the lack of a sufficient political commitment to insist on the payment of tax liabilities, especially by large taxpayers, as well as the weak capacity of tax administration and deficiencies in the tax system, particularly the vast array of tax exemptions that had been granted by presidential decree in return for favors. No doubt many favors were related to efforts to help secure the 1996 election result for Yeltsin, but many exemptions also reflected the loose controls in place at the time. Repeated attempts to deal with the revenue situation floundered, with the result that despite efforts to control spending, the deficit rose and significant spending arrears emerged.

Fiscal Reality Hits Home

Even as the IMF board was meeting on September 3, 1997, preliminary information was coming through the IMF's Moscow office that the tax collection continued to disappoint. The July tax data showed poor performance of excises and the value-added tax (VAT) with the result that cash collections for the month were slightly below 7 percent of monthly GDP, or 19.1 trillion old rubles, against a flow target for the month of 24.6 trillion old rubles. Viugin expected that the August outturn would not be much better than July. He acknowledged that catching up in September in order to meet the nine-month flow target for revenue was far from obvious. Officially, though, his authorities maintained that revenues would pick up from September on, and that they should even be able to meet the revenue floor targets for end-September. By extension, the cash revenue floor of 283 trillion old rubles for 1997 was beginning to look ambitious. The formal revenue floor for the year was set under the program with a margin at 283 trillion rubles, which differed from the budgetary revenue target of 304 trillion rubles.

Viugin agreed that it might soon be prudent to consider reviewing the revenue forecasts for the remainder of the year. In fact, he admitted informally that his staff had done some projections that suggested revenue could be well below the annual floor by perhaps as much as 40 trillion old rubles. The actual 1997 outcome was 252 trillion old rubles.

Ironically, the deficit was seen as well within the program ceiling. But poor data continued to hamper monitoring on the expenditure side of the budget. Indeed, the IMF staff and the authorities measured the deficit on the basis of below-the-line or budget financing information. The assessment at that time was that since expected spending in the federal budget in July was about 14 percent of GDP—while in fact it was just over 11 percent, as implied by the financing data—some net arrears were incurred on items other than wages and transfers to the Pension Fund (being the only two items where current arrears could be monitored, pending the introduction of the treasury control system).

The IMF staff warned that the revenue projections underlying the draft 1998 budget were starting to look too optimistic and should be reconsidered. MinFin officials did revise their estimates downward for the likely 1997 outcome, but still envisaged cash revenue of around 8.5 percent of GDP, whereas it had been only 7.3 percent of GDP in the first seven months of the year.

By way of explanation, a key issue was the intertemporal impact of tax and monetary offsets on cash revenue (that is, the moral hazard problem). While cash revenue in 1996 was about 7 percent of GDP, and 7.3 percent in the first seven months of 1997, the total revenue was much higher. In 1996, including all forms of tax and monetary offsets, the total revenue was about 9.5 percent, and in the first seven months of 1997 the corresponding figure was 10.3 percent. It seems likely that the 2.5 to 3 percent of GDP collected in noncash form during this period had at least some depressing effect on firms' willingness to clear their tax liabilities with fungible money.

In a discussion in late August, Aleksashenko offered his assessment, and as a former deputy finance minister, he probably understood more about budgetary issues than practically anyone else. Aleksashenko and Dubinin had worked together in MinFin earlier, and Aleksashenko handled most of the budget negotiations with the IMF in 1994, at least in areas where Vavilov was not involved. When Dubinin, as acting minister, was fired as one of the scapegoats following the ruble crash on "Black Tuesday," October 19, 1994, Aleksashenko resigned in protest, and wrote a scathing public letter, directly criticizing the president—a virtually unprecedented step by a senior official in Russia at that time. Aleksashenko agreed that revenue performance in 1997 was a source of concern, but he said that this was not a new story and fundamentally there was little basis, since the departure of the mission, to revise the projection for the year as a whole. Certainly, each month that went by following a below-program trend would only make it that much harder to catch up. He stressed that Chubais would not acknowledge any possibility of missing the annual target until the late October mission at the earliest. Apparently Chubais had promised Yeltsin, as part of the deal to obtain the latter's support for the 1997 sequestration budget, to collect at least the programmed amount of revenue.

Aleksashenko also wanted to disabuse the IMF of the notion that any significant revenue could be raised in the remainder of the year from any kind of "emergency revenue package"; he maintained that it had all been tried before, and anyway, anything of significance would require Duma approval. He felt that efforts to improve tax administration and collection would continue to be hampered by the attitude of the STS staff members, who viewed their basic task as assessment rather than collection and seemed to be content when taxpayers even filed a declaration. Whatever the changes at the top, these attitudes cannot be modified rapidly, and the problem was aggravated by the poor wages in the STS. Finally, Aleksashenko stressed that the new tax code would make the situation even worse since it did not go far enough (in the then-current version) to encourage compliance, yet it weakened the ability of the tax police to enforce collection.

Without the possibility of higher revenues, the question was how to cut further—relative to the draft sequestration budget—in order to observe the deficit target without incurring arrears. Aleksashenko explained that Chubais's hands were tied since he could not admit to Yeltsin that the revenue target could not be met. He argued that there would still be time to take steps (which he did not elaborate on) in the last two, normally high-spending months if a revenue shortfall were to emerge. This would need to be closely monitored, and would require some tough decisions concerning the postponement or cancellation of some budgetary cash spending. Action, however, with respect to spending commitments would be far more difficult.

The problem, as Aleksashenko explained it, was really how to control expenditure, not through legal instruments, but rather in practice. Unfortunately, in the absence of a real treasury system, there was just no system in place to ensure that there would be no new arrears. In his view, treasury head Alexander Smirnov had no idea of exactly what he wanted to achieve, so he had no idea of how to get there. Of course he would tell his boss, Chubais, that the treasury would be in place by January 1, 1998. In one sense, it was no doubt true that twenty-five hundred branches would be in place. But each one would have its own account and would operate without central control. Aleksashenko thought that even with determination and the right people, a real treasury system controlling commitments and payments was still years away. In other words, Russia's spending control problem would remain the weak point in the fiscal system. Aleksashenko's assessment turned out to be prophetic. A lack of progress in resolving this issue would be critical to what was about to unfold, as the Asian financial crisis and the resulting plunge in world oil prices started to engulf Russia itself.

Welcome Back to the Bad News

So when the Russian delegation members returned from Hong Kong in late September 1997, they arrived at their desks to face a lengthening string of bad news, as Viugin's worrying projections about revenue for the year as a whole seemed to be materializing. Rumors of Korean and Brazilian investors pulling out of Russian assets to cover their positions at home swept through Moscow, and the CBR started losing reserves—about US$0.5 billion in September and US$0.2 billion in October. Both the GKO and stock markets became more volatile.

The CBR seemed to exhibit a slightly neurotic reaction. On the one hand, the CBR management appeared to be concerned about possible contagion effects stemming from the recent currency crises in southeast Asia. It was visibly worried about not having adequate monitoring mechanisms in place, and even the data it received from banks mostly consisted of form rather than substance. It had no regular data on items such as nonresident flows in the GKO market, short-term foreign exchange positions of banks, off–balance sheet items such as guarantees and forward contracts, and unconsolidated accounts of bank subsidiaries. At his urgent request, a confidential note on currency crises and speculative attacks was prepared by IMF staff members for Aleksashenko, highlighting the implications for Russia.

On the other hand, the CBR management was also becoming more secretive, at least in regard to the IMF. Marquez-Ruarte complained to Aleksashenko in Hong Kong about insufficient information being provided in terms of coverage and timeliness, as I had done in vain some weeks earlier. The flow of information was not even up to the IMF standards of those days. Aleksashenko tried to argue somewhat disingeniously that with the switch to quarterly reviews of Russia's program, there was no longer any need for monthly data. Marquez-Ruarte quickly disabused him of this notion and suggested that the issue would have to be resolved before completing further reviews. The issue in fact continued to fester. On October 24, Marquez-Ruarte sent a clear set of proposed data-reporting requirements, in line with normal fund standards, to Aleksashenko. Proposals and counterproposals were subsequently exchanged. The issues were not resolved by summer 1998. I think that we refrained from escalating the issue because it did not seem critical enough to be a program stopper, there were other more high-profile priorities, and we did not want to unduly alarm already-nervous markets. With the benefit of hindsight, we were just too complacent.

Around this time, with growing volatility in Russian financial markets and uncertainty about the fate of the 1998 budget, there was an increasingly urgent focus on the fiscal situation both in Moscow and within the IMF. Ironically, the broader debate involving the whole range of macroeconomic and structural issues kept getting postponed.

Gaidar's Institute for the Study of Economies in Transition (an economic policy think tank founded in 1990 that he rejoined after leaving the government) had developed expertise in the analysis of tax policy. At the end of September 1997, Gaidar explained that the reasons for the decline in revenues were related to the increased ability of extractive industry to engage in what he called "tax planning." They abused the admittedly poor, existing, and contradictory tax legislation through the use of tax havens and transfer pricing. Attacking them directly through audits would be difficult and was unlikely to succeed. Better to use administrative means to force them to pay, as had been long advocated by then–first deputy finance minister Ignatiev, for instance, by denying oil companies with statutory tax arrears the right to use the government-owned pipelines for exporting oil. Gaidar also felt that some complacency had set into tax collection after the initial revenue pickup in May and June, and the handling of tax arrears and expectation of further tax offsets were negatively impacting revenue performance.

At a technical level, Viugin, in a meeting in late September 1997, thought that it would not make any sense to try to implement emergency revenue measures. In his view, the reasons for the poor cash revenue performance were deeply embedded in the institutional framework, and any type of short-term measures would only yield at best temporary results. The focus instead had to be on eliminating incentives for tax delinquency (such as arrears and offsets) and building up the STS. In particular, the STS culture had to be transformed from a focus on assessment to tax collection, as the new management was trying to do, and corruption was the major problem with customs.

The most troubling aspect of this discussion was Viugin's assessment as to why the government's hands were tied in trying to tackle the revenue problem in a more aggressive manner. He noted the "coalition" nature of the present government, and certain factions were clearly against Chubais's efforts to raise cash revenue and eliminate "shady deals."

It seems that if Chubais and his allies pushed too hard on revenues at this stage, then professionally compromising material might be made public in the media—presumably controlled by their opponents—that could undermine the whole reform effort. Viugin felt that the situation was extremely sensitive and not sustainable, with the implication being that Chubais was trying to find a political solution, but had to be careful in terms of the timing in pushing tax collection efforts. He observed that there was nothing the IMF could do in these circumstances except to continue to advocate suitable policies.

A couple weeks later Vasiliev confirmed Viugin's assessment. Vasiliev pointed out that Chubais was being increasingly marginalized by people around the president. These people (apparently including Livshits and some bankers) noted that Chubais was acknowledged by many as being a problem solver, but the big macroeconomic problems (inflation, reserves, and growth) were thought of as largely a thing of the past. Since in their view Chubais also had political baggage, Yeltsin should get rid of him soon. At first glance, the impression was that what his opponents, in trying to turn Yeltsin against the man, were really targeting the policies he supported. But given the legacy of the infighting by that point, it was actually more likely that they were trying to get rid of a particularly powerful rival.

It was thus more than coincidental when in October 1997, with markets becoming nervous as the contagion from the Asian crisis started to impact investor sentiments, the then-popular weekly television news program *Vremya* aired a segment on its Saturday night show in which anchor Sergei Dorenko accused the Chubais people of trying to destabilize the currency market by purportedly suggesting to a leading Western wire service that Yeltsin had signed an instruction to dismiss Chubais from government. At the time, the ORT network was owned by arch-Chubais foe Berezovsky.

Vasiliev, like many Russian officials dealing with the IMF and other foreign officials, made a habit of dramatizing such personal power struggles as if they were thinly veiled attacks on the policy agenda. The hope seemed to be that the IMF could mobilize support for the policies under threat, and so relieve pressure on those associated with the policies. Hence, Vasiliev said that it was only the easier problems that had been addressed (for example, controlling base money), and that the really tough fiscal and related structural measures that hit at the entrenched interests were being frustrated.

He was right, of course. In these discussions, we had the impression that Vasiliev would have liked to enlist the IMF's support in disabusing the Kremlin that Chubais had become dispensable. The IMF did not take the bait, and tried, as much as possible in the politically charged atmosphere within Moscow's beltway, to distinguish between policies and personalities.

In view of the persistence with which senior Russian officials would present the internal debate as one between good and evil in policy terms, it would seem that they might have actually believed that the IMF could have some influence on the outcome. If so, they were imagining a willingness and ability on the part of the IMF to intervene in political disputes that it simply did not have. More likely, they felt that it would help soften the IMF, at the margin, to be accommodating when circumstances did not "allow" the authorities to pursue the agreed-on policies.

Kudrin, in a meeting on October 6, said that the problem concerning monetary offsets had to be addressed, or otherwise there would be little confidence that 1998 would not be a repetition of 1997 and earlier years, with a proliferation of tax arrears used to offset budgetary arrears, and all of its adverse consequences on budgetary control. We concurred, and suggested that it would be best to organize the already widely anticipated offset operations as quickly as possible and at the same time announce a firm cutoff date. For this to be a credible move, urgent steps would need to be implemented to assert expenditure control and backload expenditures for the following year since the initial months would be the most difficult in revenue terms.

Kudrin agreed and noted that such a view was strongly held in MinFin (especially by Ignatiev, and apparently shared by Chubais). The problem was in the Kremlin (he mentioned Livshits, who was once again in the Presidential Administration), where some continued to believe that offsets were not so harmful and in any case were a necessary evil. A draft presidential decree had been prepared to make all offsets illegal beyond January 1, 1998, but the debate continued. Kudrin indicated that the IMF could help to tilt the outcome.

In a meeting on October 8, 1997, Livshits also said that he was concerned about the use of monetary offsets to pay tax obligations, because of the enormous scope for corruption and especially because they had acquired the nickname of "Livshits offsets," so he was glad that they were being discontinued. Still, Kudrin indicated that Livshits seemed to be less concerned about the use of "reverse" monetary offsets, saying that there really was no alternative. Reverse monetary offsets involved the payment of cash by the treasury through a commercial bank, which was then used to credit the tax liability of a taxpayer enterprise.

An Initial Bout of Market Jitters Erupts

On October 28, 1997, the RTS share index plunged by 19 percent, following earlier declines in New York and Hong Kong. Traders as well as the CBR stressed that the decline was not due to any Russia-specific factors. Aleksashenko was attending a conference in Berlin, where Alexander Potemkin reached him to decide on an appropriate response. The CBR did not intervene in the foreign exchange market but did purchase about one trillion old rubles of GKOs. Nevertheless yields rose sharply, on average by some 6 percentage points from 19 percent the previous day. On October 29, the Russian stock market regained most of the loss and GKO yields declined back to about 20 percent.

In order to assess the critical situation developing in Russia, especially as rumors from market sources started to express increasing concern about Russian prospects, Fischer had been originally scheduled to arrive in Moscow at the end of the mission, which left Moscow on November 1. He had wanted to see for himself how to get the program back on track and decide what signals to send the World Bank about the continuation of its adjustment lending. The World Bank had prepared a new loan to support Russia's structural reform program. Normally such program lending is only provided to a country with an operative arrangement in place with the IMF. Since the IMF program was off track,

Fischer's assessment from the IMF as the umpire on macroeconomic issues could play a crucial role in determining whether the bank would go forward with its loan. But at the last minute, because of the crisis in Korea, Fischer was unable to leave Washington, DC (since both he and Camdessus could not be absent at a time like that, and Camdessus was on a visit, initially secret, to Seoul). Fischer's trip was only postponed, though.

In the meantime, whatever complacency had been manifest in Moscow during the summer had dissipated by the fall. On November 5, a worried Aleksashenko called me to say that US$1.5 billion in CBR foreign exchange reserves had been lost through intervention in the past week. He mentioned that his contacts with foreign banks and fund managers suggested that nonresident outflows would continue, with rumors specifically about Brazilian and Korean investors. It was estimated from market sources that Brazilian and Korean investors accounted for one-third of the US$15 billion in nonresident holdings of GKO at end-September 1997. He had heard that the potential amount of nonresident net outflows could be in the range of US$4–6 billion by the end of December.

We discussed the data (and lack of information) as well as possible steps to take, specifically the question of allowing a much faster, though orderly (or controlled) rate of depreciation of the ruble should significant pressure continue. He was adamant that any sharp acceleration in the rate of depreciation would backfire since it would send a clear signal to Russian investors that the ruble was weak, and so just compound the outflow problem. I urged him to tighten liquidity and raise CBR rates at least in line with market rates. Chubais's earlier boast about Russia being considered a safe haven for investors in Asia looked like a bad joke in retrospect.

Acquiescing on Exchange Rate Policy

There was considerable discussion about an appropriate exchange rate policy for 1998, and a growing sense of urgency in October 1997 to reach a firm view so that the policy could be announced in advance to calm market concerns. The corridor (or band) regime for the ruble (which was essentially a commitment by the central bank to allow fluctuations in the exchange rate within a band that could itself adjust over time, and where the bank would otherwise intervene to buy or sell foreign exchange in order to maintain the rate within the designated band) was introduced in July 1995, following several months of pressure for appreciation. The aim was to stabilize market expectations about the exchange rate and provide an anchor for disinflationary policy. The regime had been modified to a sliding band starting in the second half of 1996, after heavy exchange market intervention in support of the ruble ahead of the June presidential elections, but also reflected an increasing desire to protect external competitiveness. For 1996 as a whole, the ruble depreciated by 16.5 percent against the dollar, compared with a depreciation of 23.5 percent in 1995. Monthly inflation continued to decline.

During fall 1997, the IMF staff considered that the exchange rate band had provided stability to the foreign exchange market since it was adopted in mid-1995, and should be maintained in 1998. In general, the staff took the view that a fixed exchange rate regime would not be optimal in seeking macroeconomic stability in a country like Russia, where the long-run equilibrium real exchange rate might not yet have been reached and where there was a high probability of substantial shocks to the economy, but that the country was not ready for a fully flexible regime until inflation was tamed.

As CBR deputy chair, Potemkin said in a meeting on October 3, 1997, that while the ultimate intention was to conduct a managed float without a preannounced target rate, at least for 1998, it was still considered to be premature to make such a move. Aleksashenko also stressed more of a political economy point, which was that a firm ruble helped to protect the CBR from political interference. In this case, the CBR could always argue with its many critics in the Duma that a tight monetary stance was needed to support the stability of the ruble. If the ruble exchange rate were no longer an anchor, he contended, parliamentarians could try to play havoc with credit policy.

All of the analysis to date indicated that the real exchange rate remained highly competitive, even if the margin was being slowly eroded. The external current account through the fourth quarter of 1997 continued to have a substantial surplus (almost 2 percent of quarterly GDP), the exchange reserves were rising, and the estimated profitability of the nonenergy tradable goods sector remained buoyant. Real GDP growth was positive for the first time in 1997 in post-Soviet Russia, and the prospects for 1998 looked promising.

Moreover, there was the prevailing view, perhaps best articulated at the time in Russia by Aleksashenko and endorsed by the IMF more broadly, that the real exchange rate, even in the short run, was not a policy variable but was instead endogenous, and depended on real factors such as capital and labor, productivity and initial endowments. If anything, in light of the prevailing lax "budget" constraints on enterprise behavior as a legacy of the Soviet economy, a hard ruble policy would act as an incentive for the needed restructuring of an antiquated capital stock and the adaptation of the labor force. It was not fully appreciated at the time that the economy was unprepared to accept the consequences of hard budget constraints in either the public or private sector.

The IMF staff and management, however, certainly felt that greater flexibility in the actual operation of the band regime should be used, especially by widening the scope of the daily intervention band, which would provide a high degree of short-term stability, but allow the rate to move over time in line with market sentiments. The exchange rate policy for 1998–2000 was announced on November 10. The timing came as an unpleasant surprise since the IMF staff still considered that the issue was under discussion, but Dubinin precipitated the announcement in an effort to calm the markets. Although advocating the utility of an early move to greater flexibility in the exchange regime, the IMF reluctantly acquiesced to the announced policy.

Under the new scheme, the exchange rate was to pivot around 6.2 (new) rubles per dollar, with a margin of +/–15 percent. This meant a widening of the band from +/–5 percent and an end to the sliding exchange rate. The narrower daily band maintained for operational purposes was to remain in place, with its total width not to exceed 1.5 percent. In practice and as a result of political paralysis, the CBR conducted a fixed exchange rate policy.

What was striking in retrospect was that there was no clearly articulated "exit strategy" that could square the circle of a needed monetary anchor, the exchange rate flexibility needed to adapt to a rapid collapse in the terms of trade as oil prices started to plummet, and the political signal needed to demonstrate that economic policy was benign, all in the midst of a gathering crisis atmosphere as the market contagion rolled in from Asia. Personally, I was always against fixing prices, even for foreign exchange, but went along with the consensus against my better instincts.

Russian Politics Come to a Boil

It seemed then that Murphy's Law must be operating: if things can get worse, they will get worse. In the middle of the Asian contagion, with confidence in the fragile institutions of government under a cloud, the last thing that was needed was a political crisis.

The plotting and intrigues, stemming from Beresovsky's fury at the result of the previous summer's auction of privatization stakes in Svyazinvest, finally broke into a full-blooded political crisis. The events are graphically described in Chrystia Freeland's book.[1] The auction of a large block of shares in Svyazinvest was heralded by Chubais and Nemtsov as the first fair auction of state property in Russia, closing the chapter on the sorry and sordid loans-for-shares "privatization" of 1995, and a sign of great things to come. The losers had a different perspective.

Freeland's interpretation sounds plausible in that Berezovsky vowed to get revenge on Chubais for what he perceived to be a blatant double-cross when Potanin's Uneximbank won the auction that he thought was supposed to have been rigged in his favor. From the time that the auction results were announced in July, the mood became ugly. Since several major newspapers and television channels were at least partially controlled by the winners and losers of Svyazinvest, the media quickly became a battleground in a mudslinging war for the Kremlin's attention. All pretenses of a free and objective press were abandoned.

Relations apparently became so tense that Yeltsin called the bickering bankers to the Kremlin and told them to cool down. It was too late. The war of words continued until Chubais seemingly outmaneuvered Berezovsky and had him fired from the Kremlin.

In the end, that may have been a political miscalculation on Chubais's part. Once again a private citizen, Berezovsky arranged for one of his paid journalists to write an exposé about alleged graft by Chubais and his associates. In the so-called book scandal, it emerged that Chubais and four others reportedly split a US$450,000 writing advance for a presumably fictitious book from a publishing company in Switzerland. Intriguingly, the book, called *Privatization the Russian Way*, was published in 1999. Whatever the facts of the case (a subject beyond the confines of my book), Berezovsky's tactic worked, at least in terms of revenge—but at a cost. Viugin had certainly recognized the potential seriousness of the situation with his earlier warning.

Of course, we will never know what would have happened had the dream team been able to retain control of the levers of power for a few more months. As a result of the book scandal, Boycko, a deputy head of the presidential administration and key Chubais aide, left the government on November 15, followed a couple of days later by Peter Mostovoi, the cigar-chomping minister responsible for state property, and others. Boycko had just been assigned special responsibilities for dealing with the revenue situation, whereas Mostovoi was an important official involved in privatization and control of state property. Kokh had been an early victim of the newspaper war, having resigned in August.

Chubais kept his job, just barely. While continuing as the first deputy prime minister, however, he lost his bastion of real power, which was control over the Ministry of Finance. Moreover, his authority, which was crucially derived from the perception of total backing by the Kremlin, seemed to be seriously dented. Already, on November 18, the Duma was threatening to block passage of the 1998 budget unless Chubais was fired. Mikhail Zadornov, the erstwhile chair of the Duma's Budget Committee, was appointed finance minister on November 20, 1997.

Chubais's enemies, having gained the president's ear, also used the occasion for some additional housecleaning in terms of Chubais allies by stripping Nemtsov of the Ministry of Fuel and Energy, which Kiriyenko took over as minister. Zadornov initially exhibited caution in endorsing Chubais's draft budget. As former economy minister, Yasin explained to me that "Zadornov continued to act for some time as if he were still a parliamentarian, an approach that probably constrained MinFin in looming internal battles over financial and fiscal policy."

The Asian Crisis Spills on to Russian Markets

Prospects for the 1998 budget and balance of payments were suddenly undermined by a dramatic drop in oil prices in November as the slump in demand from Asia started to feed through the global system. From almost US$20 per barrel for Urals blend in September, the price dropped to just above US$15 per barrel by the end of the year.

With growing concerns about the unsupportive stance of monetary policy as market pressure started to rise in the autumn, Potemkin said that the CBR recognized that high interest rates were important to maintain the confidence of resident investors. High interest rates would deter the population from moving into foreign currency (and Sberbank, the state savings bank that by itself accounted for over half of the banking system, was raising its interest rate structure, followed by other commercial banks).

Still, it was evident that the CBR was providing liquidity to the market by supporting prices in the GKO market. Potemkin agreed that it was critical to let interest rates rise, and while most of the CBR management would support the more aggressive use of interest rates to mop up excess liquidity, there was strong outside pressure from banks and businesses that were politically influential. In fact, interest rates might have to rise much further to reduce the pressure on the exchange rate.

In another meeting, on November 18, 1997, Potemkin underscored that market perceptions implied a lack of confidence in the authorities. Heavy CBR intervention in the foreign exchange market continued, amounting to an additional US$3 billion in the previous two weeks. Of this amount, an estimated US$600–700 million was to settle forward transactions, US$1 billion reflected seasonal import needs, and the rest represented capital outflows and the desire by commercial banks to cover open positions. At that time, Potemkin hoped that the worst was over, and he did not expect gross reserves to fall below US$18 billion by the end of the year. Yet the end-year reserves were US$17.8 billion.

I again suggested that some of the pressure could be taken off by allowing a higher rate of depreciation of the ruble. Potemkin stressed that the CBR would be worried by any perceptible increase in the rate of crawl: while it would do little to reduce outflows, the CBR was concerned that it could be interpreted by the market negatively and indeed accelerate outflows. He also implied that the CBR's room for maneuver was limited in any case since a substantial depreciation could negatively affect the position of the domestic banking system.

Given the important role that the exchange rate anchor had played in reducing inflationary expectations, it was felt that in the first instance, the authorities should defend the corridor regime through higher interest rates, at the same time that they pressed ahead with a credible fiscal package. Yet the IMF view by late November was that if such action failed to stem the exchange market pressure, a step devaluation would be needed, although there was some concern that in such circumstances involving a large loss of credibility, the early shift into the new band would be difficult, if not impossible. Although this position was discussed internally in the IMF, it was not communicated officially to the authorities since their policy had already been publicly announced, and it might leak with explosive consequences. They were urged to use the flexibility within the band to absorb some of the pressure.

Buffeted by falling oil prices, and against the background of nervousness on the world financial markets and plunging Russian share prices, the CBR announced that as of November 11, 1997, it would raise interest rates in conjunction with the exchange rate policy for 1998 to ward off any speculative attack on the currency. Dubinin said the temporary interest rate increase, combined with a more flexible exchange rate policy starting next year, would shore up investor confidence in Russia following the crisis on world financial markets over the previous two weeks. "This is a temporary toughening of monetary policy," Dubinin said at a joint news conference on November 10 with Chubais. "We are confident that along with our announcement on currency policy, this will orient players in the financial market."

The Russian commercial banks, though, were applying strong political pressure on their contacts in the Kremlin, which together with the general confusion hampered the effective operation of monetary policy. After some initial policy tightening at the time of the announcement, there was a loosening of the credit stance during the subsequent period in November. It seems that the lobbying by the banking interests was intense, particularly with well-placed sympathizers in the presidential administration. The bankers were clamoring that the deterioration in money market conditions had already reduced the value of the collateral used to secure foreign credits, and any further monetary tightening would lead to a serious loss for the banks on their GKO holdings.

Dubinin was apparently under enormous pressure directly from the Kremlin to accommodate the bankers. He personally believed that it was critical to keep monetary policy tight and defend the exchange rate peg, but seemed to have little choice short of resignation—which would have been catastrophic for market confidence. The temporary decline in yields on treasury bills no doubt contributed to (if not fueled) the loss in official foreign exchange reserves. The pressure on the ruble continued unabated. The announcement of the flat exchange rate band over three years did not visibly contribute to a strengthening of confidence.

A meeting of Russian commercial bankers with the CBR initiated by Dubinin on December 3, 1997, may have also been unhelpful in defense of the ruble, no doubt for the same reason noted earlier that certain key commercial bankers held sway in the Kremlin. If Dubinin had been counting on moral suasion to impress the banks, he seems to have been mistaken.

Another worrisome aspect of economic policy was seen in the desperation by the government to find international support for the ruble. There was a great deal of talk at the time about emergency loans. This seemed to display an element of panic and raised questions about whether the prevailing financial situation was indeed far worse than had been understood until then. In view of the continuing revenue shortfalls, rumors started to circulate about a possible financing package by Russian commercial banks (that is, ironically by those very banks that were supposed to have liquidity problems and therefore made it impossible for the CBR to raise interest rates) or possibly launching a new loans-for-shares scheme. All the rumors suggested a crisis brewing in the short term in either the currency market or GKO market, or both. They certainly provided scant assurance to anxious market participants that the authorities could behave sensibly.

Amid further rumors reported in some media that the government had approached several Western banks for a US$2 billion credit line to shore up its public finances, Dubinin had to vow publicly on December 3 to defend the ruble against devaluation. "The bank will in every possible way prevent jumps in the ruble rate," Dubinin told a conference of investors. Dubinin stated that the CBR's gold and hard currency reserves were about US$18 billion. The CBR's reserves had fallen by more than US$4 billion since the beginning of November, when they stood at US$22.6 billion. Reserves dwindled as foreign investors fled Russia's government debt market, selling ruble-denominated treasury bills for dollars to repatriate profits. The sharp exit from the GKO market by nonresidents increased the government's cost of borrowing and put downward pressure on the ruble. This financial pressure came as the government was scrambling to fulfill a public pledge to pay off all budgetary wage arrears by the end of the year.

The dramatic tightening of monetary policy seemed to have an immediate effect in calming the financial markets. GKO yields declined, and the pressure on the ruble subsided. Indeed, foreign exchange reserves creeped back up to US$17.8 billion by the end of the year, bolstered by a large World Bank disbursement as well as foreign exchange purchases by the CBR.

Putting the situation at the end of 1997 in perspective, while Yeltsin not only surprised some observers by surviving the year, he also infused fresh blood into his cabinet early in the year, raising hopes of real economic progress. Sadly, by the year's end, his enthusiasm had cooled. On December 19, he warned that Russians were tired of "radical" reforms.

Most state workers' wages had been paid as promised, but Chubais's future in government looked dim. Chubais himself in an off-the-cuff remark suggested that he was fed up with his meager government paycheck while getting blamed for all of Russia's problems. Yeltsin had made him a scapegoat and sacrificed him to the opposition in the past, so he was ready, but Chubais was also a seasoned survivor of fierce political infighting.

The IMF Remains Skeptical

By the end of 1997, the IMF team members working on Russia—and no doubt the fund's executive directors—felt that they had been on a roller coaster from policy pessimism to hope, then to gloom, finally ending up with a large dose of sober skepticism. The tricky domestic politics, where even the IMF itself was an issue, were hard to assess in context. The concern of the IMF, above all, was not Russian politics or politicians for their own sake but only whether there was the political will to actually apply the policies needed to bring the Russian economy on to a trajectory of sustainable growth and rising living standards.

The disappointing fiscal results, following so much promise earlier in the year when the dream team took charge, had provoked a great deal of reflection and analysis within the IMF by late in the year. In preparing for further program discussions that autumn, for instance, the IMF staff Russia team (commonly known as the mission) took the view that we should work to help the Russian authorities in the context of the prevailing program, as suitably modified, provided that a sufficiently strong fiscal package of tax administration measures could be put in place to improve the fiscal revenue situation. In that regard, clearly one of the most important single things to do would be to terminate all forms of noncash settlement as quickly as possible.

Jack Boorman, the genial, thoughtful, and principled director of the IMF's policy department, and Susan Schadler, a discerning review officer in his department who had the responsibility to cosign with the European II Department on all issues concerning Russia for the management, took the view that the size of the slippage from the fiscal targets—originally accepted because they had been presumed realistic—made completing the quarterly program review (and disbursing the tranche) incompatible with the IMF's actions in virtually any other country. They advocated stopping the program while actions were taken to address the problems and then their effects observed. Schadler had tried valiantly to influence the IMF management to treat Russia more consistently with other program countries on this and subsequent occasions. Mussa and his colleagues in the Research Department took a similar stance with a more aggressive tone, stressing the pitiful realities of the fiscal situation, the continued dismal fiscal performance, and the evident bankruptcy of the fiscal strategy that had been pursued by the IMF and the authorities in the past two years.

We in the mission believed that the Chubais team was making utmost efforts to improve revenues. Pochinok, brought in by Chubais as the head of the STS, seemed on the right track with the reform of tax administration, and Boycko had been given new responsibilities for revenues. Measures to deal with expenditure control in a more forceful manner were also under preparation.

Fischer arrived in the early evening on November 9, 1997, accompanied by Marquez-Ruarte, and proceeded directly to a tête-à-tête dinner with Chubais at a fish restaurant on Moscow's garden ring. The whole next day was filled with meetings to get a sense directly of what was being done to confront the growing problems. During the visit, markets were nervous. Indeed, Dubinin had been due to accompany Yeltsin to China, but was kept home by the brewing financial crisis.

Fischer made it clear that the review could not be completed and the tranche would be delayed because fiscal policy was so far off track as a result of revenue slippage along with the need for either huge spending arrears or offset operations, and because the formulation of specific plans—particularly with regard to cuts in spending programs by line ministries and agencies in line with the 1998 budget limits—would take time.

Chubais said that the CBR would immediately raise its interest rates and soon announce its exchange rate policy for the next three years to steady market sentiments, and agreed with Fischer that tax collection should be brought under a unified authority under Pochinok at the STS. When Chubais mentioned that the new exchange rate band would be extended for three years, Fischer responded that three years was a long time, but he understood that the final date was chosen to take them beyond the next presidential election.

Chubais also agreed with Fischer that the draft 1998 budget revenue target of 353 billion (new) rubles was "unattainable," and he would introduce a sequestration provision into the draft budget so that there would be no spending arrears next year. Chubais pushed for a January board meeting to complete the delayed review. Fischer thought it ambitious, but could provide an earlier public statement of support if a strong, credible program were devised. Chubais also mentioned the idea of extending the EFF beyond its date of expiry in March 1999, and even envisaging a precautionary arrangement (where a program would be followed that was approved by the IMF but with no money involved).

In technical discussions with MinFin and the STS, a fiscal action plan was formulated that became dubbed as the Kudrin-Fischer plan. Fischer observed that the fiscal action plan was serious, and if implemented, would help improve the budget situation. But implementation would require a sustained effort, and the effects would be slow. The Russians, not least Chernomyrdin, seemed to be determined to implement the plan, but they had been similarly determined in the past. The discrepancy in their record in terms of policy promises made to the IMF and promises kept was mediocre at best[2]. Fischer emphasized to Chubais privately that he, as the finance minister, would have to take charge of the economic program and spend more time on these issues than he had recently.

The Russians by and large did not complain about the failure to complete the review, especially since Fischer was prepared to inform the World Bank that the IMF was encouraged by the action plan and would advise in favor of the bank's disbursing if the assessment of the IMF December mission was that the macroeconomic program was coming back on track. But Chernomyrdin at one point launched into a long speech about how the IMF treated Russia more harshly than other countries. Fischer replied that this was not the usual view, and that Russia had been so far off track that the IMF simply could not have disbursed. The expressions on the ministers' faces around the table suggested they would have preferred Chernomyrdin not to take this line. Fischer left Moscow on November 11.

Fischer must have felt a strong sense of déjà vu during that late 1997 visit. He had seen it before. Much of the discussion and the concerns expressed on both sides seemed to be a repetition of Fischer's January 1997 visit to Moscow.

Such a feeling was more than warranted. After all, the encouraging progress in macroeconomic stabilization achieved in 1995 when Chubais was in charge was followed by the policy reversals in the following year. Back then it was blamed on the elections, but what was the excuse this time? Little could Fischer have suspected at that initial dinner in the Lobster Grill in January that by the end of the year, in the context of the contagion from the Asian crisis, Chubais's effectiveness as a manager would be compromised and the many promises proffered by the dream team less than nine months earlier would be sorely disappointed.

Markets Plunge and Urgent Calls for Emergency Assistance

Marquez-Ruarte warned Kudrin on November 18, 1997, that a program strategy based on the draft 1998 budget proposal assumed that financial market conditions would become more normal in the weeks ahead. In the unlikely event this were not the case, the possibility of exceptional assistance from the IMF would need to be considered.

I recall him stressing that such a situation would also require a much more substantial adjustment effort than was then being contemplated, though. In particular, the target for the budget deficit would need to be much lower than what was being proposed given the tighter financing situation and the need to convince markets of the government's seriousness. Action on other fronts, such as credit policy and privatization along with other structural reforms, also would need to be strengthened further.

The IMF took seriously the threat that in the event that financial markets deteriorated further, the possibility of exceptional assistance from the fund would need to be considered. Aleksashenko had even asked the IMF about the possibility of additional financing to compensate Russia for the external deterioration resulting from higher world interest rates.

In addition to formal reasons, Marquez-Ruarte pointed out that the substantive reason for turning down such a request was that international interest rates had not moved up significantly; thirty-year U.S. Treasury rates had actually come down. True, the interest rates faced by Russia had gone up, reflecting an exogenous element—a higher country risk due to the contagion effects of investors pulling out of all emerging markets—but also some Russia-specific effects that were related to policies followed by Russia. Marquez-Ruarte argued that the complete offset of the intervention in foreign exchange markets had in fact been feeding a continuation of the attack on the currency, and that GKO yields and other market interest rates had to be allowed to find their level independently if the exchange rate regime was to be maintained.

On November 25–26, 1997, meetings were held at the IMF headquarters with an urgently dispatched delegation consisting of Vasiliev and Aleksashenko to explain the current financial situation in Russia and discuss options for fund assistance. Vasiliev and Aleksashenko also met with Summers and his deputy, David Lipton, at the U.S. Treasury, where they discussed the possibility of a currency stabilization fund backed by the G-7.

The pair explained that the financial situation had continued to worsen in those days—the CBR lost one billion U.S. dollars in reserves on November 25 by itself, bringing reserves down to about eighteen billion. In the face of the exchange market pressure, the CBR had injected liquidity through its domestic monetary operations, and reserve money had remained basically unchanged since late October. Yields on (three-month) treasury bills had risen to about 30 to 33 percent (through end-November), from 18 to 20 percent prior to the onset of this pressure.

While indicating that additional fiscal measures were under preparation, the one area where the authorities were so far unwilling to commit to further action was with respect to monetary policy. Faced with the prospect of much higher interest rates, Aleksashenko expressed concern over the political cost to the government and its growth strategy, the cost to the budget, and the impact on the financial position of banks.

Vasiliev and Aleksashenko requested that the forthcoming mission focus on a possible early completion of the quarterly review in order to reestablish market confidence. As for financing, they said that a precautionary facility to bolster reserves would also help, but recognized that such assistance either through the G-7 or from the IMF was unlikely. They did express an interest in the IMF's new supplementary reserve facility (SRF), which according to Summers would be available in a few weeks.

At the end of November, official foreign exchange reserves, including gold, fell further to US$16.8 billion, and the authorities were beginning to panic. On December 1, Minister Yasin was dispatched to Washington, DC, and met with Fischer. Yasin painted a bleak picture. Given the gravity of the situation, the authorities were ready to raise interest rates sharply in defense of the exchange rate. But even with the aggressive jump in interest rates on the day of the discussions (the Lombard rate climbed to 36 percent, with the six-month treasury bill rate going to 35 percent), reserves were likely to fall sharply in the next two to three weeks as forward contracts matured.

When Fischer observed that there was room within the wide band to allow the exchange rate to take some of the pressure, with interest rates also taking some of the pressure, Yasin—like all interlocutors on the Russian side—asserted that it was necessary to defend the exchange rate.

Yasin confirmed that the government was ready to take tough measures on the fiscal side as well, including dramatic spending cuts such as the closure of a network of social institutions, to achieve an additional 5 percent cut in total spending, although it had not yet been discussed with the president. He stressed that IMF financial assistance was needed as soon as possible, even hoping that much larger sums of money might be made available. Otherwise, all the economic reform effort might turn out to have been wasted, given the political situation.

This was not the first time that senior Russian officials were given to this type of presentation in hopes of swaying the IMF by drawing it into the internal political dimension. The allusion, of course, was to a situation in which a refusal to assist Russia financially at that stage could lead to a social and political upheaval with unpredictable consequences, but a first victim of such a crisis would be macroeconomic stabilization.

Finally, Yasin expressed his doubts about emergency tax measures, including tighter control over major tax delinquents. He thought that only sustained improvements in tax administration would lead to a permanent increase in revenues. Some of the quick fixes that the authorities had used had culminated in perverse effects. For example, the requirement of single taxpayer's accounts had led to demonetization because enterprises were avoiding passing money through the accounts as far as possible. The single taxpayer account was a well-intended attempt by the STS to try to get the banks into the job of tax collection by requiring enterprises to maintain only one single bank account for conducting all of their cash flow, so that in the event of underpayment, the funds in the account could be readily seized. As a consequence, firms started dealing in either cash or offshore bank accounts. Although this measure should have been abolished, it was difficult to do so because of the short-term revenue loss. Personnel changes might have helped, for example, if the rumored proposal to put Fedorov, the outspoken former finance minister, in charge of the STS had become a reality.

Fischer said that the mission would look at the situation. As for even larger amounts of IMF money, he maintained that he did not know when the new facility under preparation as a result of the Asia crisis (the SRF to provide much larger amounts from the IMF in conjunction with other creditors to deserving members when faced with a capital account crisis) might be ready, nor whether it would be available for Russia. He would have to look at it closely, but Russia should not rely on it. In any case, it would at a minimum require that the agreed-on program was on track.

The IMF itself was quickly trying to assimilate the lessons from the Asia crisis. For instance, in December 1997, following a general decision to strengthen the IMF's crisis-detection system in Washington, DC, countries were asked to provide a few financial indicators on a weekly basis as early warning signals that a crisis might not be far off. These indicators would include commercial bank reserves, capital adequacy, the foreign asset position of banks, money market and foreign exchange market intervention, and net international reserves. The idea was to have this monitoring in place by the beginning of 1998. In the case of Russia, partly because of the continuing difficulties in getting cooperation from the CBR as a result of its own data inadequacies, and ironically partly because of the crisis atmosphere itself diverting attention from monitoring to crisis management, the information gaps remained significant. Even by August 1998, the IMF staff did not have information to appreciate the foreign exchange liabilities of Russian commercial banks. Had the IMF put its foot down at that stage, perhaps better and more timely information could have helped to avoid some of the mistakes that were about to be made.

Even with hindsight, it is unlikely that the IMF would have tampered with the exchange rate regime itself. No one in the IMF foresaw anything worse than a fiscal crisis—an economic program off track that would require significant fiscal efforts to bring it back into line. With the normal exchange rate indicators showing no stress, there was also no pressure to formulate, much less implement, an exit strategy.

A Reprieve Seems to Buy Time

The mission arrived back in Moscow on December 2, 1997. The just-announced monetary stance, to finally support the exchange rate policy, provided some positive momentum, and MinFin officials, led by Viugin, were earnestly working to supply more specificity to the Kudrin-Fischer plan. A skeptical Zadornov was kept fully informed but remained wary of what was under consideration, perhaps still feeling more of a parliamentarian than a minister. The mission met with Chubais, accompanied by Yasin, Vasiliev, and Viugin, on December 5. In response to the urgent request of the authorities' representatives visiting Washington, the mission was prepared to accelerate work to allow for a January 1998 board meeting to consider the delayed review and tranche, but only if all outstanding issues could be immediately resolved. Chubais assured the mission that the government was fully determined to bring the fiscal situation under control once and for all.

In order to ensure consistency between the 1998 budget approved by the Duma and a more realistic fiscal program, which could be supported by the EFF, Chubais suggested that a "special reserve fund" be included in the official budget; such a reserve fund could be drawn on only to the extent that the revenue target under the program was being fulfilled. Marquez-Ruarte responded that the IMF would be willing to discuss such an idea, although a more cautious budget based on a lower revenue target would have been preferable. Dan Citrin, at the time the ever-vigilant division chief for Russia who worked closely with Marquez-Ruarte to manage the IMF's Russia team, worried about the internal consistency of the Russia program. In this instance, he noted that the reserve fund would need to be fully specified, announced, and explicitly included in the budget voted by the Duma. Chubais demurred.

From the IMF's point of view, the credibility of the 1998 budget and the Kremlin's commitment to budgetary control was demonstrated by Yeltsin's dramatic surprise speech to the Duma on December 5, 1997, that convinced reluctant opposition deputies to pass the 1998 draft budget in its first reading. This was a dramatic step and overwhelmed the deputies; it was the first time that Yeltsin had set foot in the Duma since 1993.

The mission assessed the progress in implementing the fiscal action plan. Among the key measures that would demonstrate the resolve of the authorities were decisions to be taken the following week by the VChK against large tax debtors, including bankruptcy and the dismissal of managers in the case of state enterprises. The mission also discussed the IMF's concerns with a loan under discussion from a consortium of foreign banks that Chubais saw as a bridge to a 1998 Eurobond issue, with possible new tax exemptions for foreign investors, and the continuing problems that the IMF staff members were having in receiving information from the CBR concerning financial developments and developments in the banking system.

In concluding the meeting, Chubais stressed that the IMF's decision related to the EFF program would be critical for the government, as it would affect World Bank loans as well as financial inflows from other sources. He asked that assuming the program were brought back on track, the IMF disburse not only the next EFF purchase already before the end of December but that it also provide emergency financing of ten billion U.S. dollars to support the ruble (but hopefully not to be disbursed), in light of the considerable strengthening of fiscal and monetary policies being undertaken by the authorities. Chubais noted that this should be considered as an official request to the IMF management.

By December 12, 1997, the authorities had amassed an impressive array of measures concerning the implementation of the fiscal action plan such as treasury control over the defense and other security ministries along with the impending action against large tax delinquents, an additional new twenty-five billion rubles in revenue measures for 1998, and identified spending cuts relative to the budget approved in the first reading the previous week. Even so, the projected 1998 budget deficit under the program would amount to 4.9 percent of GDP versus the staff's view that it should be no more than 4.5 percent of GDP, not to mention an original EFF target of 2 percent of GDP in 1998.

Marquez-Ruarte's assessment to IMF management was that there was a real commitment to implement effective expenditure controls and the proposed revenue measures. The decision was made to submit the delayed sixth quarterly review under the program for board approval provided that all of the prior actions were fully implemented as agreed on.

There had also been discussions with the CBR and private financial institutions on the impact of recent financial developments on the soundness of the banking system. The CBR officials said that only one or two of the larger banks were expected to end 1997 with net losses. That being said, the CBR officials acknowledged that some large banks may have had considerable open foreign exchange positions, making them vulnerable to exchange rate depreciation, and that the reliability of figures provided by the banks to the CBR remained doubtful.

Even then, nothing was done to ensure that the data would provide, at least to the CBR management itself, a clear picture of the financial viability of the major banks. It was not for lack of effort. The CBR requested, even required, that relevant data be supplied. The truth was that the banks felt sufficiently immune to interference from the CBR to ignore its mandates.

The CBR officials reaffirmed the strategy of identifying and closing or restructuring problem banks, and stressed that the CBR would act only as a lender of last resort; any liquidity support to banks would be temporary. Yet the mission's impression was that there were strong pressures for the CBR to provide support to banks, and the situation would need to be watched carefully. The CBR's intervention in the treasury bill market in November may have been partly motivated by a desire to assist banks when the tightening of liquidity conditions was threatening to force them to liquidate their treasury bill positions and thereby take losses. I later understood that the CBR did not have full control over its own policy, and too often it was leaned on to lend to banks on terms that effectively became more than just temporary. Here again, the IMF was unaware of just how great this political pressure to distort public policy for personal profit had become, and did not have the requisite data that might have revealed what was happening. Clearly some oligarchic interests were interfering much more than Camdessus could have even imagined.

Most of the drama concerning the banks was yet to come. In the meantime, it seemed to the IMF team that the Russian authorities had clearly confronted the sizable fiscal imbalances inherited from earlier periods and were at last moving with determination to address these issues. The government had identified a set of measures that would be implemented in the weeks and months ahead to address the interrelated fiscal issues of poor revenue performance, unrealistic budgeting of actual government consumption, and inadequate treasury control of spending commitments and cash payments.

The mission was particularly encouraged by the steps to implement the government's fiscal action plan, the presidential decrees issued to end all forms of noncash tax payments and bring spending commitments under control, and the amendments tabled to the draft 1998 budget law. A safety valve for the IMF was that for the first time with Russia, the main parameters for the coming fiscal year were agreed on before the year actually began, thereby giving the IMF more room to check progress and insist on corrections to any deviations while there was still time to have an impact.

We were also encouraged by the overdue but firm CBR policy for interest rates to move without intervention by the monetary authorities. This decision and the strengthening of the fiscal policy stance were seen to help dispel market uncertainty about the course of economic policy. But underestimating the institutional vacuum as well as administrative and political constraints of the authorities, the IMF staff members were sincere in thinking that hopefully the worst really was over. In retrospect, it seems just naive.

In any case, the belated tightening of monetary policy on December 1, 1997—when the CBR withdrew completely from the treasury bill market—had the intended effect. Following the initial interest rate hike, rates edged downward during much of the rest of the month and there reportedly were some net capital inflows. The calmer market situation also seemed to have led to increased confidence among the Chubais team; its interest in a ten billion U.S. dollar loan from the fund, which had been formally requested by Chubais in early December, seemed to have been dropped.

The Sad Tale of the VChK

With hindsight, one can appreciate that the experiment with ad hoc procedures to improve tax administration would end in failure. But such was the nature of institutional paralysis in Russia that to people like Chubais, only a bold exceptional approach could yield results; maybe he was right. All the alternatives, involving tedious and long-term institution building, could not deliver short-term results.

Thus, when tax collection in cash terms collapsed in September 1996 and proved insufficient even to cover the federal government's wage bill, the creation of the VChK was announced with great flourish the following month at the authorities' initiative under the Chernomyrdin's chairmanship. The VChK's specific aim was to make a demonstrable example of large delinquent taxpayers by showing that tax treatment was equitable and transparent. The idea did not come from the IMF, where indeed there was skepticism and even regret at distracting from necessary but less spectacular institution building.

The VChK was Chubais's brainchild. It was a practical attempt to circumvent the heavy bureaucratic inertia to galvanize tax collection. Unfortunately, its abbreviation coincided with the name of a sinister secret police force set up by the Bolsheviks in 1917 to terrorize the enemies of the new regime (and was later transformed into a pillar of the Stalinist USSR, the NKVD; the KGB was its direct successor). When Lenin decreed the original VChK into existence in December 1917, he claimed the idea was to confront "sabotage" by forcing "persons belonging to richer classes" to report on their finances. It turned into a terror machine within days after that, of course. Opponents often accused Chubais of "Bolshevik approaches" to reform, citing, among other things, his preference for exceptional administrative measures. The identical abbreviations for the "Chubais commission" and the Bolshevik committee only reinforced that perception in public opinion.

The IMF's skepticism was warranted because after a few dramatic announcements and almost no action, the VChK process seemed to stop. At a meeting in April 1997, Kudrin lamented that the effort the previous autumn to bring the big tax delinquents with large tax arrears into bankruptcy under the highly publicized procedures of the VChK had been a failure, and had actually been worse than doing nothing at all. It had only been an empty label and was hardly Bolshevik. Real Bolshevism implied a readiness to resort to ruthless means to achieve the ends—clearly something that a weak government was not about to do.

Despite this abysmal experience, the key feature to be employed for demonstrating political will was once again the use of the VChK. Notably, at the December 8, 1997, VCkK meeting, chaired by Chubais (in Chernomyrdin's absence), a decision was made to take immediate actions

against two large tax delinquents: Omsk oil refinery (owned by Ber-
ezovsky's Sibneft) and Angarsk oil refinery (owned by Potanin's Sidanko).
The two refineries represented the long-anticipated litmus tests that
Chubais had been mentioning.

On December 15, 1997, Chernomyrdin left on an official visit to
Turkey without signing the December 8 VChK decision. Worse, based
on conversations with Vasiliev and Viugin, it appeared that the decision
could be in serious trouble, and even if signed, could be significantly
watered down. I cautioned that the IMF was unlikely to move forward
unless these steps, which were the only concrete actions—in contrast to
"paper" measures—were followed as agreed on. Otherwise, no one
inside or outside Russia would believe that there was finally a commitment to confront fiscal reality. Vasiliev and Viugin acknowledged these
concerns, but observed that the political pressure was enormous. It
appeared that since Chubais chaired the VChK meeting, his enemies took
the decisions in a particularly personal manner.

Camdessus sent a sharp letter to Chernomyrdin later that day. The
managing director stressed that he attached critical importance to the
decision aimed at major tax delinquent enterprises that was reached at
the VChK meeting on December 8. He stated that such a decision was
especially critical if the government was to demonstrate to large taxpayers that it meant business in its effort to enforce tax obligations. Accord-
ingly, the decisions should be immediately finalized and publicly issued,
and then fully implemented according to the specified schedule. In the
absence of this, it would not be possible to conclude that the government
was making satisfactory progress in addressing the fragile fiscal situation.
The fund management, in such circumstances, would not be in a position
to make a fully positive assessment to the World Bank prior to the consideration of its loan later that week, nor to proceed with the fund board
meeting.

On December 18, 1997, *Nezavisimaya Gazeta* (also owned by
Berezovsky at that time) published a leaked copy of Camdessus' letter to
Chernomyrdin (including the list of prior actions) on the top of the
front page. Kudrin suspected that the leak occurred in the prime minister's
office, but could not be sure. He was convinced that the leak was delib-
erately timed to further embarrass the reformers in the government.

On his return from Turkey, Chernomyrdin called Camdessus. They
spoke for over an hour and a half. The thrust of the discussion was
Chernomyrdin explaining that taxpayers had to pay, but the government
had to enforce compliance legally, and the VChK decision of December

8 to seize the assets of the two companies were illegal. At some point, when the exchange became rather heated, the prime minister claimed that the IMF staff was being misled by unscrupulous officials. He asserted that he would propose alternative measures with similar effect and convene an immediate meeting of the VChK. A meeting was indeed held on December 17, where it was decided that the two refineries should pay their tax arrears by December 25; if not, all actions would be taken to secure payment, including the seizure of assets.

On December 18, Gaidar spoke with Chubais (from India) following Chernomyrdin's phone conversation with Camdessus the previous night. Gaidar was plainly worried that any reversal by the VChK of its December 8 decision, especially now that it was public, could have the most devastating signaling effect on tax collection efforts and the reform process itself. He could not imagine any alternative measures that could have a similar impact, stressing that the real issue is not the money but rather the demonstration of political will. Any substitute measures would additionally need to compensate for the political will lost through backtracking on a previous key set of actions. And he observed that if the political costs were judged to be too great in this clear case, there would be little hope of the other difficult revenue and spending measures under the program actually being implemented. In his view, the IMF management should accept nothing less than the full and immediate implementation of the original VChK decision. Gaidar felt that Chernomyrdin cited legal constraints to obfuscate the issue: apparently there was no quorum at the December 8 meeting, but this could be easily remedied.

Gaidar was pessimistic about the outcome. He said that Chernomyrdin really did not understand the issue, being convinced by those around him that it was only about money and perhaps personal political vendettas. The only hope was to appeal directly to Yeltsin, which might require a couple of days. In the meantime, the IMF would have to consider its stance, and the World Bank would have to decide whether to postpone its board meeting scheduled for the next day.

But it was too late. Camdessus felt that in light of the actions promised by the prime minister against the designated tax delinquents, he could not object to the World Bank proceeding with its loans. In a letter to Wolfensohn, while acknowledging that the measures against the two oil companies were different from those decided on earlier, Camdessus noted that he had been assured by Chernomyrdin that the measures contained in this new decision were as strong as could be taken at this time against those two tax debtors. He went on to say that the full implementation of this approach—that is, either payment in full of all tax debts or the prompt adoption of effective actions to collect the arrears—would be a prior condition for the completion of the quarterly review under the EFF scheduled for January 5, 1998.

Pochinok, the STS head, seemed thoroughly despondent. On December 18, 1997, he thought that nothing would happen, and implicitly that it was at least partly the IMF's fault. He said privately that they were all awaiting the return of Chubais from India the next day to decide what to do—and that there could be a number of resignations. Vasiliev was also reported "ill" all of a sudden; his assistant told me that he was totally disheartened.

Meanwhile, the smear campaign against the reformers and their policies was intensifying, with the major television channels picking up and further distorting the story from the morning's paper. Livshits, for instance, was interviewed on the main channels and spoke of spies in the senior levels of the government passing on sensitive information to the IMF, which only represented foreign interests. The mood was hardly one that boded well for the program.

By late December, it appeared that the situation concerning the VChK measure was that Omsk had paid the principal of tax arrears due (including the current December tax obligations) of 640 billion old rubles by December 25, of which 420 billion old rubles was paid using monetary offsets. The accumulated interest and fines of approximately 400 billion old rubles were not paid. Little or nothing apparently was paid with respect to Angarsk. No further meetings of the VChK took place to pursue actions against other large tax delinquents. Yet Pochinok seemed pleased with the collections from some large taxpayers in December, including from RAO UES, Gazprom, and Lukoil, which the prime minister had been citing as evidence of a new tax discipline.

Despite repeated meetings, it was difficult to get a clear idea of what had happened, perhaps because all on the Russian side were embarrassed by the situation and felt that they were on weak ground in explaining the rationale for the subsequent actions. My conclusion at the time was that Chubais, MinFin, and the STS originally believed that they had the upper hand to move aggressively against large taxpayers, and even after the VChK decision of December 17, still hoped to punish the blatant nonpayment of taxes, as agreed was necessary under the program. Subsequently, the prime minister and political reality weighed in and watered down the effect.

They were just trying to put a brave face on it by citing legal constraints, perhaps accepting that this was the best that could be done at the moment. Pochinok admitted that the message sent to taxpayers was weak, at best, since in the end it was only the principal that might have to be paid, and even then—if the taxpayer was large or politically important—only if massive pressures were brought to bear. All of this raised the question of what purpose the VChK served and indeed how tax compliance could be expected to improve if a murky legal situation were allowed to thwart, when politically expedient, the efficient collection of taxes.

A decision was taken to postpone the IMF board meeting a few days, until January 8, 1998, to further clarify the situation with respect to the implementation of all the prior actions, including the VChK decisions. Right up until the time of the board meeting, unanticipated legal hurdles and procedural issues in pursuing tax delinquents kept emerging. In exchange for promises to vigorously pursue all legal options, it was decided that the Russian authorities had done everything that they could legally to pursue the tax delinquents and hopefully create incentives for higher tax compliance.

In retrospect, the outcome of 1997 was no triumph for Russia or the IMF. The story on the fiscal side was grim. The federal government collected less than 12 percent of GDP in revenue, about 30 percent less than what was targeted in the budget, and even then about 20 percent of the revenue was in the form of offsets of mutual tax and payment liabilities as well as other nonmonetary transactions, rather than cash income to the budget.

The revenue shortfall forced the federal government to adjust expenditures downward, while the deficit remained high at 7.8 percent of GDP in 1997. With interest payments rising, noninterest expenditures fell from around 21 percent of GDP in 1994 to 14 percent by 1997; subsidies, transfers to the regions, and capital expenditures were among the items most affected, whereas wages and social transfers were better maintained. The expenditures adjustment had occurred in a rather ad hoc manner, with little direction from the weak institutions responsible for budget preparation, execution, and evaluation. Attempts to maintain expenditure commitments, as opposed to cash spending, led to sequestration, the use of noncash means to settle budgetary obligations, and an accumulation of payment arrears.

With the gradual destabilization of the political situation in Russia as the year proceeded, the influence of the team of young reformers on the formulation of economic policy kept diminishing. One of the last serious successes in the fiscal area in 1997 was the adoption in July of the budget code and a special section of the tax code. The budget code was finally adopted as law in 1998. The new tax code took until 2000 to become law. Otherwise, in the second half of the year, reform efforts floundered as a fractious and distracted government ran up against increasing internal and political opposition. Owing to such developments, there were no substantial improvements in the budgetary situation in the second half of 1997. In 1997, federal budget tax revenues were only 9.1 percent of GDP.

Although the federal government was able to eliminate its budgetary wage arrears by the end of 1997, this was replaced by a sizable buildup of new arrears to suppliers of goods and services to the government. The regional and local authorities along with other government entities accumulated unrecorded arrears on government wage payments and payments to suppliers. The persistent weakness of revenue as well as the pervasive problems of ad hoc expenditure cuts and arrears reflected fundamental weaknesses in tax policy, tax administration, and budgetary management.

Moreover, the problems of weak revenue collection, expenditure control, and spending policy were interlocked. Weak tax collection was linked to persistent problems in controlling expenditures. The lack of expenditure control and the inability of the government to pay its own bills, combined with the extensive resort to noncash mechanisms to settle budgetary arrears against the arrears of tax debtors, severely undermined incentives for paying taxes in cash. Noncash tax arrangements hindered public expenditures on wages and other social commitments that could be satisfied only in cash.

Aside from the fiscal results, the other indicators of 1997 were feeble. Growth, while positive for the first time in post-Soviet Russia, was an anemic 1.4 percent, whereas in April, the IMF staff had expected a 3.0 percent increase. As the promising prospects for real change evaporated by late summer, consumer and investor confidence were too weak to sustain positive growth.

5
How a Possible Crisis Becomes Probable

Even as late as the first few months of 1998, the coming financial collapse was not preordained and, despite plunging oil prices and a dramatic reversal of private capital flows, might have still been avoided. In principle, a determined effort to confront and resolve the macroeconomic imbalances on a permanent basis could have conceivably warranted a major G-7 support package, if not a market-based rollover. But politics again unexpectedly interfered.

The Year in Perspective

The events in Russia leading up to and following the August 1998 financial crisis are well-known. That said, they warrant a retelling, not least because the received wisdom reflects a number of inaccuracies and misinterpretations. The eruption of the crisis on August 17 was not the plot of a Greek tragedy or a Strindberg drama. The outcome was not inevitable. Indeed, until the last minute, many of the key participants did not see what was about to happen. And when they did, they then mostly thought the worst would happen. But it didn't either.

To understand these developments and the decisions faced by the main players on the Russian side, in the markets, in the IMF, and in Western governments, a fundamental point—yet a disturbing one—to appreciate was the lack of information available to all of them as events unfolded. Clearly, with information, such as it was, so compartmentalized, what was known at the time by the primary players was much less than assumed by the markets and led to less than well-informed decisions.

Perhaps most critical was again the role of domestic politics in Russia, and how decisions were made (or improvised) irrespective of the economic context and seemingly impervious to the possible consequences.

There seemed to be an implicit assumption by senior Russian officials that Russia was too important, too big, and mostly too dangerous to fail. In their view, the West, via the IMF, would have no choice in the end but to come to the country's rescue. Clearly the moral hazard issues associated with "too big to fail" have returned with a vengeance in the recent sovereign European debt crisis. Certainly many market participants were operating on that assumption in both cases.

A Promising Start

There was almost a sigh of relief as the new year began. In Moscow as well as at the IMF headquarters in Washington, DC, there was a palpable feeling that an unexpectedly difficult turbulence had been successfully handled. Somewhat bruised, and still leery about future obstacles, the sentiment on all sides was that the worst was over: the Asian financial tsunami had been resisted. So as 1998 rolled in, Russia was still standing—in some respects, stronger than ever. Inflation had been all but tamed, the new, "heavy" ruble was successfully introduced and remained remarkably steady, and economic reforms seemed to be taking hold. The Mir space station, for all its troubles, was still flying, and Russia was slowly regaining its status on the international diplomatic stage, at least temporarily.

Of course, unknown to the IMF at the time, some large Russian commercial banks were borrowing significant amounts in foreign exchange from domestic counterparts but especially from abroad, pledging their Eurobonds and dollar-denominated MinFin bonds as collateral. Moscow-based commercial banks seemed to have secured short-term loans and credit lines in the range of three billion U.S. dollars by early 1998, or over 120 percent of their share capital. The banks were engaged in what appeared to be a safe, one-way bet (given the stability of the ruble) of borrowing cheaply in dollars and placing the funds in high-yielding GKO, then purchasing the foreign exchange on maturity to reimburse the loan and pocketing the profit. This was a classic carry trade operation. The banks also were starting to write forward contracts in dollars to more cautious nonresidents wishing to hedge their investments in rubles in the GKO market.

This speculative behavior by the banks was perfectly logical and even legal within limits. The problem is, as we have seen more recently in highly leveraged Western financial markets linked to U.S. real estate, that such gambles only seem to work well when prices keep rising and confidence remains positive. As much as the IMF should have suspected the exploitation of such natural investment opportunities by Russian banks, it did not have the necessary data to prove it. Nor was the CBR cooperative in providing information that it also did not seem to have readily available. This lapse was all the more surprising in view of the special supervisory unit, OPERU II, set up to closely watch the largest banks, but we now know what we did not know then: it was just a fig leaf, and the banks were reporting garbage data to it. So no warnings came. And again the IMF was naive not to have pushed more to find out. In truth, though, even the foreign investment banks that were the counterparties in these operations were in no rush to reveal the extent of their operations as long as the outlook was positive. They too did not trust the IMF with confidential and competitively sensitive information. They only came complaining worriedly to the IMF when there seemed to be looming problems.

The mood was not one of complacency, however. Rather, the main protagonists felt that they had been lucky, so no time should be lost in consolidating economic and administrative reforms.

The IMF board met on January 8, and although completing the long-delayed review with its tranche of US$640 million, it also voiced its frustration and concerns about almost all aspects of the program. This was a less than ringing endorsement by the IMF. Meanwhile, an economic program for 1998 had still not been finalized.

One welcome sign that the year had begun on a brighter note was the huge sense of relief felt in the CBR when banks opened on Monday, January 5, 1998, without a panic or crowds in the streets. On that day, the effects of the redenomination of the ruble were felt in full force. The new ruble notes and coins went into circulation, alongside the old ones, but with three zeros dropped—so ten thousand old rubles became ten new rubles, and a trillion old rubles became a billion new rubles.

The introduction of the "hard" ruble, announced by Yeltsin in August 1997, was intended to demonstrate that inflation had definitively been conquered and the stability of the currency was now assured. Since then, the government had taken pains to convince a reform-weary public that unlike two previous banknote changes in 1991 and 1993 that led to mass confusion and lost savings, no one would lose anything this time around. Yet despite a large-scale television advertising campaign aimed at assuaging the public's fears, uncertainty persisted until the final days of 1997, and hard-currency purchases by Russian savers gave rise to fears of a run on the ruble. The successful introduction of redenomination was thus seen as a sign that confidence was slowly taking hold again. In the meantime, old and new bills were both considered to be legal tender throughout 1998, and in principle the exchange of old notes for new ones was allowed at designated banks until the end of 2001.

Another encouraging policy move was the final step in the liberalization of nonresident access to the GKO and OFZ markets. As of January 1, the requirement was removed that mandated the one-month forward contract prior to the repatriation by nonresidents of the proceeds from sales of GKO. This liberalization process, which began in June 1996 when Russia accepted the current account convertibility obligations under the IMF's article VIII, was intended to deliver the benefits of globalization to Russian financial markets by providing a broader and deeper domestic market with unfettered foreign participation. The liberalization of market access was mostly a formality, since so-called gray schemes had been flourishing, which allowed most foreign investors—except some institutional investors such as pension funds constrained by prudential regulations—to participate freely in the market through Russian nominees. Indeed, one of the incentives to liberalize was to bring these unregulated practices to an end. The fact is that exchange controls, whether in Russia or elsewhere, do not work well unless they are so draconian as to be inconsistent with a market economy. The CBR move was thus an effort to at least make these operations more transparent.

Market Perceptions

The global markets were not so benign. With Asia still in a free fall, most investment banking analysts remained cautious about the Russian market in the short term. Ever since the financial turmoil in Asian markets started the previous October, investors abandoned emerging market assets for safe havens in Western markets. The Russian equity market was down almost 50 percent from its October high, and the widely anticipated post–New Year's rally never materialized. A constant flow of bad news from Asia was initially seen as keeping share prices down. "Russian markets are completely dependent on the international market and foreign flows," said Christopher Granville, head of research at United City Bank in Moscow.[1] Nevertheless, he went on to predict that the equity market would eventually recover its losses and rise 50 percent for the year, as long as the situation in Asia did not deteriorate further.

Zadornov, still wary in his new role as finance minister, was doubtful that Russia could achieve significant positive economic growth in 1998.

"To be honest, I am not a big optimist about economic growth in 1998," Zadornov told *Nezavisimaya Gazeta* in a lengthy interview on January 13. "I think the [1998] parameters will roughly follow figures for 1997." He explained that the recent market crisis had upset the government's economic plans. "The market crisis of October–November has set Russia back at least half a year," he said. "A further lowering of yields on the domestic debt market will be very difficult," added Zadornov, predicting that yields on treasury bills would not come down before the second quarter of 1998 at the earliest (even though such a pessimistic assumption was not consistent with his budget).

Interestingly, his interview was published the same day that Yeltsin, after meeting with Nemtsov at Valdai, a holiday retreat in northwestern Russia, issued a statement saying that he was instructing the government to reduce taxes and interest rates to kick-start the economy. The president wanted the government to ensure that 1998 would be the first year that Russia recorded a solid economic growth of 2 to 4 percent.[2] IMF staff members were projecting a 2 percent growth.

At the same time, despite these external concerns, the general market sentiment was that there should be a rebound based on Russia's relatively sound economic fundamentals and that equities looked cheap after the market run-down. But the prevailing view was that international markets needed to recover first. It was noteworthy that there was some concern that stock prices had been held back in part because yields on GKO remained high, drawing investors away from the equity market. Most foreign investors also stayed away from the GKO market, however, fearing the volatility of yields.

The expectation was that for rates to come down, the CBR would need to wait for foreign investors to return. In fact, following the January 1 removal by the CBR of the formal requirement for nonresidents to use a one-month ruble forward contract to exit the GKO market, a surge of new inflows was anticipated. But the lifting of the restrictions did not spark a flood of foreign money. Foreign investors and foreign hedge funds controlling Russian money offshore had been put off by the market scare the previous month and the persistently bad news coming out of Asia. In the absence of foreign funds, yields were expected to remain high, complicating the fiscal situation and compromising growth prospects.

With the cost of domestic borrowing higher than budgeted (GKO yields averaged 33 percent in mid-January) and foreign borrowing in the form of Eurobonds prohibitively expensive, budget troubles in 1998 were already looming. The budget, which was still in the Duma as the year began, assumed that the debt-servicing costs on GKO would be quickly brought down by the end of the first quarter. Given the higher cost of borrowing, there were market concerns that the government could be forced to scramble to find additional resources or sequester spending as it did in 1997 to keep the deficit in line.

There were encouraging signs for markets as well. The Russian authorities were seen as moving to clean up public finances and boost tax collection. From the start of the year, the Finance Ministry announced that it would no longer use monetary offsets for tax payments—a move that was expected to boost the collection of tax receipts in cash. Among other initiatives, the government was trying to move to a treasury system to make budget transfers directly to the regions, thus cutting out commercial banks, which had been handling the funds and been blamed for delaying payments as well as exacerbating wage arrears.

Chernomyrdin said as the year began that all budget funds would be channeled through the treasury system by June 1. The government also announced yet again its intention to start cracking down more vigorously on tax evaders, using methods such as the continuing threat to cut off oil companies from access to the valuable government-owned export pipeline if they failed to pay their taxes. But tax reform remained in limbo.

By all accounts, the most important legislative challenge in 1998 was a new tax code, and hopes were high as the new year began that some kind of tax reform package would be pushed through the Duma in the first half of the year. After the previous year's failure of the government's draft tax code, which met with stiff opposition in the Duma, it was expected that the Finance Ministry, now under the direction of Zadornov (who as chair of the Duma's relatively powerful Budget Committee had been the most vocal opponent of the tax code) would be able to persuade the Duma to back its revised proposals.

Finally, on the political side, there was a broad expectation of greater political stability in 1998, encouraged by Yeltsin's efforts to meet regularly with opposition leaders from the Duma and draw them into decision making. The greatest uncertainty on the political horizon was Yeltsin's health.

Against this general consensus view, the initial steps in January were already not encouraging. On January 16, 1998, Chernomyrdin announced some redesignations of assignments within the government. No one was dismissed, but clearly Zadornov was asserting himself since the main change was that Chubais, while retaining a responsibility for tax revenue, lost his financial oversight (probably an inevitability once he lost his ministry the previous November and since Zadornov reported directly to the prime minister). Chubais's writ was limited to economic coordination, but focusing on the medium term. Nemtsov was also formally relieved of his responsibility for oversight of the energy sector, and as reported in the *Economist*, moves were afoot to oust his protégé, Boris Brevnov, as head of UES, Russia's huge electricity monopoly.[3]

It also turned out that the closure of foreign exchange operations during the first week of January to facilitate the introduction of the redenominated ruble masked strong pressures on the exchange rate. After recovering somewhat during December, the stock market index fell sharply starting in the second week of January, apparently reflecting developments in emerging markets in Asia, and foreign exchange outflows were once again registered in the first half of the month.

CBR deputy chair Potemkin explained in a meeting on January 14, that the main reasons for these pressures were the wage and bonus payments made by the Ministry of Finance in late December. He said that the CBR monetized about US$1.2 billion of MinFin's own foreign reserves, expecting that at least part of this increase would be met by a higher demand for real money balances by the public. Instead, the increased liquidity was converted by the public into foreign exchange, and some Russian banks switched into short-term dollar assets. The net withdrawal of nonresident funds from the GKO market also continued.

The CBR responded by widening the daily intervention band for the ruble, increasing interest rates on its facilities (January 12), and selling about three billion U.S. dollars in foreign exchange reserves over the course of the month. Gross reserves fell from eighteen billion U.S. dollars at the end of December to sixteen billion at the end of January, despite the receipt of the IMF tranche and a disbursement of a loan tranche from the World Bank under its structural adjustment loan. During the month as a whole, the ruble depreciated by about 1 percent.

The CBR abstained from making any net purchases of GKO in the market and let interest rates move freely. Still, through much of January, the level of market interest rates remained broadly unchanged from end-December, with the yield on three-month treasury bills hovering in the 30 to 32 percent range. Although the third week of January was calm, devaluation rumors—reflected, for instance, in an article in *Nezavisimaya Gazeta*, a paper owned by Berezovsky at that time, comparing the

GKO market to the infamous MMM pyramid scheme of the early 1990s—swept through the markets in the last days of the month.

On January 26, GKO rates jumped to about 40 percent, causing MinFin to cancel the primary auction scheduled for January 28. This led to a sharp sell-off in the equity markets the next day, continuing a slump that brought the Russian stock market index down by 30 percent in one month.

After this early bout of near panic, market perceptions seemed to improve rapidly in early February on the back of relatively favorable news. On February 5, GKO yields dropped and the equity market rose by 7.4 percent as Yeltsin offered a public pledge to maintain his two first deputy prime ministers in place until 2000, and also signed a decree aimed at spurring foreign investment that would create special economic zones for foreign investors that invested sums of over US$250 million in Russia.[4]

Chubais and Zadornov were reporting an improving fiscal situation, which allowed the government to forego the need for net market financing in the first quarter. "The latest events on the market are occurring against a background of an improving financial situation," Zadornov said. "The IMF has ascertained that the situation in the fourth quarter [of 1997] and in January [1998] is changing in a positive direction." The problem was that by the time Zadornov had said this, it was already old news, in keeping with what was stated at the time of the early January IMF board meeting, and unfortunately was no longer applicable. Just a month after the board meeting, perceptions were changing.

Shortly thereafter, as part of a market-bolstering strategy, Zadornov was in London, where he participated in part of a G-7 finance ministers' meeting on February 21. He told reporters that "Russia is not at big risk. We pulled through our financial crisis and interest rates on the Russian market are falling." Zadornov said that he did not see any new threat from the problems faced by the Russian economy late in 1997 when contagion from Asia swept through the global markets, sapping confidence in the ruble and triggering rumors of devaluation. He said the ruble was no longer vulnerable. "Absolutely not. Our Central Bank has enough reserves to stabilize the ruble," he maintained.

The markets and observers remained apprehensive. On March 12, the credit rating agency, Moody's, downgraded Russian debt. Moody's said that Russia remained vulnerable to global market turmoil and had failed to make headway on cleaning up its finances. Another international rating agency, Fitch IBCA, withdrew an earlier threat of a downgrade on March 11 and left Russia's rating unchanged. Chubais and Zadornov were dismissive of Moody's decision. Chubais said that the agency was attempting to make up for its recent failure. "They have overlooked the Asian crisis and now are trying to compensate for this," he claimed.

Russia had overcome the worst of the market crisis, Zadornov said, predicting foreign investment would take off in April. He said that Russia's GDP would grow by 1.5 percent in the first quarter of 1998, compared with the same period of 1997, retracting his earlier warning that the crisis would set back economic growth by six months. Zadornov asserted that economic growth would be spurred by gradually declining rates on treasury bills, then at about 27 percent. GKO yields peaked at around 45 percent in January as foreign investors fled the market, selling rubles and buying dollars. "All the talk about a devaluation of the ruble is behind us," said Zadornov.[5]

While Russian leaders and senior officials may have been politically motivated in their stance on the ruble exchange rate, there was a large degree of sympathy with this position in the IMF, despite the increasingly bad news on the price of oil. Russia did not face a major balance of payments problem caused by the usual suspects of overheating nor was the exchange rate seriously overvalued. There were none of the typical factors—such as a loss of profitability of the nonoil export sector—that would suggest an exchange rate adjustment as a necessary step. Moreover, the stability of the ruble was seen as playing a key role for expectations and a guide to monetary policy, even leaving aside its political dimension.

Oil Prices Weigh Heavily on Prospects

Another factor impacting Russia's prospects as 1998 began was uncertainty about oil prices. The last time that world oil prices crashed, in the mid-1980s, the consequences for Russia were catastrophic. The Soviet Union's stagnating economy had been living on the proceeds of high oil prices since the 1970s. In a nutshell, the oil price windfall probably allowed the Soviet Union to prolong itself financially, and could be said to have given Communism another decade. Given the highly inelastic global supply and demand curves for oil, however, a small shift to lower demand in the West resulted in lower prices by the mid-1980s, and the Soviet economy felt the strain. Soviet leader Gorbachev had little choice but to seek radical solutions. Increased borrowing and the use of gold reserves only prolonged the day of reckoning. While a complex process was at work, it could be said that the cyclic slump in oil prices was a major contributing factor to the failure of perestroika policies.

The Gulf War of 1990–1991 caused oil prices to spike, and until the Asian crisis Russia's oil sector had been benefiting from a relatively buoyant global economy, which was bolstering demand against inelastic supply, keeping prices close to twenty U.S. dollars a barrel. The crisis in Asia contributed to a slump in demand and depressed prices by almost 40 percent, though. The crisis began on oil markets in November 1997, when the Organization of Petroleum Exporting Countries (OPEC) announced that it would raise production quotas by 10 pecent, to 27.5 million barrels per day from 25 million. OPEC's timing could not have been worse. The market for this increased supply collapsed when financial turmoil hit the fast-growing Asian economies.

As the year began, fears were expressed that the profits of Russian oil companies could be cut by up to 50 percent in 1998 and could cut into margins for years to come if oil prices remained low. With the export market moribund, Russian oil companies complained that they were struggling to cope with crippling statutory tax burdens and a domestic market where customers were reluctant to pay in cash. As the largest sector in the Russian economy, the oil industry had a domino effect. Other industries serving the oil sector also felt the pinch. And the effects quickly spread through the whole Russian economy, where crude oil and oil products accounted for about 25 percent of exports, and oil revenues made up 25 percent of the federal government's total tax revenue.

From the time of OPEC's announcement in November 1997, the price for Urals crude fell about 31 percent to the end of February 1998 from an average of US$18.80 in 1997. Sinking prices finally forced OPEC members and some non-OPEC producers to promise production cuts.

Other factors were also weighing on prices. The demand in Asia was still falling, and non-OPEC producers such as Mexico, but also including new entrants like Vietnam and central Asian developers of Caspian Sea reserves, were eager to step up production. The United Nations' decision to allow Iraq to double exports under the food-for-oil humanitarian program added to the problem of oversupply as well. This hit Russia especially hard since Iraq produces oil of similar quality to Russia's.

Russian producers were poised for big losses. Analysts offered different estimates, but most predictions were grave: with some of the highest production costs in the world, leaving their profitability dependent on high export revenue, many Russian producers seemed to be exporting at break-even levels, and others were exporting at a loss. Getting a barrel of Russian oil to market was said to cost up to US$13.50 per barrel when all was said and done. Operating costs ranging from US$7 to $8 per barrel were reported, the transport fees paid to pipeline monopoly Transneft added another US$4.90 per barrel, and a fixed excise tax of US$1.30 was also levied on each barrel.

Based on those rough estimates, and with prices for Russian crude averaging just over US$13 per barrel in January–February 1998, Russian producers were under pressure to cut costs and tax payments. Economics minister Urinson offered an even more sobering account when he reported in early March that Russian oil companies in total lost US$500 million on January and February exports. The situation varied widely from company to company, however, and the numbers were unreliable. In the March 4 issue of *Kommersant Daily*, Fridman, whose Alfa Group owned the Tyumen Oil Company, said that most Russian oil producers would be pushed into the red when oil prices sank lower than US$10 a barrel.

What Russian producers wanted was a quick fix in the way of huge tax cuts. There was a major debate about the real tax burden, with the producers arguing that taxes equaled one-half of revenues since many of the taxes were not based on profits but rather on volume. As the oil price fell, the tax burden grew. Since prices began falling, oil companies started to lobby for lower taxes. In January 1998, the heads of seven major Russian oil companies sent a letter to Prime Minister Chernomyrdin urging that excise taxes be halved and pipeline tariffs reduced.

The letter to Chernomyrdin, dated January 19, argued that the prevailing tax obligations would exceed the oil companies' ability to pay in 1998 by 20 percent, or 16.8 billion rubles (US$2.6 billion). The letter contended that if oil prices continued to fall, the oil industry's 1998 losses could reach as much as 27 billion rubles (US$4.5 billion) at the prevailing tax levels. "In the case of a sharp growth in this deficit, the oil companies will be forced to sharply reduce agreed upon levels of production . . . and to reduce the number of production workers," the letter warned. The IMF view was more circumspect: first, because the IMF's own *World Economic Outlook* forecast was an oil price fall of only 14 percent in 1998, and second, because the accounting for oil revenue and even production was totally opaque. In actuality, world oil prices fell by 32 percent in 1998, before rebounding by 37 percent in 1999.

Oil taxation remained a key issue after Chernomyrdin was dismissed and Kiriyenko took over the government, and it became a litmus test in the eyes of the IMF and watchful financial markets of the government's political will to resolve its fiscal problems. It was at the top of the agenda of the new Kiriyenko cabinet. One of then–acting prime minister Kiriyenko's first orders on March 30 was for a decree cutting oil excise taxes to be prepared immediately. Nemtsov agreed that oil companies needed help, saying that oil prices had fallen by 50 percent and oil companies just could not pay. The excise tax was perhaps the most dreaded of all oil taxes since it was levied on each metric ton of oil sold, irrespective of price. Another charge—the pipeline tariff—was particularly burdensome for producers shipping oil long distances to export markets.

The Russian government was immobilized at the worst possible time by the oil issue. Clearly the precipitous fall in prices was having a negative impact on oil company profits. That said, the oil companies and their supporters in the government were not forthcoming with figures that were robust enough to support their claims, and it was apparent that the situation varied significantly from company to company, and even field to field. Outside analysts were not objective in clarifying the picture either. There was also the question of why, if prices were temporarily low, the companies did not stop pumping so much (although it seemed that some were tempted to try to steal some market share from OPEC, which had agreed on cuts). At the same time, it was equally clear that there was no other large, cash-rich source of potential tax revenue except for the oil companies and Gazprom. In a fiscal crisis, the oil companies became the line of ultimate defense.

The Asian Contagion

Following the announcement of a higher refinance rate by the CBR on January 30, 1998, the financial markets were calmer. The Lombard rates were raised to 42 percent (before being reduced to 39 percent on February 17), and the ruble/dollar exchange rate remained virtually stable in February. Foreign exchange reserves declined, however, to US$15.1 billion at end-February owing to currency outflows to repay debt by MinFin, as the CBR was a net purchaser of foreign exchange.

Yeltsin made reassuring statements during a televised meeting with Chubais on February 4 (about speeding up the tax code, strengthening shareholder rights, getting tough with tax debtors, and reducing government spending and borrowing), which also helped to calm market concerns. So did the passage of the 1998 budget in its third reading in the Duma in early February. Yet the markets remained nervous, especially nonresidents, who were openly speculating that the IMF might be forced to offer Russia a big financial support package. The press was asking whether Russia would be the next domino to fall.

The persistent fiscal problems and underlying weakness in the banking sector left the market highly exposed to abrupt swings in investor sentiment. CBR officials were adamant that while foreign investors were nervous, there had been no adverse shift in residents' demand for ruble-denominated assets and the Russian banks did not have large, unhedged foreign exposure—but they proved consistently reticent to provide data to substantiate these assertions. The IMF staff reluctantly continued to accept their word for it. Indeed, the CBR officials characterized the new year bout of market fears as akin to those in early December, when despite significant alarm among many observers, a financial crisis did not materialize.

The political environment for strong adjustment and reform programs in Russia remained unclear, even after Yeltsin's vigorous annual address to the Federal Assembly on February 17, during which, after reciting a long list of commendable and urgent measures, he warned ominously that "if this government is not capable of resolving these strategic tasks, we will have a new government."

Camdessus visited Moscow, along with Odling-Smee, from February 17 to 19. Having just visited Korea, which was in a full market meltdown with devastating economic and human consequences, the IMF managing director was anxious to inform Yeltsin that if he didn't take strong, credible steps, Russia too could go the way of Korea. In all of his meetings, Camdessus stressed the lessons from the Asian experience relevant to Russia, urging the authorities to:

• tackle the fiscal situation vigorously, through tough action against tax offenders, strong support for the tax administration agencies, and strict expenditure control
• improve the climate for long-term foreign capital inflows, especially through an improved tax system (tax code, *not* exemptions for foreign investors), and an improved legal framework and contract enforcement
• do more to address the problems of governance, especially in the areas of corporate governance (a major deterrent of foreign investment), the transparency of privatization, the influence of powerful business interests over government policy, and of course tax collection
• demonstrate stronger ownership of the government's economic program, particularly in relation to decisive and consistent implementation, where word and deed too often diverged, and the avoidance of contradictory public statements on policy, which alarms markets.

Yeltsin strongly agreed with Camdessus on these points. After the earlier market turbulence, the government also had taken these lessons on board and prepared its own twelve-point action program. Camdessus agreed with the thrust of the program and urged its rapid implementation, which would have allowed the IMF to continue its financial support. Chernomyrdin and his colleagues seemed to get the message, and an action program was finalized. The government's policy statement, which would be the basis for its request to the IMF for further financial support, was almost ready for the prime minister's signature.

Politics Again Interfere

Just as it appeared that the Russian authorities were really waking up to the increasing vulnerabilities from lethargy, and were busy preparing and implementing policy measures, politics suddenly got in the way. Chernomyrdin was dismissed, seemingly abruptly, on March 23—and political limbo began. Later that day, Yeltsin named Kiriyenko as acting prime minister and asked him to form a government. The erstwhile thirty-five-year-old minister of fuel and energy, with a reputation as a bright technocrat and protégé of Nemtsov, was thrust into the unenviable position of trying to tackle the daunting economic and social problems confronting the country in the midst of a crisis with no time to make teething mistakes.

The change in government was not widely anticipated (although Kudrin said to us that very afternoon that the changes that looked unexpected from the outside were, in fact, well prepared and not a surprise to many in the government, including in MinFin). In announcing the change, the president emphasized that the action did not imply a change in the course of policy. Rather, he said that it was an effort to provide a new impulse to the reform process; in the recent period, the government had not been characterized by dynamism, new ideas, and initiative, and a new team capable of achieving real results was needed. Rumors flew in Moscow as to the real reasons behind the change, since clearly the timing was, at best, awkward and possibly even dangerous in the prevailing market conditions. These rumors ranged from Chernomyrdin stepping down from the firing line to be groomed for the presidential election in 2000, to a fit of rage on Yeltsin's part that he was starting to act prematurely presidential, notably on a recent stop in Washington, DC. There was also a rumor that this was the only way that Berezovsky—still powerful behind the scenes—could get rid of Chubais once and for all.

Nonetheless, the initial financial market reaction was broadly favorable. The ruble was almost unchanged, and the three-month GKO yields stood at 26.6 percent, against a range of 24 to 28 percent during the previous week.

In a meeting later that day, Livshits, then a deputy head of the Kremlin administration, said to me that the president wanted to assure the IMF management that the change in government did not represent any relaxation of policy—indeed, if anything, it should be seen as a reinforcement of the president's determination to pursue growth and better financial management. More fundamentally, he asserted, while politics played a role, the immediate cause for the change in government was the mismanagement of the financial situation. Revenue collection remained weak in the first quarter. Under these circumstances, it was not surprising that wage arrears reappeared and the Paris Club payments got delayed.

Kasyanov, then a deputy minister at MinFin, assured me on March 6 that the six hundred million U.S. dollars due on February 20 to Germany under its Paris Club bilateral agreement, was paid on March 4—that is, within the technical grace period provided under that agreement. He acknowledged that owing to poor organization within MinFin, with three separate departments dealing with debt as well as the VEB as the government's debt manager, and living hand to mouth without adequate cash management, it was difficult to avoid using the grace periods. In fact, to his astonishment, his deputy told him only on March 10 that an unpaid balance remained owing to MinFin's cash flow constraints. And this just days before Kasyanov was embarking on a road show to promote the issue of a deutsche mark Eurobond, on March 16.

Livshits continued that although the elimination of offsets might complicate the situation, the government had seemed almost lackadaisical in dealing with revenues. For instance, no action had been taken to implement the program measure on oil pipeline access nor had any serious meetings of the VChK dealing with revenues been held so far in 1998. There was the general feeling that no one in government was pushing this agenda or taking responsibility for revenue. Nominally Chubais had been named in early March to head a revenue commission in government, but a rumor was circulating that he would be named as the new president of UES—so much so that Fischer asked him about the rumor in a phone call on March 13. Chubais was appointed to UES on April 30.

The hapless Kiriyenko was finally confirmed on the third try on April 24, in a bitter showdown with the State Duma. The month of April was virtually wasted; the reform program stayed on paper. It took until May, and even then only after the traditional holiday season that takes up much of the first half of the month, for a new government to be formed.

Zadornov remained as finance minister, but strangely his former deputy, Viktor Khristenko, then nominally became his boss as the new first deputy prime minister in charge of the economy. Yet it soon became clear that Khristenko's responsibilities were circumscribed as Zadornov reported directly to the prime minister, and especially because Chubais was appointed to a new position as the special representative of the president to international financial institutions on June 17. Ironically, given the events that were about to unfold, Chubais had no real power in terms of domestic policies.[6]

Meanwhile oil prices continued to drop, presenting the novice Kiriyenko with some delicate decisions. The lobbying for relief by Russian oil majors was intense, and yet the needs of public finance—and any possibility of withstanding further negative market sentiments—depended critically on raising higher revenues from the energy sector (oil and gas). By the beginning of April, the average prices for Urals crude were under thirteen U.S. dollars per barrel, a 40 percent decline since November 1997, when the Asian contagion first hit the markets. On April 8, Nemtsov signaled that Russian producers were prepared to self-enforce a production cut of sixty-one thousand barrels per day in solidarity with the recently agreed-on Riyadh pact among OPEC producers—a purely symbolic measure of about 1 percent of the then-current rate of output.

In fact, an important measure to ensure compliance by the major oil companies with their statutory tax obligations was under preparation by MinFin. The idea originated with then–first deputy minister Ignatiev. The proposal was elegant and simple: if an oil company was delinquent in its taxes, it would be automatically denied access to the state-owned oil export pipelines.

As with so many of Ignatiev's innovative and practical ideas, a massive countereffort was organized by the Ministry of Fuel and Energy, which controlled the commission that allocated pipeline access on a monthly basis, to emasculate the proposal. This was hardly surprising since the new minister, Sergei Generalov, was no doubt sympathetic to the oil lobby, having just come from Yukos Oil Company. As spring 1998 advanced, it became obvious that the battle lines were drawn among economic interests in Russia on this single issue. With all other revenue sources either tapped to the full or requiring significant improvements in tax administration to start yielding results, the oil pipeline measure became the litmus test of the country's resolve to address its fiscal problem and hence a key barometer of market sentiment. Other writers, such as Freeland, Rose Brady, and Juliet Johnson, have described in some detail the reported intrigues among the so-called oligarchs, senior government officials, and Duma officials surrounding this issue.[7]

The authorities agreed to the oil pipeline measure in February, during Camdessus' visit, and it formed a key plank in their economic program for 1998. The measure was to be enforced with respect to oil shipments on a quarterly basis, starting with the second quarter. Unfortunately, Ignatiev was put in the position of having to say on March 17 that it was legally and physically impossible to implement it from April 1; he said that the MFE had already made the second-quarter allocation and legally it could not be modified.

Ignatiev suggested instead that compliance with all outstanding tax obligations as of May 1 become the criterion for pipeline decisions for the third quarter, starting July 1 (the tax data for May 1 should have been available early enough in June to assess compliance and reallocate any spare capacity to complying companies in time for July 1). He argued that the crucial element of this measure for revenue purposes would be achieved by publication of the resolution, rather than the actual distribution of pipeline access. Ignatiev alluded to, but did not explain, the nature of the problems in bringing the Ministry of Fuel and Energy on board.

The key issue of finding additional revenue had become urgent—all the more so as the Russian government had pushed spending cuts seemingly as far as they could go. In fact, the 1998 budget, which had just been signed into law by Yeltsin, was admitted to be unrealistic by the authorities. The revenue estimates could not be achieved, and even the reduced targets agreed on with the IMF were missed for the first quarter and would be missed by an even larger margin without additional measures in the second quarter. As Viugin observed at the time of the spring IMF meeting in Washington, DC, in late April, with no possibility of any further net market financing, any revenue shortfall would have to be reflected in immediate spending cuts.

The problem was that the budget authorized the commitment of and spending up to the amounts in the budget law even if there was not enough revenue to pay for it. A draft degree had been prepared in secret that would mandate the sequestration of spending beyond the available financing, but its signature was delayed at the last moment by the dismissal of the government. Each day that went by without the decree allowed the potential for new spending arrears and hence pressure for tax offset operations. As Gaidar and others cautioned, however, it would have been political suicide to have the decree issued just as the Kremlin was trying to get Duma support for Kiriyenko's appointment as prime minister. The decree was not signed until May 11.

Political sensitivity, especially in relations with the Duma, also explained the overreaction to relatively innocent comments made by then–first deputy finance minister Kudrin in an interview with the *Financial Times* on March 29, in which he admitted that in MinFin's assessment of appropriate spending cuts, there should be 206,000 jobs cut among teachers and health workers. His remarks were taken out of context and splashed over television, fueling opposition to Kiriyenko and the reformers more generally. Kudrin was only addressing the issue of redundant federal institutions with massive excess capacity. In fact, most education and health workers were employed in the oblasts and municipal governments.

Just before the key third vote in the Duma on Kiriyenko's approval, scheduled for April 24, Ignatiev again called an urgent meeting with us to explain the government's proposed temporary reduction in the oil excise tax—to reduce the rate from fifty-five to forty-five rubles per metric ton (equivalent to 7.3 barrels) until the end of the year. The revenue loss for the rest of the year, assuming a May 1 application, would be somewhat less than two billion rubles. He said that Zadornov felt that this was the minimum concession needed since the oil industry was lobbying hard for much more sweeping tax concessions.

Ignatiev was also concerned when he discovered from the IMF team that the oil pipeline resolution, which was to have legal effect with respect to May 1 tax obligations, had still not been signed when we met on April 20—and the oil companies already were complaining that the cutoff date was illegal or unfair, or both.

In their desperation to demonstrate policy momentum, there had been a flurry of activity to have Kiriyenko sign the government's policy statement for the IMF as quickly as possible—the one that had been virtually finalized by Chernomyrdin's government. Some senior Russian officials suggested that a signed statement might help bolster Kiriyenko's authority and help secure his confirmation by the Duma. Others felt that with the ruble under pressure because of the political hiatus, a signed statement might help to reassure worried markets. Kiriyenko did sign the statement of economic policy to the IMF on April 11, but it was never issued. In the absence of a viable government, too much of the package was starting to unravel.

When the IMF mission met with the finally confirmed prime minister at the end of April, he acknowledged that the change in government had taken much longer than it should have and disrupted the implementation of the program—although he also stressed that the new government would "unequivocally follow the jointly agreed course" with the IMF. The government resolved to identify new revenue measures, additional to those already in its program such as the oil pipeline measure, by mid-May to compensate for the continuing revenue shortfall.

In retrospect, the dismissal of the Chernomyrdin government and the bruising battle with the new Duma to confirm a new and inexperienced team under the bright, affable, but hopelessly overwhelmed Kiriyenko—more than any other single factor—tested the patience as well as credulity of Russian and foreign investors alike, and pushed the debt dynamics beyond the point of no return. The resurgence of the financial crisis in May seems to have been directly linked to the political limbo and lack of concrete actions to correct the financial imbalances. As a frequent visitor to Moscow from a London-based investment bank said, "When lending to the government [through the purchase of GKO], you need to be sure that you are bridging to future revenue." The new government lost credibility in this regard before it even had a chance to act.

Another Wave of Crisis Hits

It's difficult to pinpoint the catalyst to the financial market panic that followed on the heels of the traditional and long May holidays in Moscow. Perhaps it was the widely reported news of a miners' strike over wage arrears in the middle of the month, when the government for the first time that year failed to place the entire issue of GKOs at the auction on May 13, when a laudable medium-term plan was announced by the government on May 18 that was largely devoid of anything specific, or finally the spectacular failure to raise US$2.1 billion at an auction on May 26 for a controlling stake in state oil giant Rosneft, when not a single bid was received. Maybe all these factors, combined with reports that tax revenues in April had fallen, made the fiscal picture look dramatically worse.

The crisis erupted suddenly on Monday, May 18. It was the worst bout of financial market pressure in Russia since the previous December. That day, interest rates on a three-month GKO jumped to 54 percent, while the exchange rate moved to the weak end of the intervention band and the stock market index dropped by 13 percent. During May 18–22, the CBR supported the exchange rate by intervening in the foreign exchange market, and gross reserves fell to about fifteen billion U.S. dollars from sixteen billion at the end of April.

In response to market pressures, the prime minister reiterated the new government's commitment to fiscal restraint, and the CBR raised the interest rates on its refinance and Lombard facilities to 50 percent on May 19. The markets seemed to calm down, and interest rates fell back to 44 percent on Friday, May 22.

Nevertheless, the news circulating over the ensuing weekend that yet another IMF mission had come and gone, without tying up a deal with the new government, seemed to have sent the markets into a spin when they opened on May 25. The problem was that the mission had met an unexpected roadblock from Zadornov, who would not commit himself to the budget revenue numbers discussed earlier; he proposed to cut spending further in the current year without incurring arrears. Incredulous, the mission left to consult with the IMF management. GKO rates rose immediately to 58 percent, and the stock market fell by 5 percent; interest rates rose above 70 percent the following day, and the stock market continued to slide.

Investors began selling both stocks and securities, and the ruble came under intense pressure. With the government being slow to react, panic struck the markets on May 27. An attempt to auction off eight billion rubles of GKOs failed miserably, and the average yields were pushed up to a twenty-two-month high, touching 90 percent. The next day, just as Odling-Smee arrived in Moscow as a signal that progress was being made toward an agreement, the markets crashed even further. As an emergency action, the CBR raised its refinance rate to 150 percent and intervened heavily in the foreign exchange market. The short end of the yield curve exceeded 100 percent in a large GKO sell-off, the average rates rose to 85 percent, and the stock market fell by a further 12 percent (to levels not seen since 1996).

On May 29, Odling-Smee tried his best to present an upbeat press conference in Moscow as the government, supposedly in coordination, was unveiling its anticrisis program. When the government issued its anticrisis program that day, it was a bungled affair. Instead of orchestrating its release to get maximum favorable market impact with a presentation by Zadornov and Dubinin at prime time, armed with charts and tables, the plan was faxed to news agencies in an entirely routine manner late on a Friday afternoon. It was promptly ignored. It even backfired to some extent. The media seemed to be already obsessed with the idea that only a major IMF-coordinated support package could save Russia and were downright skeptical about Odling-Smee's explanations that the government's new fiscal policy could be up to the task. There was also considerable discussion of a government proposal (actually suggested by investment banks) to restructure its debt by medium- and long-term borrowing on the Eurobond market in combination with retiring short-term GKO.

Later that day, Kiriyenko put on an impressive performance in a public broadcast about his determination to bring the fiscal situation under control and announced that Fedorov would take over from Pochinok as tax minister. He also agreed to drop the proposed reduction in the oil excise tax, using as a political alibi a provision in the 1998 budget law that precludes any new measure that would reduce revenue without a substitute measure of at least equal importance. Fedorov immediately announced that major corporate tax dodgers would have until the end of June to come up with five billion rubles in back taxes, and about a thousand Russian jet-set celebrities were threatened with special tax audits.

The plot started to thicken. Up until that point, little attention had been paid to the banks. The CBR had provided assurances during the spring that the large banks were closely supervised by the OPERU II unit, which found no major causes for concern. Andrei Kozlov, a first deputy CBR chair, called me on Saturday afternoon, May 30, to meet immediately about Tokobank. The bank was unable to meet margin calls against collateral held to secure foreign credits and had been put into receivership by the CBR. It was the twentieth-largest bank and was not alone in being vulnerable to market pressures.

Kozlov said that there was a discussion within the CBR management about whether to formulate a general approach or deal with any problems on a case-by-case basis. The author was reminded of Aleksashenko's remark of a year earlier about the CBR's unpreparedness and even its inability to sort out a banking crisis, owing to a lack of trained specialists and managers. Subsequently, in June, the CBR discovered that a number of other large banks could be facing liquidity problems before the end of the year, even without a major crisis. A policy was needed.

It did not help that the Clinton White House announcement of May 31 fed expectations of a major international support package. The statement said that "the United States endorses additional, conditional financial support from the international financial institutions [IFIs], as necessary, to promote stability, structural reforms and growth in Russia."

But markets, no doubt expecting more, plunged the next day. The RTS share index fell by 13.6 percent to its lowest level since October 1996. The yields on GKO rose back up to 75 percent, and the ruble came under pressure.

Chubais and Vasiliev, as Kiriyenko's envoys, had already flown to Washington, DC, on a supposedly private visit to minimize adverse market reactions, and after official meetings on May 29, met the next day at Deputy Treasury Secretary Summers's house to devise their strategy. AP-Dow Jones already noted on May 28 (actually when the Chubais mission was in the air) that "top investors met with Khristenko and came out saying that phone calls were already made to Washington and that discussions begin that day with top western officials and Deutsche Bank on a package of large proportions, probably of around $15 billion."

The fact that the IMF had announced the completion of discussions on the long-delayed 1998 program on June 4, and scheduled a board meeting on June 18 to complete the review, seemed to have been totally discounted by the market in the growing chorus for a major support package.

Meanwhile, as markets were in a holding pattern with an emerging consensus that Russia would be safe for the summer as a support package seemed inevitable, the more parochial attention of the IMF and the Russian authorities turned next to the IMF's board meeting and the related release of the tranche. Most of the outstanding issues had been resolved. Perhaps not surprising, the oil pipeline access issue remained. Negotiations in the IMF's Moscow office continued through the night of June 8, with Generalov, Kudrin, and Viugin. My colleague and fiscal expert Tom Richardson valiantly hammered out a deal even though he was in the process of moving his family back to Washington after three years in Moscow. Those discussions continued through the next night as well. The issue was how to ensure that the mechanism would really work, and a compromise was reached on the elimination of outstanding tax arrears.

In what must have been a real slap in the face to Kiriyenko, but particularly to the earnest though hapless Khristenko, Chubais was suddenly appointed by Yeltsin on June 17 as his special representative to international financial organizations, taking over all discussions with the IMF. The intrigue behind and reason for this move were explained by our contacts as an attempt by the oligarchs to salvage what they could before Kiriyenko and his amateurs wreaked havoc. While not formally a member of the government—indeed he maintained his new position as the CEO of UES—Chubais sat on the cabinet with the rank equivalent of a deputy prime minister and a corresponding office in the Russian White House.

Whatever his real motive, Chubais's first act in his new position the next morning seemed astounding and totally unexpected. In his new office, he met with some of the major oil companies and agreed to have GR#599, the government resolution on oil pipeline access, amended as a virtual gift to the oil companies. The version signed by Kiriyenko the previous day was nullified and replaced with a new version signed by Nemstov, as acting prime minister since Kiriyenko was technically outside Moscow.

What Chubais had done was to introduce a new, brief paragraph that exempted oil shipments that had been pledged to foreign creditors from the tax provisions for pipeline access. When I called Chubais, hours before the board meeting was to start in Washington, DC, he pretended that the exemption was a small, technical issue, important in the currently nervous foreign markets with little impact on actual shipments. I told him that his action was reckless and could undermine the confidence that the IMF had shown in the effectiveness of his leadership. He reiterated that it was just a minor technical adjustment, the significance of which should not be exaggerated.

Camdessus was not amused. The board meeting scheduled for June 18 was canceled at the last minute. In order to avoid undue embarrassment that could compromise Chubais, Camdessus came up with the excuse that in addition to the pipeline access issue, there were also problems with data-reporting requirements and large taxpayers. Unfortunately, and unbeknownst to Kasyanov because of the relative compartmentalization of MinFin, a US$2.5 billion Eurobond issue was launched that day. The announcement effect of the IMF decision cost Russia an additional US$10 million. In any case, the actual extent of foreign loan pledges had to be ascertained, and not surprisingly, it suddenly turned out that a considerable portion of the oil was pledged. And while Dubinin expressed his displeasure at being blamed in part for the delay, the data problems were real. After all, the IMF did not know about the highly leveraged, short-term foreign exchange positions of the commercial banks.

The IMF board finally met on June 25, and approved the 1998 program and tranche release. The markets were not impressed, and the calls for a large support package reached a crescendo.

Meanwhile, back in Moscow, there was one last attempt to see whether tax compliance could be quickly raised. Fedorov had a peculiar manner of ensuring tax compliance, going public in his pursuit of tax delinquents and even going against Gazprom. The latter effort got him into trouble with the Kremlin, and he was apparently told to back off.

He also tried to continue the efforts started by Pochinok to rationalize tax administration. Fedorov was promoted to deputy prime minister in June, and given oversight of the Tax Police and the Federal Service for Currency and Export Control (VEK), an obscure Soviet legacy as a specialized agency dealing with foreign currency and exports. The VEK seemed in practice to have had little function other than rent seeking, and the IMF suggested several times that it be abolished, finally succeeding only in May 2000.

Relying largely on bluster to try to be effective, but without getting his own deputies in place, Fedorov was no team player. As a one-man show, he was constrained. Even experts in the IMF noted that Fedorov seemed to trust no one then at the STS headquarters. The big question was who was going to do all the work that needed to be done to implement urgent legislative and administrative reforms. His threats appeared to have some initial effect, but once Fedorov was called down over Gazprom, the pressure was off.

By the beginning of the summer, the prevalent view in the markets, the Russian government, the G-7 capitals, and the IMF was that an Asian-style financial crisis in Russia was not inevitable. By the end of July, after the approval by the IMF of the enhanced program, this would give way to a more pessimistic view of an impending crisis, probably in the autumn. The difference between those two dates was explained by initial hopes that a combination of a major external financing package and a strong "better late than never" crash policy program to change the trajectory of financing needs would avert a stampede by market participants. While keeping various scenarios under review, the IMF management and staff were relatively optimistic that this mix would do the trick. This is certainly also the feedback that Fischer and others on the IMF side were receiving from numerous market contacts. Even though the IMF's main policy development work on crisis prevention was yet to come (in part inspired by the Russian crisis), here was an early opportunity to show—if only the Russian authorities would cooperate—that crises were not inevitable.

The Panic Button and the Bolshoi Package

By early June the presumption in the market was that a support package was under preparation. Already during Odling-Smee's visit at the end of May 1998, Kiriyenko asked the IMF to explore the issue in view of the severe financial crisis engulfing the country. Odling-Smee sent a letter to

Khristenko on June 6 outlining the types of additional policy measures that the IMF would want to see in place to organize a large-scale support package for Russia. Subsequently, exploratory discussions were held in Washington, DC, on June 11–12 with Viugin and Olga Aliluyeva, economic adviser to the prime minister. Viugin sought clarification on some points, indicating that the authorities were committed to taking tough measures as necessary to restore market confidence, but noted that the majority of the proposed measures would require Duma approval and as such could prove difficult to implement in the current political climate.

Although it had been agreed to keep the discussions on the enhanced package a secret lest market expectations be disappointed, the discussions were in fact followed closely. It was, of course, in the IMF's interests to keep the discussions under wraps in order to avoid undue pressure to agree on a program irrespective of its merits in a situation where negative news could have self-fulfilling expectations. Obviously it was tempting for the authorities to do the opposite since they knew that the IMF would never want to be blamed for triggering a crisis by walking away and upsetting market expectations. Camdessus tried to downplay expectations, communicating on the sidelines of a press conference in Kazakhstan that "contrary to what markets and commentators are imagining, this [in Russia] is not a crisis. This is not a major development."[8] Fischer arrived in Moscow on June 22 with Marquez-Ruarte and a small team. Before leaving on June 24, Fischer cautioned the prime minister that this looked like their last chance to avoid an economic cataclysm.

And in a letter on June 29 to Kiriyenko, Camdessus set out the guiding principles to reach an agreement on a strengthening of the program and increased funding from the IMF. First was whether the program contained sufficiently strong fiscal measures to enable Russia within a short time to reduce its borrowing and put its recent market problems firmly behind it, and second was whether its structural reform components, together with what had already been done, would enable the economy to begin a period of sustained growth.

By late June, the situation was becoming even more perilous. A typically well-informed view from the markets was that "a [ruble] devaluation is by no means a foregone conclusion," according to Avinash Persaud, global currency strategist at J.P. Morgan in London, "but we would warn that the risk is substantial." Persaud said that the timing and size of external financial support were critical. "Too small a loan which arrives late will disappoint the market greatly," he noted.[9]

On June 26, the CBR raised its refinancing rate to 80 percent from 60 percent after GKO yields touched 75 percent, but investors continued to exit, driving the yields even higher. The government's one-year benchmark bond was trading at 82 percent on June 29. The equity market also dropped, with the RTS share index falling a further 16.2 percent over four days.

For the first time, a leading official publicly mentioned the possibility of a ruble devaluation. Zadornov told the State Duma's Budget Committee on June 29 that "if tax collection does not improve by a third [in the coming months], there will be a devaluation." Government officials were quick to deny this, saying that Zadornov's remark had been "misinterpreted," but the markets were already spooked.

Dubinin reiterated the Kremlin's stance that devaluation was not under consideration. "The government and Central Bank have enough instruments and strength to avoid devaluation of the ruble," he said. But Dubinin stressed that the crisis was real. "I share Finance Minister Mikhail Zadornov's assessment that the situation is serious," Dubinin commented on ORT television later that day.

The IMF's view of the situation at the end of June was that the risks of supporting the Russian authorities' efforts to defend the achievements of macroeconomic stabilization—low inflation and a stable ruble—were significant, but the possible costs of not doing so, to Russia, the region, and international markets, were also considerable. If the Russians were ready to bite the bullet, the IMF would also try to do its part to avoid a meltdown. Bowing to the government's emphatic preference that the current exchange rate regime should be maintained, this entailed that they would have to adopt a major additional fiscal package to convince markets that fiscal policy was on a sustainable path consistent with the exchange rate policy.

The IMF team calculated that even after the full implementation of the government's economic program for 1998 and a decline in GKO yields to an average rate of 25 percent in 1999, a further adjustment effort of 3 to 4 percent of the GDP for 1999 would be required, meaning that the new budget would have to entail significant increases in revenues as spending had already been cut to the bone. The measures to bring this about were negotiated intensively with the government between June 27 and July 12. Odling-Smee arrived for the last two days to settle the outstanding issues with Kiriyenko.

While discussing what came to be called the "bolshoi package," however, the IMF team was aware that even if such an enhanced program were immaculately implemented, it was possible that market uncertainties would lead to such financial market pressures that the current exchange rate would become impossible to defend. In such a case, there was also contingency planning involving a step devaluation and associated policies. A step devaluation was favored over a free float. Our analysis suggested that since the source of exchange market pressure came from the capital account, competitiveness issues were not particularly relevant. Hence, it was proposed that one approach to restore equilibrium in capital flows would be to calculate the exchange rate needed to allow gross reserves to fully cover base money. At the end of June, with reserves of about US$17 billion (following the Eurobond issues and fund tranche) and base money of 170 billion rubles, an exchange rate of 10 rubles per dollar seemed broadly appropriate. It was recognized that devaluation by itself would actually worsen the fiscal imbalances, unless accompanied by a large-scale debt conversion scheme. The IMF staff had also considered the possible merits of a currency board, but decided that the political will and mechanisms required for success were absent. Again, because of a fear of leaks, this analysis was not shared in writing with the government.

The crux of the bolshoi package was to convince the markets that the fiscal prospects were being brought under control. The IMF staff accepted the authorities' perspective that there was little they could do in addition to the measures already taken to date that would significantly affect the outcome for 1998. It was agreed that for the purposes of restoring market confidence, the focus should be on the policies for 1999 and beyond; if investors could see that there were iron-clad commitments to a conservative 1999 financing framework, they would accept maintaining their positions in ruble assets. At least that was the logic.

It has to be said that there was great skepticism within the IMF concerning this approach, in view of the poor track record that the Russians had displayed in earlier years. Even within the negotiating team, there was the question of why all these desirable policies, which had been under discussion for so long, were now suddenly possible? Many did not see credible evidence of any real commitment to a regime change—there were some improvements at the margin, but little more. Being so close to the action, this was certainly my view, and so I cautioned my colleagues. There was also a concern that the markets would not be so easily manipulated.

And on the Russian side, it seemed that President Yeltsin and those advising him were simply not convinced that the bold measures required were really the lesser of two evils. The senior Russian officials, such as Viugin and Kasyanov, who did believe that dramatic action was required appeared to be in the minority, but hoped that market developments would focus the minds of the doubters during the course of the negotiations.

A key practical concern of the IMF staff was that once the mission arrived in Moscow, it would become a hostage. It could not leave without either announcing its support in line with market expectations or be held responsible for the very collapse that it was seeking to avoid. As a result, it was feared that little—in terms of market-credible measures other than on paper—might emerge from the discussions, but it would be sufficient to secure large upfront financing from the IMF. The market, sensing the lack of real, tough measures, would then bolt, neutralizing the bolstering of reserves provided by the IMF. As I noted in an email of June 16, "In retrospect, it would be called a Foreign Investor Exit Facility." In a sense, of course, that is exactly what happened. The smart investors used the substantial liquidity support provided to Russia in the ensuing weeks to defend its exchange rate in order to cash out. But we were trapped, and it was too late to pull back.

The press was dominated by articles calling for a support package. As an example, William Browder, the manager of a Russian-based brokerage firm, ran an opinion piece in the *Wall Street Journal* in June calling for a US$20 billion package from the IMF. He also sent his piece to me, and I replied, "I find your views curious to say the least. If the situation is really as you describe, perhaps it would be appropriate for you and other investors to both save Russia and profit in the process by providing the '$20 billion' yourselves."

The package of additional measures under discussion focused primarily on steps to ensure a conservative and realistic 1999 budget, supported by a tight monetary stance and an ambitious structural reform program, including a plan to rehabilitate the banking system. Some of the most important fiscal measures required the enactment of legislation, and so a special session of the Duma was convened for July 13–17, well beyond the normal end of its spring session. It was clear that some of this legislation would be difficult: notably the temporary surcharge on payroll taxes, an increase in the personal income tax, a reduction of VAT exemptions, moving VAT to an accrual basis, and raising the land tax. Zadornov, who knew the Duma well, was busy lobbying deputies and assured his cabinet colleagues that the entire legislative package would probably pass. In parallel, the World Bank also negotiated a new structural adjustment loan focusing on antimonopoly, privatization, and infrastructure monopoly pricing and reforms as part of a new impetus for structural reform to lay the basis for more efficient market signals and resource allocation.

Moreover, when questioned about the credibility of the fiscal package, especially whether there were any strong, upfront measures that would demonstrate definitively the resolve of the authorities, Chubais—presumably tongue in cheek—pointed to a dramatic decision to allow the formula used to calculate quarterly pension payments to apply a reduction in the nominal pensions paid in the third quarter, which should have helped address concerns about the looming pension fund imbalances. He stressed that no other country would have the courage to undertake such a politically difficult measure. This proposed measure, as impressive as it might have been, was totally unrealistic in the Russian context. Miners had been on strike, and pensioners were demonstrating about low pensions and nonpayment. Chubais, as finance minister in 1997, had promised to get the pensions paid. Yet when pressed as to whether this could be done, he and other officials suggested that it was tough but feasible.

Another complementary element of the enhanced package was a voluntary debt exchange, aimed at substituting short-term ruble debt with longer maturities in dollars, thus relieving much of the immediate financing pressure. In theory, the idea made sense. In fact, starting in early June, the IMF team had been working on a scenario for a debt restructuring that would "bail in" private creditors. It was concluded that ideally a concerted, voluntary rescheduling would be the preferred approach. Yet the IMF was insistent that the incorporation of such an element in the package would only make sense under some specific conditions: that it was supported by a strong fiscal adjustment, that the bulk of the short-term debt was rescheduled, and that the CBR and Sberbank were also restructuring their short-term government securities in a parallel operation.

Clearly the large stock of short-term government debt was seen by market participants as the main immediate threat to financial stability. As of July 6, 1998, the nominal face value of the debt amounted to 433 billion rubles (US$69.8 billion), with a market value of 306 billion rubles (US$49.4 billion). Holdings were fairly concentrated: 30 percent by nonresidents, 27 percent by Sberbank, 21 percent by the CBR, 15 percent by resident banks, and 7 percent by the nonbank sector. On average, about 6–7 billion rubles, or a little over US$1 billion, in securities fell due each week. At every Wednesday's primary auction, MinFin was finding it increasingly difficult to roll over these maturing securities at almost any feasible interest rate. Hence the attractiveness of a debt exchange.

MinFin had chosen Goldman-Sachs to manage such an exchange of short-dated GKO/OFZs for medium-term Eurobonds. Even though the proposal came from Goldman-Sachs, the choice of this firm was probably unfortunate. While it was a top player in the Eurobond market, its experience in Russia and the GKO market was limited. Kasyanov, who was responsible for the operation, agreed with the conditions for a successful operation (although it later proved that he lacked the authority to make it happen, owing to the lukewarm support from Zadornov and Dubinin). Dubinin, in particular, was concerned about creating problems for Sberbank, which might need to be able to sell securities to obtain liquidity at a time when there were worries that the withdrawal of household deposits could intensify. Zadornov was worried that the GKO market would be further weakened, making it even more difficult to roll over maturities falling due. In fact, there was no separate operation to assure investors that the half of the securities held by Sberbank and the CBR were effectively removed from the market. Nor was there a willingness to ensure that the operation would be large enough to alter the debt dynamics.

The outcome of the special Duma session ending on July 17, rejecting some of the key legislation underlying the package, came as a surprise. So sure had the government been about the outcome that there were no contingency plans, no plan B. Alexander Zhukov, subsequently a deputy prime minister from 2004 on, but the insightful chair of the Duma Budget Committee at the time, had a different perspective. Despite his own pessimism at the outset, nineteen of the twenty-eight draft laws submitted by the government as priority legislation were passed, and three more were approved in a first reading. Zhukov observed that it was truly unprecedented for such a large body of important laws to be presented, considered, and passed in such an expedited manner. For those that were not approved, in most cases there were good reasons, including inadequate technical preparation. Zhukov also advised that convening a special Duma session in August to reconsider the rejected legislation was a mistake.

Zadornov was in a state of shock, and clearly embarrassed in front of his cabinet colleagues, who had relied heavily on his assurances that the situation was well in hand. Fortunately the news came late in the day after most markets had closed, and the initial press reports were broadly favorable since a large amount of other legislation was passed.

At a late-night meeting with Chubais, I was told that they did the best they could and the IMF could not abandon Russia now. It had not helped to dampen his assurance of fund support that earlier in the day, Mike McCurry, the U.S. White House spokesperson, observed that in President Clinton's view, the negotiations with the IMF had gone on long enough and it was time for closure. In any case, Chubais announced that he would no longer be involved and was leaving the next morning for a private trip to New York. He stated that the stalwart Khristenko—who had been totally absent from all the discussions on the enlarged package until that point—would now suddenly be responsible for straightening out the mess.

Worse news was to come. The next day, a hot Saturday in Moscow, I received an urgent call to come to the Russian White House for a meeting with Khristenko and Zadornov. Oleg Sysuev, another deputy prime minister responsible for the social bloc, was also called in. It turned out that Chubais's litmus test of political resolve—the pension reduction—had been shot down by the Kremlin as naive without even bothering to show it to Yeltsin. In other words, this and presumably other key parts of the package were assembled without Yeltsin's blessing. Poor Khristenko and his colleagues were engaged in a frantic effort to salvage the package as Chubais headed for New York.

Negotiations continued all weekend right up to the time for the scheduled board meeting on July 20. In frustration and disappointment at the outcome of the Duma session, but accepting some alternative proposals as well as a promise to reconvene the Duma again in a special session in August, Camdessus decided to proceed with the scheduled board meeting (he had little choice), but to reduce the size of the initial tranche from US$5.6 billion to US$4.8 billion. The IMF package, approved by the board, was US$11.2 billion. Two additional tranches were foreseen in September and December. The total international financing package of US$22.6 billion also included a parallel Japanese loan and disbursements from the World Bank.

This was one of those situations that some would point to as the IMF succumbing to political pressure—in this case from the United States, as some senior officials in the treasury claimed credit for "making" Camdessus reduce the size of the initial tranche as a signaling device to the Russians. While Camdessus and Fischer acknowledged that there were discussions over that weekend with many of the interested parties, as would have been expected, and several ideas were floated, Camdessus was adamant that the "rephasing of the purchase," which is a standard IMF procedure in such instances, was a step that would have been made irrespective of the U.S. Treasury's views.

Short-Lived Relief

The afterglow of the IMF decision on July 20 did not last long. The first market reactions were positive with all indicators favorable except for Eurobond prices, which continued to dive. Exhausted and relieved Russian officials made their holiday plans and set off to relax.

Another curious twist in the story was when on July 22, Kiriyenko appointed the first Communist to his cabinet in naming Maslyukov as the new minister of industry and trade. The choice of Maslyukov, until then the Communist chair of the State Duma's Economic Policy Committee, was announced by Kiriyenko at a news conference, ending months of speculation over possible candidates for the recently created post.

The markets were already jittery by July 23. It was ironic that the U.S. vice president Albert Gore, making his first visit to Moscow since Kiriyenko became prime minister, stated enthusiastically on July 24 that the Russian economy was in safe hands.

It turned out that the CBR lost US$2.7 billion in reserves in the first twenty days of July, before receiving the IMF money. During the same period, however, the money supply (base) did not shrink as the CBR inadvertently supplied credit to MinFin. This fact, unknown to the IMF staff at the time, resulted from a bitter feud between Dubinin and Zadornov in July. Faced with a disastrous financing situation, Zadornov wrote to the Kremlin that the Finance Ministry was unable to redeem maturing coupons on government bonds, or make payments to the coal sector and the army. The letters, together with CBR documents, showed that the CBR withdrew 8.7 billion rubles from MinFin's accounts on July 20 as part of repayments for treasury bills held by the CBR that had matured during the previous week. As Yasin later explained, Dubinin was correct in a formal sense, but Zadornov's pleas for attention to the government's chronic cash flow problems had been long ignored.

Thus, it was all the more curious that Zadornov, in light of the above, never was willing to share MinFin's weekly cash flow projections with the CBR or the IMF. All he provided during the negotiations on the big package were assurances that the short-term problems were manageable. It turns out that he did not even have an articulated systematic cash flow plan but rather maintained an assumption, perhaps really just a hope, that GKO holders, notably nonresidents, would roll over their maturing instruments. It was also curious that the IMF accepted those assurances at face value—although in retrospect, it was clear that the numbers the IMF was using were relatively accurate—but they depended critically on assumptions about GKO rollovers and the behavior of Sberbank, which even MinFin could not deduce.

In light of the conflict with Dubinin over the cash flow problems of MinFin, it wasn't apparent why Zadornov, in discussing his difficult cash flow situation for July and August, turned down a suggestion by the chief IMF negotiator, Marquez-Ruarte, that went beyond his authorized instructions to use US$1 billion of the initial tranche to help support MinFin's cash flow in the immediate aftermath of the debt restructuring. It had been agreed that the entire first tranche, originally foreseen as US$5.6 billion, was to be dedicated to bolstering the reserves of the CBR, thereby providing confidence to investors that the CBR had sufficient foreign exchange to continue to meet all liquidations of GKO by non-residents. Indeed, Zadornov publicly changed his tune, asserting that it had been the IMF that had refused his request. The fact of the matter was that without all the numbers, we were flying blind into a storm.

By July 27, markets were in a panic, perhaps perceiving that the financing fix was temporary and unlikely to last through the fall. The GKO yields jumped from 55 percent on July 24 (a Friday) to 70 percent, the stock market fell by 5 percent, and the ruble was trading at the band. The mood in the market was dour and seemed to be getting worse.

Every market participant appeared to have their own view as to why so much uncertainty remained: Camdessus' decision to reduce the size of the tranche (implying a lack of confidence), contradictory signals about a special Duma session, BNP's liquidation of its dollar-denominated Russian portfolio on July 23, a desire to balance the books before the summer holidays, and so on. None of the individual explanations were in themselves sufficient. Taken together, however, and combined with continuing political uncertainty (for example, Yeltsin speaking during the previous weekend about an impending government reshuffle and a "hot" autumn ahead), investors saw little reason to return to the market and instead took a wait-and-see attitude.

A major and immediate complaint was that the MinFin auction of three-year OFZ on July 22 was a disaster. The market and the IMF were taken by complete surprise. Then it was announced that an auction would take place on July 29 for thirteen billion rubles, which exceeded market expectations of MinFin's cash flow needs. In turn, this raised concerns that perhaps the liquidity needs of the government were underestimated or some new problem had unexpectedly arisen, or worse that MinFin just didn't know what it was doing.

Investors were calling for the immediate enunciation of a clear borrowing strategy that was well managed, preferably by the IMF. It is noteworthy that Aleksashenko said at the time that he didn't think that MinFin actually had a coherent strategy, but if it did, it should certainly share such a strategy with the rest of the government and the CBR. Viugin, in fact, also said that MinFin did not actually have any well-articulated cash flow estimates. He noted that various assumptions were used about financing, but the analysis was not rigorous, and that Zadornov had a better overall sense of the situation and kept information close to his chest.

Unbeknownst to most market sources at that point in time—and to most of the government and the IMF—was the stupendously bad news that Sberbank, acting on its own or under CBR instructions, redeemed the totality of its GKOs falling due in July of 12.4 billion rubles. A key assumption by Zadornov in the discussions two weeks earlier on the financing of the program was the entire rollover by Sberbank.

When MinFin became aware of this on the morning of July 28, the GKO auction scheduled for the next day was immediately canceled, and then all subsequent auctions were also canceled, virtually sealing the fate for existing GKO holders. The only choice then was between redeeming maturing liabilities with money emission or restructuring the stock of short-term debt into new medium-term instruments.

As a result, the July outturn was truly catastrophic. For the month as a whole, only 13.8 billion rubles of a total of 38.8 billion rubles in government bonds were rolled over. Of that net 25 billion rubles, about 7 billion rubles, was owed to the CBR, which while tantamount to an illegal extension of credit, was not reimbursed. But the remaining 18 billion rubles had to be paid from budget resources. As a consequence, large arrears were incurred, estimated at 15 billion rubles, including the entire monthly wage bill of almost 9 billion rubles including the power ministries.

Hard as it was to believe, the situation was even worse. As it turned out, the IMF's concerns about the GKO/Eurobond exchange materialized. MinFin officials belatedly discovered that Sberbank had been the main recipient of the exchange, using mainly August maturities, which had been assumed to be rolled over. Not only were Sberbank and CBR securities not restructured separately (into non-Eurobond instruments) but the size of the non-Sberbank exchange was small as well—too small to make a significant difference to cash flow demands in the coming weeks.

So the Russians ended up with the worst of both worlds: an exchange so limited that it left the overhang of short-term securities falling due with little hope of a rollover, while saturating the Eurobond market with a flood of new paper, provoking a collapse in prices even as other Russian markets received a temporary boost.

In a poorly executed and maybe desperate attempt to convince the markets that despite appearances, the government really was in control, a large group of key investors was invited to a meeting at the Russian White House on July 30. Kiriyenko chaired the meeting with his entire economic team to answer questions. On the hard number questions, the authorities were poorly prepared, and had no tables or charts to explain the near-term outlook.

By the end of the meeting, when investors were wondering why they had been convened so urgently from London and Frankfurt, it was clear that some convincing numbers had to be placed on the table. Fischer arrived the next night, and spent much of the weekend poring over the numbers and ensuring high-level cooperation. He told Kiriyenko that there would be no more support forthcoming from the IMF; he suggested that the Russians try talking further directly with the G-7. He left on August 2, with the feeling that the game was up.

6

How a Probable Crisis Then Becomes Unavoidable

By this point there were few options. In the absence of a large G-7 bailout, the Russians faced an excruciating choice between monetizing the debt (it was after all denominated in rubles) or forcing a restructuring/write-down of it. They chose the latter, and despite a last-ditch effort to involve the IMF, the handling of the default was a shambles. Seen from the outside, it appeared as if policy was being conducted by rank amateurs.

The Meltdown Begins

As the managing director in charge of proprietary trading at a major London brokerage with one of the largest nonresident holdings of Russian government securities explained to me at the end of July 1998, "All the key players in the Russian market are nervously watching the exit—it is critical to be one of the first ones out when the stampede begins." And as the markets remained unconvinced about Russia's ability to pull through the crisis, these players were anxiously watching each other to see who would move first.

GKO/OFZ rates climbed again by a further 4 to 5 percentage points on August 3, in the presence of no apparent bad news and several bullish indicators (Fischer's upbeat presentation on his departure and some additional decrees signed). The market view seemed to be that Russia would almost certainly limp through until the early autumn and then things would once again get ugly. If this trend continued, myopic market thinking appeared to posit that the government would be forced to either issue new securities at distressed market levels of interest rates or tap another funding source. The market opted for the latter as the most probable, not even considering a much bleaker possibility.

What market sources were saying at the beginning of August was that what investors needed, in addition to precise cash flow information, was further clarity on the latter issue—that is, what the additional sources of funding could be. Apart from the obvious privatization route to garner more resources (which would be slow and uncertain), the only even remotely realistic alternative that might calm markets at that point would have been a large loan from the G-7 or a large commercial bank package backed by the G-7.

During the week of August 3, in expectation of at least a lull in the crisis, many of my colleagues and Russian counterparts left on much-needed holidays. I was the only professional staff member left in the IMF's Moscow office (with my deputy, Alfred Kammer, on a well-deserved holiday in anticipation of a quiet month and Jonathan Anderson, due to take up the key fiscal portfolio, only arriving from China in September). And I was distracted as my wife had just given birth to our first child.

The crisis continued relentlessly. On August 4, for instance, Gaidar was urgently trying to get Paul Volcker, the esteemed former Federal Reserve chair, to Moscow in order to advise the government and the CBR how to prevent the crisis so widely anticipated after the end of the summer; Viugin was working on cash flow projections to try to convince investors that the GKO debt falling due could be repaid; and more bad news was coming in about poor revenue collection, inadequate actions against tax delinquents, Gazprom's payment of negotiated rather than statutory tax liabilities, and yet more problems in monitoring compliance with oil companies' tax payments and pipeline access.

A couple of days later, Viugin presented the MinFin's cash flow projections at a technical meeting for financial market analysts. The presentation seemed, belatedly, to meet some of the concerns for more information. Yet the consensus view was that the government would not even be able to meet the third quarter's target of nine billion U.S. dollars in GKO rollover by nonresidents, especially at the yield targets of 50 to 55 percent assumed in the projections.

Despite another big outreach session by the government at the Russian White House with major foreign bank creditors the previous week (in public relations terms, little better than the first one) and the provision of some cash flow projections for the rest of the year, investors remained cautious about bringing new money into the market, or for that matter rolling redeeming GKO proceeds into the secondary market (about 75 percent of the August 5 GKO redemptions were earmarked for repatriation). As part of the bolshoi package put together by the IMF in July, the World Bank approved a new loan called SAL3 of US$1.5 billion on August 6 and disbursed a first tranche of US$300 million. The World Bank's action also seemed to have been fully discounted by the markets. In fact, it seemed that only bad news could influence the market.

By the end of the first week of August 1998, the markets looked worse than during the lows of late June before the IMF announced the bolshoi package. The principal on the London Club debt traded at an all-time low in London, while GKO/OFZ creeped up in yield terms to the 80 to 90 percent level. By then, two additional concerns were being voiced in the marketplace. One was the wholesale liquidation of external assets by Russian banks and the effects this was having on their already-constrained liquidity. Apart from the immediate headline effect of a bank collapse, this could have negative consequences for the budget, requiring additional financing in the eventuality of a possible CBR-funded bailout package to prop up the banks. The other was a growing belief that rollovers of any sort in the GKO market were totally unrealistic, even at the then-current high double-digit yield levels, for months to come. The specter of default started haunting participants again.

A bearish market psychology had firmly taken hold, which could have led to a crisis far sooner than the fundamentals had implied just weeks earlier. Investors appeared to have become immune to continued news of fiscal improvement, and in such circumstances, dramatic initiatives were expected. Continued amateurish muddles further sapped any remaining shreds of market confidence. For instance, *Kommersant* on August 6 reported that Kasyanov—trying to steady nerves in the market—claimed that MinFin would not conduct GKO auctions for the next three to four weeks, but then Bella Zlatkis, then head of the MinFin debt department, announced the next day a GKO/OFZ auction for the following week.

Thus, some alternative source of financing was being voiced as Russia's only hope in getting out of the crisis. The numbers touted around were significantly larger than the estimates of eight to ten billion U.S. dollars mentioned by some investors even a week earlier as adequate to cover all short-term liabilities to nonresidents. By then, the market was expecting the announcement of an additional twenty billion U.S. dollars (explicitly earmarked to buy back all outstanding GKOs falling due through the end of 1998).

Such a much-touted credit was expected to give the market a tremendous boost, and help participants focus on the economic fundamentals, rather than a vague sense of unease and foreboding. The divide between the expectations of market participants and the reality of any further G-7 support, even through the IMF, could not have been greater. There was about as much chance of a further large bailout as there had been to the realization of Joseph Stalin's oft-repeated talk about a general amnesty for those in the labor camps.

Most market participants, in fact, were certain that such a package was under preparation. This certainty dictated against the GKO-Eurobond exchange. After all, the recent experience in Asia underpinned these expectations—all the more because in the case of Russia, the West and the United States in particular had too much at stake to let Russia fail. Behind these sentiments was the near certainty that Russia was too big, too important, and certainly too dangerous to take any risks of economic and social destabilization.

Little did they appreciate that U.S. Treasury secretary Robert Rubin was not about to make hedge funds good on their massive speculation in Russian securities.[1] Along with the rest of the G-7, he avoided public comment. In view of the G-7's concerns about the precariousness of the situation, the members were careful to avoid any public denial about the possibility of further financial support for fear of destabilizing the markets. Politically, however, no matter how intense the concerns, there was insufficient support for another financing package. In essence, the Russians had exhausted their remaining goodwill with respect to policy credibility.

A big commercial package of uncertain size had indeed been discussed. In early August, MinFin and the CBR reportedly had received several proposals, which they had rejected on account of cost. Well-informed investors anticipated that when faced with the choice between paying 18 to 20 percent in dollar terms versus 60 to 90 percent in ruble terms, they would inevitably reexplore this route. The only fear was that time might run out. They were still watching the exit.

That first week of August had an air of unreality—not only because of my preoccupation with becoming a *pater familias*, but because the crisis seemed still distant. Virtually everyone at that point, even the most ardent exit watchers, was certain that the crisis had been postponed until September at the earliest. Chubais, no longer with an official position, left for holiday in Ireland, Dubinin went to Italy, others were at their dachas, Camdessus went to his home in Bayonne, and

Fischer set off for the Greek islands (armed with his ever-ready cell phone).

It was also the week that Russian commercial banks were being hit with margin calls on the declining value of their collateral of Russian Eurobonds and MinFin securities (domestically issued bonds denominated in foreign currency). The real ramification of the July GKO-Eurobond exchange was finally felt as the price of Russian sovereign Eurobonds collapsed with too much paper in a nervous market. Reuters carried a detailed report of the possible credit crunch for Russian banks as early as July 30. Traders were reporting that Russian companies and banks were forced to liquidate positions to repay the substantial foreign credits falling due. For example, it was reported that SBS-Agro and Inkombank were dumping their GKO and MinFin portfolios at significant losses in a desperate effort to avoid default.

The market view was that not only was default by some of these commercial borrowers inevitable but the forced liquidations in both the ruble and dollar sectors also made it unattractive for other investors to come into the market. Owing to the virtual absence of timely information about the short-term foreign exchange exposure of the banks, neither the government nor the CBR nor the IMF took any preventive steps, other than the general approach to problem banks ironed out in the wake of the still-continuing Tokobank workout. A rescue attempt by Moscow Bank collapsed at the beginning of July, and creditors were still waiting to receive concrete proposals from Bank Menatep, which had stepped in to take over Tokobank.

The Scramble for the Exit

By August 11, there was true panic on the markets. The ruble traded high above its band; the GKO market was collapsing, with yields for three-month GKOs jumping to 205 percent from 124 percent in the previous trading session; and the bottom seemed to be dropping out of the equity market, with the RTS index plunging by 25.7 percent between August 6 and 13 to a level below April 1996. The government submitted yet another anticrisis package to the Duma, but it was reported that the Duma might turn down the government's request to convene in August to discuss the package.

On the evening of August 12, Viugin spoke to markets through information agencies. He said that MinFin had canceled all government debt auctions in August, MinFin's reserve fund for redemptions would amount to two billion U.S. dollars in August, and measures to improve the market situation in September were being prepared by the government. Meanwhile, most officials continued their holidays. There was virtually no contingency planning.

In the end, the straw that broke the proverbial camel's back was the publication of a letter by financier Soros in the *Financial Times* on Thursday, August 13, which sent Russian markets over the edge. He wrote that Russia's financial crisis had reached a "terminal" stage. Soros called for a 15 to 20 percent ruble devaluation, and then the creation of a currency board to keep the ruble pegged to the U.S. dollar or a European currency, similar to systems used in Argentina and Hong Kong. "The devaluation is necessary to correct for the decline in oil prices," Soros said, adding that the government needed fifty billion U.S. dollars in reserves to defend its currency, and calling for the G-7 to put up fifteen billion U.S. dollars to help get Russia there. He also noted that "unfortunately, international financial institutions do not appreciate the urgency of the situation." Soros, in my view, started the stampede for the exit: there was no way back, even though his proposed solution was totally unrealistic. A currency board in Russia's circumstances was nonsense since there was neither the political will nor the administrative capacity to implement the policies that would be required.

Kiriyenko played down the crisis, saying that the government would be able to pay off its debts for August and September "calmly," and that the run on the markets was based on emotions and not fundamentals. "There will be no changes in the monetary policy of the Central Bank and the Government," Kiriyenko said during a one-day trip to the city of Perm in the Ural Mountains.

Even one-month GKOs jumped to 160 percent on August 13. The international rating agency Moody's downgraded Russia's sovereign foreign debt from a rating of B2 to CAA1—a level assigned to many poor African countries. Standard and Poor's cut Russia's rating to B- from B+. The CBR admitted that the interbank market, where large commercial banks lend to each other overnight, was crippled by acute liquidity problems.

In what were murky circumstances, at least as far as the IMF was aware, the CBR provided large-scale emergency credits in rubles to several banks that were in danger of default, notably SBS-Agro. Dubinin, who had wanted to bankrupt the banks and save the ruble, faced enormous pressure to do just the opposite, thereby almost sealing the fate of the ruble as excess ruble liquidity started flooding into the foreign exchange market. The CBR also imposed limits on commercial banks' foreign exchange purchases, claiming that the measure would calm markets and would not affect ruble convertibility. Banks across Moscow restricted dollar withdrawals and closed down exchange points by the end of the week as worried Muscovites scrambled to secure hard currencies.

On Friday, August 14, the GKO and equity markets recovered marginally as Yeltsin pledged to defend the ruble while also urging the Duma to hold an emergency session to address the financial crisis. "There will be no devaluation—that is firm and definite," he said during a visit to the city of Novgorod in northwestern Russia.

Lipton, the U.S. Treasury assistant secretary for international affairs, visited Moscow on August 12–13. He at least was well received by those remaining in Moscow, unlike his boss, Summers, who came to meet senior officials in May 1998. At that time, the new protocol staff members working for Kiriyenko could not appreciate why the prime minister should meet with just a "deputy finance minister." Financial markets were spooked on reports of the snub. Lipton was amazed at the wishful thinking of those officials that he met (Zadornov and Aleksashenko), and even more by the absence of other key senior people in the midst of a market meltdown, which could have unforeseen ramifications for the future of Russia and perhaps the world. The officials argued against radical solutions, whereas Lipton stressed that time was running out—indeed, that their assumption of diminishing reserve losses could be just the opposite. He left with no doubt that the end was near.

Fischer, in contact with Lipton and me, decided to confer with Odling-Smee to see how the IMF could assist the authorities in an orderly manner to face the inevitable. From his Greek island, he contacted Chubais to suggest that Chubais and Dubinin both return to Moscow forthwith, and dispatched Odling-Smee (to be followed by a larger mission team) to Moscow, after conferring with Camdessus.

Also, on August 14, Aleksashenko urgently called me, acknowledging that the situation had become dire—the CBR had lost US$400 million the previous day and had already lost another US$500 million by the time of our midafternoon phone conversation. Reserves fell below US$16 billion. The main purchasers were residents, and the classic symptoms of a run on the currency were evident. Aleksashenko still held out hope of containing the situation without radical measures, and said that along with Viugin, he was working on a quantified approach. He stressed that any solution involving a devaluation would precipitate a change in the

CBR management, resulting in a likely loosening of monetary policy and hence still-higher nominal GKO rates.

When I later spoke with Viugin, he seemed to accept that if their approach didn't work, a more drastic alternative, such as a step-and-hold devaluation combined with a consensual restructuring of the GKO debt—should be put in place quickly. This would entail, for instance, negotiations with creditors to reschedule all the GKO/OFZ notes falling due through the end of the year for new notes of some kind, maybe even denominated in dollars, with a new and much longer maturity schedule.

It was clear that the government did not have enough money to redeem GKOs falling due on the following Wednesday, August 19. July wage and other budget arrears had still not been paid off, and spending arrears for August were being incurred. The options were stark: monetization of the debt was briefly entertained by the Russian authorities as having the worst possible consequences and was not considered further.

This would have entailed instructing the CBR, contrary to the law, which did not allow it to purchase government securities in the primary market (except under narrowly defined circumstances), to buy all of the GKO falling due in the regularly scheduled primary auctions each Wednesday. This would have resulted in a massive increase in credit to the government. The Russian senior officials, faced with such an agonizingly painful choice, felt that a stable currency and low inflation were the most notable achievements of seven years of sacrifice, and any large-scale money emission to pay off the debt would wipe out those achievements overnight, with absolutely unpredictable and possibly dangerous consequences. This only left the option of a restructuring of the short-term debt and a likely, but hopefully limited devaluation. In retrospect, given how poorly the chosen option was implemented, the monetization option might have been less disruptive.

In the midst of a crisis it is difficult to understand, much less agree on, what to do and what the results would be, even when well organized, coordinated, and fully informed. It is notable—and remarkable in hindsight—to what extent the Russian authorities themselves were flying blind going into the thick of the crisis. The necessary data on the short-term foreign currency debt simply were not collected by government or the CBR, or even more surprising, such data as was collected was not shared and tended to be highly compartmentalized. At a minimum, data were lacking on the stock of short-term foreign currency liabilities by banks including future contracts, the amount of collateral pledged including its market value, and a weekly schedule of amounts falling due (including any grace periods).

Perhaps most difficult to understand in retrospect is why the CBR and MinFin did not cooperate better in July to address the robustness or even the existence of the government's weekly cash flow projections, and discuss them with IMF staff. Viugin admitted that until early August, there were elements that he did not have and only Zadornov was privy to the whole picture. If both we and the Russian officials had been better informed and prepared, at least, the actual crisis package could have been better designed and presented, at least minimizing the widely felt external effects of Russia's financial meltdown. But maybe burnout and fatigue among the players also obscured what was actually happening.

The Climax of the Crisis

By Saturday, August 15, Chubais and Dubinin were back in Moscow. Along with Gaidar, Zadornov, Aleksashenko, and Viugin, they were the core team on the Russian side, struggling to find a solution to the crisis and advising Kiriyenko on his options. They were busy examining the various alternatives that they would share with the IMF in its capacity as a trusted adviser. The IMF's role in Russia had reached an apogee of sorts. No money was on offer; for the Russians to turn to the IMF at this time reflected either a hope against hope or a desire to share the inevitable fallout, or both.

The culmination of the crisis came much more quickly than imagined. Poor Odling-Smee. On his arrival at the Metropol Hotel at 9:30 p.m. that Saturday evening, August 15, five hours late due to bad weather leaving the United States, he had flown straight through from Washington, DC, and without even stepping out of the car, he was whisked away with me to a private dinner. The setting was Arkady Murashov's Liberal Democratic Club on Bolshoi Nikitski Street in Moscow. Murashov was a Gaidar supporter from the early days and politically active in liberal party politics. His club was an appropriately discreet place for that evening's conversation. Chubais and Gaidar represented the authorities. Odling-Smee was accompanied by Odd Per Brekk, the then–deputy division chief for Russia at the IMF. Sitting at a singular roundtable in the back room of the Liberal Democratic Club, it was getting late; there was no time to lose. The meal was largely overlooked as Russia's representatives wanted to quickly reach a conclusion. Kiriyenko was awaiting their report.

With their backs to the wall, that dinner—from the Russian side—represented the last thread of hope that the outside world might still come to the rescue. The Russian representatives understood that coming away from the dinner empty-handed would mean only one thing: a financial and ultimately economic meltdown that could overnight destroy the meager achievements of Yeltsin's tenure in power, and possibly force the country down a path that could endanger the planet. But the foreigners sitting at the table already knew that there would be no last-minute miracle. The only issue was how to face the inevitable collapse while minimizing the panic among the population with its possibly unpredictable consequences for Russia and the world.

There was a review of the options. Odling-Smee had been hoping for bold policy proposals, perhaps in conjunction with a commercial financing operation. But his two Russian hosts had neither new initiatives nor financing to suggest. In that case, Odling-Smee concluded, there could be no question of opening markets on Monday without an announced plan to avert financial default and collapse of the ruble. After sighs of dashed hopes, I suggested to Chubais that the next steps were to conduct "damage control," but he shot back, with a cringe on his face, that it was rather an issue of "disaster control."

There seemed to be two basic issues to address immediately as well as a number of related questions. Clearly, the first issue was to work out a deal with creditors to restructure the stock of GKO/OFZ falling due. There was no question of a repudiation of the debt; the only issue was how to stretch out the payments in line with the country's capacity to pay. Unanticipated, it would be seen as a forced or unilateral debt restructuring, which would have enormous financial and legal implications. Since such an announcement would come as a shock to the markets, the run on the currency could only get worse, and so it might be impossible to maintain the exchange rate within the narrow band.

Gaidar, however, observed that a devaluation of the ruble was impossible, even if desirable, since it would directly contradict what the president had just said publicly the previous day. A way would need to be found to provide political cover for a more flexible exchange rate. Other questions discussed related to any new policy measures and the full implementation of outstanding program measures, the possible use of capital controls, and the implications for the Russian banking system.

As there was no question of any additional financial assistance from the IMF, its role was really to provide some outside advice and, ideally in the view of the authorities, to be seen as supporting the unprecedented steps that the government was about to take. Presumably, the public stance of the IMF would play a critical role in shaping external political and market perceptions of the Russian actions.

Before Chubais and Gaidar concluded this somber dinner discussion to report its conclusions at a postmidnight meeting with Kiriyenko, Odling-Smee queried whether the G-7 members could be asked for direct help, since now they would be staring down the certain prospect of market failure affecting their own financial systems as well as the uncertain plight of Russia. No one really knew how the Russian population would react. Cataclysmic consequences seemed to loom as a possibility. Chubais said that he would try one more time overnight with the G-7. It was agreed to meet the next morning with Zadornov and Dubinin.

In retrospect, it is extraordinary to think of two nonofficial Russians meeting in a back room to plot Russia's financial fate. They had been delegated to deal with the final decisions, maybe as a way of absolving the existing authorities from recommending the dreaded radical steps that all wanted so badly to avoid. Yet this is the way that it worked. Maybe official government representatives would have been reluctant to confront the issue in such a direct way, or take responsibility for the consequences.

The emergency measures took shape over the course of Sunday, August 16. What was disturbing is how few officials were involved in the discussions. In a supposed effort to maintain strict secrecy, the small clique of senior officials did not wish to enlarge their circle. It meant that financial experts and lawyers, who could have helped to design a more defensible and perhaps palatable package, were sidelined. I had taken the precaution to alert MinFin's highly paid, foreign debt advisers to be available for the weekend in case there was an urgent need for them. They stayed in Moscow, but their advice was never sought by their principals. Still, while I personally saw no unusual activity at the Russian White House, the contention of other writers is that the oligarchs and other bankers were mostly well informed and even contributed to elements of the final package. In looking back, there were more chefs in the kitchen than we could have imagined, even though officials who should have been involved had been excluded by design, or more likely by omission—another example of amateurs running the show.

Following the morning technical meetings, we met with Kiriyenko early on Sunday afternoon. There was broad agreement on the essential steps to adjust the exchange rate corridor and renegotiate the maturing GKO-OFZ debt with creditors. As a seeming aside, Aleksashenko mentioned the logic of imposing a temporary moratorium on the repayment of foreign loans by Russian banks, which had provided forward cover for nonresident GKO holders.

Kiriyenko concluded that he saw no other alternative, and waiting to announce the plan could only destabilize the markets and the population even further. He left by helicopter to confer with the president just outside Moscow. It was agreed to meet later that evening to review what could be announced before the markets opened the next day.

In the late afternoon, while Kiriyenko was conferring with Yeltsin, two curious developments transpired. One was when Fedorov visited us at the Metropol Hotel. He knew what the inner group was hatching as a scheme, and thought that it was an enormous mistake. Fedorov urged the IMF to withhold its support and engage in further thinking—since in his view, it was not too late.

Fedorov seemed to be the only senior Russian official prepared to talk about additional measures, perhaps even a currency board arrangement, and extraordinary steps to find commercial financing. He complained that his colleagues wouldn't listen to him and that thinking was dominated by a small, self-serving cabal. While we were sympathetic to his concerns, Odling-Smee observed that we could not dictate even if we wanted to because we had no leverage at that point and noted that the government had already decided on its package after weighing the alternatives. It was not our proudest moment.

The other unexpected discussion was a phone conversation with Camdessus as he was leaving his house in Bayonne for Paris. It suddenly seemed that Camdessus, who had been broadly supportive of the approach taken by the Russian authorities, was raising last-minute but serious concerns with a possible forced debt restructuring. Odling-Smee would have to go back to the prime minister and explain the conditions for the public endorsement of the package by the IMF.

The discussion during that evening meeting, instead of focusing on a draft of a statement that the IMF side had still not seen, became heated about what was perceived by the Russian side as last-minute sabotage, or at least abandonment, by the IMF. Stressing that he had just returned from securing the president's acquiescence to the inevitable that the IMF team was supporting a few hours earlier, Kiriyenko blurted out that it would be impossible to return to the president.

With or without the IMF, there could be no turning back. But Kiriyenko said that the IMF endorsement would be critical to the way in which the package would be perceived. Clearly Odling-Smee was in a tough spot.

Based on later conversations with Camdessus, Fischer, and Odling-Smee, it appears that there had been a misunderstanding in terms of nuances concerning what it was that the IMF would be endorsing. The fact is that with Camdessus on holiday and Fischer actively telemanaging the discussions from the IMF side, the managing director understood that a Paris Club–type of approach to creditors would be sought—that is, essentially a consensual agreement to convert short-term government securities into longer-term instruments.

It was only when Summers called Camdessus that morning in Bayonne, suggesting that the IMF might want to support a forced restructuring (while emphasizing that it was not a U.S. government position), that the latter understood fully what the Russians were proposing. It seems that the Americans had been conducting some orchestration from behind the scenes. Frustrated, Summers then initiated a conference call with Secretary Rubin (patched in from an airplane) and Camdessus later in the day that only confirmed Camdessus' fears. He made it clear to the Americans, and asked Odling-Smee to make it clear to the Russians, that the IMF would not facilitate a unilateral default.

As Argentina was to reveal four years later, the absence of predetermined mechanisms for the restructuring of sovereign debt can lead to greater economic disruption for the debtor and creditors alike than would be necessary if there were agreed-on procedures in place. For the first time since the 1930s for a major country, Russia was about to pave the way in forcing the restructuring of sovereign domestic fixed-interest securities. What was interesting, since there is a prevalent view that the IMF was under U.S. Treasury orders with respect to Russia, was that Camdessus clearly disagreed with the "private" suggestions of the treasury secretary and insisted on an alternative course of action in keeping with the closest proxy for international rules, which was the Paris Club; maybe this was not so surprising, though, since Camdessus had been a former president of the club.

Late that Sunday night Chubais came to Odling-Smee's room at the Metropol, where they proceeded to call Camdessus, who was by that time in Paris before flying on to Washington, DC, the next day. During the forty-five-minute call, I could only hear Chubais's side of the discussion. Angry, frustrated, and even menacing, Chubais tried to prevail, but Camdessus refused to budge. In the end, it was agreed that the government's statement would make no mention of the conditions for a debt restructuring but would invite creditors to participate in elaborating an approach. In exchange, Camdessus would issue a mild statement of support.

They agreed to meet early the next morning again, before the statement was to be announced to the media. The Russian officials wanted to secure if not a statement of support, at least a statement from the IMF that would express "understanding" of the difficult steps taken.

Given the focus on this one issue, we didn't even get to see a draft of the statement the next morning in Kiriyenko's office. Although the hurried discussion was clearly more cordial than that of the previous evening, the focus was once again on the issue of GKO-restructuring conditions. The statement was issued at 9:30 a.m. on August 17. The government's plan provided for three sets of measures:

• introducing a new ruble corridor to disguise a floating exchange rate for the ruble with its depreciation to roughly nine rubles per dollar by the end of the year
• introducing a three-month moratorium on the repayment of Russian banks' external debt
• a compulsory GKO/OFZ debt-restructuring scheme to be negotiated with creditors.

At the time of the meltdown, the Russian government had a domestic (ruble-denominated) debt of about 340 billion rubles, then equivalent to about US$55 billion, and a sovereign foreign debt of about US$150 billion, two-thirds of which had been inherited from the Soviet days. To this could be added commercial bank obligations, including future ruble contracts worth about US$6 billion that had been signed with Western investors seeking to hedge against devaluation risk. There was an obvious fear in the markets that a massive series of Russian defaults would trigger financial shock waves throughout the world economy.

Markets, having just opened, plunged. Since the whole operation had been so poorly coordinated, the markets were not told to close promptly, and some trading continued until midmorning on the MICEX, the main Russian stock exchange—an issue that became the subject of a number of lawsuits. Responding to this unprecedented financial collapse, once the news was confirmed by MinFin later in the morning, the MICEX Directorate suspended trading, clearing, and settlement operations for all derivative instruments, including foreign currency futures contracts. The prevailing sentiments in the markets, in Russia and abroad, were shock and confusion. The shock, despite abundant leaks over the previous weekend, was understandable.

Less comprehensible was the confusion reflecting the amateurish preparation of the package without even involving the government's own foreign legal and investment advisers until after the announcement. Likewise, senior financial officials at MinFin and the CBR were unaware of the decisions, and no thought had been given to talking points for the media. No mechanism was established from the outset to explain the practical implications of the announced package, or deal with a multitude of queries from worried investors and their lawyers. In the meantime, the IMF issued its statement of lukewarm support for the authorities' actions.

Monday, August 17, 1998, is now etched in the contemporary history of Russia—perhaps as significant a date as December 25, 1991, when an independent Russia emerged from the collapse of the Soviet Union. Many pondered at the time whether the experiment in forging Russia as a modern, democratic, market-oriented country had failed.

Enough has already been written about this period in the aftershock of the government's announcement. While the thesis of this book is that August 1998 was a watershed for the Russian economy, the singular event that transformed all the previous prevarications of the Russian authorities into their worst nightmare, it should be apparent that in the immediate aftermath, the underlying causes of the crisis were still there, although their economic and political forms were now modified.

The August crisis was set to remain a key factor for Russian economic and political development for a long time to come. The world was also shocked, and the impact of Russia's debt default and unilateral moratorium on debt payments reverberated in global markets, almost culminating in a major international financial crisis.[2] It might have made a substantial difference in perceptions if it had been clarified at the outset that only domestic ruble-denominated securities were involved and all external obligations as well as domestic dollar-denominated securities would be paid in full as scheduled.

Owing to the intervention of the IMF, the package announced on August 17 did not include a specific domestic government debt-restructuring scheme but nevertheless elicited a massively negative response from the financial markets. The announcement of the proposed GKO-restructuring terms was postponed several times at the IMF's insistence so that creditors could be consulted and a mutually agreeable approach could be developed. The IMF team was insisting that in addition to a consensual restructuring of the GKO debt, the associated terms should not involve any unfinanced gaps for 1999. There were also major concerns about legal issues and the related standstill on private sector external debt as an extension of the moratorium on bank liabilities.

A proposed restructuring scheme was finally published by the government with a one-week delay. The amount of frozen domestic sovereign debt totaled 265.3 billion rubles (US$42.2 billion at the exchange rate as of August 14). What remained in circulation was a total of 75 billion rubles of OFZ maturing in 2000–2001.

The stock market plunged by a further 29 percent in just a week, and a major concern was holding the exchange rate within the new corridor (the ruble depreciated by 10 percent, from 6.3 rubles per dollar to 7 rubles per dollar, by August 19 on the interbank market, although trading on the street for cash dollars was reportedly exceeding 9.5 rubles per dollar). The gross foreign reserves fell to US$14 billion. Further downward pressure on the ruble was being driven by a rapid expansion of credit as the CBR extended liquidity to relieve pressure on the commercial banks.

In a briefing to the IMF board on August 19, Camdessus observed that it was important to acknowledge that the Russian financial crisis was exceptional not only for Russia but also for the IMF and indeed the entire world. While close cooperation between the Russian authorities and the IMF staff had been maintained during the period when the emergency measures announced on August 17 were being formulated, the measures—in terms of both content and timing—were entirely the choice of the Russian authorities themselves.

He went on to say that the IMF would have preferred a different course of action. First, the involuntary rescheduling of debt was undesirable not only for Russia's credit worthiness but also for the global financial system. Second, devaluation should be considered in the context of a fully formulated monetary and fiscal policy, for the success of which devaluation was deemed to be indispensable. Third, any emergency measures would best have been postponed until after the Duma had met to consider the full package of measures agreed on by the government in July. The Russian authorities had, however, decided that Russia could not wait and drastic steps had to be taken immediately.

Camdessus also noted that a devaluation is always an indication of a failure in policy, not just of the country, but of the system as well. Fischer observed to the IMF board that the August crisis represented the spectacular failure of Russia's economic program supported by the IMF.

A hastily assembled IMF mission arrived at the beginning of the week, as Odling-Smee left Moscow. The team was there to provide technical support to the authorities in trying to design steps to minimize the negative impact of the crisis. Inconsequential meetings were held that week on the various poignant issues such as GKO debt restructuring or the banks, but senior officials seemed incapable of making any decisions. That said, on August 20, the CBR announced a policy of guaranteeing household deposits in Russian banks (if these deposits were transferred to Sberbank). The Duma did meet in a special session but considered no legislation. Its focus was limited to attacking the government for its handling of the crisis. Meanwhile, the government was in a state of paralysis, and the Kremlin was completely silent. In almost all of the meetings, no one had a plan or even much of a sense of responsibility. There was a definite *fin de règne* atmosphere.

Only Fedorov, who was still the head of the STS and a deputy prime minister, was trying to work out a deal on the GKO restructuring, but he couldn't get access to the data from MinFin. For instance, in a meeting with the mission on August 21, he contended that there could be one last round of money creation by the CBR in the form of targeted credits to distressed banks and the government to repay its arrears and settle outstanding short-term debt obligations—much like the original monetization option. Recognizing that such a course of action would be inflationary, he suggested that inflationary expectations could be dampened by carefully publicizing that the purpose of the operation was only to clear the overhang of nominal claims on the government and banks, after which there would be a drastic tightening of credit policy.

The Denouement: Political and Economic

Five months to the day after he was plucked from relative obscurity to head Russia's government, Kiriyenko and his administration were unceremoniously dismissed on August 23. Chernomyrdin was called on by Yeltsin to form a new government. It seemed that after the reckless adventure with a young band of amateurs, the reins of power were returning to the tested and steady hands of experience and stability. Surely one aspect of the appointment was to try to calm public fear, which was growing by the day.

In retrospect, though, it appears that at least in part, the extent of the economic dislocation that followed in the wake of August 17 derived mainly from the power vacuum created by Yeltsin's decision to dismiss the government. Without firm leadership and control over activities in the "frozen" financial markets, the implausible silence of the Kremlin simply amplified the uncertainty, and fed rumors of intrigues and plotting, with some even suggesting an oligarch-inspired move to bring Chernomyrdin in to replace Yeltsin, who might "retire" early. Other rumors circulated that the crisis was triggered by that very intent in the first place. One rumor was that the fall of the Kiriyenko government was orchestrated by Berezovsky, because he and the other top bankers feared that the government would strike a fair deal between domestic and foreign creditors. By convincing the president to dismiss Kiriyenko, and lobbying hard for Chernomyrdin to replace him, the banking oligarchs could feel safe from the threat of equal treatment for Western investors.

This conspiracy theory was given added weight by Nemtsov, who claimed that the government had been preparing to bankrupt some of the politically powerful yet economically weak banks and oil companies, allowing others, including Westerners, to take over.[3]

It soon became clear that Chernomyrdin did not have any strategy for extracting Russia from the quagmire it was in. Almost his first step as acting prime minister, after initially attempting to lobby the Duma for support and before its vote on his confirmation, was to seek an urgent meeting with Camdessus. Although Camdessus understood well that the new acting prime minister was clutching at straws, he felt that accepting the meeting might at least steady nerves for the unpalatable tasks that any Russian government would be facing in those difficult days.

The managing director at first proposed a meeting in Paris, but it was difficult to create an alibi for such a meeting in the middle of the crisis. Then, under the cover of a prearranged meeting with Ukranian president Kuchma, it was decided to meet privately at a dinner in Foroz, the presidential dacha in the Crimea (now part of Ukraine after the dissolution of the USSR), where Gorbachev had been held as a prisoner of the aborted putsch some seven years earlier. On the evening of August 25, Chernomyrdin flew off to his secret rendezvous with Camdessus in Crimea, accompanied only by Mozhin, Fedorov, and Aleksashenko. After a much-too-long dinner with Kuchma talking about football, the private discussion began after midnight, focusing on dealing with a collapsed banking and payment system, tightening monetary policy, and defending the exchange rate. The only concrete measure explored was a possible windfall tax on exporters profiting from the ruble devaluation.

Finally, Chernomyrdin spoke at length about a Duma strategy and timetable.

On August 28, the Duma rejected Chernomyrdin in its first consideration of his nomination, and did so again on September 7. Meanwhile, the financial markets remained in crisis mode, and the CBR suspended foreign exchange trading on the MICEX for a second straight day on August 28. In fact, the last quoted official rate was 7.86 rubles per dollar, which was both obsolete and confusing since no transactions could take place at that rate, whereas the market rate had reached about 10 rubles per dollar. Irate depositors were besieging closed banks such as SBS-Agro, panic buying was spreading in markets and shops, food hoarding was taking place, it was hard to find cash dollars at exchange points, and queues were visible for the first time since the end of the immediate post-Soviet collapse.

Urgent decisions needed to be made on the remaining core of a banking system, and the CBR had to announce its intention to let the ruble float freely—and preserve its remaining reserves for a time when exchange rate stability could be secured through supportive fiscal and monetary policies. Up until that point, those policies, such as they were, accommodated an acceleration of inflation.

Espoused by Fedorov, who remained proactive in trying to find workable measures, the idea of a currency board was being actively promoted. Fedorov even prevailed on Domingo Cavallo, the architect of Argentina's currency board and initially successful stabilization, to visit Moscow to try to convince officials and public opinion of its merits. Cavallo arrived in Moscow on September 1, and traveled on to Kiev, where the fallout from the Russian crisis was severe.

Indeed, a chorus of international opinion was calling for the adoption of a currency board arrangement, including not only the usual proponents such as Steve Hanke but Soros and others as well. Little did these well-meaning observers seem to understand that they were trying to place the proverbial cart before the horse. If Russia did not have the political maturity and discipline to honor its most basic fiscal obligations, what hope could there be that it would accept the even more constraining consequences of a currency board?

As many of those senior officials confided, a currency board might sound like an attractive idea in the midst of a crisis, but it was probably impossible to implement—at least under the prevailing political regime. In addition, it would require Duma legislation (which seemed utopian given the overall hostility) and would need to be carefully prepared. While ready to explore the possibility in the context of a real, strong policy package, there was little enthusiasm in the IMF for such an improbable solution.

A particular Russian variant of a possible policy approach, pushed by Fedorov, was to have one large round of money issue—or what he called "controlled emission"—in order to solve the outstanding debt problem, and then lock in to a currency board supported by the IMF and the international community. For the IMF, this was a nonstarter. Planning for a currency board after a deliberate policy of hyperinflation, in the political environment that would likely exist in Russia at least until the scheduled 2000 presidential elections, and with fiscal policy in disarray, was just plain unrealistic. As noted earlier, Federov would have favored the option of monetizing all the GKO instead of the default, as he tried to explain during his visit to us at the Metropol, but this was the option explicitly rejected as too radical.

On August 28, a senior official in the reformer wing of the government said to me in a private discussion that he concluded that the current management of the country had come to the end of the road. There would be no confidence whatsoever in a new Chernomyrdin government because of its responsibility for the country's plight (few people actually blamed Kiriyenko, who was seen as having to deal with the mess left behind by his predecessor) and even more so because there was no confidence in Yeltsin.

This senior official thought that there was truth in the rumor that Yeltsin might resign and this was indeed behind the decision to change the government. Reportedly backed by the oligarchs led by Berezovsky, the plan was for Yeltsin to resign in the autumn, and for Chernomyrdin to take over and then call a presidential election early in the new year. It was not clear why Yeltsin would do this, but that seemed to be the political strategy. As a consequence, no bold economic initiatives could be expected. Price and exchange controls were instead likely. Public behavior seemed to reflect the plausibility at least of those types of measures.

As the crisis deepened, regional governors had been introducing emergency measures. In Krasnoyarsk Krai in Siberia, Governor Lebed had signed a resolution to hold down prices "using administrative methods," a television report said. It was reported that the authorities in the far eastern city of Vladivostok had banned deliveries of food to areas beyond the port city, and there had been talk of introducing rationing there. In

Russia's Kaliningrad enclave on the Baltic, the governor announced a suspension of tax payments to the federal authorities.

The regional budgets also suffered from the crisis. The spending of the regions declined from 18.2 percent of GDP in 1997 to 14.8 percent. It dropped another 1 percent of GDP in 1999 to 13.8 percent. One of the main factors in the reduction was the decline in subsidies for housing and municipal services, from 3.5 to 2.7 percent of GDP.

On September 1, after having spent US$9 billion of its foreign exchange reserves in an effort to defend the currency in July and August, the CBR announced that it would no longer support the ruble exchange rate on the MICEX. The next day the official rate established on the MICEX was 10.9 rubles per dollar, as against the upper limit to the band announced on August 17 of 9.5 rubles per dollar. The CBR made the case that given the weakened financial situation of banks as a result of losses on assets and the temporary moratorium, the collapse of the GKO market removed the key instrument for redistributing liquidity among the banks.

The CBR allowed favored commercial banks to use their frozen GKOs as collateral for loans, which were promptly used to buy dollars. Over four days, from August 17 to 21, the CBR disbursed a total of fifty-six billion rubles. As a result, the banks facing problems in honoring their liabilities triggered a chain reaction in the form of a massive run on bank deposits and a sharp rise in the demand for foreign currency. In turn, this aggravated the financial standing even of those banks whose stability had not been questioned.

Duma opposition to the return of Chernomyrdin appeared to be overwhelming. Russia's economic and political crisis deepened on August 30, when the Communists said they would vote against Chernomyrdin's appointment as premier as well as oppose a reportedly informal agreement previously worked out between the Kremlin, Duma factions, and the government in dealing with the economic collapse. Opposition to Chernomyrdin, as Yeltsin's candidate for prime minister, came to be considered as a proxy for opposing the president.

In an act of semirebellion, the Duma seemed poised to back Moscow mayor Luzhkov as its candidate for the premiership. The ambitious mayor had his eyes set on the presidency, and this ultimate prize suddenly seemed to be within his grasp if he could first secure the position of prime minister. In desperation, Yeltsin's advisers abandoned Chernomyrdin's candidacy, and the then–Kremlin chief of staff Valentin Yumashev suggested instead the candidacy of Primakov, the wily foreign minister, as the lesser of two evils since he was probably more pragmatic, predictable, and inclined to compromise. Yeltsin in the end accepted Primakov, who was approved by the Duma on September 11.

With the intention of providing a new departure to economic policy inspired by experts from the late Gorbachev era, the new prime minister proceeded to effect major personnel changes in the upper reaches of government. Maslyukov was given the overall direction of the economy as first deputy prime minister, harking back to his old days at the Gosplan, and Shokhin, the ever-opportunistic "reformer," was brought back into government based on his reputation at knowing how to extract money from the IMF and World Bank with minimum strings attached. Zadornov retained his position, although with much-reduced clout— being mistrusted by all for the financial disaster. He was seemingly desperate to keep his MinFin portfolio even at the price of working with Shokhin and then Maslyukov.

Dubinin resigned formally as head of the CBR on September 7, and Alexashenko's days as acting chair were limited. More than anyone else, even Kiriyenko, Dubinin felt the weight of responsibility for the crisis and the numerous policy mistakes that led to it. He thought that everyone had let him down, even supposed friends and supporters. He was crushed. In some ways, though, Dubinin must have also been relieved. I recall him saying that being CBR chair was a dangerous business given the powerful vested interests that had to be resisted, and shots that were fired at his apartment in 1996 and again in 1998 appeared to underscore the point.

Eventually, during the course of the autumn, Potemkin and then Kozlov left. Potemkin later became the president of MICEX, although he was made the scapegoat when the market crashed in September 2008. Kozlov returned to his old position at the CBR when Ignatiev moved to head the CBR. As we know too well, he was gunned down in cold blood in September 2006, presumably in retaliation for his withdrawal of bank licenses. Nadezhda Ivanova, head of the bank's general economics department, was removed from the CBR board (although she was later reinstated when the management changed), and the professionalism of the CBR suffered. MinFin, with Zadornov, Kasyanov, Ignatiev, and Viugin, then became the primary professional institution in formulating economic policy.

With an ironic sense of timing, President Clinton flew to Moscow on September 1, for a previously scheduled visit whose agenda had obviously been reshuffled at the last minute. His new agenda contained one principal, and pressing, item. This was an urgent plea to Russia to adopt tough measures to stop its chaotic economic slide and not turn back the clock to the "failed policies of the past." "Today's financial crisis does not require you to abandon your march toward freedom and free markets," Clinton said in a speech. Implicit in his urgings seemed to be a warning: if you don't take this path, don't expect any more money out of us. At that time, Clinton certainly had other things on his mind as he was facing impeachment by the U.S. House of Representatives on charges of perjury and obstruction of justice in relation to the Monica Lewinsky scandal.

Worries about International Contagion

IMF concerns about the possible international ramifications of the Russian crisis proved to be warranted. Within weeks there was a run on the currency in Brazil, and Ecuador defaulted on some of its foreign debt by early 1999. Moreover, in September and early October, indications of heightened concern about liquidity and counterparty risk emerged in some of the world's deepest financial markets. A key development was the news of difficulties in and ultimately the near failure of a major U.S. hedge fund—Long-Term Capital Management (LTCM)—which had large, highly leveraged positions across a broad range of markets along with substantial links with a range of U.S. and European financial institutions.

Although a private rescue of LTCM, organized with the help of the New York Federal Reserve Bank, was announced on September 23, the market reverberations intensified in the ensuing weeks as previous positions were unwound, and as concerns increased about the extent to which other financial institutions might be in trouble or face a need to unload assets into illiquid markets at distressed prices. In response to these developments, market volatility increased sharply and there were some significant departures from normal pricing relationships among different asset classes.

These developments were a particularly visible manifestation of a global move by investors to close out open positions and reduce leverage in the wake of the heightened market turmoil provoked by the sudden risk aversion emanating as the direct consequence of the crisis in Russia. In response, the U.S. Federal Reserve moved to cut interest rates on three occasions beginning in late September. These moves sent a clear signal that the U.S. monetary authorities were prepared to move aggressively, if needed, to ensure normal market functioning. Starting in mid-October, a significant degree of calm returned to the financial markets. Indicators of reduced liquidity and heightened counterparty risk were substantially, though not completely, reversed, and exchange rate volatility declined somewhat.

The G-7 deputy finance ministers, worried about alarming signals on the world markets and especially concerned about the financial collapse in Russia, held a meeting in London on September 14. Odling-Smee briefed the ministers and then flew on to Moscow to meet with Primakov. Odling-Smee's message was unrepentant: the August collapse should not lead to the conclusion that the whole course of reforms was ill conceived. Rather, the problem was that Russia achieved insufficient fiscal adjustment and structural reform. The IMF thus would not support a strategy that departed from the reform course, which if anything, should be accelerated. As Fischer later remarked,

The Russian devaluation and debt restructuring set off a huge crisis for the rest of the emerging markets. One has to wonder how people can both have been investing at triple digit interest rates and expecting that in the end the West would find the money to enable Russia to continue to pay. Surely they should have understood that the markets were telling them something. Actually, there may be an explanation. The people who did not expect Russia to be able to pay were already out of the market. Those who remained in the market were the optimists, who thought that somehow the market had got it wrong. Those were the people who appeared genuinely shocked when Russia could no longer pay.[4]

Gerashchenko was appointed CBR chair on September 12. More precisely, the colorful ex-Soviet banker was reappointed, having served as CBR chair from 1992 through most of October 1994, and even earlier as the last chair of the Soviet Gosbank. The legacy of his earlier stint as CBR chair remains controversial even today. The fact is that he did try to channel direct central bank credit to enterprises during summer and fall 1992 in an effort to stimulate domestic production. But once he realized that the credits were misdirected and wouldn't be repaid, he quickly turned off the tap. Steeled by his strongly, if single-mindedly, monetarist first deputy, Tatiana Paramonova, the two resisted the powerful pressures to reflate and engineered an impressive deceleration of money growth. Indeed, the resulting pressures on some banks may have been directly responsible for the sudden but short-lived ruble collapse in October 1994, also known as Black Tuesday.

In any case, Gerashchenko certainly was not the world's worst central banker, as Sachs ignobly called him, but—like many central bankers in a politically charged environment—he was simply trying to survive. He also brought Paramonova back to her old position to control monetary policy. After Black Tuesday, Paramonova became the acting chair of the CBR until Dubinin was appointed a year later, in November 1995. She played a key role during that time as a monetary hawk who resisted the enormous outside pressures to ease liquidity, brought inflation down dramatically, and stabilized the exchange rate. Gerashchenko also, unfortunately, brought in some anachronistic elements to some crucial management positions such as bank supervision and reform, the international department, and foreign exchange regulation. On September 18, the CBR repeated the monetary injection, allowing favored banks first to borrow twenty-seven billion rubles, with which they could settle their debts, and then to repay those loans with basically worthless GKO. Foreign GKO holders were excluded from such operations.

Following the collapse of a large number of banks in the aftermath of the 1998 crisis, the authorities made little use of the power granted within the existing legal framework to place ailing banks under administration. There was neither the political will nor the administrative capacity, despite a surge of foreign technical assistance. By the time these banks were subjected to bankruptcy procedures, they had become mostly empty shells. All of the assets had been stripped, and only the debts remained on the balance sheets. A bank restructuring agency—the Agency for Restructuring Credit Institutions (ARCO)—that was created in late 1998 with much fanfare involving IMF and World Bank advice, had relatively little to do with the major banks.

Hints of Scandal Emerge

In retrospect, it would have been surprising if there had not been significant controversy given the scale of the financial collapse in Russia. After all, the new Russian prime minister was engaged in a high-profile campaign against "profiteers," calling for the prosecutor general's office to seek out and punish such people. What was unexpected was the amplitude of the seeming hysteria reached when "scandals" started to emerge in the wake of the crisis. The remarkable media feeding frenzy probably deserves a serious study in its own right, including what in my view was unwarranted self-righteousness on the part of much of the foreign press.

The first scandal—of the many of increasing ferocity to develop over the next year or so—surrounded some remarks made by Chubais in an interview on September 8, 1998, with *Kommersant*. His comments gave rise to a *Los Angeles Times* report about deceiving the IMF in which the question "Do the authorities have the right to lie?" was juxtaposed with the IMF, and was misinterpreted as if the lying was directed at the IMF. Other than journalistic sleight of hand and misinterpretation, it was clear from the text that Chubais did not say that the authorities lied to the IMF but rather that they were able to "get away with it." He was obviously referring to the authorities' misleading the population at large about whether or not there would be a devaluation. Chubais issued a clarification, which the *Los Angeles Times* declined to publish. In any case, the notion itself is almost nonsensical in that the IMF was fully engaged with the Russian authorities in their efforts to cope with the consequences of insufficient fiscal adjustment in the context of a serious deterioration in external circumstances. The IMF executive board, management, and staff knew plainly that the whole operation was risky, but decided to go ahead in July with the big support package in full knowledge of those risks.

This was only the first of many efforts in Russia and elsewhere to exaggerate or present a one-sided view of events to feed the prejudices of those who felt strongly that Russia was on the wrong track.

Days later, while the Chubais scandal was still hot—indeed raising heated questions in the U.S. Congress (whose opinion often seemed to be the target of the scandal mongers)—another one broke out. On September 21, based on an interview with the BBC, wire services started carrying a story that Venyamin Sokolov, an auditor in Russia's Accounting Chamber (which reports to the Duma), said that billions of dollars in aid sent by the West had been wasted. Some of the press reports contained allegations that Russia's disbursement from the IMF the previous July may have been misused.

Sokolov almost immediately said that he had been misunderstood, and the Accounting Chamber had not carried out any audit on the spending from the July tranche—and he clarified that he was saying nothing new. He was simply reiterating his own view of what he had been claiming in public for many months: that Western aid had been misused in many ways—because Western aid, including IMF money, was used to finance the budget, and he was sure that budgetary spending had gone astray, frequently through corruption. He had made a presentation along these lines the previous spring to a number of groups in Washington, DC, including on Capitol Hill. It should be noted that especially at that time, the Accounting Chamber was a politicized body with each auditor representing a political faction in the Duma. Sokolov himself had been appointed by the Communist faction.

Sokolov's remarks as well as those by Chubais received undue attention, at least in Moscow, as a result of an effort to identify those responsible for what went wrong, and who could be blamed for the economic and financial crisis. A common line of attack that seemed to be emerging even at that early stage was that money was stolen or misused. The situation was reminiscent of an inquiry by the Federal Security Bureau, a successor to the KGB, launched in October 1994 in the wake of Black Tuesday, when the ruble collapsed. Security investigators and police were sent in to uncover a supposed dark, criminal conspiracy to spin immense personal fortunes out of the destruction of the Russian currency. Yet Black Tuesday was caused not by criminal gangs but instead by the government's own inconsistent monetary and fiscal policies.

One reflection of this was an accusation by Russia's then–prosecutor general, Yuri Skuratov, on September 20 that the CBR had misused billions of dollars disbursed by the IMF in July. On September 21, Dubinin published a denial in which he explained how IMF money had been placed, as usual, in foreign exchange reserves, apart from the agreed-on amount that was transferred to the budget, and he claimed that the CBR could account for every cent of the IMF loan.

It should be rather obvious that there is no meaningful way in which the use of IMF financing could or should be tracked, unlike in the case of project loans, since it was used for general balance of payments and budgetary support. Yet it was also perhaps understandable that some Russians, particularly those opposed to the Kiriyenko government, such as Skuratov, viewed a major reduction in reserves as an improper use of money. As it turned out, these scandals were only a warm-up for what was to come later. The net result of these brewing scandals was that the IMF as well as Russian officials had to spend an inordinate amount of time and energy fending off attacks rather than concentrating on preventing spreading chaos.

Prospects for an Economic Collapse

The rush of events, the feeling of being pulled down into a financial black hole, and the seeming lack of anyone in charge all certainly laid the basis for the overwhelming impression as the crisis unfolded in mid-August that the outlook for the future would be, at best, bleak. Many commentators spoke of growing unrest amid a return to Soviet-style shortages with unforeseeable consequences. It seemed like the immediate task was to avoid—or at least minimize—a total economic collapse.

Primakov and his team, representing an alternative to the failed reforms, hardly appeared up to the task. Nevertheless, his reassuring presence as the head of the government during those disturbing times, with the increasing possibility that he would even become the next president, steadied nerves. In many ways, at least seen from the outside, that was about it. Despite much talk about dirigisme, such as an anticrisis plan drafted by previously underemployed academics, mostly from Soviet times, which was presented to the new government on September 15, in the end Primakov took no action. And still the collapse did not happen.

At the time, just after the events of August, the prospects for hyperinflation and economic collapse were real. After all, as noted above, even Fedorov was promoting the idea of some novel approach he called "controlled money emission." In any case, Fedorov (who ultimately was not included in the Primakov government) was at least trying to find a way out of the crisis, which only seemed to deepen into September with a further aggravation of the economic and financial situation arising from the devaluation of the ruble and the erosion of confidence in the Russian currency.

A devaluation of the ruble by two-thirds leading to a spike in prices of imports and a continuing injection of liquidity in the face of a collapsing demand for ruble money accounted for a rapid rise in consumer prices. In August prices rose by 3.7 percent and in September they increased by 38.4 percent.

Eventually, the rate of inflation slowed down concurrently with a temporary appreciation of the ruble. This was largely due to the monetary policy pursued by the CBR starting in late September with Paramonova in charge. In August, however, a loose monetary policy had no doubt exacerbated the pressures on the ruble. There was practically no change in base money in August despite the fact that the CBR had spent about six billion U.S. dollars out of its foreign exchange reserves. Apparently, the contractionary effects of the foreign exchange losses were fully offset as a result of operations with government debt and the disbursement of stabilization loans to commercial banks.

The population's apprehension reached a crescendo by early September 1998. The problems in obtaining cash dollars and even cash rubles had a sharp adverse impact on the retail trade, especially small traders working on a purely cash basis. Moreover, imports, especially of consumer goods, almost came to a halt without a settlement system in place.

Queues formed, and the specter of Soviet times descended on Moscow and other major cities. As veterans of such crises, the Russian population remained calm and even resigned. Answers were expected from the Kremlin along the lines of Lenin's proverbial "What is to be done?" and "Who is to blame?" but no answers came.

That said, ironically, it seemed that the situation outside Moscow and other big cities was not so severely affected. The point often made is that having not benefited much from the upswing, these places were largely immune to the financial implosion as well. In fact, some of the regional banks, which had not borrowed abroad because of limited market access and did not hold much government paper, survived in better condition than virtually all the big Moscow-based banks that had participated in GKO financing.

The poor preparation for dealing with the aftermath of the crisis, the lack of leadership from Yeltsin on down in addressing urgent issues, and the political limbo that was allowed to fester for almost a month after August 17 were all startling breaches of public confidence as seen from the outside, even if many Russians grudgingly accepted such passivity as almost normal. During this period, some oligarchs and others with large outstanding loans were engaged in asset stripping, and others were moving whatever assets they still had in Russia offshore. Although perhaps not in all cases, these moves were at least tolerated, if not abetted, by the authorities.

Urgent actions were required for dealing with defrauded depositors, a collapsing payments system, falling tax revenues, asset stripping, and many unhappy investors. The delays in the announcement of terms to be agreed on with creditors for the restructuring of GKO/OFZs were wearing thin whatever residual support Russia still enjoyed among investors with a view to the long term. Likewise, the temporary moratorium on the foreign credits of banks was equally subject to widespread abuse. Threats and counterthreats, including litigation and the possible invocation of cross-default clauses, proliferated. The staff members at CSFB, the largest private foreign investor in Russia, were irate at being excluded from discussions on debt restructuring, and David Folkerts-Landau, the economist for emerging markets at Deutsche Bank in London who had been decidedly bullish on Russia prior to August 17, as he was so sure of an international bailout, purportedly engaged in a curious and bitter attempt to reinterpret events in a conference call with investors on August 26. One investment banker was famously reported to have remarked, "I'd rather eat nuclear waste than invest again in Russia."

The problem on the government side was that no one was clearly in charge. It was obvious that Kiriyenko's team and the CBR management were doomed after August 17. Then the fiasco with Chernomyrdin only had the effect of unnecessarily prolonging the limbo. In fact, until Primakov was confirmed by the Duma on September 11, all the members of the government were "acting" rather than confirmed in their positions—hardly a recipe for encouraging the initiation of bold policies in the midst of a crisis.

Maslyukov, having briefly served in the Kiriyenko government, was made responsible for economic policy, but initially Shokhin was brought back into government as a deputy prime minister in charge of financial policy, meaning obtaining money from abroad, which could only mean from the IFIs, following the crisis. There had obviously been a bitter clash of views between Zadornov and Shokhin, with Shokhin insisting that Zadornov was responsible for the crisis and had to be dropped from the new cabinet. Shokhin didn't get his way, but it was clear that Zadornov would have to trim his sails to remain in government.

The IMF's previous experience with Shokhin, when he occupied a similar position in 1992–1994, was not a happy one. Famously ambitious, cynical, and clever, yet with an uncanny intuition and sense of timing, his seeming one objective during that earlier time had been to get money from the IMF with as few conditions attached as possible. In the context of a country with what the IMF staff would call a particularly poor track record at the time, Shokhin's own credibility was especially low.

During his ten days back in the government, Shokhin suggested that Russia's debts to the Paris Club should be netted out against the nominal one hundred billion U.S. dollars that Russia was owed by former Soviet client states such as Nicaragua, Angola, North Korea, and Iraq. Claiming that it had been a mistake for Russia to join the Paris Club in 1997, he went on to propose to negotiate mutual offsets of the Russian obligations to the Paris Club and the obligations to Russia of the countries with which the Paris Club had conducted negotiations on rescheduling debts with the possible outcome being a zero option.

That said, the IMF staff members were trained to assess policies, not personalities, and so a mission, headed by Marquez-Ruarte, met with him on a number of occasions during his ten days in government. Suddenly, on September 25, shortly after a final meeting in which Marquez-Ruarte made it clear that the economic program supported by the IMF approved the previous July was virtually dead, and no money would be disbursed until a new policy framework could be negotiated and a track record of actual performance recorded, Shokhin resigned. Maslyukov himself effectively took over the responsibility for relations with the IFIs.

An anxious world looked on as Russia seemed to drift in autumn 1998. Discussions with the IMF and the World Bank about ways to revive financial support continued during the annual meeting in Washington, DC, at the beginning of October where the Russian delegation, headed by Gerashchenko and Zadornov, met with Camdessus on October 3. They continued in Moscow in late October, and again in the second half of November. Plans were discussed, including Maslyukov's anticrisis program on October 28. But the two sides were far apart and indeed not even speaking the same language—despite excellent interpreters from the IMF Moscow office. The IMF held an informal seminar on November 30 in Washington attended by academics and experts to seek the views of others—which was somewhat unusual for the IMF in those days, and underscored the difficulty in formulating appropriate steps in such a risk-charged atmosphere.

Educating Maslyukov, a gregarious, well-meaning, but economically illiterate man, was an uphill endeavor. His instincts as a Soviet manager and then minister were to draw up a plan based on the best conceptual scheme and then have it implemented under close government control. He had no feel for the market, much less for market economics. Maslyukov certainly did not understand the world of finance, which in Soviet economics played little more than a bookkeeping role. Even less did he appreciate the role of the IMF, admittedly a misperception shared with Primakov and other top government officials. That entire fall, Maslyukov and his colleagues kept asking for the IMF to disburse the remaining amounts "promised" the previous July, and the IMF staff members kept trying to explain that disbursements were tied to performance under an economic program whose main goal was medium-term sustainability.

Meanwhile, despite the numerous consultations with Soviet-era experts and other erstwhile advisers, including Communist Duma deputies, and the rhetoric, which kept sounding as if a new national plan was about to be announced, the government actually displayed a high degree of pragmatism—perhaps despite itself.

In the government's caution not to make things worse, almost no decisions were taken. Yes, eventually a scheme to restructure GKO debt was announced in November, with Primakov signing the resolution on the restructuring of GKO on December 15, and Kasyanov bravely tried to salvage Russia's reputation in the Paris Club. The Paris Club had even considered the possibility of barring Russia's future participation as a creditor or invoking the default clause in the 1996 agreed-on minutes since the IMF program was irretrievably off track. Despite payment problems and a complete lack of government focus on the issue, Kasyanov tried to cope. The CBR also announced plans—but little more—for dealing with the banking collapse, although formally it went through the motions of establishing ARCO at the insistence of the IFIs and began a few limited operations with secondary banks in 1999. But Paramonova, ever vigilant about the monetary base, kept a tight rein on credit. Some of her less economically conversant colleagues on the CBR's new management team raised the surrender requirement on export proceeds to 75 percent and tightened foreign exchange controls (both measures being ineffective and economically costly).

The consequence of government inaction was, perhaps unintentionally, to run a tight macroeconomic policy. With no financing available, the government could only spend what it received in the form of revenues. That said, MinFin officials downplayed proposals to inflate and performed a major role in stabilizing the situation.

Since little was being done about the present, the focus of discussion in the government shifted, also by necessity in view of the timing, to the aggregates of the draft 1999 budget. It became the basic assumption of the Primakov government's policy stance that the revenue projections were optimistic, and so real spending would have to be cut drastically as implied by its draft budget, and even then impartial observers and the IMF were skeptical that the targeted deficit would be financeable.

Indeed, Primakov intervened directly with the IMF mission when he became irritated with continuing reports from his staff of posturing by the mission, whose concerns with the budget proposals were seen as merely a pretext to withhold the promised money. There was a showdown with Marquez-Ruarte on November 21, when Primakov insisted on a face-to-face meeting. On both sides, the discussion did little to advance understanding, and Primakov, following his instincts that this was really a political problem, appealed directly to the G-7 to stop the charade using the IMF team as its pawn.

Primakov then and later did not accept the IMF's position at face value. When Primakov had asked about the availability of the undisbursed amount of the IMF credit, Marquez-Ruarte told him that the agreed-on program was so far off track that its basic targets and objectives were no longer achievable. Instead, he suggested focusing on a new program for 1999 to address the immediate macroeconomic stabilization problems, advance structural reforms, and deal with the banks and debt restructuring—and noted that what Maslyukov was proposing was inadequate. He also criticized aspects of the government's emergency economic plan of October 31, which would actually make the fiscal situation even worse and entail a move away from the market-oriented policies needed to establish economic growth in Russia.

Primakov's view was completely different. He said, in sum, that the IMF—as the financial conduit of the G-7—had promised a large amount of money to Russia. This money was now urgently needed in the context of circumstances even more difficult than envisaged when the program was approved in July. The new government was not responsible for the postcrisis mess and should not be punished for the transgressions of its predecessors. In view of the explosive social and political tensions, Russia had done as much as could possibly be expected of any IMF member in similar straits. Therefore, withholding the money was obviously a politically motivated decision by the major shareholders of the IMF. These views were articulated in great detail in his book about his period as head of the government.[5]

Primakov started mustering his forces by calling his former friends who were still foreign ministers in several G-7 countries as well as contacting a couple of heads of state. For instance, on the afternoon of November 24, U.S. ambassador James F. Collins was summoned by Primakov, who complained that the IMF was making demands inconsistent with what Vice President Gore had written earlier. Collins said that the Gore letter was perfectly consistent with what he understood about the IMF's views. A well-placed G-7 source suggested that the prime minister was trying to stir doubt to gain some kind of tactical advantage. Similarly, Primakov put in a call to French president Jacques Chirac the previous day to complain about the IMF and the promised tranche. Chirac then raised the issue with German chancellor Gerhard Schröder, with whom he was meeting anyway, before Chirac returned the call.

In view of the degree of misunderstanding and the involvement of concerned shareholders, Camdessus flew into Moscow on December 1, for a day of meetings with Primakov and members of his government. The managing director delivered broadly the same message as Marquez-Ruarte, but perhaps in a more diplomatic way—holding out the hope that, of course, a program would be designed that the IMF could support. There were just technical details that needed to be clarified and agreed on. One such detail was the deeply felt desire of the new tax minister, Georgy Boos, who was close to Mayor Yuri Luzhkov, to cut the rate of the VAT and reach negotiated settlements with all the large taxpayers (a practice he contended was the norm previously, but he was simply proposing to make it more transparent). Camdessus weighed in on the debate, strongly advising against both steps.

Meanwhile, backtracking in other areas proliferated as entrenched bureaucratic interests realized that there was no practical opposition so long as the "facts" could be presented in line with the new government's loosely formulated philosophy. For example, the VEK—supposedly abolished by Kiriyenko with its functions incorporated, where appropriate, into other structures—got a new lease on life. Its managers claimed that there was an overwhelming need to control prices and the quality of traded goods as a source of capital flight. Whereas in actuality it was known that the principal source of large-scale capital flight was the abuse of perfectly legal transfer pricing and the use of offshore units. A similar example arose when a government meeting in late November chaired by Maslyukov made "an important political decision" to resume attracting foreign loans with a Russian government guarantee. The practice had been stopped earlier in 1998 as an original condition under the IMF's 1996 three-year program. The fact is that enterprises receiving imported goods financed by foreign trade credits with a sovereign guarantee did not repay, and the loans thus became liabilities of the government (and hence an unbudgeted subsidy to the enterprises). It was particularly hard to resist pressures from so-called friendly governments that tried to promote their exports and were only too pleased that the Russian authorities were prepared to provide guarantees, so making it much easier to reopen in a major way this source of fiscal irresponsibility.

7

The Surprising Postcrisis Recovery

The political and economic aftermath of the August crisis took a surprising turn. Based on historical experience and expectations, the world waited for first an economic meltdown in Russia and then a bitter, revengeful political reaction. And events did start out in that direction. Then nothing happened. And then, from this limbo, the economy began to rebound and politically, in the end, Yeltsin was able to ensure a peaceful transition of power. With the new millennium approaching, the Russian economy was starting to boom.

Overview of 1999

As the year began, there was little to cheer about. Although initial indications were that the economy and society had escaped perhaps the worst of the immediate fallout that could have resulted from the crisis of the previous August, the prospects for the period ahead were nonetheless disheartening.

The experiment with economic reform and the rapid transformation of the Russian economy into the globalized economic system seemed to have utterly failed. It could no longer be said, as Chubais did already in 1997, that the move to a market economy was irreversible. If anything, under Primakov, with solid backing in the Duma from the Communists and other left-wing and nationalistic political factions, the limited reforms were soon to be undone by likely price and exchange controls. At the time, Gaidar was quoted by Interfax as contending that it was hard to say how long the "government of communists" would take to "destroy elements of a free market economy in Russia." The impression was that the game was up. A millenarian cataclysm appeared about to descend.

Moreover, on the political front, it seemed that Yeltsin had lost his political grip and that Primakov was destined to be elected in the presidential elections scheduled for the following year. On September 30, 1998, another potential contender, Moscow mayor Luzhkov, in Blackpool as a guest at Prime Minister Tony Blair's Labor Party conference, said that he too would consider running for president if there were no other qualified candidates. For the Russian people, the hope for a better tomorrow continued to be postponed.

The IMF also shared this gloomy assessment of economic prospects. Under the highly unlikely condition that some of the more sensible policies suggested by the IMF would be pursued, it projected that the economy could grow by 3 percent, at best; if not, it was expected that economic activity would more likely decline by 2 percent or more. That was without taking into account all of the things that could go wrong under such precarious circumstances. Being close to the action, I anticipated retrograde policies that would cause the economy to implode.

One proposal in the new government was to make the domestic use of dollars illegal—a measure that would have wrecked the fragile economy. Fortunately other urgencies intervened, and time ran out before such a measure could be applied. Another dangerous idea that seemed to have intuitive appeal to the new government was a proposal by Boos, the new tax minister, to pursue an ad hoc approach to tax collection. His idea was to negotiate individually with each of the large corporate taxpayers, and agree on what they could and should pay in practice. Fortunately, in this case as well, time ran out before Boos could go too far with his brainstorm, which would have undermined several years of efforts to build an effective tax administration based on a respect for the law. Boos said that of course he understood these concerns, but realistically his approach was the only practical method to raise revenue under the circumstances.

In dealing with the Primakov government, the IMF staff members were criticized by Maslyukov for suggesting that his proposed budget policies relied excessively on cuts in real spending and hence were unrealistic. The prime minister saw the IMF position as a political tactic to withhold the money, and the mistrust was never eliminated. But it turns out that the IMF, along with everyone else, was wrong about the trajectory of economic recovery that would generate sufficient revenue to sustain spending.

The factors in the recovery were the resilience of the Russian private sector, the role of the depreciated ruble, and ironically the total disillusionment with Russia abroad as the country was seemingly plunged into scandal—at least sufficiently to make investors and the IFIs wary of further involvement. There was some evidence that outside Moscow and a few other major cities, the economic damage of the collapse was more limited. Thus the financial collapse did affect the large city banks, but had a more limited impact beyond the financial sector—just as much of the country had really not benefited from what had come before. Even the drop in government spending was attenuated by the limited reach of the budget in the first place.

Moving Up the Learning Curve

Primakov and his allies in government obviously felt that the outside world was conspiring against them as 1999 began. It seemed that the country was being punished at the behest of Wall Street bankers who were dictating policy to the U.S. government and the G-7. The fact that the U.S. Treasury secretary was Rubin, a quintessential Wall Street mandarin, did little to dispel this interpretation in the Russian White House.

Furthermore, it appeared that NATO was dictating policy concerning the former Yugoslavia, which with its Slavic orthodox people in Serbia, a historic Russian ally, touched raw nerves in the Kremlin. Under these circumstances, misunderstandings with other countries and the IMF intensified. Primakov was convinced that the IMF's stand was inevitably part of a political tactic (whatever Camdessus might have said to the contrary).

Primakov called Camdessus on January 12, and mandated Maslyukov to fly to Washington, DC, two days later with Paramonova and Viugin to straighten things out and bring home the money. Not motivated so much by the desire to disburse its resources but instead increasingly concerned about the policy drift in Russia, the IMF worked toward a compromise. Maslyukov returned empty-handed yet at least encouraged. He prepared his own draft policy memorandum, which was discussed with the IMF staff, and when the IMF mission said that the policies set out in the draft were not concrete enough, Maslyukov proposed a list of specific measures (on February 10).

Meanwhile, Primakov and his officials continued to work the phone with calls behind the scenes to the prime minister's high-level foreign contacts. For a couple of months already, within the IMF, there had been speculation as to what was really going on. One vein was that Primakov, who was a clever diplomat and well informed by his advisers, knew perfectly well what the real situation was, but was playing a coy game to try to get what he wanted (IMF money and support) at a minimum cost. For a man whose experience was to see all negotiating situations in zero-sum terms, this was the most likely explanation for his stance. Moreover, with people in government who knew IMF policies and procedures well such as Zadornov and Viugin, it just didn't seem possible that Primakov really could not have understood.

Yet there was a nagging doubt—or he played his game awfully well, since he really didn't appear to understand. The point is that the IMF was in a delicate position. It did not want to block, or be seen as blocking, possible progress of any reforms under Primakov based on its inability to communicate effectively; nor did the IMF wish to be duped into lowering its conditions for resumed financial support. With Russia still teetering on the edge of the precipice, the stakes for getting it right were large.

As it turned out, the people who could have explained matters were not trusted by Primakov's inner circle of advisers. U.S. ambassador Collins had become so convinced that the prime minister really did not understand that he took the initiative to suggest a low-key private lunch with Deputy Foreign Minister Georgy Mamedov, a trusted adviser to Primakov, and Kasyanov, the very day that he was appointed as a first deputy finance minister, on March 1, 1999. Later, in 2000, when Kasyanov became prime minister and was routinely castigated in the press as a "Berezovsky" man, I would recall that lunch. Logically, it seemed to me that if Primakov trusted Kasyanov to the extent of making him an envoy, and given his well-known antipathy for Berezovsky, how could people seriously think that Kasyanov "belonged" to anybody? By the end of the lunch, the situation seemed to be much clearer. It was an unusual step by the U.S. embassy that, until then, was not directly involved in bilateral Russia-IMF issues, but reflected the serious concerns of the ambassador himself.

It had been a frank discussion. I set out my personal view as to how—in its relations with the IMF—Russia had reached the present impasse, how this kind of situation had been avoided in other countries, the need to agree on a common technical assessment, and what the options might be. What I said was nothing new, but I had the advantage of explaining it directly to a key member of the inner circle, in an atmosphere of cordiality, and with Kasyanov confirming broadly what was said. Mamedov was convinced, and said so later in a note that he sent to me.

Camdessus and Primakov had an immediate exchange of correspondence, and a mission arrived in Moscow a few days later (now headed by Gerard Belanger, a laconic Canadian) and made further progress in Moscow in trying to transform this better understanding into concrete program measures.

In the meantime, the Kosovo war had begun. Primakov, who was due in Washington for an official visit to the United States on March 23, returned to Moscow in midflight when he received word that NATO planes had begun bombing Serbia. This U.S. decision, among conspiracy-minded Russians, seemed almost timed to sabotage Primakov's visit. Rumors circulated in elite circles that Yeltsin was so upset, serious consequences were only narrowly averted.

Primakov himself obviously saw the IMF's squeamishness as just camouflage for its principal shareholder. In his book, he observed that "bomb attacks on Yugoslavia by NATO under U.S. leadership were made when the Cabinet was in office. This did not create the best international climate for the Cabinet's work. Little optimism, too, was generated by the protracted discussions with the IMF, with the same USA standing invisibly behind its back."[1]

With Russia seemingly isolated in the world, Primakov phoned the managing director to explain his decision to abort his U.S. visit and insisted that discussions were needed. Camdessus, in a dramatic gesture, arrived in Moscow on March 27. At the end of the visit, an agreement with the IMF was announced, even though an unusually large number of details still remained to be agreed on at a technical level.

During the visit, there was an extraordinary debate on budgetary policy, with Camdessus resisting real wage and spending cuts of the scale proposed by the government. Primakov complained about being outflanked on the Left—hardly his impression of the IMF. The point that Camdessus was pushing was that dramatic real cuts in wages and pensions were not sustainable over time, and could not be accepted as a credible basis for budgetary policy. In a subsequent meeting with Maslyukov, Belanger was even accused of being a socialist. Primakov relates these conversations in his book.

During these discussions, which continued in April in both Moscow and Washington, DC, the Russian negotiators were divided. The tension between Maslyukov and Zadornov was palpable as Zadornov's patience at playing second fiddle to an amiable but bungling Maslyukov was wearing thin. The situation was not helped by the reportedly partial information and especially ill-informed views of one of Maslyukov's principal advisers.

But finally, before the long May holiday season began, Russia's 1999 budget was belatedly adopted by the Duma. It contained no financing. Revenues equaled spending except for foreign debt payments, which were financed through the CBR. The budget looked better than it really was, however. For one, almost by an accident of legislation, the VAT-sharing formula was altered, significantly raising the allocation to the federal budget, thereby forcing the regions to adjust. At least this was its real effect. In the area of cosmetics, Zadornov had cleverly excluded interest payments on the government's debt portfolio, notably to the CBR, and provided for minimal amounts for the new foreign debt service. The unintended consequence was to starve the CBR of income, effectively undermining the effectiveness of monetary policy.

The Primakov government never reached an agreement with the IMF, and the scandals circulating about Russian financial malfeasance were taking up more and more time in order to understand what was and was not true, including with regard to the reportedly stolen IMF money (see below).

Another Change in Government

A taciturn Yeltsin seemed resolved to his political fate, cloistered inside the Kremlin (or actually at one of the presidential dachas near Moscow). Primakov seemed to be an unstoppable political force, especially having aligned himself with Moscow mayor Luzhkov, when he became the head of a newly created electoral bloc called Fatherland–All Russia.

It was clear to many observers that Yeltsin did not appreciate being upstaged by his prime minister and was increasingly concerned with the succession issue. There were even those who still argued that he meant well and was discouraged that Primakov seemed so intent on turning back the clock, thus undoing the results of reforms painfully achieved. In March, Alexander Voloshin was appointed as chief of staff in the Kremlin, after a series of periodic changes. Voloshin, as a bright, reasonable, hardworking, and well-organized person, quickly became the powerful manager of the Kremlin, bringing stability and much-needed organizational skills to the execution of the presidential agenda. He also arrived in time to help block the Primakov-Luzhkov bandwagon.

At the end of April, in a little-noticed change at the time, Vadim Gustov, a close friend of Primakov, was dismissed as a deputy prime minister and Stepashin, an earnest and hardworking senior official, became a first deputy prime minister. Stepashin's promotion and greater public visibility was made embarrassingly evident on a televised broadcast of a meeting on May 5 where Yeltsin, at the outset, stopped procedures until Stepashin was properly seated, reflecting his new and higher rank.

A few weeks later, in a largely unanticipated move (but then surprises were becoming a Yeltsin habit), Primakov was dropped and Stepashin was appointed prime minister. This change did not go smoothly at first, though, because there was confusion as to whose name had been put forward.

"The flap" actually occurred right in the middle of a parliamentary session. It was Wednesday, May 12—one of the two days a week that the Duma had for plenary sessions. In the morning Gennady Seleznyov, the speaker, told the deputies that he had received a telephone call from Yeltsin about his next candidate for the prime minister position, and that the candidate was going to be named officially later in the day. It became known immediately that Yeltsin was naming Nikolai Aksyonenko, the railroad minister, for the job. Though Seleznyov didn't initially say so in the Duma, he leaked the news to reporters and aides.

When an official letter from the Kremlin arrived in parliament a little later, naming Stepashin, Seleznyov was astonished and publicly commented that Yeltsin didn't know what he was talking about. Seleznyov called it an example of Yeltsin's inconsistency and inability to think clearly. Others (especially right-wing deputies) remarked on this as a sign of acute struggle within the Kremlin administration between its "reasonable" group and an aggressive clan of corrupt officials and oligarchs.

In his book, Yeltsin is quite rational in his explanation that he had already envisaged Putin as his successor, but didn't want to float his name around too early.[2] And in that specific situation, he just wanted to confuse the legislators (presumably because they seemed to be in opposition to his every move by that time). What really happened, of course, still remains murky. It was yet one more example of the seemingly byzantine nature of political economy in Russia, adding to an increasing wariness by the G-7.

Somewhat surprisingly, the Duma acquiesced to the change. Stepashin, coming from the power ministries, was also seen as reassuring, but with more of a human touch and suspected reformist tendencies. There ensued a messy transition, especially concerning the economic portfolios.

Maslyukov and Boos were out. There was considerable speculation about the post of first deputy prime minister in charge of the economy.

At first it was thought that Zhukov, the chair of the Duma Budget Committee, would get the post. Then Zadornov was appointed instead on May 25, but he resigned three days later when it became clear that he would not be allowed to keep his MinFin portfolio. In the end, Kasyanov became finance minister, and Khristenko returned as a deputy prime minister dealing with economic issues. But Zadornov agreed to be the president's special representative to the IFIs.

Stepashin did not make a big impression as the head of the government. His style, affable and attentive, seemed—in the absence of strong political backing—to lack the decisiveness needed to get things done. Partly no doubt to repair relations with the IMF and perhaps in part in an effort to bolster his image, when Camdessus decided to visit Saint Petersburg to participate in a conference on June 15–16, Stepashin seized the occasion (it may have also been a case of local pride since he was from Saint Petersburg).

Stepashin acquitted himself well in those discussions and advanced the negotiations on the government's economic program sufficiently to secure tentative support for finalizing an agreement on a new standby arrangement from the IMF. Camdessus explained what he felt was needed to bring all the diverse elements of the program together, and spoke frankly to Gerashchenko about FIMACO, a financial subsidiary of Eurobank in Paris that was at the center of the misreporting to the IMF (see below).

Meanwhile, it turned out that the procrastination on a range of issues was starting to be felt. Problems with the government's cash flow had been masked by ad hoc steps involving intragovernment debt obligations taken by Zadornov, who had kept his cards close to his chest so that even his deputies did not have the full picture. Thus, Kasyanov confided that he was not pleased at the real situation he discovered when he took over as minister at MinFin. Zadornov's sleight of hand in the 1999 budget of not showing the debt service falling due was only one aspect of the problem.

There were also a number of unresolved problems in the banking system. A large international effort to provide massive amounts of technical assistance, coordinated by the IMF and World Bank, seemed to only result in an ever-growing pile of paper and unimplemented recommendations (it should be noted that a number of senior Russian officials complained that they perceived that much of the technical assistance was really supply driven rather than demanded by the authorities).

Against this backdrop, Russia's long-discussed economic program for 1999 was being finalized. It reflected Maslyukov's imprint, especially on the structural side, where the World Bank had accepted a minimalist set of feasible measures rather than insisting on a desirable set of measures. The program also contained measures applied to the banking system, where the CBR was noticeably unenthusiastic, as well as measures to shed light on the FIMACO issue through audits and corrective actions.

There was also the fact that the 1999 budget, being unrealistic in terms of revenue projections, required additional measures. These were discussed over dinner during Belanger's mission in June 1999 at the MinFin dacha near Barvika, just outside Moscow. The issues were resolved, and after some further toasts, Mozhin provocatively asked me who the best Russian finance minister was—right in front of Kasyanov and Zadornov. Fortunately, to avoid a diplomatic incident, I had the sangfroid to answer "Witte," the late nineteenth-century finance minister under the czars who is broadly acknowledged as the great reformer of Russian finance.

In a sense, Russia's economic program was loosely constructed. Some of the elements, especially on the structural side—the World Bank's area of responsibility—needed to be more fully specified. These issues should have been resolved during a final round of discussions, but were swept under the proverbial rug as the IMF staff members got sidetracked by a purely technical issue of their own making about the timing of the proposed tranches under the new program. This issue generated much heat along with a number of phone calls between Zadornov and Fischer, and even between Stepashin and Camdessus on July 2.

The IMF board met on July 28. A new seventeen-month standby credit was approved. I accompanied Zadornov, who came to Washington, DC, to "bring home the money." When a last-minute problem arose over a prior action involving Sberbank's refusal to accept an outside strategic review, Zadornov made a personal promise to Fischer to resolve the outstanding issues related to the Sberbank audit as soon as he returned to Moscow—but in fact, it took another year before the issue was resolved. By then it emerged that some of the bank and IMF staff member's alarmist concerns about Sberbank's viability were exaggerated. Not only were audits eventually conducted that met governance concerns with transparency but, more important, they revealed that Sberbank was solvent as an ongoing concern. That said, it still continued to pose questions as regards longer-term issues of the effectiveness of monetary instruments and the transparency of the CBR.

The tranche of US$640 million, which was disbursed on July 30, turned out to be the final tranche that Russia received from the IMF.

Another tranche had been intended for disbursement based on program performance as of the end of September. But the tranche was never disbursed despite satisfactory macroeconomic performance as of that date. One of the other conditions was adequate clarification of whether there could have been any other possible offshore operations with the CBR's reserves of a related nature to those using FIMACO. The results of a PricewaterhouseCoopers audit needed to be available by the next review, but Gerashchenko feigned misunderstanding (despite a letter that he had signed to Camdessus agreeing to the further analysis—which by the way, confirmed that there were no other related operations). As a result, the tranche was delayed until the next PricewaterhouseCoopers report was ready, although by then other unanticipated problems arose.

Yet Another Change in Government

The mood in Moscow, as the almost-sacred August retreat to the dachas began, was one of resigned fatalism. The economy seemed to be doing a little better than originally expected (the IMF projected a revised real growth rate of 3 percent), a banking system of sorts was working to ensure payments (although there was still minimal scope for intermediation between savings and investment), and the problem of barter and nonpayments at least did not seem to be getting any worse.

On the political front, Stepashin was seen as a well-meaning but weak head of government, trying to please his interlocutors and avoiding tough decisions. As an eventual replacement for Yeltsin as president, he seemed totally unsuited—a perception that was underscored by the opinion polls (for what they were worth) that showed that Primakov would swamp Stepashin in a presidential election. If anything, the power of Primakov and Luzhkov was undiminished and indeed unstoppable. The implication, less than ten months from the scheduled elections, was for a mediocre future at best for the Russian economy, not to mention Russia's role in the world.

Still, confounding the conventional wisdom yet again, Yeltsin dismissed Stepashin after only eighty-two days in office and replaced him with the relatively unknown Putin on August 9. Putin, a former KGB operative in the GDR and later a deputy mayor of Saint Petersburg under the liberal mayor Anatoly Sobchak, originally had been brought to work as Pavel Borodin's deputy in the Kremlin by Kudrin in 1996.[3] There he rose to be deputy chief of staff before being asked, in July 1998, to take charge of the Federal Security Bureau. Subsequently, Yeltsin appointed him as head of the powerful Security Council. Putin was approved by the Duma on August 16, 1999. As the fourth prime minister in a little over a year, the appointment was met with a yawn. Speculation was growing that Yeltsin might find a way around the constitution to run for a third presidential term, in the absence of any viable alternative candidate.

Initial impressions of the new prime minister were favorable, although cautious. Much of the previous government was left in place, notably Kasyanov at MinFin and the CBR management. Gennadii Bukaev, a real-life senior tax official who had a solid reputation for his work in the difficult environment of Bashkortistan, replaced Pochinok at the Tax Ministry, while Pochinok took over the troublesome labor ministry portfolio. Putin took an interesting initiative late that autumn in asking German Gref, a former associate from his Saint Petersburg days and a senior federal government official, to carry out a thorough analysis of the economic problems confronting the country and formulate a detailed plan over a ten-year time horizon to resolve the issues, including a short-term action program.

In some ways, this initiative resembled the usual device of Russian leaders to formulate plans and programs, just as Primakov's government had done a year earlier. This time seemed different in that Gref was charged to use the best talent in the country and abroad, ignore ideological predispositions, and especially suggest concrete steps to achieve the program objectives on which there should be a large degree of consensus among the experts. It was also unusual in that the study was being conducted outside the government itself. Gref was mandated a commission, with Nabiullina as his deputy (called back from her challenging job in the private sector at a Russian credit-rating agency), and provided offices in the posh headquarters of Smolensky's failed SBS-Agro bank, across the river from the Kremlin.

When Odling-Smee made a visit to Moscow in early November (and after a breakfast with Chubais in the Metropol), he met with Putin for the first time on November 3. Chubais was right that Putin seemed more focused and decisive than his predecessor, but also perhaps less charming—the latter quality having presumably tipped the Kremlin in favor of Stepashin rather than Putin in the earlier reshuffle. The relatively new prime minister appeared to be especially well briefed on the background and current status of relations with the IMF.

He clearly understood the role that the IMF could play in terms of facilitating Russia's access to capital markets and official financing, including debt relief.

In terms of policy, Putin was quite explicit. He explained that the government's approach to further reform was to proceed in a sequenced manner. He observed that it was important to draw lessons from the failures of the past when attempts to introduce broad-based reforms across a range of issues served to create coalitions of opponents who could form a united front and overwhelm inherently weak governments. This approach, which may have been warranted at an initial stage, should be avoided. It was now important to take one issue at a time and keep potential opponents of reform guessing. Putin asserted, for instance, that of course Gazprom would be reformed, but only in good time.

A Benign Backdrop

History, like life itself, is about timing. It's hard to say what might have been had the economic situation been less favorable at the time of the passage of power from Yeltsin to Putin. Maybe it was just luck that the economy was soaring, seemingly irrespective of the policy paralysis. Indeed, it would have been difficult to imagine a more favorable set of economic circumstances, at least against the backdrop of eighteen months earlier, than those prevailing at the beginning of 2000.

The economy was thriving. The strengthening of oil prices, rising to US$25 per barrel for Russian Urals blend by late January 2000, played a significant role, but still not as critical as widely believed. Consumer spending and investment were also expanding rapidly. The causes for this growth were rooted in a number of factors, notably the significant overshooting of the real exchange rate of the ruble, providing a large margin of undervaluation that sharply increased the profitability of domestic production as against imports. In fact, at a technical level, one of the more intriguing questions of that period is why the level of imports remained so low. It had been widely predicted, including by the IMF based on the experience in other countries, that import penetration would start to move back to precrisis volumes quickly once the real rate of the ruble started to appreciate toward its earlier level as rapid inflation eroded the benefits of the nominal exchange rate depreciation.

With wages restrained, profits, as a percentage of the GDP, rose from a low point—in modern Russian statistics—of 4 percent in 1995 to 8 percent in 1999, and then to 12 percent in 2000. And the recovery seemed to be becoming more broadly based, not just in Moscow and other big cities, as Russian companies started and expanded operations. Moreover, with virtually no dependence on domestic or foreign financial markets, Russia was largely immune to adverse external developments.

In line with what was becoming the usual pattern, the IMF projections (admittedly along with almost everyone else's) were way off. The reader will recall that the IMF had originally forecast a real growth rate for Russia in 1999 of -2.0 percent without measures. That number had been revised around midyear to a positive 3 percent. The actual growth rate turned out to be an impressive 6.4 percent. Its projections for 2000 were off by almost the same difference. At the beginning of 2000, the IMF— along with most analysts—was projecting GDP growth of about 3 percent. Again, the IMF staff members were constrained in their initial projections to use the commodity price assumptions in the IMF Research Department's *World Economic Outlook*, which predicted an oil price decline, not a further increase. The outcome was 10 percent, one of the most impressive growth rates in the world, although admittedly from a low base.

And a similar story applied to 2001, when the IMF experts were preoccupied with the seeming contradiction of a loose monetary policy with a managed nominal exchange rate, which could cause a sharp real appreciation of the ruble, stopping investment and growth in its tracks. At least this was a welcome change from the almost-overwhelming focus on fiscal policy that dominated the dialogue in the 1990s. The IMF projected real growth, again, of no more than 3 percent. The final result was growth of 5.1 percent against the backdrop of a worldwide slow-down, making Russian performance again one of the most impressive in a subdued global context.

Political Limbo

It was indeed fortunate for Putin and his new administration that as he became the acting president on January 1, 2000, the economy was so benign. There were no immediate emergencies, and no crises even on the distant horizon—abstracting of course from the tragic situation in Chechnya, which was more in the realm of a merciless quagmire. International experience, much less that of the tortured path of the post-Soviet Russian economy, taught that such becalmed periods do not usually last long. What the IMF and most other observers did not realize at the time was that Russia was heading toward a paradigm shift, in good part owing to the legacy of the 1998 crisis.

One only has to recall, with a new presidential election suddenly brought forward—as required by the constitution—to March 26, that the central question (which became a cliché) was, Who is Mr. Putin? Putin seemed to personify Winston Churchill's characterization of Russia as "a riddle wrapped in a mystery inside an enigma." That winter of 2000, however, Putin's performance as a candidate showed him to be competent, energetic, serious about both strategy and tactics, and remarkably adaptable. During the election campaign, Putin managed to convince each major constituency that he sympathized with its own aspirations. To reformers, he appeared a quiet reformer; to oligarchs, a guarantor of their positions and possessions; to the security forces, one of their own; and to the people, an ordinary father, just like them.

What seemed to stand out as attributes, as Russia and the international community came to know Putin better, were the characteristics of realism, pragmatism, and patriotism. No previous Russian leader had ever spoken to his compatriots with such brutal candor. A striking example was in a special document, "Russia at the Turn of the Millennium," published on the Kremlin Web site on December 30, 1999, in lieu of a typical new year's greetings, in which Putin said that Russia would be mistaken not to recognize Communism's accomplishments. "But it would be an even bigger mistake not to realize the outrageous price our country and its people had to pay for that Bolshevist experiment." He went on to compare Russia not to the United States, not to the great nations of Europe, but rather to Portugal. As Putin stated bluntly, "To reach the production level of Portugal and Spain, two countries that are not known as leaders of the world economy, it will take Russia approximately fifteen years if the GDP grows by at least eight percent a year."

Putin's diagnosis of Russia's predicament was harsher than that of Russia's fiercest Western critics. He argued that Russia's very survival was at stake—threatened by forces of disintegration should Chechen separatism spread through the Caucasus into central Russia. Even the nemesis of the Russian authorities, the U.S. Central Intelligence Agency, as late as April 2004, was reporting in a forecast for the next decade that Russia could disintegrate into as many as eight separate states. Putin's disgust with and disdain toward earlier Russian governments for the country's loss of authority and credibility was palpable. And in acknowledging Russia's poverty, he noted that its per capita GDP fell into the lower half of nations in the world and risked falling further to the level of developing countries.

To address these failings, Putin's prescription was straightforward. Russia must strengthen the state to assure survival as a country as well as restore the government's capacity to enforce its laws and decisions. Russia's great challenge for the next generation was one of economic reconstruction. He and his advisers believed that this effort would take at least a generation.

Putin argued that the only way Russia could achieve such levels of growth was through greater integration with the global economy and its associated institutions, including the IMF, the WTO, and global capital markets. Russia had, he said, "entered the highway by which the whole of humanity is traveling. Only this way offers the possibility of dynamic economic growth and higher living standards, as world experience shows. There is no alternative to it." Finally, Putin maintained bluntly that in order to enter the global economy and attract foreign investment, Russia had to adopt a cooperative posture toward the United States and the West, without sacrificing Russia's vital interests. And he said these things, and seemed to mean them, more than eighteen months before the infamous September 11, 2001, and well before he'd had a chance to master the issues that he would be called on as president to resolve.

There was almost no policy substance to measure the man to his words, however. In fact, caution and hard work had seemed to be his style ever since he became prime minister the previous August. It would be difficult to identify any significant new measures or forthright decisions during his incubation period, other than perhaps the establishment of a novel, high-level think tank, nominally outside the government, to formulate a strategy for the country in consultation with domestic and foreign experts, or Putin's controversial decree to pardon Yeltsin and his family of any wrongdoing while in office. This long political limbo until Putin asserted power in summer 2000 was hardly indicative of what was to come.

Against the backdrop of a benign economy and an uncertain political transition, for members of the acting government—most of whom were confirmed in their jobs in May—the whole first half of 2000 appeared to be just an act of treading water. All of the emphasis was squarely placed on looking forward. A couple of examples should suffice here, while also demonstrating the changing role of the IMF in its relations with Russia, even if this was not fully appreciated at the time. In retrospect, Chubais's contention to Camdessus in Hong Kong in September 1997 of a friendly divorce seemed belatedly to be coming true.

On January 10, to his own surprise, and that of most observers, Kasyanov came out of Putin's office at the Russian White House as the only first deputy prime minister and thus effectively the acting head of government. By chance, his first meeting in his new function when he returned to MinFin was with me. He asked for the discreet assistance of the IMF in suggesting priorities in formulating the future government's economic program.

Kasyanov was at that time, along with many others who had seen grand plans come and go, skeptical about what Gref's Center for Strategic Policy would be able to propose in terms of concrete, coherent, short-term priority measures. A few weeks later, in early March, Kasyanov, clearly conveying the impression that he was assured of his continuing postelectoral direction of the government, asked for practical advice from the IMF in dealing with the restructuring of the banking system, exchange controls, and debt management, where there was a problem of conflict of interest with the VEB. Kasyanov was also seeking the advice of other experts, both Russian, such as Gaidar's Institute for the Study of Economies in Transition, and outside, such as the World Bank. Gref's commission, which was transformed into the Center for Strategic Policy, was active in consulting with these and other relevant experts.

If anything, the attitude of the outside world to Russia deteriorated further as the first round of the presidential election, scheduled for March 26, approached. The disappearance of a Radio Liberty journalist named Andrei Babitsky in Chechnya on January 26 did not help. It was widely reported in the West that Babitsky had been killed by Russian troops for his alleged pro-Chechen sympathies. When he reemerged in mysterious circumstances in Dagestan on February 25, the further damage to Russia's low international esteem had already been inflicted.

The appearance was that of a dangerous country with undisciplined security forces assuming control and giving orders to pursue a policy of an autocratic state that would buck no criticism. It seemed at the time to be virtually an article of faith that this episode was orchestrated by the Kremlin. In a sense, what seemed to have happened, at least in terms of the exercise of central authority, is symptomatic of the kinds of issues faced by the Russian authorities in implementing other policies, including economic policy. For as hard as it was to believe, supposedly even the Kremlin did not know at first what had happened to Babitsky and could not locate quickly the local field commander presumably involved.

To say the least, it was embarrassing that the public could glimpse the weakness of the military chain of command, and moreover, that it should be revealed in practice to be so weak in a country with more than five thousand nuclear warheads. In essence, though, what had happened reflected the underlying weakness of central authority in post-Soviet Russia and sheds light on the enormous difficulty in actually implementing policy decided at the center.

Putin was elected in the first round and was inaugurated as president on May 7. Controversy surrounded the results, with allegations that Putin's close margin of victory (with just over 52 percent of the first-round vote) over Zyuganov was more than just a suspicious coincidence. Kasyanov was confirmed as prime minister on May 17. Most of the appointments to the cabinet were more or less expected. Kudrin was appointed finance minister and also as a deputy prime minister on May 18. There had been some speculation as to whether Gref would be rewarded with a major role in the new government. In the end, he was given the enlarged functions of the former ministries of economy, trade, and industry. Until almost the time of the announcement, it had been thought that Bugrov, theretofore Russia's executive director to the World Bank and Kasyanov's choice, would be given the Economics Ministry, and indeed he had flown to Moscow in that belief, only to be told on landing that Putin had given the position to Gref. In an atmosphere of skepticism, especially in the West, much of the speculation revolved around whether a group of trusted cohorts from Saint Petersburg, Putin's native city, would run the government in practice, and more specifically appointees from the state security organs, or whether Yeltsin holdovers would successfully resist the assault on their monopoly of power. There was additional speculation about reported tensions among Kasyanov, Kudrin, and Gref. While it was perhaps not an ideal government team in terms of managerial abilities, the differences seemed to have been much exaggerated—especially when viewed in hindsight.

Yet even during this period of political limbo, economic policy was still discussed. Much of that discussion between Russian officials and the IMF team, however, was limited to technical issues concerning an appropriate macroeconomic framework. Furthermore, the IMF team focused its attention and resources on the preparation of papers to be presented to an inaugural conference on the modernization of the Russian economy in a ten-year perspective, organized by Yasin at the State University Higher School of Economics in early April. Perhaps unwittingly because so many of the IMF staff members assigned to the Russia team had changed, this involved largely a reinvention of the analysis and recommendations, still largely relevant, that had been prepared in late 1995 to lay the basis for Russia's EFF program that began in early 1996.

Meanwhile, Russia's tough friend and activist, Camdessus, retired as managing director from the IMF on February 15, as he had announced a few months earlier. In view of the bitterly contested succession struggle among Europeans, and between Europeans and others—with the United States assumed to have veto power—no immediate successor was appointed by the time Camdessus left, and so Fischer became the acting managing director. Horst Kohler took up the post of managing director on May 1.

Fischer, in his capacity as acting managing director, opened the Higher School of Economics conference on April 6, and later met with Putin and other senior government officials. He was encouraged by what he heard, but still concerned that there was so much to be done. Indeed, despite the lack of a fully functioning government until July at the least, the IMF fielded four missions in the first six months of the year, even though much of the time could not be said to be productive. This was most clearly seen in the seemingly endless and inconclusive discussions with Ignatiev (who was still first deputy finance minister until he replaced Gerashchenko, who resigned as head of the CBR in mid-March 2002) and Paramonova on financial policies, and with the IMF team still focusing on the outstanding structural policies from the defunct 1999 program. Nevertheless, a useful dialogue on nonprogram issues began to be established.

The Window of Opportunity

For onlookers to the Russian economic scene, all too aware of the pitfalls of the past, there seemed to be no time to lose. For the IMF and Western governments supporting Russia's transformation, one of the keenest lessons of the rocky road of the 1990s was how, with political will in such short supply, timing could be such a critical consideration. With a relatively favorable external economic environment (with the continuing effects of the undervalued ruble combined with strong oil prices) and the expected usual honeymoon period for a new government, a small window of opportunity was available for pushing through some difficult and major reforms. Clearly that was the thrust of Fischer's advice when he met with Putin in April, and Odling-Smee's when he met with Kasyanov and members of the new government on May 19.

Politely but firmly, the new Russian authorities resisted the pressure from well-intentioned outsiders. No doubt the favorable external circumstances allowed them to step back and reconsider new approaches. An unexpectedly buoyant revenue situation, combined with a tight 2000 budget (and improving expenditure control), also provided a cushion for the authorities. The work by Gref and his colleagues along with the large number of experts consulted on an appropriate approach to future reforms led to the formulation of a homegrown economic strategy for the first time in post-Soviet Russia with only limited input by outsiders. For some outside observers, especially in Europe, expecting that no good could come from Russia, such news was interpreted as yet another indication of Russia's withdrawal from the world, and hostility and indeed ingratitude for foreign support.

Putin again repeated what he had said earlier (when he was prime minister) about learning the lessons from the past difficulties in implementing reforms. His conclusion led him to favor a sequenced approach, which would have better chances of success. When pushed by the IMF to use the honeymoon period to ram, if necessary, key legislation through the Duma—for instance, via an omnibus bill—before the beginning of the summer recess at the end of June, he voiced an unexpectedly frank assessment of his view of the political process in Russia.

Putin told us that unfortunately, the standing of parliament and government institutions generally in Russia was low. Clearly, running roughshod over a new Duma would hardly enhance the parliament's reputation or help to attract better candidates for political office in the elections to come, on which the future of Russian democracy would be based. As the newly elected president of Russia, Putin did not want one of his first official acts to be abusing the Duma and treating it as a mere rubber stamp. Putin said that in view of the widespread skepticism in the West about his administration's intentions, such an approach suggested by the IMF could be used by Russia's many critics in the West to prove their point.

While appreciating the astute observations of the new president, the IMF remained of the opinion that this was a risky strategy, relying on the hope that the external context would remain benign for a few years to come. Experience had taught that such an assumption could rarely be taken for granted. Of course, as we now know, the external economic environment not only remained favorable but also generally improved further over the subsequent years until the abrupt collapse of global financial markets in the second half of 2008. Putin turned out to be right tactically, although in retrospect he did not use the opportunities created to pursue the desirable structural reforms.

A conversation with Voloshin, the president's chief of staff, a little later in summer 2000 confirmed in somewhat practical terms the way in which the priorities were established, echoing a much earlier conversation with Putin when he was prime minister. The discussion was specifically about why banking reform was not being made a top policy priority given the obvious problems in the sector and the impact on future economic activity.

Voloshin patiently explained to me that first of all, everyone from Putin on down—including Gerashchenko—perfectly well appreciated the problem and what needed to be done. All the hand-wringing and most of the eagerly proffered advice of foreigners were not necessary. Voloshin went on to observe that even though growth was currently being fostered by productivity increases and investment financed by internal cash flow, it was clear that in the longer term Russia, like other countries, would need to finance investment through the efficient intermediation of domestic savings via a developed, domestic banking system and financial markets. This was a key point made years ago by Russia's best macroeconomist, Evgeny Gavrilenkov, the chief economist at Troika Dialog investment bank and a professor at the Higher School of Economics. No one quarreled with this. The only issue was one of timing.

At that moment (in August 2000), it was difficult to justify the use of a large amount of political capital when the ruble exchange rate was stable, reserves were increasing, inflation was decelerating, the payment system was operating, and household deposits were protected (at Sberbank, as the Russian Deposit Insurance Agency—the equivalent to the U.S. Federal Deposit Insurance Corporation—was established only in January 2004). Instead, the president saw as his top priorities the resolution of major problems in the reform of the military, the regions, and then the judiciary.

Voloshin wondered if any G-7 leader would seriously question whether those were not the highest priority, on which all else depended. He finally noted that it was the role of the president to deal with questions of state; the government should deal with the economy. That is how Putin intended to govern.

A Paradigm Shift Begins

It was a slow start. It seemed to take forever for the new government to get itself organized. An IMF team that returned to Moscow in July (the fifth mission of the year) to work with the new government found that only three senior officials had been appointed and confirmed in their positions at Gref's new superministry, which was an amalgamation of the old ministries of economy, trade, and industry. On July 26, the Russian authorities finally approved their priority program for the period remaining through the end of 2001.[4] Even after some strong resistance in parts of the government, the program turned out to be close to the earlier versions prepared by Gref's center and charted an ambitious structural agenda to be implemented over the following sixteen months.

Meanwhile, the Kremlin was much quicker in moving forward its own agenda for reform. Already in May, Putin was in discussion with the military, and a major restructuring and downsizing of the military was announced by Defense Minister Igor Sergeyev at the beginning of June, and after an embarrassing public row within the general command, Sergei Ivanov was appointed as the new defense minister in September, the first nonmilitary person to hold the post, although Ivanov had formerly been a KGB general.

In July, Putin announced his plan for ensuring the equitable application of federal law in all parts of the country, and proposed sweeping reforms of the federal parliament's upper chamber as well as curtailing the powers of regional and local authorities. He also appointed his own representatives to seven superdistricts, corresponding to the already-existing military districts, whose job it was to ensure the conformity of local and federal law, and act as ombudspersons when complaints arose about official treatment by government representatives or state institutions in the regions.

Russia's new president got a foretaste of how difficult it was, even supposedly with sufficient political will, to get desirable policies implemented in practice. A notable example at the beginning of his administration underscored the central theme of this book about the dispersion of power, and the weak central authority to monitor and control events—even when these were considered to be priorities.

After he won the election in late March, Putin decided that it was important to send a strong, if mainly symbolic, signal of his intentions to the country. Recognizing that there would be insufficient time, realistically, to table new legislation that could pass between the time of his May inauguration and the end of the Duma's spring session in late June, he identified a draft law concerning landownership as a feasible piece of legislation. A liberal version of the bill had already been tabled in the Duma and discussed in committee (as well as competing illiberal alternatives). Putin issued a formal order that the government should give priority to the passage of this piece of legislation. It was recognized that the practical implications would be limited since land rights were protected in the constitution and applied through earlier decrees. Yet in the absence of a law, which had been politically impossible in the old Duma, the regime was uncertain, which severely constrained operations in most regions. Nothing happened. In fact, it was only a year later, during the extension of the spring Duma session in July 2001, and after direct presidential intervention, that the law was finally passed. The new land code strengthened the legal basis on which urban land could be transferred and held, including by nonresidents, and facilitated the transfer of state-owned urban land to private ownership. Putin described the process of issuing instructions, in the face of strongly entrenched interests and incompetent bureaucrats, as the equivalent of pouring water on to sand.

Perhaps another, more sinister example of the weak state was when Gusinsky was arrested on June 13, when he was called in to testify at the federal prosecutor general's office. He was released after three days and went into exile shortly thereafter. While the story about Gusinsky (and the other oligarchs) is beyond the scope of this narrative, this particular episode was indicative not only of the already-mentioned practical problem of the Kremlin (and the government) with the chain of command and keeping subordinates under control but also perhaps more damagingly of the perceptions that the exercise of political power in Russia could be so arbitrary in practice, with seemingly no recourse.

While some aspects of his arrest remain obscure, it seems fairly clear that Putin and at least some of the upper echelons of the Kremlin were taken by surprise, notwithstanding the legions of conspiracy theorists in Russia and elsewhere to whom it was self-evident that Gusinsky's arrest was the result of a centrally orchestrated plan. That said, although the form and timing may have been embarrassing to Putin, clearly the substance was not. Putin was in the midst of touring the Prado Museum on an official visit to Madrid when he was asked by a journalist about the arrest. His off-the-cuff response, that whoever had ordered this was certainly not doing him a favor, was an understatement. Not surprisingly, Putin's image—especially outside Russia—as a sinister and manipulative autocrat seemed to be confirmed. And certainly, the stories about the stifling of the freedom of the press emanating from judicial actions against the independent television company NTV (and TV6) were yet to come.

Not all of the news was bad. The one piece of legislation, more under the control of Kudrin at MinFin, was the introduction of a modern tax code. Much of the legislation had already been considered in the Duma. One of the problems was to deal with the multiple amendments that had been tabled. In a frantic effort at the end of an extended spring session, most of part 2 of the tax code (containing the new tax structure and applicable rates) was passed. This timing was critical since it was the deadline for laying the legal basis for the following year's budget. If the bill had not been passed, another whole year would have been lost.

As it was, with the introduction of a flat 13 percent personal income tax starting on January 1, 2001, Russia became a tax haven of sorts. While a flat tax is inherently regressive, the reality was somewhat more nuanced since the highly progressive rates in place in the past were rarely paid owing to deductions and actual collection averaged 12 percent of reported incomes. Also, the new law was applied with a high threshold to shield low incomes from any tax liability at all. Still, a hefty payroll tax to finance the pension and other social funds remained as well as corporate income tax, VAT, excise duties, and various minor taxes.

Working with a New Government

The lethargy with which the government was getting itself organized surprised me. After all, Putin had been acting president since the beginning of the year and prime minister since the previous August. His election was almost a foregone conclusion. With Kasyanov appointed effectively as the acting head of government in January, the two had plenty of time to focus on strategy and personnel issues, so they could have moved rapidly to put a team in place and implement priority measures. But other than the push for the tax code and the skeleton of a new administration, it was not until the end of the summer dacha season, in late August, that the new government finally took shape.

It seemed clear that MinFin was no longer as dominant as it had been in developing economic policy in previous governments. While it still had a key control function, and its role in budget preparation and implementation was growing (especially as the treasury function under the formidable Tatiana Nesterenko, who had been brought in by Zadornov, became fully operational), its strategic role was weaker. In part, this reflected Kasyanov's own financial expertise and that of his staff in the prime minister's office, and the move of crucial MinFin people like Lubov Kudelina to defense and Arkady Dvorkovich to MinEcon, the earlier departure of Viugin, and the preference of senior officials like Ignatiev to focus on technical rather than policy questions. Lastly, Kudrin, an intelligent, dedicated, and unpretentious official, initially felt more comfortable working on the budget than the broader issues related to financial policy, although—like Kasyanov and many other competent officials—he learned to grow with the job.

For instance, in July 2000, during a conversation with me that covered both administrative issues such as the establishment of a consolidated MinFin debt department and who might head it as well as broader issues such as abolishing antiquated currency regulations like the foreign exchange surrender requirement, while agreeing that all of these were administratively simple, logical, and timely steps, Kudrin was visibly uncomfortable in dealing with them. He seemed to feel that the public debt department was a Kasyanov project and the other questions had to be treated with kid gloves (especially while the Duma appeared to be intent on constraining the CBR's independence).

More than ever, it appeared that the locus for strategic thinking had shifted to MinEcon, especially with deputy ministers Nabiullina and Dvorkovich working under Gref as well as the legacy of Gref's agenda from his Center for Strategic Studies. Even without a major operational role, MinEcon had essentially become the primary institution in the formulation of economic policy. Even in 2010, I still consider MinEcon as the locus of strategic thinking, at least by the mediocre standards seen elsewhere in government.

The discussions on an economic program that could be supported by the IMF continued once the new government was in place in late July 2000. But there was too much baggage, especially the transparency conditions imposed by the G-7 in the 1999 program, to try to revive the program. In any case, most of the discussion was concentrated on dealing with projected macroeconomic imbalances stemming from such a strong balance of payments. Oil prices had continued to rise while imports remained largely restrained. Long debates ensued with Ignatiev about the strength of the balance of payments, in which he argued at great length that the current strength could not be sustained. In fact, the 2000 outcome was even stronger than the IMF team had been projecting that July.

The real policy conundrum, and why officials were arguing so much in an uncustomary manner about the external balance, was the implication for the money supply and inflation if reserves rose rapidly in an effort to prevent a nominal appreciation of the exchange rate. The dilemma became a parochial question of which institution, MinFin or the CBR, would be responsible for the requisite degree of sterilization of the net inflows. In the end, agreement with the IMF on a new program was getting close, but then it was axed by Paramonova, who staunchly stated that the CBR could do no more because of a threat to its income position.

This may seem a strange way for a central banker to debate. Yet in the Russian context, there was a basis for her concerns. It should be recalled that after the 1998 GKO default, the CBR's stock of government bonds—which constituted the bulk of its assets—was illiquid at best and possibly worthless. On one level, the concern was that the CBR was bankrupt depending on the valuation of those assets. With the terms imposed by Zadornov in autumn 1998, the income stream on the CBR's stock of government assets implied insolvency. This modest income on the outstanding stock was not enough to cover operating expenses, much less open-market operations, at the prevailing interest rates. Zadornov had again ensured that such lending was at substantially below-market rates, or only 1 percent. Hence, the CBR found itself in the contradictory role of refraining from necessary policy positions because of its overriding concern about its balance sheet.

This was an unusual situation for a central bank, whose main focus should be the conduct of monetary policy. If there is a hole in its balance sheet because of government policy, then the budget will eventually have to plug it. But as so often in Russia, things were not so simple. The Duma had a number of concerns of its own with the CBR, including its purported extravagance and lack of transparency. This reputation was enhanced by an elaborate refurbishing in mid-2000 of the main bank building in the center of Moscow to which even its original nineteenth-century elegance could not aspire.

Among these concerns, there was the prevailing impression that the CBR's large (but secret) stock of nongold precious metals provided more than enough income to sustain this high living for years to come. At best, the Duma wanted to shed light on these operations; at worst, it wanted to bring the CBR to heel by curbing its independence. In the meantime, the CBR's overall level of professionalism took a sharp drop as impeccably professional senior staff members like Konstantin Korischenko and Andrei Cherepanov left. Korischenko later returned under new management in 2002 after Gerashchenko's departure, but then became president of MICEX after the stock market disruptions in September 2008.

The government program approved in late July 2000 represented the best-prepared, comprehensive, and practical plan for economic modernization (as the Russians liked to call it) ever devised. So much so that at least a couple of senior officials were surprised that the fund had not said anything publicly about the positive nature of the new program when it was announced. For one thing, many of the people involved in its drafting had been involved in the earlier IMF-supported programs, and had a pragmatic view of what was needed and what could actually work given the inevitable implementation difficulties in Russia. Senior officials all shared a common view that political will—which was in such short supply in the past—was no longer the main obstacle; rather, likely difficulties could come from the limited administrative capacity to carry out policies, especially on a sustained basis.

There seemed to be some emerging difference of opinion between the IMF and the Russian authorities on the priority economic measures. Each side was formulating its own list of desirable measures with limited overlap. To a large extent, the formal divergence was misleading since there was broad agreement on what was needed in the area of macroeconomic policy. The IMF, however, stuck in a backward-looking mode owing to the political concerns of its dominant members, was adamant that the long-festering transparency and governance issues should be prioritized.

In fall 2000, I asked Nabiullina, as the first deputy economy minister at the time and the key person on structural issues, about this difference in views. She replied that as far as some of the specific transparency measures for the CBR, it was clear that these would be done, if deemed reasonable, and it was not necessary to include them in the government's program. On fiscal issues, she thought that the main issues were the tax code and the draft 2001 budget, in which she felt that the results should be considered satisfactory by the fund staff. This was not entirely the case since the draft budget did not attempt to regularize the financial relations between MinFin and the CBR, as suggested by the IMF.

On banking and nonpayments, she said that the situation was more complex. In terms of banking, even the IMF experts seemed to have shifted their focus from bank restructuring to operational issues that needed to be addressed in order to avoid a future banking crisis. Nabiullina noted that the debate had moved on to other issues. In fact, Viugin pointed out to me at that time that beyond even the measures set out in the government program, there was high-level consideration being given to additional steps to accelerate banking reform, such as empowering the CBR to close banks without recourse to the courts, imposing minimum capital requirements, abolishing the surrender requirement, and loosening capital controls. Viugin recognized that implementation of such an ambitious program would require a change in CBR management, which he considered just a matter of time. He became the CBR's first deputy chair in 2002 responsible for monetary policy.

Similarly, on the nonpayment question, Nabiullina remarked that the World Bank had seemed to shift its focus as well. She believed that a shift in focus was needed anyway because the problem itself was no longer critical. Furthermore, by then it was recognized that nonpayments was a manifestation of improper budgeting provisions and soft budget constraints that really had to be addressed through a number of microeconomic measures, including a specific program to reform Gazprom.

Nabiullina, after conferring with Gref, asked how the fund staff members might view the structural part of their program, and whether it would warrant fund support more or less as it was formulated. Relatively little attention had been devoted to structural issues (other than fiscal) in discussions with the May and July IMF missions because of the debate on appropriate macro policies and a lack of preparedness on the Russian side. She thought that perhaps some of the IMF's key concerns could reasonably be reconsidered in light of the new circumstances—including the continuing strong macroeconomic performance—and also wondered how the debate in the IMF about the appropriate focus of structural policies initiated by the new managing director, Kohler, would affect IMF thinking about a new program. Most of all, she asked that the IMF staff members seriously assess the government's own program and try to work from that basis; after all, she noted that it was Fischer who suggested to Putin that a Russian-formulated program would be welcome.

While continuing to work closely together, and with World Bank staff members from Washington increasingly identified with coordination on the structural agenda, progress was slow. Collaboration between the staff of the two neighbors on Nineteenth Street in Washington was not particularly as cordial on the working level as it should have been, but that is a long and tangential story. The slow pace was in part because the attention of the IMF staff members was on emerging macroeconomic problems and sidetracked by the reports of the scandals, but also because the Russian authorities and the IMF (and World Bank) staff had different policy priorities when it came to the structural agenda. The IMF wanted to bring to closure long-festering issues such as the banking sector, natural monopolies, and transparency concerns more broadly, whereas the authorities felt that a sequenced approach should first emphasize business deregulation along with tax and administrative reforms. As a consequence, there was limited scope to discuss, much less agree on, structural issues. Finally, over a year after the default, the London Club completed the exchange of twenty-one billion U.S. dollars in new Eurobonds for thirty-two billion U.S. dollars of canceled GKO/OFZ debt on August 25.

That August was a miserable time for Russia. The economic news, which was continuing to improve, was constantly swamped by unrelated disasters. First there was the bloody explosion on August 8 in a major central metro station in Moscow at Pushkin Square. A few days later, on August 12, the Kursk submarine sank suddenly in seemingly mysterious circumstances in shallow water in the Barents Sea with all crew lost. And the Ostankino television tower, from which all major channels in Moscow broadcast their signal and the tallest structure in Russia, caught fire on August 27. In addition to the destruction and deaths, the capital was without television (except for limited cable service). All this certainly seemed to convey the impression that Russia was doomed. Stories about crumbling infrastructure and the hopelessness of future prospects were pervasive.

Pouring Water on to Sand

I've already noted Putin's problem in getting policies implemented or preventing grandstanding by his subordinates. I also stressed that the problem was hardly new, and indeed was an inherent characteristic of the collapse of the CPSU and hence central authority in post-Soviet Russia. One positive aspect of the attitude to government personnel in the new administration, however, was a first attempt to provide some security and continuity to the work of the government, while delineating the responsibilities and rights of government employees. Perhaps an initial modest step was simply the fact that as of 2000, the political merry-go-round stopped, and ministers and government officials actually started to have an opportunity to mature in their jobs.

In turn, this raises the long-standing issue of why is it so difficult to find the right people in Russia to devise and implement sound public policy. This has been an all-too-critical part of the period of gloom and revival covered in this book—and remains unresolved even today. For example, in March 2009, Medvedev launched a search for qualified people who could constitute an administrative reserve to fill senior government positions.

Indeed, fully appreciating this point is crucial to an understanding of what has happened and is likely to happen in Russia. Limited administrative capacity is probably the most serious bottleneck in implementing Russia's economic programs, much less any additional, more-ambitious measures under consideration. Voloshin, for one, was strikingly candid about his concerns. He underscored that Russia just didn't have enough competent professionals in the government at all levels—thus, for instance, the speculation about a major cabinet reshuffle in spring 2001 was nonsense, in his view, because the question was, Who would be better than the present crew? And at the lower levels where daily decisions need to be made and followed, he was despairing. He entreated that any suggestions for civil service reform would be welcome, but recognized that it would make little difference in the short run. Voloshin acknowledged, for example, my criticism of the government's backtracking on energy restrictions in September 2001 was a good case in point about a new policy (to use targeted budgetary subsidies instead) that simply was not implemented. This was because the few good managers were distracted with day-to-day issues, and it had then become a situation of fait accompli as the short harvest and northern supply seasons were already under way. This was evident, say, in the case of a letter to Khristenko from Camdessus concerning the former's pledge to ensure deliveries to the Northern Territories before the summer in order to avoid a repetition of emergency credits as in previous years. The letter was leaked, and the actions were not implemented in time.

Kasyanov also explained to me the difficulties in finding good, experienced staff members for work in government during his time as prime minister. He recognized that this weakness constituted a major impediment in dealing with the IMF in the past, not to mention perceptions by international markets and creditors. But he simply had little time or even ability—short of micromanaging his ministers—to get involved in appointments below the level of minister. As an example, he pointed to his frustration during the November 2000 mission when he heard that it was going nowhere and wanted to find a way to get involved. Kasyanov called a meeting of the Russian negotiators, but the meeting was reportedly a disappointment. Nowhere was the problem of professionalism more evident than in the fiasco in dealing with the question of Paris Club payments at the beginning of 2001 (see below).

The long-standing nature of the staffing issue was well established. For instance, during a much earlier visit to Moscow in November 1997, Fischer had been informed of discussions about whether personnel in the economic block of the government should be changed. Most people to whom he spoke believed that taxes would be collected better if Aleksashenko became head of the STS. Aleksashenko had been offered this job by Chernomyrdin and refused, citing the need to remain at the CBR. The other person mentioned as tough, able, and probably willing to take the job was Fedorov. But Chernomyrdin had been deeply insulted by some incautious remarks made by Fedorov and would not offer him the job, even though Fedorov had apparently agreed to apologize and promised to behave.

This sensitive issue of staffing and efficient organization of government has long been recognized as a key problem in Russia. It figured prominently as one of the three critical sets of reforms originally envisaged by Gref's Center for Strategic Studies in early 2000, but it was never implemented. Gref's proposed state reform program was comprised of a number of fundamental reforms: the development of the federal districts, intergovernmental fiscal reform, judicial reform, deregulation, and civil service and administrative reform. Drawing lessons from the poor track record of reform implementation in post-Soviet Russia, Gref concluded that it would not be possible to achieve the results hoped for in the areas of economic and social reform without also implementing a set of radical, deeper institutional reforms. The practical problems related to his insight have been all too clear subsequently.

So why, then, has so little been heard about this reform, while major attention has rightly been paid to related reforms such as judicial reform and deregulation during Putin's first administration? The answer appears to be that the reform team had understood the lessons from the earlier efforts in this area, and had decided to approach the development of reforms carefully from both a strategic and tactical perspective. A lot of effort during Putin's presidential tenure went into building a broad consensus within the government and the presidential administration around the strategic objectives for, and priorities of, reform of the civil service system, to create a modern, merit-based, and corruption-resistant civil service. Even by the middle of 2010, due to the continuing clash of aims and interests within the governing class, little other than some higher salaries had been achieved.

8

The Friendly Divorce

One Last Chance

From the Russian side, with a growing self-confidence from formulating and implementing its own homegrown economic policy program, the further strengthening of oil prices in autumn 2000, better economic results (and more important, some initial signs in some areas even outside of large cities that everyday life was starting to improve), the desirability of finalizing a program with IMF support was fading fast. The government no longer saw it as a top priority, but merely a worthwhile objective. And even here, the motivation was mainly to ensure the financing of the 2001 budget, in which the IMF and especially a rescheduling of debt service maturities falling due to Paris Club creditors were assumed when the draft budget was formulated during summer 2000. This budget assumption resulted from inertia since the government's key parameters for budget planning—as in many countries—had to be fixed almost six months before the budget year, and circumstances could change radically in the interim. So it was with the 2001 budget.

The balance of payments projections of the July 2000 IMF mission indicated a hypothetical financing gap for 2001 of three billion U.S. dollars, which would emerge in the absence of debt rescheduling. This financing need was consistent with the financing gap in the 2001 budget projection. Critically, the projection assumed that the sharp rise in oil prices would not be sustained—an assumption in line with the IMF's *World Economic Outlook* (and one that IMF missions were more or less obliged to use in their country work)—but also because of the expectation that imports would start to surge toward their early 1998 levels with growth accelerating and the appreciation of the real exchange rate. The IMF staff noted in its report the unusual degree of uncertainty in making the projections (this had become a usual mantra in every projection for the balance of payments for Russia in the past ten years).

In making our calculations, the IMF assumed that Russia would require another arrangement covering 2001 in order to secure a debt-rescheduling agreement with Paris Club creditors as a group and especially with Germany as the largest sovereign creditor. In fact, the Paris Club normally requires a debtor country seeking a restructuring of debt service maturities to have an IMF program in place before providing debt relief. The staff report on the July mission, called the Annual Article IV Consultation, was discussed by the IMF board on September 15, 2000. Creditor country representatives on the board were not happy with the staff conclusion about the need for three billion U.S. dollars in debt relief in 2001, especially in view of further increases in oil prices, but broadly supported the staff's conclusions.

A couple of weeks later and three long years after those heady days in Hong Kong, the IMF annual meeting was again held outside Washington, DC—this time in Prague. The Russian delegation was headed by Finance Minister Kudrin. As had started to become a regular feature of big international economic gatherings subsequent to the confrontational WTO meeting in Seattle in December 1999, the Prague one grabbed the headlines with demonstrations and disruptions to the normal business of the meetings. On the last day, the Russian delegation—considering that nothing would be lost in terms of the substance of the meetings and in an effort to leave the meeting security perimeter early to catch a flight back to Moscow—tried to get to their awaiting cars without a police escort, only to regret the effort when Kudrin was mugged and a couple of others were hurt.

During the rest of autumn 2000, the debate over monetary policy and the effective sterilization of reserves (that is, mopping up the ruble liquidity created by central bank purchases of dollars) continued with little progress. Meanwhile, it turned out that Russia was coping relatively well with the strong balance of payments pressure: the IMF staff members had been right that such pressures were likely to grow, not diminish, but MinFin's Ignatiev and CBR's Paramonova were also right that the sharply higher-than-expected government budget surplus and increasing demand for ruble money helped to sterilize those pressures. But especially, what salvaged the argument was that private capital outflow not only continued unabated (so much for the effectiveness of Russian exchange controls) but also was considerably higher than expected. The sterilization of the ruble counterpart from acquiring foreign exchange reserves was carried out not by the CBR, or even MinFin, but by the Russian private sector moving its funds offshore.

Another seemingly unresolved issue with the IMF was what to do about the restructuring of the banking system. As the CBR rightly pointed out, the issue had moved on since the August 1998 banking collapse as well as the many alarmist concerns about permanent damage to payments and even the viability of Sberbank. In retrospect, there had been too much focus by the IMF and World Bank on a few large, Moscow-based banks as if they were representative, but mainly because there was a tendency—based on the experience in other countries in Asia, Latin America, and Eastern Europe—to exaggerate the importance of Russia's banking system to the economy.

There had not been much of a real banking system in the normal sense of the word. Even in mid-1998, before the crisis, excluding cash held by the population and deposits at Sberbank, broad money in Russia was only 3 percent of the GDP, which was hardly enough to influence the macroeconomy one way or another in a significant way. Ironically, a major weakness of the Russian economy—the fact that the people did not trust their own currency—actually became a strength in these circumstances, since much of the population, especially outside Moscow, were largely unaffected by the direct consequences of the economic crisis. An indicator of the degree of mistrust was also that the estimated amount of U.S. dollar banknotes held in Russia exceeded the total value of ruble broad money.

As an illustration of the basic concern, I often tell the following story. One time I was asked by the editor in chief of a leading Russian weekly magazine what exactly it was that the IMF wanted Russia to do. I said to him, "Sergei, you're presumably a middle-class Russian who wants his country to be a secure and prosperous place for his family. You tell me what policies your government and central bank would need to follow for you to be persuaded to receive your salary in rubles [not in dollars as was then the practice], keep your money on deposit in a Russian bank, and invest your savings in Russian assets. If you can tell me what those policies are, I am sure that they are close to what the IMF is looking for." Sergei, a classic skeptic, responded as most did to my query: "I wouldn't believe anything they do; it is much easier to convince you gullible foreigners than it would ever be to convince me."

Thus, my personal measure of when the Russian economy will definitively turn the corner has always been when Russian residents choose to hold rubles, not only for small transactions, but also for big-ticket items and savings, as measured by the demand for money (using broad ruble money as the proxy) to the levels prevailing in other medium-income economies in central Europe of at least 50 percent. In 2000, I found it discouraging that demand was still at an average level of 12.5 percent of GDP. Since then money demand has risen steadily, mirroring the de-dollarization of the economy. By 2008, money demand rose on average to 32.7 percent of GDP, and despite a dip with the financial instability in early 2009, money demand rose marginally to 33.8 percent by the end of the year. In view of the economic trauma in 2009, the mere fact that money demand did not collapse was an encouraging improvement. Nevertheless, until we witness a convergence with average European levels, I remain of the view that no matter how impressive the policies, low money demand is indicative of a basic lack of confidence of Russians in their own country's economic future.

Back in 2000, the chances of an agreement with the IMF seemed to be fading by the day, especially since as autumn proceeded, oil prices stayed high (for instance, by November 2000, Brent Crude averaged $32.55, or an increase of 32 percent from a year earlier), and Russia's external current account performance continued to improve. This had the consequence of making an agreement with the IMF difficult to justify in terms of balance of payments need, which is one of the key conditions for a program. In practice this means that the use of IMF financial resources has to be linked to an assessment that the balance of payments, even after appropriate policy adjustments, cannot be financed from normal market sources in the short term.

This background set the stage for a lunch at Café Pushkin between Viugin and me on Saturday, October 28, which had been requested by the prime minister. Although Viugin was the chief economist at the Troika Dialog investment bank at that point, he maintained a quasi-official role as an adviser to the prime minister. Viugin wanted to see what the real possibilities of an agreement with the IMF might be and what the implications of that were for the Paris Club. I suggested to him that the likelihood of an agreement seemed slim, and that perhaps, in my personal view, it was time for the Russian authorities to accept the inevitable, and declare positively that further financial support from the IMF was not needed under the current circumstances and the Paris Club creditors should be paid as scheduled. My perspective at the time was not shared by most of my IMF colleagues.

No doubt owing to inertia, a further round of talks in mid-November proved inconclusive, with the usual focus on macroeconomic imbalances as well as the stance of budgetary and monetary policies in 2001. Again, the appropriateness of the proposed monetary stance (which assumed a limited reserve accumulation) meant that an inordinate amount of time was taken in projecting the balance of payments with MinFin's Ignatiev. Hence, the last arrangement with the IMF (the one approved in late July 1999) expired automatically, while the 2001 budget that still assumed a Paris Club rescheduling became law.

Missteps and Muddle

For those responsible for financial policy in Russia, the beginning of 2001 was a total confusion. And it was symptomatic of all the weaknesses, lack of managerial skills, and communication skills that have plagued post-Soviet Russian economic policy formulation. Having assumed that three billion U.S. dollars of debt service due to the Paris Club creditors would be rescheduled and so not paid by the budget in 2001, and having secured a tentative recognition of the financing need by creditors at an early stage, the Russian authorities had every reason to assume that certain categories of debt service falling due to the Paris Club would be rescheduled in 2001, as they had been every year since 1992. In fairness to the initial Russian position, trying to change some basic assumptions in the budget law at an advanced stage (the draft budget generally is finalized by late August, and forwarded to the Duma for consideration and adoption) was analogous to turning around the proverbial supertanker.

The Russian authorities considered the Paris Club debt rescheduling a done deal, with three billion U.S. dollars in financing (or money not spent on debt service and so available to finance other budgetary expenditure). As a point of principle, the Russian side felt that its request to creditors was modest in light of the agreed-on language concerning Russian debt among the G-7 at its Cologne summit in June 1999. Kasyanov, as the brand-new finance minister at that time, was proud of the language adopted, which asserted that a "generous and definitive solution to Russia's Soviet-era debt problem should be found once economic policies were deemed to be sustainable." Recognizing that the international attitude toward Russia might make such a "definitive" solution premature, the Russia side was only asking for a rescheduling of debt service, not any debt reduction.

Moreover, the IMF mission had worked during the autumn on the basis of that assumption, which had been endorsed, however reluctantly, by the IMF board in mid-September. During bilateral discussions in Prague and elsewhere in early fall, the assumption had not been challenged. In fact, in a meeting with a German delegation in Moscow in early November, the Russian representative, Deputy Finance Minister Sergei Kolotukhin, reported that the Germans were only concerned that the request should not entail any debt reduction or forgiveness.

Of course, what had happened in the meantime was a further considerable strengthening of the Russian balance of payments. Between the end of June and end of December 2000, the CBR's foreign exchange reserves rose by six billion U.S. dollars despite significantly higher capital outflows. When the IMF team reworked the numbers in November and shared these with the creditors in the Paris Club, it became clear that it would be almost technically impossible for them to justify exceptional financing to Russia in such circumstances. The low esteem and mistrust for Russia generally, and the more specific fear that Western public opinion would perceive any financing to Russia at that stage as tantamount to Western support for the Russian actions in Chechnya, certainly played a role. The Russian delegation was told informally about the Paris Club concerns in early December.

The Russian side was incredulous. Kudrin sent a letter to the Paris Club on December 29 requesting a tentative approach to rescheduling for the following year, which was rejected by the creditors, who asked to be paid in full. The Russians felt sore about Western hypocrisy and broken commitments. The reactions in Moscow varied between telling the creditors that it was too late technically to pay, to explaining that it was now the law and could not be changed, to a refusal on political grounds to cave in to Western demands. The stakes were high. Some large maturities started falling due in late January; if not paid, Russia would be in default and a crisis would ensue.

Western opinion was clear. Russia did not need any debt rescheduling for 2001. If there was a problem later on, then the question could be reconsidered. In any case, there was no agreement with the IMF so a rescheduling request was a mute point.

In Moscow, some were pushing for brinkmanship, arguing that the West had always given in to Russian intransigence in the area of financial policy. But the main activity in Moscow was to assign blame for this national embarrassment. The whole affair had been badly handled with a midlevel MinFin official offhandedly mentioning a "decision" not to pay debt to the Paris Club in the first quarter pending further discussions with creditors. Other officials in the government, not directly involved in the issue, also weighed in, just adding to the public confusion. Many looked to Kasyanov as the traditional official associated with the Paris

Club, and in public statements he emphasized that Russia's reputation might suffer as it was too late to adjust the 2001 budget, at least for the first quarter, but he made it clear to the IMF that Kudrin was in charge. In turn, it was also apparent that the budget people and the debt people in MinFin had different views.

To stir things up, Putin's economic adviser, Andrei Illarionov, bravely weighed in with a public attack on the government's formal position and confusion on January 17, 2001. He said that Russia could and should pay, like a normal country, and the government's position was not only untenable but humiliating as well. The issue had to be raised with the president. It was sorted out as Russia dropped its request and promised to pay all obligations falling due, while noting that the government would want to return to the issue later. Illarionov called it the end of "another dream."[1] The Russian budget would have to be financed in some other way (which turned out to be rather easy in light of higher oil prices and much faster economic growth).

The Economy Takes Off

There was obviously a growing divergence between the views of the Russian authorities and the IMF on a range of issues. This reflected greater professionalism and experience on the Russian side as well as its willingness to assert its views when new financing to be unlocked by an IMF program was no longer at stake.

For instance, the Russian authorities and the IMF diverged in their assessment of what was needed concerning the introduction of the so-called flat tax. IMF staff members were clearly skeptical in summer 2000 when the idea was being formulated in the context of the draft 2001 budget law, and were concerned about a serious loss of revenue. In January 2001, Russia introduced this dramatic reform of its personal income tax, becoming the first large economy to adopt a flat tax.

The tax code of 2001 replaced a conventional progressive rate structure with a flat tax rate of 13 percent. Over the following year, while the Russian economy grew at just over 5 percent in real terms, the revenues from the personal income tax increased by over 25 percent in real terms. Besides this revenue-yield performance, advocates also have credited the flat tax with beneficial changes in the real side of the economy. The Russian experience appeared to be so successful that many other countries followed suit with their own flat rate income tax reforms.[2] One study found that the flat tax reform was instrumental in decreasing tax evasion in Russia, and that to a certain extent, the greater fiscal revenues starting in 2001 could be linked to increased voluntary tax compliance and reporting. It also discovered that the productivity effect on the real side of the economy was positive, although smaller than the tax evasion effect.

Likewise, many IMF staff members were initially skeptical about the introduction of deposit insurance for banks, arguing that it was premature and the conditions might not be appropriate at that stage. They also expressed misgivings about Minister Kudrin's proposal to establish an oil stabilization fund, again suggesting that the conditions for a successful operation were not yet in place.

Surely one of the most unexpected results of 2000 was the extraordinary economic performance registered as the year ended. Real growth clocked in at 10 percent, the second highest in the world that year, and well in excess of the 3 percent projected by the IMF as the year began or even the 4 percent estimated at the time of the consultation discussions in midyear. In the main, the margin of undervaluation of the ruble was not fully appreciated, nor was the significant productivity increases that could be engendered from better organization and management of the existing factors of production even without large new investments.

Despite the favorable news, the IMF forecasts for 2001 were for a decelerating rate of growth. As the year began, the IMF was again projecting a 3 percent growth rate. Illarionov was even more extreme. He maintained, as the figures for the first two months were produced, that the economy was already entering a recession caused by the overvaluation of the ruble, which was stopping investment and growth. As it turned out, nothing of the kind was going on; Illarionov was simply committing the common mistake of reading too much into the most recent numbers—a point that I tried to make to him in March, but without much success. The Washington-based IMF staff tended to share his concerns about the effects of the real appreciation of the ruble and continued to call for significant sterilization measures. The actual outturn was significantly better at 5.1 percent, especially considering the international context of serious weakening on a global scale. Again, Russia's relative economic performance was one of the best in the world.

Russia and the IMF to Remain Friends

After nine years of attempted reforms in post-Soviet Russia, it appeared that real, positive change was finally taking place. And while it may not have been in line with the exact priorities favored by the IMF, on the whole the Russians were moving in the right direction. These developments reflected at least the beginnings of a sense of maturity on the part of the Russian financial authorities, and the confidence and expertise to develop and apply appropriate economic policy measures.

In retrospect, the relationship between Russia and the IMF had already begun to change in fall 1999. The essential factor in this change was a switch from an intense focus and close collaboration on economic programs to confront immediate macroeconomic imbalances, to a more consultative mode, advising the authorities on options with an emphasis on crisis prevention. In IMF jargon, it was the start of a switch from "program" mode to "surveillance" mode, and is considered perfectly normal and even desirable in the IMF's relations with its members.

This shift was hardly perceptible at the time. Clearly, the CBR and MinFin as well as the IMF staff were focused on efforts to complete the review under the program and release the associated tranche. At the Ministry of Economy and elsewhere, however, there were initial steps to rethink priorities. Sustained higher oil prices helped.

It was merely a coincidence that this change started just as Putin arrived in the premiership—unless history should reveal that both events, while independent, reflected a maturing of Russian society and its leadership, at least relative to the early phases of the post-Soviet era.

Cynics would no doubt remark that a loosening of the ties was inevitable once the IMF no longer dangled the carrot of more money. Not that the cynics were entirely wrong, but there were other reasons for the change in the IMF's relationship with Russia.

The most important point was that the economy was starting to respond positively to the combination of the completely unintentional but effective shock therapy administered by the Primakov government along with the stimulus effects of the undervalued ruble, the firming of oil prices, and critically, the cumulative effects of the many policy measures taken earlier to improve economic, monetary, and budgetary management. After recording real growth in the first half of the year of 0.6 percent (at an annual rate), the economy bounded by 11.7 percent in the second half of 1999. Budget revenues were growing even more rapidly, and MinFin was capable of meeting its expenditure commitments on a current basis and even eliminating the stock of payment arrears, at least at the federal level.

Having survived for over a year with only one tranche of IMF money, the authorities realized that they could indeed continue to live and possibly even thrive without periodic injections of IMF money. Of course, the government was paying minimal amounts on its restructured domestic debt and virtually nothing to the CBR on outstanding credits, while also benefiting from earlier reschedulings of payment obligations to the Paris Club.

A second factor had to do with changes in key people on the Russian side. On September 2, 1999, Zadornov announced his resignation as special representative to the IFIs to take up a position as counselor to the management of Sberbank—an irony that was not lost on the IMF. This proved to be a temporary position as Zadornov was reelected to the Duma in the December 1999 elections and became the chair of the Subcommittee on Banking of the Budget Committee. Barely a month later, on October 8, Viugin announced that he was leaving MinFin to become the chief economist at Troika Dialog, the Moscow-based investment bank. With their departures, a kernel of the experience with the IMF and the design of economic programs vanished. Ignatiev, who also had dealt with the IMF on a large range of technical issues over the years—but critically, not on the full range of strategic questions—was called on to add the IMF to his already-heavy portfolio. It was clear that he did not relish the addition of this new responsibility on top of an already-busy agenda.

On the IMF side as well, partly as a result of the consequences of the August 1998 crisis and the stinging criticism of the IMF in regard to Russia, a more cautious attitude developed. This shift from a proactive to a more neutral stance was hastened by the aftermath of the scandals. Meanwhile, the World Bank was becoming increasingly engaged, partly as a result of the dynamic leadership asserted by bank president Wolfenson in forging a working relationship with Putin, but also because of the additional human and financial resources being devoted to the work on Russia.

A growing sense of public outrage in the major Western countries cannot be discounted. A series of scandals erupted in 1999, each giving rise to a plethora of negative editorials in the world's leading newspapers, and consequently, even friendly governments felt under pressure to demonstrate resolve in addressing the apparent flourishing of lawlessness and criminality in Russia, which seemed to be spilling over into these very Western countries.

The eruption of the BONY scandal in August 1999, from no less an authoritative source than the *New York Times*, especially shook the Clinton administration. On August 19, a *New York Times* article by business reporter Timothy O'Brien appeared on the front page with the incredible scoop that up to ten billion U.S. dollars, again including IMF money, had been money laundered through BONY in an elaborate operation run by the Russian mafia.[3] Almost as incredible was when, sometime later and after considerable damage had been done, on January 17, 2000, O'Brien published an article inside the *New York Times* in which he retracted some of his earlier assertions, and suggested that the *New York Times* and other press may have been set up by an unreliable source. The charges and countercharges, which have continued ever since, have been mainly conducted through the media instead of the courts.[4] The point for my story here is less the possibility (though serious) of criminal wrongdoing and more the growing suspicion of corruption that accompanied the discussions of Russian financial matters.

After the resignation of Rubin as treasury secretary, Clinton nominated Summers. There were concerns in the treasury that Summers's congressional confirmation hearings in September could come unstuck over the issue of Russia. The fear was that sensitized by the scandals, congresspeople could use the hearings to voice their concerns about Russia and its financial system with which Summers had been involved. Treasury officials had developed a set of conditions that could be considered to address possible congressional concerns with Russian "transgressions." These conditions mainly focused on steps to promote transparency and avoid conflicts of interest. In the face of some hard questioning on Russia, even though Russia itself was not the major focus of the hearings, Summers offered up the proposed conditions and pledged that he would insist that they be incorporated into the Russian program before the United States voted for IMF approval of the next tranche. In actuality, shortly thereafter, these very suggestions were tabled by the United States at a meeting of G-7 finance ministers in late September. U.S. Treasury representatives insisted that the Russian authorities accept those conditions into the outstanding program conditions as agreed on with the IMF. This led to an acrimonious debate within the IMF and the G-7, and then with the Russians of course.

Reluctantly, the Russian delegation to the annual meeting of IMF in Washington, DC, accepted this extraordinary additional program conditionality on September 25, 1999. It was humiliating for the IMF that it had to justify that this new conditionality was a logical extension of what was already required for completing the delayed review based on end-September performance. Obviously, after such a blatant interference by major member countries into disbursement conditions under a pre-existing agreement, the credibility of the IMF as a technical institution suffered badly. For most Russians, it only proved what they had long known or at least suspected: that the IMF was just a political tool of its major shareholders.

Yet the coup de grace in changed perceptions of the Russia-IMF relationship was the Western reactions to the second Chechen war. The incursion into Dagestan by Chechen troops in late August (taking an entire town as hostage), followed shortly thereafter, starting on September 9, 1999, by mysterious and highly destructive apartment bombings in Moscow and other cities, marked the beginning of a large-scale Russian attempt to reassert its control over Chechnya, seemingly regardless of the cost in human and material devastation.

At least until the calamitous events of September 11, 2001, the international media reports were for the most part damning of Russian brutality and inhumanity. The reaction of public opinion in the West was one of shock and horror. Political leaders, especially in European countries such as France, became even more critical of Russian policy in all aspects, including economic.

It was in this context that an agreement was reached with IMF mission chief Belanger in late November 1999 that could have paved the way for the completion of the delayed review and disbursement of the next tranche. The agreement more or less was in line with its negotiating brief, previously approved by the IMF management prior to the departure of the mission. Belanger reported the successful conclusion of the negotiations to the IMF management by the time of the Thanksgiving holiday in the United States.

In the meantime, between the approval of the brief and the completion of negotiations, the political reaction in the West was provoking public concerns about the role of the IMF and other Western financial sources. It was against this background that Camdessus made a comment to the press in late November that seemed to link the completion of the review and Chechnya. The Russian authorities asked for clarification. Livshits, who at the time was the Kremlin's G-7 Sherpa, was dispatched to Washington. In an extraordinary display of cold professionalism, as Fischer later described the event, the managing director met with Livshits on December 3, and after observing that the conditions were not satisfactory for the completion of the review, he warned the Russian authorities not to politicize the situation. The next day, Camdessus made a public statement concerning the unfulfilled outstanding conditions. The list, while plausible on a literal reading, was little more than an alibi and hardly in keeping with the normal practices of the IMF.

What happened in terms of outside political pressures in late November 1999 stands in stark contrast to summer 1998. It seems to be a popular notion that there was enormous political pressure brought to bear on the IMF in summer 1998 to provide large-scale financial support to Russia. Indeed, some senior officials in G-7 governments, most notably in the United States, wanted the Russians to believe that they were responsible for the IMF largesse. Both Camdessus and Fischer remarked to me in separate interviews that this attempt to take the credit was readily understandable. But it should be obvious that there was really not much of an issue of outside political influence over decisions that the IMF was inclined to take in any case on their own merits. The same governments that were so eager to take the credit for IMF disbursements before the crisis in 1998 were just as happy to use the IMF more anonymously to take the blame for withholding disbursements when it suited their political interests. Clearly, in my view, the IMF caved in on this issue in November 1999 from political pressure.

Fischer observed to me that it was the most blatant example of political interference in an IMF decision during his seven years in management. Many Western commentators, including senior U.S. officials such as Lipton, said that it would have been unconscionable to allow a disbursement at that time, which would have been seen as tantamount to Western financing of Russian aggression in Chechnya.

Camdessus himself, in an interview for this book, said that it was not really a question of political interference as such but rather of political perceptions. As far as the Russians were concerned, they must have understood that with respect to delayed or still-outstanding program conditions subject to the next tranche, in view of the obvious international context, the implementation of these conditions must be seen as exemplary, no less.

Camdessus claimed that these instructions to Belanger's mission were clear; while what the Russians were proposing was broadly satisfactory, it was not exemplary—and certainly not enough given Russia's dodgy track record and international scrutiny. But Camdessus also admitted that as a human being, he was glad to have found an excuse to suspend IMF support in view of what he understood was happening in Chechnya. He made a further point that he had purposefully intended to send a clear signal to the Russian authorities, as he had already announced his retirement from the IMF, that the days of the proactive and available

IMF financial support were over for good. My problem was that I had to explain his understanding at the time of these developments to a puzzled and angry Kasyanov in a private meeting on December 17, 1999.

As noted in the previous chapter, both the IMF and Russian sides had developed the habit over the years of discussing appropriate economic policies and cobbling together annual programs that the Russian government would agree to implement and the IMF would support financially. This momentum continued once the initial bitterness on both sides subsided after the dramatic midnight resignation announcement of President Yeltsin on New Year's Eve 1999. Nevertheless, the miscommunications between IMF and Russian officials continued to grow in fall 2000, once an operational government was in place following the long lull of elections in May 2000 and then the summer holidays.

For instance, an IMF mission in late November 2000 was confused by crossed signals received from the authorities. Kasyanov had suggested directly to me, and less directly to the mission, that a new agreement with the IMF was not needed. With no Paris Club debt restructuring in the offing, there seemed to be little to be gained from a new agreement—and indeed something could be gained by the perception and boost to confidence that Russia no longer needed the IMF. With no financing need, any IMF-supported program would have been considered "precautionary," which in IMF jargon entails that no money would be provided unless there were a serious deterioration in the balance of payments for reasons outside the control of the authorities (such as a drop in oil prices). Since Kudrin was formally charged with relations with the IMF, though, Kasyanov did not contradict him in front of the mission; he just dropped hints. But privately he told Kudrin that if he could get an agreement with the IMF with no real conditions attached, then it would be acceptable. The bottom line was no policy conditions for IMF support that the authorities were not already going to do anyway in their own program.

Kudrin persisted in trying to elaborate such a program, and the IMF played along. Even after the departure of the mission, discussions continued with Kudrin well into April 2001 before it was finally accepted that there would be no program. It was confusing because Kudrin obviously wanted a program for his own reasons, and the IMF staff involved also wanted to elaborate a program. I recall that the mission had even reported to the IMF board, based on the discussions with Kudrin, that a program was being finalized and would shortly be submitted for approval. It was only when the program that Kudrin presented to the government failed the test that Kasyanov had laid down that it was apparent that it had been a nonstarter from the beginning.[5]

And Kasyanov was right. Russia did not need an IMF program, only its friendly advice and cooperation. A new relationship needed to be forged, not based on the tensions of a negotiated framework, but rather on a more trusted adviser role to counsel Russia in managing its own economic destiny. At least for the immediate future, and recognized for the first time in post-Soviet Russia, the country no longer was dependent on foreign financing, and foreign advice could now be accepted in good grace along with that of increasingly sophisticated Russian advisers.

Such was the seeming abruptness of this change—at least as seen from the outside—that the IMF staff continued in program mode for a while longer. An experienced senior official, Siddharth Tiwari, who had worked in the IMF's Moscow office in the mid-1990s, joined the Washington-based team in January 2001, and started to redirect the attention from programming to high value-added research and advice. The Moscow-based IMF representatives, headed by my successor, Poul Thomsen, from March 2001 also switched gears and developed a new, constructive dialogue with the Russian authorities at a policy as well as technical level.

Meanwhile, as 2001 proceeded, and buoyed by continuing favorable circumstances, the economy grew and business-government relations started to become more transparent. Despite the intrigues surrounding Gusinsky and Berezovsky, Russia was perceived as becoming more of a possibly stable emerging market economy and increasing its integration with the world. Domestic financial markets started to function again, the stock market soared, and foreign reserves jumped.

During the course of 2001, the feeling that Russia was starting to become what the Russians call a "normal" country—with the attributes of the functioning institutions of other more-or-less democratic, market economies—was almost palpable. Grinding poverty, arbitrary administration, and bureaucratic incompetence still dominated daily life, and scandals continued to erupt on a too frequent basis. But there was also at the time the perception that at the margin, slowly things were getting better. Even the debates about police abuse, crime, and government corruption seemed to involve greater transparency and public debate, much as in other countries. Unfortunately this relatively optimistic perspective didn't even last for the length of Putin's first term as president.

Fischer made one last visit to Moscow, on June 18–19, as part of the IMF management. Putin, besides jokingly offering him a job if he wanted one, found the value-added component of the discussion to be in line with what Russia needed from the IMF in future, and he welcomed him back on a future visit. When Fischer left the IMF in February 2002, he took a position as vice chair of Citigroup in New York. He is now the governor of the Bank of Israel.

The World Seems to Shift Gears Again

Prior to the arrest of Khodorkovsky in October 2003, perceptions, at least the external perceptions of Russia, had again become positive. Maybe this was yet another swing of the pendulum in the gloom-euphoria cycle in relation to Russia—in fact, it didn't last long, and external political perceptions, but not business, started to swing back to the negative the following year. And while this positive mood swing appeared to be gathering steam already in summer 2001, it received a decisive boost after the infamous attacks on the United States on September 11. The contrast in external perceptions before and after September 11 was striking. Before then, the Western press was castigating Bush and other Western leaders for their naivety in dealing with Putin. That changed on September 11, when Bush said that the first call received from a foreign leader was from Putin, saying that in addition to his shared sense of outrage, he would ensure that Russian forces stand down despite the U.S. move to the highest level of alert, and would call off a large-scale military exercise about to commence lest it confuse the situation. Two weeks after September 11, Putin lent strong support to the U.S.-led coalition against terrorism by offering the use of Russian-controlled air corridors, providing intelligence sharing, and dropping any objections to the U.S. use of central Asian bases. A few weeks later he went even further, announcing the closure of Soviet-era bases in Cuba and Vietnam.

Behind such initiatives were concerns about the very real threat facing Russia of unrest along its long borders in the Caucasus and central Asia—and the incentive of warmer relations with the West. Another, more compelling reason was the stark fact that after more than a decade of neglect, the country's armed forces were overstretched.

In October 2001 Kohler made his initial visit as IMF management, and Anne Krueger, his first deputy (and successor to Fischer), visited Moscow in March 2002. In both cases, the visits signaled the new cooperative approach to Russia, treating it as a respected member of the IMF as well as an important element in the global and regional economy with responsibilities that extended well beyond its own borders.

In the period that followed, Russia, like other members with outstanding liabilities to the IMF, was subject to postprogram monitoring with twice-yearly missions to ensure that policies continued in place that could generate the resources to repay the fund. Then, on January 31, 2005, Russia prepaid all of its remaining debt to the IMF of US$3.3 billion (paid out of the stabilization fund). By doing so, as Kudrin explained at the time, Russia was able to save US$204 million in interest that would have accrued on its debt under the original schedule, and that instead would be allocated to the implementation of social and economic projects in Russia. In 2005, Russia also agreed to allow the ruble to be used in the IMF's financial plan to lend to other countries in need. This change in fortune stood in sharp contrast to six years earlier when it was unclear whether Russia under Primakov would default or not on its debt service to the IMF. And since then, Russia became a creditor to the IMF, and in 2009 agreed to purchase US$10 billion worth of IMF bonds along with Brazil and China.

In the years that followed, the IMF role in Russia was transformed into what is considered normal in financially significant members. The fund continued to field occasional missions and has written some excellent analytic reports about the Russian economy.[6] The IMF maintains a small office in Moscow with Odd Per Brekk now at its head and remains a source of technical advice for government officials. Russia, through both the longevity and influence of Finance Minister Kudrin and Mozhin as Russia's executive director in the fund, but also clearly because of its relative economic size and success, had achieved a relative status by 2010 that seemed almost to justify perhaps belatedly its designation as a BRIC (Brazil, Russia, India, and China) country and a prominent role in the G-20. This change in status was clear when the Russian chair, breaking ranks with the G-7, took the lead for emerging market and developing countries when Russia unsuccessfully nominated the former Czech prime minister and central banker Josef Tosovsky for the post of IMF managing director in August 2007. Former French finance minister Dominique Strauss-Kahn was elected, but the Russian initiative was appreciated by the increasingly important and vocal emerging market members of the IMF.

By the middle of 2010, despite a difficult global economic context, the Russian economy has started to grow again and broaden its base—

although clearly facing continuing spillover from the process of global deleveraging, especially the sovereign debt crisis in Europe, and the related volatility of oil and other commodity prices. Disinflation has been working, and with lower interest rates, creditworthy borrowers have greater access to bank credit. In a low-debt economy like Russia, there is scope for productive investment and growing consumption. Productivity increases will hopefully lay the basis for long-term growth and diversification, needed all the more in light of the declining demographic trend despite a tiny and unexpected uptick in 2009. In a world of greater volatility, if Russia can maintain a steady course, then its international role, including in the IMF, will be enhanced, not only in determining the next managing director, but also even more in the development of appropriate policies where Russia and the other BRICs are not only among the world's largest creditors but the major locomotives for world growth as well. The role reversal from defaulting debtor to a leading creditor in a little over a decade is nothing short of extraordinary.

9

The Legacy of the Crisis

Thus far, the focus has been on the factors that led to the 1998 financial collapse and its immediate consequences as well as the end of the IMF's financial role in supporting Russian economic policy reforms. Now I turn to the obvious questions about the longer-term legacy of the crisis—seen from the vantage point of more than twelve years later—and whether the lessons of that earlier calamity have been applied in facing the financial turmoil that began in late 2008.

The Latest Crisis Is Not a Rerun

Seen from the perspective of mid-2010, looking at the financial devastation and then the subsequent rebound of Russian financial markets and economy over the past year or so, many in Russia and beyond wondered if they had been in for a repeat of the 1998 crisis. This has been no time for complacency about Russia or the global economy. With most of the OECD countries in the process of debt deleveraging and even a clutch of them turning to the IMF, Russia was certainly not immune. Despite the initial overshooting relative to other emerging markets in 2009 and the poor initial credit ratings, however, I would contend that Russia is much better placed than most countries to become steadily stronger.

No doubt the virulence of the sudden collapse of the Russian equity and bond markets between August 2008 and March 2009, the abrupt reversal of seemingly unstoppable economic growth, the flight of foreign investors with the resulting hemorrhage of foreign reserves, and the pressure on the ruble exchange rate and subsequent depreciation of the rate by 35 percent relative to the U.S. dollar between November 2008 and January 2009 all strongly echoed of the events of over twelve years ago.

There are indeed many similarities. Once again Russia was in a situation in which the financial and economic meltdown was provoked by external factors. The Russian crisis of 1998 was a direct result of the Asian crisis of late 1997, which led to a massive drop in Russia's terms of trade and made the fiscal trajectory increasingly untenable. In a similar way the recent global crisis, which this time emanated from the United States and other advanced economies, had similar effects—resulting in plunging oil prices and a flight to safety by investors worldwide to the security of U.S. Treasury assets. Of course, all emerging market economies were impacted to varying degrees. And the combination of the drop in the oil price and the sudden reversal of capital put Russia in an extremely precarious situation—just as in spring and summer 1998.

Mood swings among foreign investors in their perceptions of Russia also played an important role then, as now, involving the media, rating agencies, regulators, and shareholders. Poor communication skills among Russian senior officials were in evidence in both situations. Lastly but powerfully, the long memories of the Russian people who have endured—at least until early in the last decade—almost a century of mostly perverse economic policies inspire them to expect the worst whenever financial variables, especially the exchange rate, come under pressure. This book is ample testimony to the need to address public mistrust through the maintenance of sound and stable policies.

I find it interesting that the crisis also revealed how—even over a decade ago—Russia evolved rapidly from the isolation of Soviet times. I mention this to underscore the point that Russia is fully integrated into the global system now. And it already was to a considerable extent even twelve years ago, with capital inflows and nonresident purchases of government bonds, which were so important to the financing of the budget back then.

Yet the differences between the recent financial collapse and 1998 are, in my mind, even more striking. There are several, and they are crucial to stress, although I will elaborate further below.

One difference is the lessons in fiscal conservatism learned by the authorities. The Achilles' heel in the 1990s was low and inadequate tax collection. The tax system was ineffective, and even minimalist budgets were always underfinanced. That became particularly evident in July 1998, when revenue was not sufficient to pay the army in cash. This lack of fiscal discipline stemmed from a combination of inadequate administrative structures little evolved from Soviet times and a lack of political will. The oil stabilization fund created in 2004 was a direct legacy.

Another major difference from the period leading up to and just after the 1998 crisis—one that the Russian authorities have really taken to heart—is that the Kremlin stopped the political merry-go-round. One of the hallmarks of the 1990s was political instability. Only President Yeltsin remained throughout most of that decade. In the period between March 1998 and August 1999, there were five prime ministers. Finance ministers also changed, from Chubais, to Zadornov, to Kasyanov, and then to Kudrin, over roughly the same period. There was government instability with poorly paid and motivated officials caught among various factions fighting for power as well as oligarchs and the so-called red directors of state companies, who were a powerful political force. Since 2000, there has been relative political stability. In addition to this, Russia is one of the few countries in the world where there is an experienced team of people who have learned about crises the hard way and are still in major policy positions.

Another important distinction between the recent crisis and the last one is that reluctantly, and maybe a little bit late in the game, the CBR let the exchange rate go. In late 1997 when the Asian crisis was breaking out and oil prices were starting to take a hit, for strictly political reasons, the Russian government did not want to even insinuate that the exchange rate could be changed. In fact in November 1997, it announced a continuation of a new ruble corridor for three years. In retrospect, this was a huge mistake: the government locked itself in.

In Russia, between November 11, 2008, and January 22, 2009, the CBR engineered a slow, but controlled and effective devaluation of the ruble that allowed a large amount of the reserves of the CBR to be transferred to Russian companies and the population. By so doing, fewer companies would be subject to default and were able to repay foreign loans. The population could convert savings into dollars if it wanted. This time, instead of most of the money fleeing the country, there was instead a transfer of foreign exchange from the public sector to the private sector. Kudrin estimated that about eighty billion U.S. dollars of the two hundred billion that the CBR lost between August 2008 and January 2009 actually went to the accounts of companies in the private sector, which helped to cushion the blow. So allowing the exchange rate to adjust when there were major terms of trade shock has been critical in dealing with the current crisis.

A final difference is that in 1998, the IMF and the international community were forthcoming with large amounts of money to help bail out Russia. Today, the Russian government understands that there's nobody to bail it out. It is on its own. That also helps to avoid wishful thinking or hoping for some kind of almost-divine intervention that obviates the need for decisive action.

Russia, like some of its Asian near-neighbors, learned valuable lessons from the crises of the late 1990s. The substantial foreign exchange reserves and large fiscal surpluses channeled into an oil stabilization fund have provided crucial buffers to cushion the impact from the contagion emanating from Wall Street. These buffers distinguish Russia's more benign circumstances from other countries in the region. Indeed, even after the reserve loss in late 2008, Russia still has the third-largest reserves in the world and has become one of the largest creditor countries globally. When Russia sits at the table of the G-20, it is in a strong financial position. Furthermore, the fiscal stimulus to confront the latest recession led to a budget deficit that could be entirely financed without resort to borrowing in 2009. Unlike in most Western countries or among the new EU members, Russia has low foreign debt levels in most sectors.

What does this mean? Russia has learned some hard lessons. But it is now even more globalized that it was a decade ago. And while better placed than most countries, certainly better positioned than many of its neighbors, it remains subject to the same contagion effects. In fact, despite the greater inherent resilience of the Russian economy, it is often viewed as a greater risk by market participants than its neighbors. In my view, once the country fully recovers from its first post-Soviet experience of a normal business cycle, a sustainable resurgence is the more likely outcome. Some modesty is in order, however: if the conventional wisdom, even among experts, could be so repeatedly wrong about the short-term prospects for economic developments in Russia, what credibility should be attached to future prognoses?

The assessment of the legacy of the 1998 crisis is confounded in some sense by the rapid success of the unanticipated recovery starting in 1999. A recovery in oil prices was only a part of the story. In any case, it is not a simple question of cause and effect. And notwithstanding Russia's official redesignation as a market economy by both the United States and the EU in 2002, and its upgrade by Moody's to investment grade in October 2003, some still continue to question whether the transition is really complete. Even if Russia is clearly Europe's biggest and most populous country—and no doubt someday it will be the richest—it is evident that much remains to be done and the outcome is not preordained.

Perhaps the noncontroversial part of the legacy concerns the incomplete reform agenda, although it begs the question as to why so much remains to be done, and indeed, whether the reform process itself has really become irreversible. More contentious aspects of the legacy that seem to linger from the 1990s relate to the role and influence of the West, the appropriateness of the advice provided by outsiders including the IMF, and the string of financial scandals that appeared to undermine Russia's chances of achieving a credible reputation on the global stage.

The Economic Legacy

A major factor in Russia's emergence on the world stage has been its new role as a global economic power. Although it cannot yet be seen as a fully developed economy, Russia is certainly considered an energy superpower, and the continuing search for energy security has increasingly seen the West (and China) turning, albeit reluctantly, to Russia's huge natural resource reserves. Between 1999 and 2008, Russia was demonstrating economic growth rates that were well above those of advanced countries—a factor that propelled it to become the eighth-largest economy in the world by the end of 2009, according to IMF data. Even with this kind of performance, it has not been enough to catch up significantly with Portuguese living standards, as Putin had hoped back in 2000.

The increasing oil revenue going into the stabilization fund, at least until the correction starting in late 2008, has allowed the Russian government to pay down Russia's sovereign external debt to 3 percent of the GDP—one of the lowest ratios in the G-20. It also means that many of the Western nations that lent money to Russia until the 1998 crisis now have little financial leverage. In fact, Russia has become increasingly a major net creditor and its foreign exchange reserves have substantially recovered from the low of US$384 billion in April 2009.

Another important factor in Russia's resurgence is the huge opportunity that Russia's emerging middle class constitutes for sellers of Western goods, and the massive boost being given to the international capital markets by the arrival of Russian companies and investors. All of this adds up to Russia increasingly becoming an economic power on the global stage. This trend, while admittedly interrupted by the impact of the global financial turmoil starting in late 2008, is likely to continue.

In evaluating the post–1998 crisis economic performance, the key issue is whether the population has benefited from the country's economic growth over the past decade. Overall, this period contains a number of economic successes. Until late 2008, millions of Russians were transformed into the middle class, unemployment had fallen, poverty was reduced, and debt was low on average, even if inflation remained a problem. Of course, the recent financial crisis presented a major challenge, with the indicators for poverty and unemployment deteriorating, while forcing the government to reconsider the assumptions underlying the economic model for future diversification and growth.

Putin was appointed prime minister just twelve months after August 1998. The economy was showing some signs of recovery, owing to the significant impact of currency devaluation, yet the viability of this growth was not considered by the IMF to be strong at the time. Today, it is a much different economic environment. Russia's economy ranked as only the twenty-third largest in the world in 1999.[1] GDP in 2010 is expected to reach more than US$1.5 trillion, or a rise of more than seven times the reported figure in 1999. The average salary had increased to US$682 a month as of March 2010, even after the devaluation of the ruble, and up from US$52 a month in January 1999. The population's real disposable income more than tripled between 1999 and 2010, even if it was negatively affected during 2009.

In 1999, Russia was still negotiating with its foreign creditors on restructuring its sovereign foreign debt, which then amounted to more than 70 percent of GDP. In August 1999, Russia agreed with the Paris Club of creditors to restructure US$8.3 billion of debt. In 2000, Russia signed a debt-restructuring deal with the London Club of creditors. For several years, there was talk of the "2003 problem," when foreign debt payments were set to peak. Yet by 2005 and 2006, Russia prepaid US$37 billion to the Paris Club. Reflecting a greatly reduced debt burden, the spread on Russian securities (as reflected in J.P. Morgan's emerging market bond index) narrowed to just over a hundred basis points by May 2008, from the more than three thousand basis points in early August 1999—although in the context of the global financial meltdown, the spread reached over eight hundred basis points in December 2008, before narrowing again. By March 2010 it had returned to about 158 basis points.

The stabilization fund was set up in 2004 as a tool to save windfall oil revenues for the future. Furthermore, the fund was established to serve as an important tool for absorbing excessive liquidity, reducing inflationary pressure, and insulating the economy from the volatility of raw material export earnings, which was one the reasons for the 1998 crisis. To prevent high inflation rates the fund was invested abroad only, at least until the latest crisis. The fund's revenues are oil-export duties and taxes for the extraction of natural resources starting when the oil price exceeds US$27 per barrel (Urals blend). By mid-2010, the fund, which is managed by the Finance Ministry, but was split in two at the end of January 2008 (between a reserve fund and a national welfare fund), still amounted to about US$130 billion, even after significant drawdowns to finance the budget deficit and the anticrisis package. The establishment of the fund was an important achievement for Finance Minister Kudrin, and had become an essential element of dollar sterilization.

With the recent global crisis, the fund has become symbolically the clearest positive legacy of the 1998 default as it demonstrated that Russia had committed itself to a discipline of saving oil revenues for the future and reducing its foreign debt. The transparent process of accumulation and management of the fund has become a clear manifestation that Russia pursues prudent fiscal policies, and is planning ahead. Ironically, the IMF was initially skeptical about the ability of the Russian authorities to manage such a fund prudently along the lines of the Norwegians. Anticipating the worst, the IMF cautioned that the necessary conditions for the successful operation of a fund were not in place and only later, as its success in practice was established, accepted that it had been a useful step. Accumulated foreign reserves, along with the size of the stabilization funds, clearly embody the strength potential of the Russian economy.

The total elimination of Russia's chronic budget deficits of the 1990s was another important consequence of the 1998 financial meltdown. In 2008, the federal budget surplus was over 4 percent, compared with a 1.2 percent deficit in 1999—an achievement in itself after the 1998 fiasco. In late July 2007, a three-year budget that would be the envy of many other countries from the point of view of rational fiscal management was approved for the first time. Moreover, the procedures for directing oil-related tax revenues above a certain oil cutoff price to the stabilization funds have been strengthened in order to try to reduce budgetary dependence on oil. In view of the volatility of oil revenues, budget spending has been kept to relatively modest proportions compared to other economies, although creeping up to about 20 percent of GDP. Of course, Russia—along with the rest of the world—was surprised by the sudden loss of revenue during the recent global crisis and the Keynesian need to relax its overall fiscal stance. And as part of the coordinated G-20 strategy to cope with the crisis, Russia played its part by switching from the 2008 fiscal surplus to a deficit in 2009 of 6 percent of GDP.

Certainly the sudden exit of capital, triggered by the deterioration in the global financial environment reinforced at the same time in August–September 2008 by the perception of increased political risk in financial relations with Russia, complicated the conduct of macroeconomic policy. The ruble, after its depreciation, stabilized and even started to appreciate again through the second half of 2009 and into 2010 even while the CBR was buying dollars in order to avoid a higher nominal ruble exchange rate. So, while still well below their peak at almost US$600 billion in June 2008, foreign exchange reserves have recovered to over US$460 billion by May 2010.

The campaign to improve tax discipline and fight tax evasion became one of the most distinct features of the post-1998 crisis economic policy. The tax code, adopted in 2000, represented a major breakthrough in fiscal administration in Russia, reducing the tax burden as well as establishing a more streamlined system of budget revenues and expenditures. Indeed, since its adoption, the government has not attempted to revisit any major personal or corporate taxes (other than energy), which has provided a high degree of security and safety for both domestic and international investors, and helped to attract capital to Russia. The 13 percent flat personal income tax rate remains among the lowest in the world.

Postcrisis Russia has also gone a long way in securing government control while improving financial and business discipline over the state-controlled companies—including Gazprom and Rosneft, which were helped to grow much larger than they had been in 1999, although there have been increasing investor concerns about the spread of state control after 2004, the lack of transparency, governance problems, and associated longer-term inefficiencies for the economy if state corporations continue to play a major role. The role of the siloviki and others benefiting from close relationships with the Kremlin remains a source of serious concern. At the same time, the government has moved ahead with the gradual reform and privatization of key assets in other sectors—including the reform and liquidation of RAO UES and the initial public offerings (IPOs) of Sberbank and VTB as well as Rosneft itself. Only time will tell whether it will work, but in late 2009, the government announced firm plans to privatize significant state holdings through IPOs if the market conditions are suitable and to dismantle the special legal status of state corporations.

By July 1, 2006, Russia had fully liberalized its capital accounts, following the liberalization of its current account a decade earlier. This essentially completed the country's transition into the globalized financial system just before it started to implode less than two years later, and was a highly significant reform at the time, securing Russia's place among the world's most open and fastest-growing economies. That said, Russia's inclusion in the group of financially liberalized economies is a mixed blessing. I believe that the complete liberalization of foreign-exchange controls was instrumental in the era of the post-1998 crisis reversal of capital flight into strong capital inflows and has contributed to the major repositioning of Russia in the global financial markets. It also meant that some Russian borrowers could go on a borrowing binge and make the country vulnerable to a sudden change in global market sentiments, as we saw starting in late 2008.

Despite the fact that Russia is still not a member of the WTO, it has become a much more open economy since 1998. On the consumption side, the limited availability of some foreign-made goods was an important achievement of the late Gorbachev and Yeltsin administrations after decades during which consumers were limited to Soviet-made goods. Now the extensive availability of foreign goods of all kinds is taken for granted, as it is in any "normal" country.

The liberalization of consumption has been a critical component of the postcrisis economic revolution since it has also permitted the restructuring of the economy. For example, despite the government's efforts to protect domestic automotive producers, Russians increasingly prefer foreign cars—produced both in Russia and abroad—to domestic brands, which puts severe competitive pressures on traditional producers. Russian companies, on the other hand, increasingly compete on the international markets and actively seek international expansion.

Inflation has been reduced from 36 percent at the end of 1999, but has remained an important concern for monetary authorities ever since. That said, the sudden shift to a deflationary global environment has contributed no doubt to the significant dampening of inflation beginning in the second half of 2009. Yet inflation still represents a challenge for the Medvedev administration, given expected utility rate adjustments and especially the inflows of foreign currency, coupled with the authorities' reluctance to move to direct inflation targeting and a floating exchange rate. The fact that the annual inflation rate fell to 8.8 percent by the end of 2009 was encouraging, but it must be brought down to the level prevailing in major financial centers if the ruble is to remain attractive. As of May 2010, it was down to 6 percent.

Since 1999, Russia succeeded in dramatically reducing the level of poverty. The proportion of the population living below the subsistence level had declined to 14 percent by 2009 from 30 percent in 1999. Nevertheless, with the global crisis and its impact on Russia, poverty levels are estimated to have risen again and many of the new middle class have been repressed. A large part of the government's anticrisis efforts were focused on countering that reversal.

The government also conducted key market reforms in the monetization of social benefits. The system of the provision of in-kind privileges existed as a rudimentary legacy of Soviet times, and added to the complexity and opacity of a significant proportion of government operations. It was a system prone to corruption as well. Reforms conducted in 2005, however unpopular at the time, were an essential step in simplifying the government's social expenditures. The government has also attempted to reform the pension system—with limited success so far. Most people chose not to select a manager for their individual pension accounts, and the authorities reportedly believe that employees are not encouraging their employers to make contributions to the pension accounts. Yet the introduction of pension reform was of paramount importance, even if it is just one piece of a fully funded system.

In 1999, there were 8.6 million unemployed in Russia, and unemployment amounted to 13.2 percent. Significant underemployment (short hours and involuntary unpaid leave) was also a characteristic feature of the system. By the end of 2008, the number of unemployed had dropped to almost 4 million, with the unemployment rate at 6.2 percent, although the number rose quickly again, like elsewhere, during the global crisis. By the end of 2009, it stood at 8.2 percent, after peaking at 9.5 percent in February 2009.

Russia is the second-largest destination for immigrants in the world after the United States, attracting workers from most CIS countries, and this trend may have been only partially reversed as a result of the global recession. Indeed, if there is any progress in economic integration between Russia and the CIS, it is in the labor market. The long-term trend counterbalances the nationalistic domestic political mood, which often results in the effective closure of certain professions to foreigners. Over the medium term, Russia will need foreign labor to sustain high growth rates, and cheaper foreign workers should help to maintain flexibility and competitiveness in the domestic labor market.

The Determinants of Growth

Much of the commentary about the extraordinary and unexpected positive performance of the Russian economy since the 1998 crisis—at least until the fourth quarter of 2008—refers rather simplistically to oil prices, confusing perhaps simultaneity with causation. The critics may be right if they focus on the financial markets, notably the RTS share index, which closely tracks oil prices—not surprising, since over 50 percent of the index consists of oil companies. But when looking at real GDP, it's a different and more complex story. Otherwise, how can one explain that real growth in 2003–5, when oil prices averaged US$30 per barrel, was higher than in 2006–8, when oil prices averaged US$70 per barrel? This and other lingering aspects of Russian economic performance need to be considered.

Besides the oil price, some would argue that oil production was driving GDP. In his 2008 book, Marshall Goldman presented a chart plotting changes in oil production and GDP. At first glance, a noneconomist might be led to believe that there was a statistically significant relationship. In my view, though, his chart just proves that Russia's growth is not only an oil story since real GDP was growing much faster in 1999–2008 than oil production.[2] In fact, domestic consumption was driving GDP growth as the dominant factor.

After ten years of rapid economic growth, even in the face of an adverse global environment in the past year, Russia's economic performance until late 2008 could have claimed to be somewhat of a miracle. This performance is especially striking for a large country since there is some evidence to suggest that large countries would tend to have slower growth rates relative to smaller neighbors because of lower spillover effects, although China would seem to be in a league of its own. And as the case of China, Ireland, and South Korea, economic miracles seem to be frequently rooted in these countries' past underperformance, which often leads to higher than expected economic growth. This process is based in part on the shift from economic fragmentation to integration. The dynamism of these economic miracles is frequently linked to the release of the "unobserved reserve": the reduction in the shadow economy, or the inflow of capital and labor resources from abroad.

Integration has played a significant role in Russia's economic growth over the past decade. In this context, the role of high oil prices in the country's expansion, although important, should not be exaggerated. And it is also now clear that capital inflows and excessive credit expansion were starting to fuel an unsustainable boom (or bubble) in some sectors, such as construction and automobiles.

I would stress that Russia has largely avoided the resource curse that has historically affected economies heavily dependent on the export of natural resources. The creation of the government's stabilization fund in

2004 has helped Russia avoid the resource curse by following a policy of fiscal discipline; the government did not give in to the temptation to spend money from the stabilization fund on populist social programs. This fiscal policy was presumably made possible by a reasonable degree of popular support for the government's economic policy course.

It also seems to me that there are significant hidden reserves that could fuel continued growth due to the return of capital and labor from abroad, the decrease of the shadow economy, and Russia's increased role in the global economy. Admittedly, this upside can be exploited to the fullest only if macroeconomic stability and structural policies lead to further economic integration.

In the early to mid-1990s, one of the explanations advanced for the precipitous decline in Russia's GDP was "disorganization"—a concept characterized by a fragmentation of nonmarket production links between enterprises.[3] This disorganization resulted in an economic system that was dubbed the "virtual economy," and was characterized by supply disruption, nonpayments, and barter.[4]

After the 1998 crisis, disorganization increasingly gave way to economic integration characterized by the formation of market-based links between interdependent enterprises. This was happening at the microeconomic level of individual companies and also across regions after years of widespread regional protectionism and trade barriers. The creation of a unified economic space free of trade barriers was likely a key factor that stimulated the country's economic growth along with the incorporation of sizable chunks of the shadow economy into the official sector as well as the return of flight capital and migrant workers.

With respect to capital flows, the growing volume of foreign direct investment was to a major degree driven by the return of capital that left the country back in the 1990s. The share of foreign direct investment coming to Russia from places like Cyprus, the Virgin Islands, and Luxembourg—believed to harbor the bulk of the country's capital flight—has been as high as 40 percent. Another trend, though less pronounced, is the return of the "human capital" that had left the country in the 1990s. This process is particularly important for growth and productivity in the services sector, most notably in information technology and financial services.

The integration of parts of the gray economy into the official sector was a critical development in the past ten years, no doubt assisted by more modern tax administration and the flat personal income tax. Finally, the country's integration into the world economy has increased in the past five years, as evidenced by the significant rise in the ratio of foreign direct investment to GDP to over 4 percent, or about seventy-three billion US dollars in 2008, before plunging to thirty-eight billion US dollars in 2009. There is great potential to further increase Russia's global economic integration, especially with respect to the country's accession to the WTO. Hopefully, this desirable goal, which has been delayed by political posturing, can be achieved in the near future. Russia is the only major economy that remains outside this organization.

The key economic priority in Russia is to return to the high economic growth rates that it achieved between 1999 and 2008. There are reasons to believe that this growth, while negative in 2009, will remain high provided that the global economic environment becomes more benign. This would result from a further shift in the country's development from fragmentation to integration. Of course, these adjustment factors will not fuel higher productivity on a continuing basis, and higher levels of productive domestic investment are required. Even the financial turmoil spilling over from international markets starting in September 2008 may have a longer-term positive impact as domestic interest rates rise in real terms; a move toward positive real rates, but lower nominal rates, will help to ensure that new investment is channeled to more productive uses. For instance, the higher investment recorded in 2007 and early 2008, guided by negative real rates, probably reflected large elements of a bubble economy. The main point that I want to stress is that high oil prices are not the sole explanation for Russia's growth performance.

The focus of this book has been on the Russia story. Russia certainly had its unique features, but the crisis itself was hardly an isolated incident. The 1990s were littered with a slew of crises ranging from Mexico in 1995, Thailand, Korea, and Indonesia starting in 1997, Brazil starting soon after Russia, Ecuador in early 1999, Turkey in late 1999, and Argentina by 2001. Like Russia, all these countries shared to varying degrees what could be seen in retrospect as an overdependence on foreign debt financing by either the public or private sectors in conjunction with exchange rate rigidity. There is a large literature on all these related crises.[5] The latest sovereign debt crisis in Europe, notably in Greece, is distinguished by the fact that the debt at issue is domestic, as was Russia's in 1998.

Political Legacy

Undoubtedly, Russia has changed radically since the time of the 1998 crisis. During most of this time, Putin was either prime minister or president. By 2010, Russia was considered economically successful (even if under temporary pressures) and politically strong, at least by Russians—a drastically different self-perception from that of 1998. Seen from the perspective of the crisis twelve years ago, the change is truly dramatic and almost completely unexpected. The explanation of this development remains controversial. For instance, what was Putin's role?

Aslund has argued that Russia's current economic success is the result of a critical mass of economic reforms undertaken in the 1990s: deregulation, privatization, and eventually financial stabilization. From a historical perspective, he notes that it is impressive that Russia built a dynamic market economy in only seven years.[6] The Russian financial crash of 1998 delivered the catharsis that Russia unfortunately needed to adopt responsible fiscal policies. In Aslund's view, Putin was not the generator of Russia's current economic success but rather its beneficiary and custodian. Putin also greatly benefited from high international oil prices.

During Putin's first term, the economy was the area of his overwhelming success. Russia's economy grew quickly, foreign debt was paid down, capital flight turned into strong private capital inflow, and significant progress was made in fighting poverty and unemployment. Yet Putin was more than just the beneficiary of earlier reforms. He also decisively built on those with far-reaching changes in the form of a new tax code (with its 13 percent flat rate personal income tax), land reform, and consistently prudent budget laws.

In retrospect, it now seems clear that beginning in 2000–2001, the influence of oligarchs and factions outside the executive was significantly reduced.[7] Although the methods may have been developed as events unfolded, one objective of the new administration was to limit significantly the autonomy of the oligarchs, and deprive them of the political resources and access to executive structures that they had in the 1990s.[8] This was accomplished by both coercive and cooperative methods.

Most observers of Russian politics would consider the Yukos affair, which began with the arrests of the Yukos oil parent company's top shareholders Platon Lebedev and Khodorkovsky in June and October 2003, respectively, as a watershed moment, marking a transition from one model of state-business relations to another. At the time, Yukos was Russia's largest private company and top oil producer.[9] Following Lebedev's and Khodorkovsky's arrests, the company was dismantled by the authorities and sold off to state-controlled enterprises. Lebedev and Khodorkovsky were tried and convicted for tax evasion and fraud. In my view, like most observers, the whole affair reeks of political manipulation, whatever the possible merit of the legal issues, especially in view of the second trial in 2010.

It is no doubt true that in terms of economic policy, less was achieved during Putin's second term. Perhaps the major new initiative was the monetization of social benefits, whose introduction in January 2005 was controversial and poorly executed. Frustration at the government's inept handling of national projects for housing and health led the president to turn their management over to a special commission headed by the chief of the presidential administration, Medvedev (who then became a first deputy prime minister in November 2005). Judicial, administrative, and military reforms were all stymied by internal feuding among various factions close to power and a lack of strong leadership under Prime Minister Mikhail Fradkov, which were only marginally addressed by his short-term successor, Viktor Zubkov, from September 2007 to May 2008. Then again, in many countries, the second presidential term is often less productive than the first one.

Perhaps Putin's second term would have been more productive in policy terms had Kasyanov remained as prime minister. After all, despite a fractious cabinet, important policies were implemented by the government under his mandate. No doubt his familiarity with economics helped inform his judgment.

I had a frank discussion with Kasyanov about some of the difficulties in implementing policy in 2002, about halfway through his mandate. He was cautious generally about what had been achieved by that time in the Russian economy. From his vantage point as prime minister, it was clearer than ever just how much remained to be done, especially in the areas of administrative, judicial, structural economic, and political reform policies. And yet the political dimension, involving the various factions, lobbyists, and public opinion, could not be ignored. Financial stabilization, while a clear achievement, was not solid at that time, and the real transformation of the economy was still too limited to Moscow and Saint Petersburg. Kasyanov spoke at length about the dire situation in much of the country and used the analogy of a ticking time bomb. His government needed to proceed expeditiously, albeit carefully. This task was all the more difficult in light of the limited number of devoted, honest, and competent senior civil servants. That said, Kasyanov was impressed with the rapid increase in the level of professionalism displayed by enterprise managements and the resulting change in the attitude of businesses toward the government. In the past, in his opinion, business only asked for money or a special deal—a prime example being the oligarchs. Now increasingly they would lobby for policy changes as in other countries.

I observed that a skeptical world seemed to have suspended judgment on Russia and was certainly not prepared to give the authorities the benefit of the doubt; it was waiting for results. In fact, in relative terms, this skepticism had worsened since the objective circumstances were so much more positive than in, say, late 1999. Kasyanov felt that this was unfair since so much had already been achieved—not only macroeconomic stability, but also the new tax code, natural monopoly reforms, and labor market policies were all laying the basis for real structural transformation.

The problem was that the inheritance was so heavy and so little was done to significantly advance the structural agenda that Kasyanov felt as if they were still only at the beginning. Every day he was confronting a myriad of tough decisions; mistakes were made, of course, and implementation had been problematic. It would take time for the cumulative effect to be felt, but it was hard to accelerate the process without a major risk of error or political misjudgment. Unfortunately the big, simple measures had been done; the rest were technical and small. In this regard, Kasyanov spoke glowingly of his working relationship with Putin. Perhaps the president didn't always agree, but he listened, asked the right questions, and was supportive of what the government was trying to do. Obviously, a little over a year later, the close relationship ended.

On February 24, 2004, Kasyanov was called on by the president to tender his resignation. As Kasyanov later recounted, at first he didn't fully appreciate the intended timing. After all, with the first round of a presidential election less than two months away, Kasyanov readily agreed that after the election, the resignation of the government would be completely normal. To Kasyanov's amazement, Putin shook his head and made it clear that he meant that the government should resign immediately. The prime minister, bewildered, had no choice but to accept, and he resigned.

Kasyanov said that he later understood that some faction close to the president suggested that he was being disloyal and entertaining the possibility of standing in the presidential election himself. Maybe he should not have been so surprised after his spirited and public defense of Khordorkovsky on at least two occasions after his arrest in late October 2003. Clearly, whoever was behind the arrest was capable of setting up Kasyanov. Although Kasyanov vigorously denied having any presidential ambitions at that time, he did not have a personal relationship with his boss and was unable to appeal.

I have always found it interesting that few ministers ever seem to resign on issues of principle or policy in most modern governments in any country. Even in Asia where there is more of a tradition of resignation, resignations only seem to occur when there is some embarrassing revelation, not over issues of principle. It is no less the case in Russia. But there must have been trying times for government members in the period covered here. In retrospect, just as examples, it is almost unimaginable that Chubais would have resigned when the VChK failed to apply the government's tax policy to the oil companies in 1997, or Zadornov when Boos, with Primakov's backing, set out to negotiate individual tax agreements with major taxpayers in early 1999, or Kiriyenko when the Duma did not support his proposals, which were the last possible way to avoid a default in July 1998. It is not easy to appreciate the motives: perhaps a combination of loyalty, patriotism, innate optimism, and hubris.

It is all the more surprising, then, that the only occasion I can recall since the 1998 crisis when a Russian political figure resigned voluntarily was when Voloshin, the powerful Kremlin chief of staff since March 1999, resigned in late October 2003, soon after Khodorkovsky's arrest. Voloshin, both publicly and in private, has always denied that there was a connection or any other point of principle involved, but I have always presumed that he just did not want to embarrass the president. Of course, there was the resignation of presidential economic adviser Illarionov, who admittedly played a more marginal role, when he dramatically announced his departure on December 27, 2005, saying that "the country has stopped being free and democratic," and "therefore it is absolutely impossible to remain."

By the time that Medvedev was inaugurated as president in May 2008, some of the burning issues—including Chechnya and political instability—that had been a focus of public concern earlier in the decade, hopefully had become issues of the past. On the negative side, however, there was—and still is—little clarity on what may be expected from a Russian president who seems to enjoy almost unlimited power. Even now, halfway through the presidential term, significant uncertainty remains about whether the tandem of Medvedev with Putin as prime minister will be effective in delivering those most highly prized policy objectives, especially as a legacy of the 1998 crisis: stability and prosperity. Surprisingly, their popularity hardly suffered from the 2009 crisis since it seems that most people blamed the problem on outside forces.

Perhaps one of the unintended, unexpected, and troubling legacies of the post–1998 crisis, with much of the Russian population yearning for stability, was the increasing role of the siloviki as a major factor in Kremlin politics. The term actually applies to disparate clans and groups associated with the various security services at one time or another. Their role, even perhaps more than that of the oligarchs, has appeared to be a destabilizing force undermining the political stability that Russia enjoyed over the past few years. Events were beginning to unfold that would be inconceivable in a genuinely stable political system. Ironically, in my view, it was Putin's consolidation of presidential and siloviki power that complicated the search for a solution to his own succession problem in 2007. The feuding among the groups grew especially intense as the end of Putin's mandate approached without clarity as to his postpresidential role. The scramble for assets intensified. While it is never welcome, perhaps the fallout from the global crisis at least constrains the rewards available for asset-grabbing siloviki. Indeed, the intention to proceed with the privatization of state holdings through IPOs could be interpreted positively as a sign that the siloviki think it prudent to cash out before Russia becomes too "normal" like other countries where transparency and the rule of law prevail most of the time.

The internal weakness of the vertical power in the Kremlin is ironic, although completely consistent with the thesis set out in this book. In that sense, it would appear to show that little has changed since the 1998 default. It is ironic because the one perception, perhaps above all, to distinguish Putin's administration from the chaotic 1990s under Yeltsin was being able to project an air of authority, a man in charge of the situation. Instead, the lack of progress on reforms, some highly publicized, unsolved murders, and other bad news may have been a reflection of the president's relative weakness.

I feel sure that Putin has been all too aware of the problem. After all, even before the split of the old Soviet KGB, there were at least two competing factions: the First Chief Directorate or foreign intelligence, and the domestic group. Almost as riven as their counterparts in the Washington intelligence community, these camps never really trusted each other, never cooperated willingly, and officers from different factions would rarely even befriend each other. The growing animosity and rivalry between various Kremlin factions could continue to be a destabilizing force in Russian politics under President Medvedev, although presumably he and Prime Minister Putin are attempting to contain these forces.

External Perceptions and the Role of the Media

There is the Russian reality in all of its complexity. Then there are the public perceptions of this reality, especially as seen from abroad, many of which seem to border on the simplistic. A narrative covering this period of the relations of a Russia emerging from the tutelage of the IMF would not be complete without some discussion of the role of the media, particularly since I believe the disparaging reports in the press played a significant role in alienating Russia in terms of public opinion, which then had political ramifications and eventually hastened the early termination of the IMF lending operations.

The Western press, at least in part, was certainly taking its cues from the Russian press. Kasyanov told me during a conversation in early 2001 that he regretted the fact that his government got little credit for the positive steps given the prevailing attitude of the media. Part of this might be due to a lack of professionalism among journalists, but in his view, it was also clearly the fault of government: much damage was self-inflicted through poor media relations and a lack of discipline in the government when speaking to the press. Yet Kasyanov asserted that with limited human resources in managerial positions, the government should not divert its attention to public relations. It must focus on substance, assuming that perceptions would later fall into line. His words, in retrospect, seem prescient, especially since our conversation followed the embarrassing flap over the Paris Club payment issue.

Some parts of the Russian media had obviously less than honorable intentions in perpetuating unhelpful rumors in late 2000 and early 2001 about an impending change in government, without any basis other than the speculation of a few political pundits and other journalists. That said, it was understandable that almost any talk of a shift had a public resonance because of the rapid merry-go-round of ministers and prime ministers in the period immediately preceding the 2000 election. But the media fed on itself. Having become so accustomed to a virtual game of musical chairs in government and given the dearth of real news—except for those real professionals who actually carefully researched and prepared their stories—the media managed to keep the story of impending changes on the front pages for months.

In much the same way, but perhaps more maliciously, the media created a whiff of scandal surrounding Kasyanov personally, dubbing him a "Berezovsky" or "Family" proxy, and applying a "Misha 2 percent" label. When I asked Kasyanov about how such rumors might affect his government's work, say, in meetings with other heads of government when he could imagine what was contained in their briefing books, he asserted that there were clearly some parties whose interests were served by undermining the credibility of the authorities. Unfortunately, these perceptions do have real consequences since they affect the attitudes of other governments and the markets, and they did indeed make the eventual recovery of the Russian economy harder than would have presumably otherwise been the case. This was especially problematic when such stories then got picked up and propounded by the Western press as if they were true.

The irresponsibility of the media was not limited to its coverage of the Russian government. Perhaps even more germane to this narrative was the manner in which even the high-quality international press would pick up on stories, often without much foundation, and report them as fact. I would single out the *Financial Times* and the Moscow-based staff of the *Wall Street Journal* among the rare exceptions that tried to verify and report as accurately as possible. It almost seemed that because the stories involved a combination of two controversial subjects, Russia and the IMF, they were sensationalized as a matter of course. Or at least that was certainly my perception.

The scandals of 1999 have already been summarized. The reporting about the US$4.8 billion tranche, although thoroughly dissected and disproved point by point to the satisfaction of the U.S. government and other major IMF shareholders, still lingers on, and even now continues to impinge on the reputation of Russia and the IMF in public perceptions. In part, this is because there were never any official retractions in the press. But maybe this is more because the accusations were reported as front-page news, while the detailed analysis underlying the refutation was relegated to inside pages of a much more upscale press. Hence, the broader public only really knows what was originally reported, and even has the impression of a cover-up or conspiracy since the "scandal" seemed to have no consequences and no one was punished.

The treatment of the BONY scandal was in some ways even worse. It followed the same pattern. At least the *New York Times* journalist originally responsible for the story later issued a retraction for most of what he had said earlier, although admittedly under peculiar circumstances.[10] Not that the retraction did much good since it was not widely reported in the international press. And the FBI and the U.S. Department of Justice never issued apologies.[11] No one wanted to admit that millions of U.S. taxpayer dollars were spent in pursuit of a money-laundering hoax. Nor did congressional staff members who jumped on the accusatory band wagon retract their positions publicly.

Following the usual pattern, these unfounded and sensationalized stories stuck. They were picked up worldwide in the press, which cited reputable sources in the quality press of the United States or Europe, and the reports then took on a life of their own. The stories also were reflected back to Russia, where stories reported in the foreign press are assumed to be true by definition.

Perhaps the most egregious case of an outright lie reported as fact was when a now-obscure Moscow-based weekly, *Literaturnaya Gazeta*, citing an anonymous Kremlin source, published an article in November 1999 alleging that Camdessus personally received a large bribe in return for providing financing to Russia. Of course, the Kremlin denied that anyone could have ever said such a thing and profusely apologized, and the editor of the newspaper issued a retraction. But that didn't stop the *Corriere della Sera*, a reputable Italian daily, from reporting the initial story and making no mention of the later retraction.

10

History Is Not Doomed to Repeat Itself

The 1998 crisis represented the apogee of the IMF's involvement in Russia's transition to a "normal" country. It was a humbling lesson for the IMF and a wake-up call for Russia. The lessons learned helped to ensure that the impact of the recent global recession, as bad as it was, was not worse. It was also the fateful tipping point in Russia's prevarication in deciding to become a modern, market economy. The future is of course uncertain, but the ground has been laid for a new generation of young Russians to avoid the mistakes of their parents.

It was not overly dramatic of Fischer to remark that when the history of the previous century is written in 2050, the question of the IMF's contribution will not be judged on the basis of the Asian crisis, or Mexico or Brazil. Rather, history will judge the IMF on the basis of the role it played in the transformation of Russia. Fischer was not referring to the 1998 crisis, which was not the IMF's finest hour, nor the programs themselves, which consistently underperformed after 1995. Fischer meant, I believe, that the IMF tutelage helped to steer Russia in a better direction than could have been expected under the circumstances.

As Nabiullina, now the economy minister, observed, the IMF's contribution to Russia was at least substantial in one area. Surprisingly, this had nothing to do with the money or even the policy recommendations themselves based on best international practices. Rather, in her view, the lasting contribution of the IMF has been in the form of a change in cultural attitudes, not unlike the introduction of blue jeans or chewing gum. The IMF brought a new and coherent way of analyzing problems and then trying to find pragmatic solutions to a Russian governing class that, in short order, mastered the new culture as if it were a new dance step.

The Lessons from the 1998 Financial Crisis

In retrospect, August 1998 should be considered the definitive watershed moment for the Russian economy, much more so than Black Tuesday on October 19, 1994. In the case of Black Tuesday, the plummeting ruble served as a siren call to the Kremlin that macroeconomic stabilization could no longer be ignored. But the subsequent policy adjustments were too modest relative to what was required, and efforts were later relaxed as more favorable external factors bred complacency. The August 1998 crisis was much more cathartic, instilling more long-standing lessons, even if complacency inevitably also reared its head. That crisis and its aftermath constitute a definitive turning point in Russia's long-awaited reintegration into the global economy.

Because of the relatively fortuitous outcome, Russia and the world are different now. In terms of what might have been but did not occur, the counterfactual outcomes could have been distinctly different and much more dramatic. The 1998 crisis could have prompted the Russians to turn inward again. There certainly were those close to power then who were suggesting that the 1990s were a failure, Russia's post-Soviet attempt to participate in the globalized economy was a mistake, and autarky was a better solution.

This book has argued that the 1998 crisis was not inevitable. The oil price decline that started in late 1997 in the wake of the Asian crisis fundamentally compromised the fiscal balance, and the authorities were challenged to adjust fast enough to the looming financing hole. That said, at several points the authorities could have possibly turned back from the edge of the abyss before the bottom fell out. Certainly, the hasty decision to announce a new corridor for the ruble exchange rate in November 1997 was such an occasion, as probably were the decisions to change the finance minister in November 1997 and the whole government in March 1998. But domestic politics kept interfering with possible solutions. Perhaps, in retrospect, by the time that the Kiriyenko government was installed in April 1998, it was already just too late. That crisis encapsulated the high point of Russia's involvement with the IMF. Even when no more money was forthcoming, the Russian authorities appealed to the IMF for its advice and moral support in facing the cataclysm.

As Viugin tellingly noted, the World Bank should have been the appropriate institution to support Russia in its transition to a market economy, but he added that whereas the World Bank was a bank, concerned with its credit rating and the quality of its portfolio, the IMF in his view was really a more politically sensitive instrument. All the more curious, then, was the irony that the IMF was called on to play a central role in helping Russia with its economic transformation, but its real impact was marginal (albeit cumulatively perhaps not insignificant)—with the seeming contradiction explained by weak and ineffective government policies. Again, as Viugin explained, the IMF could be no more effective than the government that has to actually implement its economic program advice.

Why did the IMF persist in its support of successive programs in view of their blatant disregard? Political pressure from the G-7 to continue would be too simple an answer as well as redundant since I believe the IMF was really committed to try to make Russia's economic programs work. I think more profoundly there was a genuine fear that alternative scenarios could have been worse. It reminds me of the dilemma facing the Obama administration in dealing with the global recession: what it did may not have made things much better, but doing nothing or little could have led to something truly terrible. So it was probably fortunate that a scenario of letting Russia tough it out was not tested in 1996–1998. IMF management feared fallout in the world financial system and criticism from its member nations if Russia was left dangling on its own. For this the IMF deserves, I believe, some understanding.

While no doubt much of the world, watching the comings and goings of missions, had the impression of often-confrontational relations between Russia and the IMF, yet this was not in fact the case. There was a constant dialogue between the IMF and the Russian authorities, and it included the provision of technical as well as policy advice on a broad range of economic issues. And despite varying external economic and even political circumstances over the years, the legacy of this dialogue continues.

Indeed, while the IMF may have frequently seemed critical of the authorities' policy stance (and it is true that more could always have been done better and faster), it also acknowledged just how much was accomplished in Russia's integration into the globalized economy. That the road was tougher than originally anticipated is now apparent, but it is also remarkable that the debate about what needed to be done seems to have been so clearly won by those arguing for low inflation in a liberalized market economy as the best basis for ensuring sustainable growth and development—notwithstanding the faltering pace of reforms in recent years that ensured the impact of the recent global recession was worse than it should have been.

Looking back, Russia's 1998 crisis could be viewed as a precursor to the feared contemporary concern with sovereign debt crises where an initial liquidity problem is transformed into a solvency issue. In Russia's case, the lesson from the 1998 crisis was almost self-evident: politically weak regimes with lax fiscal policy and especially high levels of debt held by nonresidents are particularly vulnerable to shocks or changes in market sentiment. By 2009, it seemed that significant foreign currency debt would be itself enough to send countries to the IMF for emergency assistance; and by 2010, the contagion had spread to the domestic debt of Greece and others.

The international chain reaction to the specific events in Russia should have been contained through better cooperation rather than ad hoc intervention by national financial authorities, particularly the U.S. Federal Reserve. The problem was that there was simply no internationally agreed-on framework then—or now for that matter—to mitigate the adverse effects of a crisis of confidence while ensuring an orderly working out of the financial implications of a default on sovereign debt. Earlier efforts by the IMF to address this lacuna were effectively vetoed by the Bush White House, which considered any mandatory and legally binding international framework as limiting its preferred philosophy of volunteerism. U.S. government officials no doubt really believed that the era of big global debt crises was over so such an approach would be redundant. In any case, since the Russians defaulted on domestic debt, it is not clear how an agreed-on framework for debt resolution might have helped. There is abundant debate on this issue.[1]

Is Russia a Special Case?

In view of independent Russia's starting conditions at the outset of 1992, notably a bankrupt treasury, the collapse of the command economy, and disrupted economic relations, it was not too surprising that the initial efforts at stabilization and growth were stymied. Those conditions were arguably worse than the ones that prevailed in the Central and Eastern European countries that emerged from behind the Iron Curtain some twenty years ago. The expectation at the time was, nevertheless, for a sustained rebound in Russia once the monetary overhang and resources misallocated under the Soviet state-control system had been addressed. But it didn't happen.

I attribute the explanation underlying the frustrating rate of progress in achieving the goal of Russia as a society ruled by law in a market economy to the fact that Russia experienced not just economic and political dislocation but also an enormous power vacuum following the collapse of the CPSU. In effect, the central authority of the state disappeared, notwithstanding formal appearances to the contrary. It has still not fully recovered, despite the sometimes heavy-handed attempts of Putin's supporters to reassert state power. Even this explanation, however, may be incomplete.

It may be that there is just too much to do. Some fatalists in Russia would contend that their country suffers from a curse of historical dimensions, with the legacy of the Soviet era as merely the latest installment in a string of bad luck. And more objective observers could sympathize with the unique nature of the multitude of challenges facing the country. Even with the most enlightened leadership, the tasks appear almost overwhelming. So with mere mortals as leaders, the crisis of 1998 does not appear so unexpected—nor that its lessons were not fully assimilated in order to minimize the effects of the global recession that hit Russia so hard at the end of 2008.

Until the 1998 crisis, those in the political class in Russia seemed to operate as if they could quarrel among themselves and fight over assets oblivious to the consequences. Perhaps in reaction to living under the centralizing principles of the Communist regime and dominant police state for seventy-four years, central authority was discredited and weak. Strong centripetal forces were seemingly pulling the country apart. As a result, legislation, even good laws, had little practical effect. The civil service was demoralized, bloated, and yet underpaid. Tax collection was desultory and totally inadequate to finance even a limited government function, much less the wholesale transformation required by the circumstances. The state had neither the will nor the means to be effective. The 1998 crisis was the wake-up call; Russia had to choose between the kleptocapitalism of a banana republic or the tough adjustments to become a modern state. Yasin, a former economy minister and the teacher of many of the senior officials now responsible for the economy, contends that the former was not really an option and eventually would have led to possibly tragic political consequences. In some ways, the events that precipitated the 1998 crisis came in time to prevent Russia from veering off in a really dangerous direction. At the same time, it is hard to argue that the lessons have been fully learned; too often, especially after the willful destruction of Yukos as Russia's largest oil company in 2004, the country has seemed to revert too readily to a regressive posture.

And so we are where we are now. While acknowledging that it could have been much worse, though, is not to say that we are necessarily content with the current state of affairs in Russia, or Russia's relations with its immediate neighbors, much less Russia's seemingly fraught relations with the West. Perhaps in an ideal world, we wouldn't be where we are today,, but I would contend that we are lucky compared with most of the probable counterfactual outcomes. In fact, in contrast to my friend Freeland, who in fairness wrote her book just after the 1998 crisis, I would say that the outcome in Russia has been the bargain of the century.

Indeed, Russia's recent story disproves determinists and buries those remnants (still sputtering in the West) of romantic Marxism. No nation is condemned. Salvation is possible with the right economic signals and some luck that applies to any enterprise in life—real leadership exercised in the right circumstances and at least a spell of fair weather. Unfortunately the reverse is true as well, which is why Russians cannot allow themselves to become complacent as many started to do too soon after the 1998 crisis was well behind them. Only now is it obvious that time and resources were squandered that could have helped to insulate the country more from the latest global turmoil.

The 1998 crisis may have inoculated many Russians from the worst excesses prevalent in advanced economies during the past decade, but it remains unclear whether a new generation will resist the temptation to spend in excess of income financed by debt. How those lessons can be instilled in future generations remains a challenge. As H. G. Wells once said, "History is a race, a race between education and catastrophe." Hopefully Russians will remain immune to the type of extreme forms of financial bubbles that seem to have enticed so many in the some Western countries in recent years, although the recent financial turmoil has also revealed a too large—if not systemically critical—number of Russian banks and affluent businesspeople with too much debt. For most Russians, it is as if the 1998 crisis provided immunity to overborrowing and risk taking, but we do not know yet how long the inoculation will last.

Challenges of Macroeconomic Management

When the recent global financial crisis started in 2008, with the United States and many OECD countries plunging into recession, the question arose in financial and analytic circles as to whether the BRICs were decoupled and could continue to grow without a major negative impact.[2] This issue was always an economic and practical nonsense. It seems to me that anyone who has studied economics would understand that a decline in aggregate demand in one country will affect its trading and financial partner countries, so decoupling is not binary. But more critically, some countries were never coupled to begin with. This is largely true about China and India, but is also the case for Russia. In Russia, like China, rising domestic demand is the main determinant of GDP growth. The export sector is not the significant driver of growth. After all, Russia started the 1990s as totally decoupled. Suddenly, after more than seventy years of relative autarky, Russians started to reintegrate rapidly into the globalized economy of the modern world, enough so as to be already vulnerable to external forces in 1998.

The international financial crisis has been concentrated mostly in developed economies, where the stability of financial systems is essential for economic growth, in contrast with low-income emerging economies in which the financial system, as important as it may be to investors (especially nonresidents), has not sown deep roots in the real economy, which remains more self-financing and so where real sector activity is more insulated from financial market turmoil. The latter more aptly characterized Russia in 1998, when a host of financial institutions collapsed but the nonfinancial sector trod on and resumed growth almost immediately after the devaluation.

More recently the irony should not be lost that Russia, along with other major emerging markets, was caught in a trap of its own making. For most of the past decade the country was creating large excess savings manifested in huge budget and balance of payment surpluses. And where was the money going? Because there wasn't a broad, deep, efficient financial market in Russia, the money was invested in the United States or Europe, yet Russian companies would then go to U.S. and European banks to borrow the money they needed for their operations. For Russian entities the size of Rusal, Rosneft, or Gazprom, the domestic market was not large enough to borrow the amounts of money required for their investment programs. So even though Russia was generating huge foreign exchange surpluses, Russian companies and banks were assuming the foreign exchange risks—borrowing their own money back, in a sense—to the profit of the Western intermediaries. There was thus an irony here that really has to be assimilated.

In sum, the government and the CBR demonstrated that they learned the lessons from the 1998 financial crisis, and did not squander the nation's wealth through the budget. Instead, the Russian authorities used that wealth to guarantee the stability of the financial system and economy, and let the capital markets decide where to allocate money, though perhaps encouraged by state-controlled institutions, especially since Putin's second term. This is not dissimilar to the approach that contributed positively to growth in other successful developers such as Japan, Korea, and even Germany at earlier stages. Clearly, Russia is now almost fully integrated into the globalized economy, and both the global inflation spike of 2008 and the subsequent financial meltdown impacted Russia with full force.

Despite a deflationary environment in advanced economies in 2010, inflation still remains a policy concern in Russia as in some other emerging countries. With inflation at single digits in the middle of 2010, it is imperative that the price level does not rise again under the influence of overly expansive macroeconomic policies, especially excessive budgetary spending.

Even though it virtually ties with Saudi Arabia as the world's largest oil producer, with no spare capacity, Russia cannot influence world prices. The oil price spiked in July 2008. Oil at one point reached US\$141 per barrel. Oil prices subsequently collapsed as the extent of the global recession became apparent. By mid-February 2009, oil was about US\$40 per barrel or back to the level of prices in late 2004. Although oil prices have recovered since then—remaining in a range of roughly US\$70–80 per barrel—considerable volatility is anticipated in the future. Russia's external balances and indeed future economic growth will depend in large part on how the exchange rate is managed in line with changes in the terms of trade.

According to a somewhat optimistic scenario, Russia could become the world's fifth-largest economy by 2020, and its per capita income could catch up with Portugal's. The ruble could eventually become one of the world's reserve currencies and Moscow a financial center. Russia would become a major economic power, along with its other BRICs counterparts, and could potentially have an even greater and hopefully more benign influence than the former Soviet Union.

However, such a scenario does not seem likely at this juncture, and not just because the global economy may not recover soon from the debt overhang, nor Russia from its relative international political isolation following the events of the Caucasian War in August 2008, even with the "reset" of relations with the United States.

Furthermore, to what extent can it be called an economic miracle if many Russians are living below the poverty line and the middle class is not yet enjoying the benefits of economic progress, such as long-term and cheap mortgage loans? The fact is that Russia's 2009 GDP per capita in purchasing power parity terms was about US$15,039, which is little more than Chile or Mexico. In these terms, according to IMF data, Russia is ahead of all the countries of the CIS, but trails behind Estonia and Lithuania, let alone those of Western Europe. On the other hand, compared to the situation eighteen years ago, Russia has seen an economic miracle. Its virtue is its dynamically growing market.

The question is whether this positive move will be paralleled by a resumption of confidence of foreign investors and ordinary Russians. In this regard, aside from politics, the government faces major challenges. Officials are well aware of the structural problems in the economy, the still-excessive share of the oil and gas sector in the GDP, and the average monthly wage, which is barely seven hundred U.S. dollars. Yet senior officials are sincere in believing that the momentum and scale of macroeconomic growth can soon result in a qualitative change in the country's economic climate. Indeed, the government's strategy up to 2020, originally adopted in early 2008 but subsequently revised to take into account the global recession, envisaged a bold shift away from a resource-based economy to a knowledge-based one relying on massive new investment. It is far from clear whether this approach can really increase total factor productivity, and much attention will need to be paid to the enabling conditions for such development. In the revised strategy, which assumes even greater oil price volatility, this need for diversification has been accentuated.

Since the 1998 crisis, economic performance has been driven in significant measure by a competitive ruble, high commodities prices, and increasing integration effects fostering productivity. None of these effects can be expected to last. The problem, seen in international experience, is that the best time to introduce needed but possibly painful reforms is when all goes well, which can facilitate their adoption. But good times also encourage the belief that difficult measures can be deferred. So the easier it is to push ahead with reform, the less likely this is to happen. Russia's impressive economic performance can allow the country to act on reforms or it can take away the desire to do so. The key question for Russia is which of these tendencies will prevail.

We have already discovered some of the answers as the contagion from the Wall Street meltdown hit Russia in late 2008: financial market reforms, for example, were woefully incomplete to cope with the stresses. During the boom years, there didn't seem to be an urgent need to reform the banking sector and the financial markets. Russia needs to develop a much larger, broader, and more efficient domestic financial system. This includes banks and markets for all kinds of securities, equities, and bonds. That's going to be critically important anyway if President Medvedev is serious about making Russia a major financial center and if he wants the ruble to become an international reserve currency.

The agenda is so large and the means so relatively limited that Russia's leadership must wonder if it is even worth contemplating. Perhaps the leadership would be better to content itself with a gradual evolution fueled by resource-based riches, even at a cost of a less liberal, more authoritarian society, and indeed of greater risks in terms of both freedom and economic security for future generations of Russians. But in a world of highly volatile commodity prices, this would seem to be a recipe for pauperization.

Just in the economic domain, the Russian leadership realized that for the country to compete effectively in global markets, far-reaching reforms were still pending in areas such as business regulation, the labor market, public administration, civil service reform, landownership, and the financial sector. It was not just a question, as it was in the Yeltsin era, of getting legislation passed; a more cooperative Duma ensured that the bottleneck to reform was no longer mainly in the parliament.

The problem was increasingly with implementation. Medvedev, Putin, and their advisers fully understood the magnitude of the social challenges to their proposed policies. After the earlier experience with economic dislocation under Yeltsin, most Russians are unlikely to accept without question the need for further personal discomfort in the name of market reforms, and if such reforms were pursued seriously, it could encumber the authorities' credibility and will to pursue all of the other needed changes in Russia in other spheres, such as the reform of the business culture that still stymies the development of small and medium enterprise, much less foreign investment. Top-down wishful thinking like the grandiose idea of creating a Russian version of Silicon Valley at Skolkovo, near Moscow, is just a waste of money without the real reforms just mentioned.

Looking Forward

At this juncture in 2010, there appear to be three main economic issues, depending on the time horizon. In the short term, the concern is how to cope with the impact of the global recession and the relative volatility in Russia's terms of trade. By itself, Russia can only do so much. It has no control over oil prices or the fate of the U.S. dollar. As a global phenomenon, when the international system is rudderless, the challenge for political economy is especially serious. Much will depend on U.S. and E.U. policies and a fine balance in the gradual withdrawal of the exceptional measures taken to cope with the crisis by governments around the world. The major uncertainty arises from whether the United States and the European Union will be able to reconcile the political pressure to sustain growth and employment through expansive policies against the bond market vigilantes as well as a conservative backlash demanding a rollback in government support.

In the world's largest debtor economies, the repricing of risk could play havoc with still-overvalued assets and the deleveraging of credit, causing the U.S. and E.U. authorities to equivocate in an effort to forestall the possibility of a serious collapse. To insulate the economy to some extent, it is critical that the Russian authorities allow the exchange rate to continue to reflect changes in the terms of trade and move toward a more flexible regime in practice.

Over the medium term, the key issue is whether the Russian economy can insulate itself better from the contagion effects of the economic problems in other countries and markets. Russia would seem to be particularly vulnerable to a significant fall in energy prices, but a sharp drop in oil prices to a level that might hurt Russia—say, a sustained price below US$55 per barrel as posited by Troika Dialog—appears unlikely. It is particularly worrisome that the breakeven price of oil for the budget to balance has risen from about US$30 per barrel in 2003–2004 to an estimated US$100 per barrel in 2010. Scaling back of budgetary spending is critical for Russia to avoid its own new debt crisis at some point in the future.

Over the long term, perhaps the crucial economic issue is the choice of the development model and how to sustain economic growth. Russia's long-term risks are connected to what could be relatively low productivity, which seems inherent in its growth model focused on a massive increase in investment including by the state sector (which unfortunately has a record of generating more waste and corrupt bureaucracy than growth) and the government's intentions to continue expanding energy exports. The extraction of natural resources remains one of the most capital-intensive sectors in Russia (along with real estate, which is overpriced, utilities and social services, which are still subsidized, and transportation, which is also subsidized, and includes oil and gas pipelines). That said, investing heavily in oil and gas extraction in order to sustain export growth could lead to a deceleration of overall economic growth in the long term, as happened in the 1970s and 1980s after the Soviet

Union started investing in Siberian oil and gas fields, building export pipelines, and expanding energy sales abroad. With a declining population as a damper, the productivity of a dwindling workforce must rise.

Certainly Medvedev has been saying almost all of the right things about economic policy. Can he and his government deliver more than fine sentiments in the period ahead? One scenario is benign: he and Putin mean what they say, and, perhaps in the usual muddled way, will do it as well over time. This is a reasonable scenario, but not a given. More likely, and as seems to be increasingly the case in practice, is what I would call the Japanese political model: that is, the example of a single dominant party in power for a long time that is riddled with powerful factions, which divvy up ministries, contracts, and even sectors among themselves. It was Japan's Liberal Democratic Party in the 1960s and 1970s, somewhat like Mexico until the late 1990s, or at best Singapore. It is obviously not so benign, although it need not be stagnant. In saying this, I am not implying that Russia has to radically change its political system if the country doesn't want to. But it does mean that the rules of governance, the rule of law, transparency, efficient and fair judicial procedures, and bankruptcy and contract enforcement need to be developed.

Hopefully Medvedev will be able to get a policy grip on these considerable challenges. If Russia wants to return to more than 7 percent annual growth over the long term (the desirable rate of growth needed to double GDP every decade, and the famous goal set by Putin in May 2003 to double GDP by 2010), then it must focus less on expanding energy exports. Growing amounts of energy will be needed to support domestic manufacturing and private consumption. That said, investment should flow to those sectors promising higher productivity and offering higher value-added output.

This would be only likely to happen after relative price distortions (i.e., energy prices being lower domestically than on world markets) are eliminated and the politicized approach to exporting energy were to change. Government guidance suggested that this was to occur by 2011, but it is now being postponed because of the volatility in global energy prices. Given that the budget surpluses have disappeared, at least temporarily, a significant revision to economic policy over the medium term can be expected.

It is certainly an understatement to assert that there was widespread skepticism about Russian economic reforms both inside the country and outside in the 1990s. Indeed there still is. These past eighteen years have certainly been a difficult time, but there have been important achievements in Russia. Among them, of course, is the remarkable and rapid entrenchment of democratic aspirations in a country with virtually no historical experience of democratic traditions. I am particularly impressed with how most Russians have rejected ideologies of almost any kind after the failed experiment conducted there during much of the twentieth century.

Most fundamentally, a consensus finally emerged among the Russian establishment—and is now firmly embedded in the economic program of the government and in Medvedev's Kremlin—that the process of transition is irreversible. It is widely accepted that the establishment of a genuinely market-based economy should continue to be an overriding policy objective, and that this is the right road to sustained growth and future prosperity in Russia.

The implementation of laws and regulations has often been inconsistent, and remains incomplete. But one cannot deny that many of the institutional underpinnings of the market economy have been put in place. What remains as policy priorities start from a quite different base than from that of the beginning of the transition process.

As I have tried to stress, however, the starting conditions bequeathed by the late Soviet era cast a long shadow, and the list of what remains is impressive. To begin with, there is the problem of a pervasive and consistent rule of law. Not only are some laws still contradictory; law enforcement officials seem to feel that they have a perogative to interpret the laws as they see fit. The administration of justice is nontransparent, and the presumption of innocence sometimes seems derisory.

Although it is a vast improvement over the Soviet and earlier times, law-abiding citizens cannot be assured of basic freedoms. And the lack of a sense of social responsibility, or even civic duty, appears to be a perverse overreaction to the state-imposed mandate of social solidarity during the Communist era. But too readily, Russian officials seem to have forgotten that government ultimately is for the people, and citizens are not their subjects.

Administrative reform at all levels is needed. Honest, motivated civil servants are required to carry out the new agenda of economic regulation while the state withdraws from control. Urgent steps are needed to prevent abuse of power and especially pervasive corruption, which is reportedly a problem at all levels. Administration should function according to transparent rules, not the discretion of the administrators. Medvedev's good intentions need to be implemented in practice.

And critically, Russia remains far too beholden to one or two people at the top—a country ruled by individuals rather than by laws. Perhaps relative to what has happened elsewhere in, say, some parts of ex-Yugoslavia or Belarus, Putin was an exemplary leader who tried hard to pursue a reform agenda. But what happens if Prime Minister Putin retains too much power, or Medvedev or his successor turns out to be less benign than Putin? Institutionally, the system is too fragile to ensure the basic objectives of an open, liberal state on a sustainable basis. There is a chronic need to develop the attributes of civil society as well as alternative sources of opinion and information. While many of the past controversies involving the Russian media may have been at heart about financial issues (who, even in Western countries, can afford to subsidize the quality press and television?), it should be government policy to foster a thriving independent media.

The Russian government, indeed any Russian government, would be challenged to address all of these issues at the same time. Trying to establish the appropriate priorities and sequencing with less than perfect leaders with poorly trained or motivated officials is daunting. Moreover, Russians are still trying to establish their post-Soviet identity after the loss of empire, borders, and trade and financial relationships less than a generation ago. They are understandably pulled in different directions. And the Russian leadership has to face these challenges while fighting against poverty and growing inequality in a large, but depleting population with high and possibly unrealistic expectations.

Medvedev's Russia

One of the key lessons from the 1998 crisis is how readily domestic politics not only interferes with good policymaking but also can even be self-defeating. In this respect, Russia faces tough choices. With a system of power that still confers too much authority to the top of the pyramid, the way ahead is neither obvious nor predestined. The world economy is not necessarily benign. Russia's luck, along with that of other countries, could run out.

These are not abstract issues. They are practical questions for Russians themselves, first and foremost, and they cut right to the heart of whether or not Russia is going to realize its full potential as an economy and a society.

Russian society needs to build strong institutions to become a nation of laws. It takes time, and will be hard, as the history of other countries have demonstrated. How President Medvedev and a new generation of younger Russian leaders respond to these challenges will shape Russia's economic future through 2020 and well beyond. It's entirely possible that Russia could become, as some predict, the fifth-largest economy in the world within the next decade. It's entirely possible that Russia could diversify beyond oil and gas, and make its mark in other sectors, especially high technology. It's also possible to miss the moment or fail to take full advantage of it.

The risks ahead are considerable—in part because we simply do not know how global political and economic events will unfold. Perhaps the key point to keep in mind is the profound mistrust and even cynicism of the Russian people. Yes, at the margin, demand for ruble money may be rising and capital is again returning after the recent global crisis, but most affluent Russians still trust foreign banks with their large assets. Unlike outsiders, who seemed to quickly forget the crisis of August 1998, Russians themselves have long memories. The decades of self-inflicted social experimentation represent a humiliation for many and a source of inherent distrust of authority for practically all Russians. This skepticism is not overcome in a decade or even two. Perhaps the most daunting task facing the Kremlin in the period immediately ahead is to overcome this profound mistrust about the future. How it handles the recovery from the recent global recession will be an important test of whether the lessons of 1998 have been internalized.

Appendix I: Data on Economic Performance

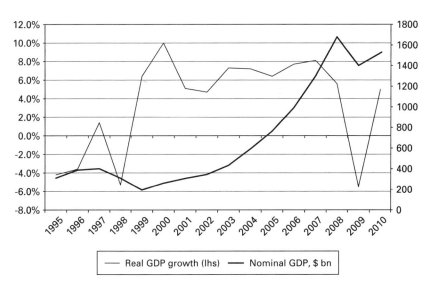

Figure A1.1
Economic growth
Source: Troika Dialog

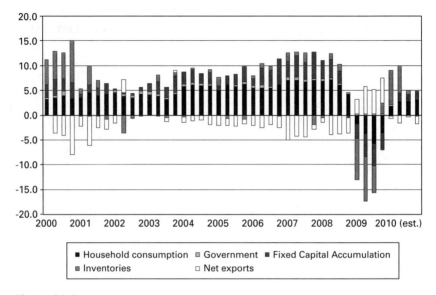

Figure A1.2
Contributions to GDP (%)
Source: UBS (Moscow)

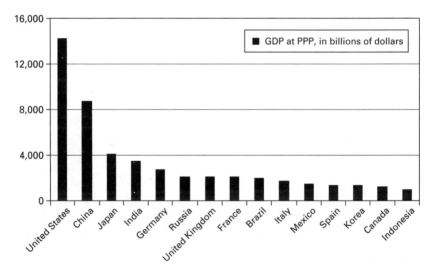

Figure A1.3
Global GDP, 2009 rankings
Source: IMF, UBS (Moscow)

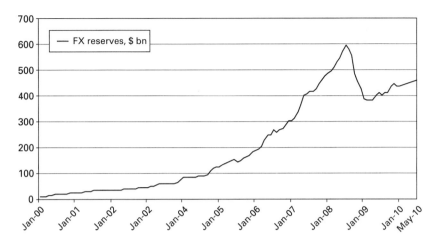

Figure A1.4
External reserves
Source: CBR

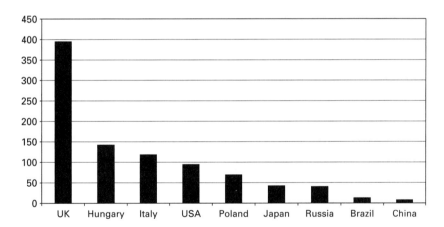

Figure A1.5
Total external debt (as a % of GDP), 2009
Source: Troika Dialog

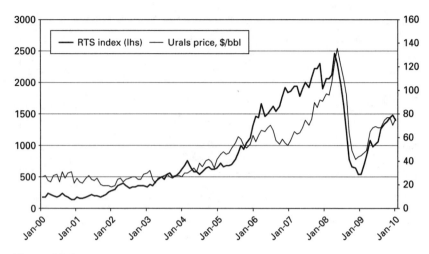

Figure A1.6
Oil price and the stock market
Source: Bloomberg, UBS (Moscow)

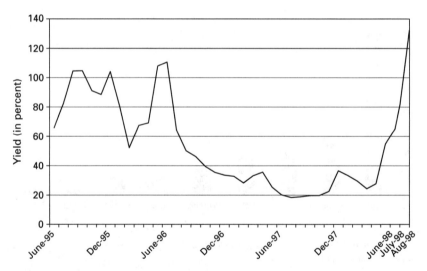

Figure A1.7
Russian government treasury bonds GKO yields (average monthly yield, June 1995–August 1998)
Source: Troika Dialog

Table A1.1
Russia: Key economic indicators

	1994	1995	1996	1997	1998	1999	2000	2001	2002	2003	2004	2005	2006	2007	2008	2009	2010 estimated
Nominal GDP, US$ billion	275.5	313.7	391.7	404.9	271.2	195.9	259.7	306.6	345.5	431.5	591.8	764.0	989.3	1288.6	1670.3	1225.8	1520
Real GDP, % annual change	−12.7	−4.0	−3.6	1.4	−5.3	6.4	10.0	5.1	4.7	7.3	7.2	6.4	7.7	8.1	5.6	−7.9	5.2
Budget balance, % GDP	−9.8	−5.9	−8.5	−7.8	−4.4	−1.2	2.4	3.0	1.8	1.7	4.1	7.5	7.4	5.3	4.1	−6.0	−3.3
Stabilization fund, $ billion[1]	—	—	—	—	—	—	—	—	—	3.7	18.8	43.7	89.1	156.8	225.1	152.1	102
CPI, % annual change	213.6	132.2	21.8	11.0	84.5	36.6	20.1	18.6	15.1	12.0	11.7	10.9	9.0	11.9	13.4	8.8	6.0
Money demand (M2/GDP)	10.1	10.7	13.0	14.5	14.4	11.9	12.5	14.7	16.3	19.3	21.4	22.9	26.4	32.1	32.7	33.8	36
Unemployment rate, %	7.4	8.6	9.6	10.7	11.6	11.5	10.0	8.8	8.0	8.6	8.2	7.6	7.2	6.5	6.2	8.4	8.0
Average gross wages per month, ruble thousands	0.2	0.5	0.8	1.0	1.1	1.5	2.2	3.2	4.4	5.5	6.8	8.6	10.7	13.6	17.1	18.8	21.3

Table A1.1
(continued)

	1994	1995	1996	1997	1998	1999	2000	2001	2002	2003	2004	2005	2006	2007	2008	2009	2010 estimated
Real disposable income, % annual change	13.0	−15.0	1.0	5.8	−15.9	−12.3	12.0	8.7	11.1	15.0	9.9	11.1	1.3	10.4	2.7	1.9	5.0
Current account, % GDP	2.8	2.2	2.8	0.0	0.1	12.6	18.0	11.1	8.4	8.2	10.0	11.0	9.5	5.9	5.9	2.0	2.5
Gross external reserves (excluding gold), $ billions	2.5	14.1	11.3	12.9	7.8	8.5	24.2	30.4	44.1	73.2	120.8	175.9	294.9	465.0	412.5	416.7	500
Rubles/$ exchange rate (end of period)	2.2	4.6	5.1	5.8	9.7	24.6	28.1	29.2	31.4	30.7	28.8	28.3	27.2	25.6	24.9	31.8	29.2
Urals, $/per barrel (average)	15.4	16.9	20.4	18.5	12.0	17.3	26.9	23.1	23.7	27.2	34.1	50.3	61.1	69.5	94.8	61.4	75.0

Source: RosStat, Troika Dialog
1. The fund was split in 2008 with estimates for the aggregate balance of the new two funds.

Appendix II: A Description of Names

This appendix contains a selective who's who of the main Russian protagonists involved in the narrative, identifying them according to the position that each held during the 1997–1999 period.

1. Nikolai Aksyonenko was the minister of railroads under President Yeltsin as well as a close associate of Yeltsin.

2. Sergey Aleksashenko was a deputy finance minister and became the first deputy chair of the CBR from 1995 to 1998.

3. Olga Aliluyeva was an adviser to Prime Minister Kiriyenko during his short time in office.

4. Boris Berezovsky was best known for his role as a Russian oligarch, media tycoon, and prominent political broker. He also held the position of the deputy secretary of the Kremlin's Security Council from 1996 to August 1997.

5. Georgy Boos, a close associate of Moscow mayor Luzhkov, was the tax minister in the Primakov government from September 1998 to May 1999.

6. Maxim Boycko was a key ally of Chubais who was responsible for privatization as head of the Privatization Center and also served as a deputy head of the presidential administration under Chubais.

7. Boris Brevnov was the head of RAO UES, the state electricity monopoly, from April 1997 to April 1998.

8. Andrei Bugrov was the executive director of the World Bank representing Russia.

9. Gennady Bukaev was the tax minister in Kasyanov's government.

10. Andrei Cherepanov was the deputy head of the CBR's foreign exchange department.

11. Viktor Chernomyrdin, a former Soviet minister for the gas industry who helped to form Gazprom, was prime minister from December 1992 to March 1998. From 2001 to 2009, he was Russia's ambassador to Ukraine.

12. Anatoly Chubais, a leading reformer, was responsible for privatization in Russia until he was named the head of the presidential administration in July 1996. In March 1997, he then became the first deputy prime minister and minister of finance, and a year later became the head of the state electricity monopoly, RAO UES.

13. Andrei Denisov has been a journalist and later editor with *Vremya Novostei* since 2000.

14. Oksana Dmitrieva was a deputy in the State Duma, and was labor and social development minister in 1998.

15. Sergei Dorenko was a leading newscaster on ORT television in the late 1990s.

16. Sergei Dubinin was the acting finance minister until late October 1994, and then became the chair of the CBR from 1995 to 1998.

17. Arkady Dvorkovich was an adviser on economic issues at MinFin, and later became a deputy economy minister and then the economic adviser at the Kremlin.

18. Boris Fedorov was a reformist finance minister from 1993 until 1994, when he resigned. He worked for the EBRD and then the World Bank, and was in the State Duma between 1994 and 1998. In 1998 he became the tax minister and a deputy prime minister. He died in November 2008.

19. Mikhail Fradkov, a former trade minister in the late 1990s and then head of the tax police, was the prime minister from March 2004 to September 2007.

20. Mikhail Fridman, one of the youngest Russian oligarchs, founded the Alfa Group Consortium along with Peter Aven.

21. Yegor Gaidar was the acting prime minister from June 15, 1992, to December 14, 1992, and the first deputy prime minister from September 1993 to January 1994. As the head of the Institute for the Study of Economies in Transition, he continued to play a major advisory role to the government, especially in 1995–1998. He died in December 2009.

22. Evgeny Gavrilenkov was the acting head of the Russian Bureau of Economic Analysis and the director of the Institute of Macroeconomic Research and Forecasting at the Higher School of Economics (and is now the chief economist at Troika Dialog investment bank).

23. Sergei Generalov became the minister of fuel and energy in 1998, having previously held senior positions at the Yukos oil company and the Menatep bank.

24. Viktor Gerashchenko was the chair of the Soviet central bank and then the CBR during much of the Perestroika period, in the early 1990s to October 1994, and then again from September 1998 to March 2002.

25. Mikhail Gorbachev was the last president of the Soviet Union.

26. German Gref was the founder of Center for Strategic Development, and became the minister of economics and trade from May 2000 to September 2007. He currently is the president of Sberbank.

27. Vladimir Gusinsky was a Russian oligarch with significant and influential media holdings.

28. Sergei Ignatiev was a first deputy finance minister from April 1997 to March 2002, and has been the chair of the CBR since that time.

29. Andrei Illarionov was the founder and director of Moscow's Institute for Economic Analysis from 1994 to 2000, and then became an economic policy adviser to the Kremlin and G-8 Sherpa until his resignation in 2005.

30. Sergei Ivanov, a former KGB general, was the minister of defense from March 2001 to February 2007, a deputy prime minister from November 2005 to February 2007, and has been the first deputy prime minister since February 2007.

31. Nadezdha Ivanova was a member of the CBR's board of directors and head of its general economics department.

32. Vladimir Kadannikov, a leading red director as the chief executive officer of the Autovaz car company, served as a deputy prime minister for a year in 1994.

33. Mikhail Kasyanov was the prime minister from May 2000 to February 2004, having served in various positions in the Ministry of Finance beginning in October 1993, most notably as the deputy minister responsible for external debt and later as the finance minister.

34. Mikhail Khodorkovsky, the founder of the Menatep bank, bought oil assets in the loans-for-shares scheme in 1995 and created the Yukos oil company.

35. Viktor Khristenko was a MinFin deputy minister and became a deputy prime minister in 1999, and since March 2004 has been the industry minister.

36. Sergei Kiriyenko was the first deputy and then the minister of fuel and energy before serving as the prime minister from March to August 1998.

37. Alfred Kokh was appointed the head of Russia's State Property Committee, acting as Russia's privatization chief, succeeding Chubais in September 1996. He left the position on August 13, 1997, after the privatization auctions (loans for shares).

38. Sergei Kolotukhin was the deputy general manager of the state-owned Vneshtorgbank in 1998 and later became a deputy finance minister.

39. Konstantin Korischenko was the head of the securities department of the CBR.

40. Aleksander Korzhakov was Yeltsin's bodyguard and became one of his closest associates until being fired in June 1996.

41. Andrei Kozlov was a first deputy chair of the CBR responsible for banking supervision and was murdered in Moscow in September 2006.

42. Leonid Kuchma was the president of Ukraine from 1994 until the Orange Revolution in late 2004.

43. Lyubov Kudelina was a deputy minister of finance, and was appointed the deputy defense minister for financial and economic issues in 2001.

44. Aleksei Kudrin was the head of the financial control doctorate in the Kremlin from August 1996 until he joined MinFin as the first deputy minister in April 1997. In May 2000, he became the minister of finance and also a deputy prime minister.

45. Anatoly Kulikov was the interior minister from 1995 to 1998.

46. Alexander Lebed, a former lieutenant general, placed third in the 1996 Russian presidential election, with 14.5 percent of the vote nationwide. He later served as the secretary of the Security Council and governor of Krasnoyarsk Krai, Russia's second-largest region. Lebed held the latter position until his death in a helicopter crash.

47. Platon Lebedev, a former CEO of Group Menatep, is best known as Khodorkovsky's business partner.

48. Alexander Livshits was the chief presidential aide on economic affairs from 1994 to 1996 and from 1997 to 1998, a deputy prime minister and the finance minister from 1996 to 1997, and the deputy chief of presidential administration from 1997 to 1998.

49. Oleg Lobov was the secretary of the Security Council in the Kremlin from 1993 to 1996, and was seen as a close adviser to Yeltsin at the time.

50. Alexander Lukashenko has been the president of Belarus since 1994.

51. Yuri Luzhkov has been the mayor of Moscow since 1992.

52. Tatiana Malkina was a journalist and doyenne of the Kremlin press corps, and is the author's wife.

53. Georgy Mamedov was a first deputy minister of foreign affairs and an adviser to Primakov.

54. Aslan Maskhadov was a leader of the Chechen separatist movement and the third president of Chechnya.

55. Yuri Maslyukov was a deputy in the Communist faction of the State Duma, and became the industry minister in the Kiriyenko government and the first deputy prime minister under Primakov.

56. Dmitry Medvedev, president since May 2008, was appointed the first deputy prime minister in November 2005, after having served as head of the presidential administration and chair of Gazprom.

57. Aleksei Mozhin was appointed Russia's representative to the IMF in 1996 and still serves in that capacity on the IMF executive board.

58. Arkady Murashev was a young liberal reformer and an associate of Gaidar, and in 1990 founded the Center for Liberal Conservative Policy.

59. Elvira Nabiullina was in various positions at the Economy Ministry, including as a deputy minister until 1997. After serving in think tanks, she returned to the ministry in 2000–2003 as its first deputy. Between 2003 and September 2007, Nabiullina chaired the Center for Strategic Development and the commission for Russia's 2006 presidency in the G-8. In September 2007, she was appointed the minister of economic development and trade.

60. Boris Nemtsov was a governor of Nizny Novgorod, and became a first deputy prime minister and minister of fuel and energy in March 1997 until April 1998.

61. Tatiana Nesterenko, a former deputy in the State Duma, was appointed the head of the Federal Treasury starting in November 1999.

62. Vladimir Panskov was the minister of finance from late 1994 to August 1996.

63. Tatiana Paramonova was the acting chair of the CBR in 1994–1995, and later served in other senior positions in the CBR.

64. Valentin Pavlov was the Prime Minister of the Soviet Union from January to August 1991. He was one of the leaders of the August Coup that attempted to depose Mikhail Gorbachev in 1991.

65. Vladimir Petrov was a first deputy minister of finance in the early part of the 1990s and was responsible for the budget.

66. Alexander Pochinok was the tax minister as the head of the STS in 1997–1998, and later served as the minister of labor and held other senior positions in government.

67. Vladimir Potanin, an oligarch, founded the Interros holding company, including the Uneximbank, and served as a deputy prime minister from August 1996 to March 1997.

68. Evgeny Primakov was the prime minister from September 1998 to May 1999. He was also the last speaker of the Supreme Soviet, and the Russian foreign minister from January 1996 until September 1998.

69. Vladimir Putin became the prime minister in August 1999 and the acting president on December 31, 1999, when President Yeltsin resigned, and then president from May 2000 until May 2008, when he again became prime minister.

70. Igor Rodionov, a former army general, served as the defense minister from July 1996 to May 1997.

71. Nikolai Ryzhkov served as the chair of the Council of Ministers of the USSR (or Premier of the Soviet Union) from September 27, 1985, to January 14, 1991, during the era of glasnost and perestroika under Gorbachev.

72. Gennady Seleznyov, a Communist Party member, was the speaker of the State Duma from 1996 to 2003.

73. Igor Sergeyev was the defense minister from May 1997 to March 2001.

74. Alexander Shokhin was a deputy prime minister for a short period in 1998, the minister of economics and the first deputy prime minister in 1994, and the minister of labor and employment and a deputy prime minister in 1991–1993. He is currently the president of the Russian Union of Industrialists and Entrepreneurs.

75. Yuri Skuratov was the prosecutor general from 1995 to 1999.

76. Alexander Smolensky, an oligarch banker, was the head of SBS-Agro.

77. Anatoly Sobchak was the first democratically elected mayor of Saint Petersburg until 1996.

78. Oleg Soskovets was a deputy prime minister and the overseer of Russian industry in the Chernomyrdin government until 1996.

79. Sergei Stepashin was the justice minister, serving from 1997 to March 1998, and the interior minister, holding that office from March 1998 to May 1999, when he became the prime minister until August 1999. After a period in the State Duma, he became the head of the Russian Accounts Chamber.

80. Oleg Sysuev was the deputy prime minister responsible for the social sector in 1998.

81. Yakov Urinson was first deputy economy minister from 1993 to 1997, and a deputy prime minister and the economy minister from 1997 to 1998.

82. Dmitry Vasiliev was the head of the Federal Commission for the Securities Market from March 1996 to October 1999.

83. Sergey Vasiliev was a deputy minister of the economy and the first deputy head of the government administration in 1998.

84. Andrei Vavilov was a first deputy finance minister from 1992 to 1997, and an acting minister in October–November 1994.

85. Oleg Viugin was a senior official in the Ministry of Finance, including as a first deputy minister, and later served as the first deputy chair of the CBR and the head of the Federal Financial Markets Service.

86. Dmitri Volkov was a journalist with the newspaper *Sevodnya*.

87. Alexander Voloshin was the head of the Kremlin presidential administration from 1999 until his resignation on October 29, 2003.

88. Yuri Voronin was a deputy in the State Duma.

89. Evgeny Yasin was the founder of the Higher School of Economics and served as the economy minister from 1994 to 1997.

90. Sergei Yastrzhembsky was the press secretary for the Yeltsin administration.

91. Boris Yeltsin served as the president of the Russian Federation from June 1991 until his resignation was announced on December 31, 1999.

92. Valentin Yumashev succeeded Chubais as the head of the presidential administration in the Kremlin in March 1997 until December 1998. In 2002 Yumashev married Tatyana Dyachenko, Yeltsin's youngest daughter.

93. Mikhail Zadornov became the minister of finance in November 1997, succeeding Chubais, until May 1999. Previously he was the head of the State Duma Budget Committee.

94. Viktor Zubkov was the prime minister from September 2007 to May 2008, and is now the chair of Gazprom.

95. Gennady Zyuganov was head of the Communist Party of the Russian Federation.

Appendix III: A List of Abbreviations

What follows is an explanation of the main abbreviations used in the narrative:

1. BIS is the Bank for International Settlements in Basel.
2. BONY was the Bank of New York, now the Bank of New York Mellon.
3. BRICs stands for the grouping of Brazil, Russia, India, and China. The term was coined by Goldman Sachs in 2003.
4. CBR is the Central Bank of Russia.
5. CIS is the Commonwealth of Independent States, a grouping of a large subset of the constituent republics of the USSR.
6. COMECON stands for the now-defunct Council for Mutual Economic Assistance, a Soviet-era organization to facilitate trade and economic integration among the Soviet satellite states and the Soviet Union.
7. CPSU was the Communist Party of the Soviet Union.
8. CSFB was Credit Suisse First Boston, a prominent investment bank.
9. EBRD stands for the European Bank for Reconstruction and Development.
10. EFF is a credit facility of the IMF that supports a three-year program and has a longer repayment schedule with the intention of promoting an ambitious structural transformation while continuing economic stabilization, usually after a one-year standby credit.
11. EU is the European Union.
12. FIMACO was a financial company subsidiary, registered in the Channel Islands, of Eurobank in Paris, which in turn was owned by the CBR. Eurobank and other foreign operations were originally established in Soviet times to facilitate trade, but became increasingly redundant in Russia's post-Soviet market economy.
13. G-7 stands for the grouping of the seven-largest so-called advanced economies, comprising the United States, Japan, Germany, France, the United Kingdom, Italy, and Canada, joined by the EU. With the addition of Russia, it became the political G-8. These countries, along with China, India, Brazil, and a few others, constitute the G-20.
14. Gazprom is the largest company in Russia, and the principal producer and distributor (as well as exporter) of natural gas.
15. GDP stands for the gross domestic product of a country, which measures the value-added of all domestic output of an economy.

16. GKO (Gosudarstvennykh Kratkosrochnykh Obligatsii) are short-term zero-coupon Russian government treasury bills. OFZ (Obligatsyi Federal'novo Zaima) are coupon-bearing federal loan bonds. Both are issued by the Russian Finance Ministry. GKO were introduced in May 1993 as noninflationary instruments for financing the budget deficit. OFZs were introduced in June 1995 to complement the GKO market as an instrument with medium- and long-term maturity.

17. Gosplan was the ubiquitous and powerful Soviet planning ministry. Its main task was to plan, organize, and execute economic activity based on five-year plans approved by the Central Committee of the CPSU.

18. IFC stands for the International Finance Corporation, a private sector financing subsidiary of the World Bank.

19. IFIs stands for international financial institutions, and is usually a shorthand reference to the IMF, World Bank, and related regional financial agencies.

20. IMF is the International Monetary Fund.

21. Interfax is one of the main Russian news agencies to emerge in post-Soviet Russia.

22. LTCM stands for Long-Term Capital Management, which was a major U.S. hedge fund.

23. MFE stands for the Russian Ministry of Fuel and Energy.

24. MICEX is the Moscow Interbank Commodity Exchange, originally established in 1988. It has since evolved into one of the major equity, bond, financial derivative, and currency exchanges.

25. MinFin stands for the Russian Ministry of Finance.

26. MSCI stands for the Morgan Stanley Country Index, which is a commonly used reference as it aggregates average performance over a large basket of countries.

27. NATO is the North Atlantic Treaty Organization.

28. OECD, based in Paris, is the Organization for Economic Cooperation and Development.

29. OPEC is the Organization of Petroleum Exporting Countries, an oil cartel that controls about one-third of global oil production. Russia is not a member.

30. OPERU II was the supervisory unit in the CBR in the late 1990s, responsible for monitoring the performance of the fifty-largest banks in Russia.

31. RAO UES was the post-Soviet electricity monopoly in Russia. It was broken up into a number of successor companies and then liquidated in 2008.

32. RTS is the Russian Trading System whose RTS Index is the main benchmark for the Russian securities industry and is based on the exchange's 50 most liquid and capitalized shares.

33. SCC stands for the Russian State Customs Committee, which assesses and collects custom duties.

34. SRF is the IMF's Suuplemental Reserve Facility which was created at the end of 1997 to provide financing for exceptional balance of payments difficulties due to a large short-term financing need resulting from a sudden and disruptive loss of market confidence. Russia's July 1998 drawing from the IMF used some SRF resources.

35. STF stood for the Systemic Transformation Facility, which was a temporary financing facility within the IMF in 1993–1995 to help support the former Soviet states.

36. STS stands for the Russian State Tax Service, which is the federal tax ministry.

37. TA is the abbreviation used for technical assistance, including training, provided by various international institutions to their members as well as by national governments and regional organizations such as the EU.

38. TNK is the Russian Eastern Oil Company, now jointed owned with British Petroleum.

39. USSR stood for the Union of Socialist Soviet Republics.

40. VAT is value-added tax, one of the main sources of budgetary revenue in Russia and in Europe.

41. VChK was the emergency tax commission created in 1996 to try to target tax collection from major problematic taxpayers.

42. VEB stands for the Vneshkombank, which was the Soviet external trading bank and is now a state development bank.

43. VEK stands for the Federal Service for Currency and Export Control that was finally disbanded in 2000.

44. WTO stands for the World Trade Organization.

Notes

Foreword

1. Michel Camdessus is the former managing director of the IMF and governor of the Banque de France.

Preface

1. A possible exception would be Finch 1989. David Finch, the late director of the IMF's central policy department, resigned in 1988 purportedly over the almost-overt political pressure to lend financial support to Egypt and Poland on exceptional terms in that same year. There is also the case of Claudio Loser, a former head of the IMF's Western Hemisphere department, who recounted his views on the Argentine crisis to a journalist, who then published the account, but only in Spanish, in 2004. See Tenembaum 2004.

2. There is the relatively recent example, however, of a more technically oriented compendium of IMF success stories; see Brau and McDonald 2009.

3. Other studies already cover much of this ground. See, for instance, Owen and Robinson 2003, which was prepared by the IMF Russia team members; Aleksashenko 1999; Gould-Davies and Woods 1999; Kharas, Pinto, and Ulatov 2001; Odling-Smee 2004; Pagé 2000; Sachs and Pistor 1997.

4. A typical example was a diatribe by Tayler 2001, where the author equated Russia to "Zaire with permafrost." More thoughtful assessments can be found in Billington 2004; Colton and McFaul 2003; Fish 2005; Jack 2004

Introduction

1. See, for example, "A New Sick Man," *Economist*, June 5, 2009. Delpech 2007 warns thoughtfully of the dangers from such oversimplification.

2. Lucas's book, *The New Cold War: Putin's Russia and the Threat to the West* (2008), is a particularly articulate and well-informed view of Russia as a disappointing and even menacing failure that missed a historic opportunity to join the West.

3. There is, of course, an abundant literature available that covers this ground much more thoroughly than I can in the context of this book. See, for instance, Aron 2007; Aslund 1995; Brady 1999; Braguinsky and Yavlinsky 2000; Cohen 2000; Gaidar 2007; Kotkin 2001; McFaul 2001; Shleifer 2005; Sutela 1998.

4. For example, Uriel Procaccia (2007) explains the failure of market reforms in post-Soviet Russia as a function of the religious, literary, philosophical, folk-traditional, and musical chasm between Russia and the West: "As long as Russia is going to preserve its ancient affinity to the values represented by the Orthodox Icon, the market economy, privatization, and a host of other occidental manifestations of the human spirit will be kept at bay."

5. Gaidar 1996.

6. Mau and Starodubrovskaya 2001.

7. Aslund 2007.

8. McFaul 2001. There were other exceptions as well, such as Mau and Starodubrovskaya 2001; Daniels 2000; Shliefer and Triesman 2000.

9. Graham 2002.

10. Strobe Talbot, although not an economist, made an insightful point in this regard in a speech at Stanford University on November 6, 1998, when referring to Yevgeny Primakov and his new government in late 1998 that "the economic rules that the custodians of the Russian economy are threatening to defy are not so much 'Western' as they are a matter of simple arithmetic."

11. Cohen 2000.

12. Shevtsova 1998.

13. Reddaway and Glinski 2001.

14. Lucas 2008.

15. Kotkin 2008.

16. Aron 2000, chapter 11.

17. Gaidar 1996.

18. Nagy 2000.

19. Mau and Starodubrovskaya 2001.

20. Stiglitz 2002.

21. Mau 2000. Also Dabrowski, Gomulka, and Rostowski 2000.

22. Gaidar 2007.

23. Kaletsky 2007.

1 Russia and the IMF

1. For some background on IMF operations, see <http://www.imf.org>. The IMF web site contains abundant information on the history of the IMF, its financial facilities, and its lending operations in individual member countries in support of economic policy programs.

2. Boughton 2001.

3. Odling-Smee 2004; Owen and Robinson 2003; Zadornov and Lopez-Claros 2002.

4. IMF, World Bank, OECD, and EBRD 1991.

5. Viktor Chernomyrdin was a former Soviet minister for the gas industry who helped to form Gazprom and served as prime minister from December 1992 to March 1998.

6. See Aslund 2001.

7. For references on procedures for the use of IMF resources, see <http://www.imf.org>.

8. For reference, see the Russia program documents, available at <http://www.imf.org/external/country/RUS/index.htm>.

9. Nixon 1992.

10. Aslund 2001.

11. See Layard and Parker 1996.

12. See, for instance, Brady 1999; Hedlund 1999; Klebnikov 2000; Wedel 2001.

13. Christensen 1993. Also see Westin 2001.

14. Aslund 2001.

2   Growing IMF Involvement

1. Red directors were the powerful managers of large productive facilities left over from Soviet times, many of whom received effective control and ownership through the so-called spontaneous privatization of 1988–1991, and who often were in collusion with the authorities in the regions where their operations were located. *Oligarchs* is the term applied to a group of Russian entrepreneurs that took advantage of the economic chaos and administrative loopholes in the late 1980s and early 1990s to build substantial business groups.

2. Solnick 1998.

3. Treisman 2010. But also see Goldman 2003.

4. See, for example, Hedlund 1999.

5. See, for example, Freeland 2000; Hoffman 2003; McFaul, Petrov, and Ryabov 2004.

6. See, for example, Hedlund 2001.

7. Shleifer and Treisman 2000.

3   Russia Seems to Be Turning a Corner

1. Aslund 1995.

2. Mozhin's unusual longevity in his post, since 1996 (and as alternate executive director from the time Russia joined the fund in 1992), connotes a sense of the confidence that he has won from all sides. In 2010, he was the most senior of the G-20 executive directors.

3. The actual budget figures in the text follow the convention of using IMF definitions, which until adopted by the government starting with the 2001 budget, varied from those used by the authorities.

4. See Talbott 2002.

5. Gaddy and Ickes 1998.

6. *New York Times*, June 22, 2001.

7. Treisman 2010.

8. IMF 1997.

9. For more on the Asian crisis, see, for example, Blustein 2001; Muchhala 2007.

4 Hope Disappointed

1. Freeland 2000.

2. See, for example, the views expressed by Fischer on program implementation, available at <http://www.imf.org/external/np/speeches/1998/010998.htm>.

5 How a Possible Crisis Becomes Probable

1. *Moscow Times*, January 13, 1998.

2. *Interfax*, January 13, 1998.

3. *Economist*, January 30, 1998.

4. *Prime-Tass*, February 5, 1998.

5. *Moscow Times*, March 13, 1998.

6. For an interesting assessment of how this happened, see Freeland 2000.

7. See Brady 1999; Freeland 2000; Johnson 2000

8. *New York Times*, July 17, 1998.

9. *Moscow Times*, June 30, 1998.

6 How a Probable Crisis Then Becomes Unavoidable

1. Rubin 2003.

2. For a detailed analysis of the international consequences of the Russian crisis, see IMF 1998. For a detailed analysis of the episode of international contagion more generally, see IMF 1999. Also see Komulainen 2000; Sgard and Zlotowsky 1999.

3. *Financial Times*, August 26, 1998.

4. Fischer, then–first deputy managing director of the IMF, in a speech at the Higher School of Economics, Moscow, June 19, 2001.

5. Primakov 2001.

7   The Surprising Postcrisis Recovery

1. Primakov 2001.

2. Yeltsin 2000. For more background, see Desai 2006.

3. Timakova, Kolesnikov, and Gevorkyan 2000. A different view of the transition is contained in Baker and Glasser 2005; Shevtsova 2007.

4. Government Directive No. 1072-r was signed by Prime Minister Mikhail Kasianov on July 26, 2000.

8   The Friendly Divorce

1. For details, see Denisov 2001a.

2. See Gorodnichenko, Martinez-Vazquez, and Peter 2008, as well as a related article by Yakovlev 2006.

3. O'Brien 1999.

4. Even after BONY settled the case in 2005 with a small fine in the U.S., the Russian SCC then sued for US$22.5 billion from BONY in May 2007, accusing it of helping to illegally transfer a total of US$7.5 billion out of Russia in the 1990s. A settlement was only reached in late 2009, whereby BONY, without admitting guilt, agreed to pay legal fees equivalent to the US$14 million that it had paid the U.S. government in 2005.

5. An interesting version of this story can be found in Denisov 2001b.

6. For a comprehensive list of reports, see <http://www.imf.org>. Also see World Bank 2009.

9   The Legacy of the Crisis

1. At nominal exchange rates.

2. Goldman 2008.

3. Blanchard 1997.

4. See Gaddy and Ickes 1998; Woodruff 1999.

5. See, for example, Pettis 2001; Krugman 1999; Lane, Ghosh, Hamann, Phillips, Schulze-Ghattas, and Tsikata 1999; Lindgren, Baliño, Enoch, Gulde, Quintyn, and Teo 1999.

6. Aslund 2007.

7. See Herspring 2005; Sakwa 2004; Shevtsova 2003.

8. MacKinnon 2007; Zudin 2002.

9. Peregudov 2005.

10. O'Brien 2000.

11. O'Brien 2005.

10   History Is Not Doomed to Repeat Itself

1. See, for example, Collyns and Kincaid 2003; Goldstein 2008; Reinhart and Rogoff 2008; Roubini and Setser 2004.

2. Wilson and Purushothaman 2003.

References

Aleksashenko, Sergey. 1999. *The Fight for the Ruble: An Insider's View*. Moscow: Alma Mater.

Aron, Leon. 2000. *Yeltsin: A Revolutionary Life*. New York: St. Martin's Press.

Aron, Leon. 2007. *Russia's Revolution: 1989–2006*. Washington, DC: American Enterprise Institute for Public Policy Research.

Aslund, Anders. 1995. *How Russia Became a Market Economy*. Washington, DC: Brookings Institution.

Aslund, Anders. 2001. "We Did Too Little." *Moscow Times*, February 5.

Aslund, Anders. 2002. *Building Capitalism: The Transformation of the Former Soviet Bloc*. Cambridge: Cambridge University Press.

Aslund, Anders. 2007. *Russia's Capitalist Revolution: Why Market Reform Succeeded and Democracy Failed*. Washington, DC: Peterson Institute.

Aslund, Anders, Peter Boone, and Simon Johnson. 1996. "How to Stabilize: Lessons from Post-Communist Countries." Brookings Papers on Economic Activity. Washington, DC: Brookings Institution Press.

Baker, Peter, and Susan Glasser. 2005. *Kremlin Rising: Vladimir Putin's Russia and the End of Revolution*. New York: Scribner.

Billington, James H. 2004. *Russia in Search of Itself*. Washington, DC: Woodrow Wilson Center Press.

Blanchard, Olivier. 1997. *The Economics of Post-Communist Transition*. Oxford: Clarendon Press.

Blustein, Paul. 2001. *The Chastening: The Crisis That Rocked the Global Financial System and Humbled the IMF*. New York: Public Affairs.

Boughton, James. 2001. *Silent Revolution: The International Monetary Fund, 1979–1989*. Washington, DC: International Monetary Fund.

Brady, Rose. 1999. *Kapitalizm: Russia's Struggle to Free Its Economy*. New Haven, CT: Yale University Press.

Braguinsky, Serguey, and Grigory Yavlinsky. 2000. *Incentives and Institutions: The Transition to a Market Economy in Russia*. Princeton, NJ: Princeton University Press.

Brau, Eduard, and Ian McDonald, eds. *Successes of the International Monetary Fund: Untold Stories of Cooperation at Work*. New York: Palgrave Macmillan, 2009.

Christensen, Benedicte. 1993. *Russia's External Debt*. Washington, DC: International Monetary Fund.

Chubais, Anatoly. *Privatization: The Russian Way*. Moscow: Vagrius, 1999.

Cohen, Stephen F. 2000. *Failed Crusade: America and the Tragedy of Post-Communist Russia*. New York: W. W. Norton and Company.

Collyns, Charles, and Russell G. Kincaid. 2003. "Managing Financial Crises: Recent Experience and Lessons for Latin America." Working paper. Washington, DC: International Monetary Fund.

Colton, Timothy J., and Michael McFaul. 2003. *Popular Choice and Managed Democracy: The Russian Elections of 1999 and 2000*. Washington, DC: Brookings Institution Press.

Dabrowski, Marek, Stanislaw Gomulka, and Jacek Rostowski. 2000. "Whence Reform? A Critique of the Stiglitz Perspective." CEP discussion papers. London: Centre for Economic Performance.

Daniels, Robert V. 2000. *The Anti-Communist Revolutions in the Soviet Union and Eastern Europe*. New York: Routledge.

Delpech, Therese. 2007. *Savage Century: Back to Barbarism*. Washington, DC: Carnegie Endowment.

Denisov, Andrei. 2001a. "Bogatye e Negordye." *Vremya Novostei*, January 22.

Denisov, Andrei. 2001b. "Rossia e MVF ne raspeshutsya." *Vremya Novostei*, March 26.

Desai, Padma. 2006. *Conversations on Russia: Reform from Yeltsin to Putin*. New York: Oxford University Press.

Economist (editorial). 2009. "A New Sick Man." *Economist* (June 5).

Finch, C. David. 1989. *IMF: The Record and the Prospect*. Princeton, NJ: Princeton University Press.

Fish, Steven M. 2005. *Democracy Derailed in Russia: The Failure of Open Politics*. New York: Cambridge University Press.

Freeland, Chrystia. 2000. *Sale of the Century: Russia's Wild Ride from Communism to Capitalism*. New York: Crown Publishers.

Gaddy, Cliff G., and Barry W. Ickes. 1998. "Russia's Virtual Economy." *Foreign Affairs* (September–October).

Gaidar, Yegor T. 1996. *Days of Defeat and Victory*. Moscow: Vagrius Publishers. English translation in 1999 by the University of Washington Press.

Gaidar, Yegor. 2007. *Collapse of an Empire: Lessons for Modern Russia*. Washington, DC: Brookings Institution. Translated from the Russian edition.

Goldman, Marshall, I. 2003. *The Privatization of Russia: Russian Reform Go Awry*. New York: Routledge.

Goldman, Marshall, I. 2008. *Petrostate: Putin, Power, and the New Russia.* Oxford: Oxford University Press.

Goldstein, Morris. 2008. *Financial Regulation after the Subprime and Credit Crisis.* Washington, DC: Peterson Institute for International Economics.

Gorodnichenko, Yury, Jorge Martinez-Vazquez, and Klara Sabirianova Peter. 2008. "Myth and Reality of Flat Tax Reform: Micro Estimates of Tax Evasion Response and Welfare Effects in Russia." National Bureau of Economic Research working paper 13719.

Gould-Davies, Nigel, and Ngaire Woods. 1999. "Russia and the IMF." *International Affairs* 75 (1) (January): 1–21.

Graham, Thomas. 2002. *Russia's Decline and Uncertain Recovery.* Washington, DC: Carnegie Endowment for International Peace.

Hedlund, Stefan. 1999. *Russia's Market Economy: A Bad Case of Predatory Capitalism.* London: UCL Press.

Hedlund, Stefan. 2001. "Russia and the IMF: A Sordid Tale of Moral Hazard." *Demokratizatsiya* (Winter).

Herspring, Dale R., ed. 2005. *Putin's Russia. Past Imperfect, Future Uncertain,* 2nd ed. Boulder, CO: Rowman and Littlefield, 2005.

Hoffman, David E. 2003. *The Oligarchs: Wealth and Power in the New Russia.* New York: Public Affairs.

IMF. 1997. *World Economic Outlook* (October).

IMF. 1998. *World Economic Outlook* (October).

IMF. 1999. *World Economic Outlook* (May).

IMF, World Bank, OECD, and EBRD. 1991. *A Study of the Soviet Economy.* Vols. 1–3. Washington, DC: IMF, World Bank, OECD, and EBRD.

Jack, Andrew. 2004. *Inside Putin's Russia: Can There Be Reform without Democracy?* New York: Oxford University Press.

Johnson, Juliet. 2000. *A Fistful of Rubles: The Rise and Fall of the Russian Banking System.* Ithaca, NY: Cornell University Press.

Kaletsky, Anatole. 2007. "It's the West That's Starting This New Cold War— Russia's Belligerence Is Hardly Surprising." *Times*, June 7.

Kharas, Homi J., Brian Pinto, and Sergei Ulatov. 2001. "An Analysis of Russia's 1998 Meltdown: Fundamentals and Market Signals." Brookings Papers on Economic Activity. Washington, DC: Brookings Institution.

Klebnikov, Paul. 2000. *Godfather of the Kremlin: The Decline of Russia in the Age of Gangster Capitalism.* New York: Harcourt.

Komulainen, T. Korhonen, I., ed. 2000. *Russian Crisis and Its Effects.* Helsinki: Kikimora Publications.

Kotkin, Stephen. 2001. *Armageddon Averted: Who Lost the Soviet Union?* New York: Oxford University Press.

Kotkin, Stephen. 2008. "Myth of the New Cold War." *Prospect* (April).

Krugman, Paul. 1999. *The Return of Depression Economics*. New York: W. W. Norton.

Lane, Timothy, Atish Ghosh, Javier Hamann, Steven Phillips, Mariane Schulze-Ghattas, and Tsidi Tsikata. 1999. "IMF-Supported Programs in Indonesia, Korea, and Thailand: A Preliminary Assessment." IMF occasional paper 178. Washington, DC: International Monetary Fund.

Layard, Richard, and John Parker. 1996. *The Coming Russian Boom: A Guide to New Markets and Politics*. New York: Free Press.

Lindgren, Carl-Johan, Tomás J. T. Baliño, Charles Enoch, Anne-Marie Gulde, Marc Quintyn, and Leslie Teo. 1999. "Financial Sector Crisis and Restructuring: Lessons from Asia." IMF occasional paper 188. Washington, DC: International Monetary Fund.

Lucas, Edward. 2008. *The New Cold War: Putin's Russia and the Threat to the West*. London: Palgrave Macmillan.

MacKinnon, Mark A. 2007. *The New Cold War: Revolutions, Rigged Elections, and Pipeline Politics in the Former Soviet Union*. New York: Random House.

Mau, Vladimir. 2000. *Russian Economic Reforms as Seen by an Insider: Success or Failure?* London: Royal Institute of International Affairs.

Mau, Vladimir, and Irina Starodubrovskaya. 2001. *The Challenge of Revolution: Contemporary Russia in Historical Perspective*. Oxford: Oxford University Press.

McFaul, Michael. 2001. *Russia's Unfinished Revolution: Political Change from Gorbachev to Putin*. Ithaca, NY: Cornell University Press.

McFaul, Michael, Nikolay Petrov, and Andrey Ryabov. 2004. *Between Dictatorship and Democracy: Russia Post-Communist Political Reform*. Washington, DC: Carnegie Endowment for International Peace.

Muchhala, Bhumika, ed. 2007. *Ten Years after: Revisiting the Asian Financial Crisis*. Washington, DC: Woodrow Wilson Center for International Studies.

Nagy, Piroskha M. 2000. *The Meltdown of the Russian State*. Cheltenham, UK: Edward Elgar, 2000.

Nixon, Richard. 1992. "Save the Peace Dividend." *New York Times*, November 19.

O'Brien, Timothy. 1999. "Activity at Bank Raises Suspicions of Russian Mob Tie." *New York Times*, August 19.

O'Brien, Timothy. 2000. "Doubts Raised about Source in Bank of New York Inquiry." *New York Times*, January 17.

O'Brien, Timothy. 2005. "Bank Settles U.S. Inquiry into Money Laundering." *New York Times*, November 9.

Odling-Smee. John. 2004. "The IMF and Russia in the 1990s." IMF working paper 04/155 (August). Washington, DC: International Monetary Fund.

Owen, David, and David O. Robinson, eds. 2003. *Russia Rebounds*. Washington, DC: International Monetary Fund.

Pagé, J.-P. 2000. "Peut-on aider la Russie? Une économie entre déconstruction et renouveau." *Les études du CERI* (64) (March).

Peregudov, Sergei P. 2005. "Novyi etap v otnosheniiakh biznesa i vlasti." January 13. Available at http://www.politcom.ru/2005/analit200.php.

Pettis, Michael. 2001. *The Volatility Machine*. Oxford: Oxford University Press.

PricewaterhouseCoopers. 1999a. "Report on Relations between the Central Bank of Russia and the Financial Management Company Ltd (FIMACO)." August 5. (This report is no longer available for public viewing.)

PricewaterhouseCoopers. 1999b. "Report on the Funds Transferred to the Central Bank of Russia by the IMF in July 1998, and the Use, by the Central Bank of Russia, of Those Funds between July 1 and September 1, 1998." August 17. (This report is no longer available for public viewing.)

PricewaterhouseCoopers. 1999c. "Report on the Statistics Compiled by the Central Bank of Russia for the IMF in the Period from January 1, 1996 to September 1, 1998." August 17. (This report is no longer available for public viewing.)

Primakov, Yevgeny. 2001. *Vosem mesyatsev plus . . .* [Eight Months Plus . . .]. Moscow: Mysl.

Procaccia, Uriel. 2007. *Russian Culture, Property Rights, and the Market Economy*. Cambridge: Cambridge University Press.

Reddaway, Peter, and Dmitri Glinski. 2001. *The Tragedy of Russia's Reforms: Market Bolshevism against Democracy*. Washington, DC: United States Institute of Peace Press.

Reinhart, Carmen M., and Kenneth Rogoff. 2008. "This Time Is Different: A Panoramic View of Eight Centuries of Financial Crises." Working paper. Cambridge, MA: National Bureau of Economic Research.

Roubini, Nouriel, and Brad Setser. 2004. *Bail-Ins versus Bailouts: Financial Crises in Emerging Markets, Private Sector Involvement in Crisis Resolution, and Alternative Approaches to Debt Restructuring*. Washington, DC: Institute for International Economics.

Rubin, Robert. 2003. *In an Uncertain World: Tough Choices from Wall Street to Washington*. New York: Random House.

Sachs, Jeffrey, and Katharina Pistor. 1997. *The Rule of Law and Economic Reform in Russia*. New York: Westview Press.

Sakwa, Richard. 2004. *Putin: Russia's Choice*. London: Routledge.

Sgard, J., and Y. Zlotowski. 1999. "Economie politique du desastre, le choc d'aout 1998 en Russie." *Critique Internationale* (3) (Spring).

Shevtsova, Lilia. 1998. *Yeltsin's Russia: Myths and Reality*. Washington, DC: Carnegie Endowment for International Peace.

Shevtsova, Lilia. 2003. *Putin's Russia*. Washington, DC: Carnegie Endowment for International Peace.

Shevtsova, Lilia. 2007. *Russia—Lost in Transition: The Yeltsin and Putin Legacies*. Washington, DC: Carnegie Endowment for International Peace.

Shleifer, Andrei, Maxim Boycko, and Robert Vishny. 1997. *Privatizing Russia.* Cambridge, Mass.: The MIT Press.

Shleifer, Andrei. 2005. *A Normal Country: Russia after Communism.* Cambridge, MA: Harvard University Press.

Shleifer, Andrei, and Daniel Treisman. 2000. *Without a Map: Tactics and Economics Reform in Russia.* Cambridge, MA: MIT Press.

Solnick, Steven L. 1998. *Stealing the State: Control and Collapse in Soviet Institutions.* Cambridge, MA: Harvard University Press.

Stiglitz, Joseph. 2002. *Globalization and Its Discontents.* New York: W. W. Norton and Company.

Sutela, Pekka. 1998. *The Road to the Russian Market Economy: Selected Essays, 1993–1998.* Helsinki: Kikimora Publications.

Talbott, Strobe. 2002. *The Russian Hand.* New York: Random House.

Tayler, Jeffrey. 2001. "Russia Is Finished." *Atlantic Monthly* (May).

Tenembaum, Ernesto. 2004. *Enemigos: Argentina y el FMI.* Buenos Aires: Norma.

Timakova, Natalya, Andrei Kolesnikov, and Natalya Gevorkyan. 2000. *First Person: An Astonishingly Frank Self-portrait by Russia's President.* New York: Public Affairs.

Treisman, Daniel. 2010. *The Return: Russia's Journey from Gorbachev to Medvedev.* New York: Free Press.

Wedel, Janine R. 2001. *Collision and Collusion: The Strange Case of Western Aid to Eastern Europe.* New York: St. Martin's Press.

Westin, Peter. 2001. *The Wild East: Negotiating the Russian Financial Frontier.* London: Pearson Education.

Wilson, Dominic, and Roopa Purushothaman. 2003. "Dreaming with BRICs: The Path to 2050." *Global Economics Paper* 99 (October 1).

Woodruff, David M. 1999. *Money Unmade: Barter and the Fate of Russian Capitalism.* Ithaca, NY: Cornell University Press.

World Bank. 2009. *Doing Business in Russia 2010* (October).

Yakovlev, Andrei. 2006. "The Evolution of Business—State Interaction in Russia: From State Capture to Business Capture?" *Europe-Asia Studies* 58:7.

Yeltsin, Boris. 2000. *Midnight Diaries.* New York: Public Affairs.

Zadornov, Mikhail, and Augusto Lopez-Claros. 2002. "Report on the Changes That Have Taken Place and Assessment." *Europe Intelligence Wire* (October 1).

Zudin, Aleksei. 2002. "Rezhim Vladimira Putina: kontury novoi politicheskoi sistemy." Carnegie Moscow Center white paper (April).

Zudin, Aleksei. 2006. "Gosudarstvo i biznes v Rossii: evoliutsiia modeli vzaimootnoshenii." *Neprikosnovennyi zapas* (6).

Index